Julie Meloni
Michael Morrison

Sams **Teach Yourself**

HTML and CSS

in **24** Hours

Eighth Edition

SAMS   800 East 96th Street, Indianapolis, Indiana, 46240 USA

Sams Teach Yourself HTML and CSS in 24 Hours, Eighth Edition

Copyright © 2010 by Sams Publishing

International Standard Book Number: 0-672-33097-0

Library of Congress Cataloging-in-Publication Data
Meloni, Julie C.
  Sams teach yourself HTML and CSS 24 hours / Julie Meloni, Michael Morrison. – 8th ed.
      p. cm.
  Rev. ed. of: Sams teach yourself HTML and CSS in 24 hours / Dick Oliver, 7th ed., 2006.
   ISBN 978-0-672-33097-1 (pbk.)
  1. HTML (Document markup language) 2. XHTML (Document markup language) 3. Cascading style sheets. I. Morrison, Michael, 1970- II. Oliver, Dick. Sams teach yourself HTML and CSS in 24 hours. III. Title.
   QA76.76.H9404526 2010
   006.7'4–dc22
                    2009046100
Printed in the United States of America
First Printing: December 2009

Trademarks

Warning and Disclaimer

Bulk Sales

Sams Publishing offers excellent discounts on this book when ordered in quantity for bulk purchases or special sales. For more information, please contact

U.S. Corporate and Government Sales
1-800-382-3419
corpsales@pearsontechgroup.com
For sales outside of the U.S., please contact

International Sales
international@pearson.com

Acquisitions Editor
Mark Taber

Development Editor
Michael Thurston

Managing Editor
Patrick Kanouse

Project Editor
Jennifer Gallant

Indexer
Ken Johnson

Proofreader
Dan Knott

Technical Editor
William Wolff

Publishing Coordinator
Vanessa Evans

Composition
Mark Shirar

Book Designer
Gary Adair

Contents

PART V: **Appendixes**

APPENDIX A: **HTML and CSS Resources on the Internet**

APPENDIX B: **HTML and CSS Quick Reference**

About the Authors

Julie C. Meloni is both the technical director for i2i Interactive, a multimedia company located in Los Altos, CA, and a scholar working in the field of Digital Humanities. She has written several books and articles on Web-based programming languages and database topics, including the best-selling *Sams Teach Yourself PHP, MySQL, and Apache All in One.*

Michael Morrison is a writer, developer, toy inventor, and author of a variety of computer technology books and interactive web-based courses. In addition to his primary profession as a writer and freelance nerd for hire, Michael is the creative lead at Stalefish Labs, an entertainment company he co-founded with his wife, Masheed.

We Want to Hear from You!

As the reader of this book, *you* are our most important critic and commentator. We value your opinion and want to know what we're doing right, what we could do better, what areas you'd like to see us publish in, and any other words of wisdom you're willing to pass our way.

You can email or write me directly to let me know what you did or didn't like about this book—as well as what we can do to make our books stronger.

Please note that I cannot help you with technical problems related to the topic of this book, and that due to the high volume of mail I receive, I might not be able to reply to every message.

When you write, please be sure to include this book's title and author as well as your name and phone or email address. I will carefully review your comments and share them with the author and editors who worked on the book.

Email: webdev@samspublishing.com

Mail: Mark Taber
         Associate Publisher
         Sams Publishing
         800 East 96th Street
         Indianapolis, IN 46240 USA

Reader Services

Visit our web site and register this book at **informit.com/register** for convenient access to any updates, downloads, troubleshooting hints, or errata that might be available for this book.

Introduction

In 2009, it is estimated that more than 1.5 billion people have access to the Internet, including 220 million in the U.S. alone. Throw in 338 million Chinese users, 55 million German users, 48 million British users, 38 million Russian users, and 67 million Brazilians, and you can see the meaning of the word "world" in the term World Wide Web. Many of these Internet users are also creating content for the Web—you can be one of them! Although accurate measurements of the total number of web pages are difficult to come by, Google's most recent data indicates they hit the 1 trillion mark of indexed pages in the middle of 2008.

In the next 24 hours, hundreds of millions of new pages will appear in accessible areas of the Internet. At least as many pages will be placed on private intranets, where they will be viewed by businesspeople connected via their local networks. Every one of those pages—like the more than 1 trillion pages already online—will use Hypertext Markup Language (HTML).

As you complete the 24 one-hour lessons in this book, your web pages will be among those that appear on the Internet. These lessons will also help you develop one of the most valuable skills in the world today: mastery of HTML.

Can you really learn to create top-quality web pages yourself, without any specialized software, in less time than it takes to schedule and wait for an appointment with a highly paid HTML wizard? Can this relatively short, easy-to-read book really enable you to teach yourself state-of-the-art web page publishing?

Yes. In fact, within the first two lessons in this book, someone with no previous HTML experience at all can have a web page ready to place on the web.

How can you learn the language of the Web so fast? By example. This book organizes HTML into simple steps and then shows you exactly how to tackle each step. Every HTML code example is listed directly before a picture of the web page it produces. You see how it's done, you read a clear, concise explanation of how it works, and then you immediately do the same thing with your own page. Ten minutes later, you're on to the next step.

After 24 hours of work, you're marveling at your own impressive pages on the Internet.

Beyond HTML

This book covers more than just HTML because HTML isn't the only thing you need to know to create web content today. The goal of this book is to give you all the skills you need to create a modern, standards-compliant web site in just 24 short, easy lessons. This book covers the following key skills and technologies:

▶ XHTML (eXstensible Hypertext Markup Language) is the current standard for web page creation. Every example in this book is fully XHTML-compatible. Where applicable, HTML 5 is also covered.

▶ All the examples in the book have been tested for compatibility with the latest version of every major web browser. That includes Apple Safari, Google Chrome, Microsoft Internet Explorer, Mozilla Firefox, and Opera. You'll learn from the start to be compatible with the past, yet ready for the future.

▶ There is extensive coverage of Cascading Style Sheets (CSS), which allows you to carefully control the layout, fonts, colors, and formatting of every aspect of your web pages, including both text and images. When it comes to creating eye-popping web pages, CSS goes far beyond what traditional HTML pages could do by themselves. For example, did you know that CSS allows you to specifically tailor the information on a page just for printing, in addition to normal web viewing?

▶ Hours 10 through 12 introduce you to multimedia applications and their use, including where to find industry-standard software you can download and try free.

▶ The technical stuff is not enough, so this book also includes the advice you need when setting up a web site to achieve your goals. Key details—designing an effective page layout, posting your page to the Internet with FTP software, organizing and managing multiple pages, and getting your pages to appear high on the query lists at all the major Internet search sites—are all covered in enough depth to get you beyond the snags that often frustrate beginners.

Attention to many of these essentials are what made the first seven editions of this book bestsellers, and this updated edition—the first for this title since 2005—is no different. All of the examples have been updated and a significant portion of the content has been revised to match new examples and new technologies.

Visual Examples

Every example in this book is illustrated in two parts:

▶ The text you type to make an HTML page is shown first, with all HTML and CSS code highlighted.

▶ The resulting web page is shown as it will appear to users who view it with the world's most popular web browsers.

You'll often be able to adapt the example to your own pages without reading any of the accompanying text at all.

All the examples in this book are standards-compliant and work with Apple Safari, Google Chrome, Microsoft Internet Explorer, Mozilla Firefox, and Opera. While all of the screenshots are taken in Firefox, rest assured that all of the code has been tested in all other browsers.

You will also find the use of colors within code examples and when elements of code appear in the explanatory text. These colors highlight the different bits and pieces of code both to enhance your familiarity with them and to call attention to their use.

▶ HTML tags are displayed in dark blue.

▶ HTML comments are displayed in brown.

▶ CSS elements are displayed in green.

▶ HTML attribute names are displayed in light blue.

▶ HTML attribute values are displayed in magenta.

Be aware that the colors of certain terms change depending on their context. For instance, when CSS elements are used within the style attribute of an HTML tag, they will be color-coded as HTML attribute values (magenta) rather than CSS elements (green).

Special Elements

As you complete each hour, margin notes help you immediately apply what you just learned to your own web pages.

TIP	NOTE	WARNING
Tips and tricks to save you precious time are set aside in "Tip" boxes so that you can spot them quickly.	"Note" boxes provide additional information about the topics being discussed.	When there's something you need to watch out for, you'll be warned about it in "Warning" boxes.

Q&A, Quiz, and Exercises

Every hour ends with a short question-and-answer session that addresses the kind of "dumb questions" everyone wishes they dared to ask. A brief but complete quiz lets you test yourself to be sure you understand everything presented in the hour. Finally, one or two optional exercises give you a chance to practice your new skills before you move on.

HOUR 1
Understanding How the Web Works

Before learning the intricacies of HTML and CSS, it is important that you gain a solid understanding of the technologies that help transform these plain-text files to the rich multimedia displays you see on your computer or handheld device when browsing the World Wide Web.

A file containing HTML and CSS is useless without a web browser to view it, and no one besides yourself will see your content unless a web server is involved. Web servers make your content available to others who, in turn, use their web browsers to navigate to an address and wait for the server to send information to them. You will be intimately involved in this process, as you must create files and then put them on a server to make them available in the first place, and you must ensure that your content will appear to the end-user as you intended.

A Brief History of HTML and the World Wide Web

Once upon a time, back when there weren't any footprints on the moon, some farsighted folks decided to see whether they could connect several major computer networks together. I'll spare you the names and stories (there are plenty of both), but the eventual result was the "mother of all networks," which we call the Internet.

Until 1990, accessing information through the Internet was a rather technical affair. It was so hard, in fact, that even Ph.D.-holding physicists were often frustrated when trying to swap data. One such physicist, the now-famous (and knighted) Sir Tim Berners-Lee, cooked up a way to easily cross-reference text on the Internet through "hypertext" links.

WHAT YOU'LL LEARN IN THIS HOUR:

▶ A very brief history of the World Wide Web

▶ What is meant by the term "web page," and why that term doesn't always reflect all the content involved

▶ How content gets from your personal computer to someone else's web browser

▶ How to select a web hosting provider

▶ How different web browsers and device types can affect your content

This wasn't a new idea, but his simple Hypertext Markup Language (HTML) managed to thrive while more ambitious hypertext projects floundered. *Hypertext* originally meant text stored in electronic form with cross-reference links between pages. It is now a broader term that refers to just about any object (text, images, files, and so on) that can be linked to other objects. *Hypertext Markup Language* is a language for describing how text, graphics, and files containing other information are organized and linked together.

NOTE

For more information about the history of the World Wide Web, see the Wikipedia article on this topic:
http://en.wikipedia.org/wiki/History_of_the_Web.

By 1993, only 100 or so computers throughout the world were equipped to serve up HTML pages. Those interlinked pages were dubbed the *World Wide Web (WWW),* and several web browser programs had been written to allow people to view web pages. Because of the growing popularity of the Web, a few programmers soon wrote web browsers that could view graphical images along with text. From that point forward, the continued development of web browser software and the standardization of the HTML—and XHTML—languages has lead us to the world we live in today, one in which more than 110 million web servers answer requests for more than 25 billion text and multimedia files.

These few paragraphs really are a brief history of what has been a remarkable period of time. Today's college freshmen have never known a time in which the World Wide Web didn't exist, and the idea of "always-on" information and ubiquitous computing will shape all aspects of our lives moving forward. Instead of seeing web content creation and management as a set of skills possessed only by a few technically-oriented folks (ok, call them "geeks" if you will), by the end of this book you will see that these are skills that anyone can master, regardless of inherent geekiness.

Creating Web Content

You may have noticed the use of the term "web content" rather than "web pages"—that was intentional. Although we talk of "visiting a web page," what we really mean is something like "looking at all the text and the images at one address on our computer." The text that we read, and the images that we see, are rendered by our web browsers, which are given certain instructions found in individual files.

Those files contain text that is *marked up*, or surrounded by, HTML codes that tell the browser how to display the text—as a heading, as a paragraph, in a red font, and so on. Some HTML markup tells the browser to display an image or video file rather than plain text, which brings me back to the point—different types of content are sent to your web browser, so simply saying "web page" doesn't begin to cover it. Here we use the term "web content" instead, to cover the full range of text, image, audio, video, and other media found online.

In later lessons, you will learn the basics of linking to or creating the various types of multimedia web content found in web sites. All you need to remember at this point is that *you* are in control of the content a user sees when visiting your web site. Beginning with the file that contains text to display or codes that tell the server to send a graphic along to the user's web browser, you have to plan, design, and implement all the pieces that will eventually make up your web presence. As you will learn throughout this book, it is not a difficult process as long as you understand all the little steps along the way.

In its most fundamental form, web content begins with a simple text file containing HTML or XHTML markup. XHTML is another flavor of HTML; the "X" stands for eXtensible, and you will learn more about it as you continue through the lessons. The most important thing to know from the outset is that all the examples in this book are HTML 4 and XHTML compatible, meaning that they will be rendered similarly both now and in the future by any newer generations of web browsers. That is one of the benefits of writing standards-compliant code: you do not have to worry about having to go back to your code sometime in the future and change it because it "doesn't work." Your code will likely always "work" for as long as web browsers adhere to standards (hopefully a long time).

Understanding Web Content Delivery

Several processes occur, in many different locations, to eventually produce web content that you can see. These processes occur very quickly—on the order of milliseconds—and occur behind the scenes. In other words, while we might think all we are doing is opening a web browser, typing in a web address, and instantaneously seeing the content we requested, technology in the background is working hard on our behalf. Figure 1.1 shows the basic interaction between a browser and a server.

FIGURE 1.1
A browser request
and a
server response.

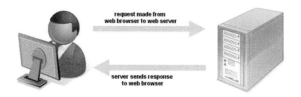

However, there are several steps in the process—and potentially several trips between the browser and server—before you see the entire content of the site you requested.

Suppose you want to do a Google search, so you dutifully type **http://www.google.com** in the address bar or select the Google bookmark from your bookmarks list. Almost immediately, your browser will show you something like what's shown in Figure 1.2.

FIGURE 1.2
Visiting www.google.com.

Figure 1.2 shows a web site that contains text plus one image (the Google logo). A simple version of the processes that occurred to retrieve that text and image from a web server and display it on your screen is as follows:

1. Your web browser sends a request for the index.html file located at the http://www.google.com/ address. The index.html file does not have to be part of the address that you type in the address bar; you'll learn more about the index.html file in Hour 2, "Publishing Web Content."

2. After receiving the request for a specific file, the web server process looks in its directory contents for the specific file, opens it, and sends the content of that file back to your web browser.

3. The web browser receives the content of the index.html file, which is text marked up with HTML codes, and renders the content based on these HTML codes. While rendering the content, the browser happens upon the HTML code for the Google logo, which you can see in Figure 1.2. The HTML code looks like this:

```
<img src="/logos/logo.gif" width="384" height="121" border="0"
alt="Google"/>
```

The tag provides attributes that tell the browser the file source location (src), width (width), height (height), border type (border), and alternative text (alt) necessary to display the logo. You will learn more about attributes throughout later lessons.

4. The browser looks at the src attribute in the <img/> tag to find the source location. In this case the image logo.gif can be found in the "logos" directory at the same web address (www.google.com) from which the browser retrieved the HTML file.

5. The browser requests the file at the http://www.google.com/logos/logo.gif web address.

6. The web server interprets that request, finds the file, and sends the contents of that file to the web browser that requested it.

7. The web browser displays the image on your monitor.

As you can see in the description of the web content delivery process, web browsers do more than simply act as picture frames through which you can view content. Browsers assemble the web content components and arrange those parts according to the HTML commands in the file.

You can also view web content "locally," or on your own hard drive, without the need for a web server. The process of content retrieval and display is the same as the process listed in the previous steps in that a browser looks for and interprets the codes and content of an HTML file, but the trip is shorter: the browser looks for files on your own computer's hard drive rather than on a remote machine. A web server would be needed to interpret any server-based programming language embedded in the files, but that is outside the scope of this book. In fact, you could work through all the lessons in this book without having a web server to call your own, but then nobody but you could view your masterpieces.

Selecting a Web Hosting Provider

Despite just telling you that you can work through all the lessons in this book without having a web server, we actually recommend that you work with a web server. Don't worry— obtaining a hosting provider is usually a quick, painless, and relatively inexpensive process. In fact, you can get your own domain name and a year of web hosting for just slightly more than the cost of the book you are reading now.

If you type **web hosting provider** in your search engine of choice, you will get millions of hits and an endless list of sponsored search results (also known as ads). There are not this many web hosting providers in the world, although it might seem like there are. Even if you are looking at a managed list of hosting providers, it can be overwhelming—especially if all you are looking for is a place to host a simple web site for yourself or your company or organization.

You'll want to narrow your search when looking for a provider and choose one that best meets your needs. Some selection criteria for a web hosting provider are

> ▶ **Reliability/server "uptime"**—if you have an online presence, you want to make sure people can actually get there consistently.

> ▶ **Customer service**—look for multiple methods for contacting customer service (phone, email, chat) as well as online documentation for common issues.

> ▶ **Server space**—does the hosting package include enough server space to hold all the multimedia files (images, audio, video) you plan to include in your web site (if any)?

> ▶ **Bandwidth**—does the hosting package include enough bandwidth so that all the people visiting your site and downloading files can do so without you having to pay extra?

> ▶ **Domain name purchase and management**—does the package include a custom domain name, or must you purchase and maintain your domain name separately from your hosting account?

> ▶ **Price**—do not overpay for hosting. You will see a wide range of prices offered and should immediately wonder "what's the difference?" Often the difference has little to do with the quality of the service and everything to do with company overhead and what the company thinks they can get away with charging people. A good rule of thumb is that if you are paying more than $75 per year for a basic hosting package and domain name, you are probably paying too much.

Here are three reliable web hosting providers whose basic packages contain plenty of server space and bandwidth (as well as domain names and extra benefits) at a relatively low cost. If you don't go with any of these web hosting providers, you can at least use their basic package descriptions as a guideline as you shop around.

▶ A Small Orange (http://www.asmallorange.com)—their "Tiny" and "Small" hosting packages are perfect starting places for the new web content publisher.

▶ DailyRazor (http://www.dailyrazor.com)—their RazorLIMIT and RazorSTARTER hosting packages are full-featured and reliable.

▶ LunarPages (http://www.lunarpages.com)—the Basic hosting package is suitable for many personal and small business web sites.

One feature of a good hosting provider is that they provide a "control panel" for you to manage aspects of your account. Figure 1.3 shows the control panel for my own RazorPRO hosting account at Daily Razor. Many web hosting providers offer this particular control panel software, or some control panel that is similar in design—clearly labeled icons leading to tasks you can perform to configure and manage your account.

FIGURE 1.3
A sample control panel.

You might never need to use your control panel, but having it available to you simplifies the installation of databases and other software, the viewing of web statistics, and the addition of e-mail addresses (among many other features). If you can follow instructions, you can manage your own web server—no special training required.

Testing with Multiple Web Browsers

Having just discussed the process of web content delivery and the acquisition of a web server, it might seem a little strange to step back and talk about testing your web sites with multiple web browsers. However, before you go off and learn all about creating web sites with HTML and CSS, do so with this very important statement in mind: every visitor to your web site will potentially use hardware and software configurations that are different than your own. Their device types (desktop, laptop, netbook, smartphone, iPhone), their screen resolutions, their browser types, their browser window sizes, their speed of connections—remember that you cannot control any aspect of what your visitors use when they view your site.

Although all web browsers process and handle information in the same general way, there are some specific differences among them that result in things not always looking the same in different browsers. Even users of the same version of the same web browser can alter how a page appears by choosing different display options and/or changing the size of their viewing windows. All the major web browsers allow users to override the background and fonts specified by the web page author with those of their own choosing. Screen resolution, window size, and optional toolbars can also change how much of a page someone sees when it first appears on their screens. You can ensure only that you write standards-compliant HTML and CSS.

Do not, under any circumstances, spend hours on end designing something that looks "perfect" on your own computer—unless you are willing to be disappointed when you look at it on your friend's computer, the computer in the coffee shop down the street, or on your iPhone.

You should always test your web sites with as many of these web browsers as possible:

- ▶ Apple Safari (http://www.apple.com/safari/) for Mac and Windows
- ▶ Google Chrome (http://www.google.com/chrome) for Windows

- ▶ Mozilla Firefox (http://www.mozilla.com/firefox/) for Mac, Windows, and Linux

- ▶ Microsoft Internet Explorer (http://www.microsoft.com/ie) for Windows

- ▶ Opera (http://www.opera.com/) for Mac, Windows, and Linux/UNIX

Summary

This hour introduced you to the concept of using HTML to mark-up text files in order to produce web content. You also learned that there is more to web content than just the "page"—web content also includes image, audio, and video files. All of this content lives on a web server—a remote machine often far away from your own computer. On your computer or other device, you use a web browser to request, retrieve, and eventually display web content on your screen.

You learned the criteria you should consider when determining if a web hosting provider fits your needs. You also learned the importance of testing your work in multiple browsers once you've placed it on a web server. Writing valid, standards-compliant HTML and CSS will help ensure your site looks reasonably similar for all visitors, but you still shouldn't design without receiving input from potential users outside your development team—it is even more important to get input from others when you are a "design team" of one!

Q&A

Q You've said "web content" instead of "web page," but I hear people refer to "web pages." So what do they mean? And how are these terms different from a "home page" or a "web site"?

A The metaphor of the World Wide Web as a library has always been easy for people to understand; in that library, individual web sites are books, and the individual content files on web sites as "pages." A "web site" is comprised of one or more pages that are created together and related in content. A "home page" usually means the first page people visit when they look at a web site. Problems arise, however, when people say "visit my web page" when really they mean "come to my web site"—sites are full of pages. Referring to a collection of web content as a page instead of a site can tip someone off that you really don't understand how the web works—either because you don't understand the way web content works together to create a site, or because you've planned, designed, and implemented a site in which your content really is all on one page!

Q I've looked at the HTML "source" of some web pages on the Internet and it looks frighteningly difficult to learn. Do I have to think like a computer programmer to learn this stuff?

A Although complex HTML pages can indeed look daunting, learning HTML is much easier than learning actual software programming languages (such as C++ or Java). HTML is a markup language rather than a programming language; you mark-up text so that the text can be rendered a certain way by the browser. That's a completely different set of thought processes than developing a computer program. You really don't need any experience or skill as a computer programmer to be a successful web content author.

One of the reasons the HTML behind many commercial web sites looks complicated is because it was likely created by a visual web design tool—a "what you see is what you get" or "WYSIWYG" editor that will use whatever markup its software developer told it to use in certain circumstances—as opposed to being hand-coded, in which *you* are completely in control of the resulting markup. In this book, you are taught fundamental coding from the ground up, which typically results in clean, easy-to-read source code. Visual web design tools have a knack for making code difficult to read, and also for producing code that is convoluted and non-standards compliant.

Workshop

The workshop contains quiz questions and exercises to help you solidify your understanding of the material covered. Try to answer all of the questions before looking at the "Answers" section that follows.

Quiz

1. Define the term *web content*.

2. How many files would you need to store on a web server to produce a single web page with some text and two images on it?

3. What are some of the features to look for in a web hosting provider?

Quiz Answers

1. Web content is a term that describes the full range of text, image, audio, video, and other media files delivered from web servers to web browsers.

2. You would need three: one for the web page itself, which includes the text and the HTML markup, and one for each of the two images.

3. Look for reliability, customer service, web space and bandwidth, domain name service, site management extras, and price.

Exercises

▶ Get your web hosting in order—are you going to go through the lessons in this book by viewing files locally on your own computer, or are you going to use a web hosting provider? Note that most web hosting providers will have you up and running the same day you purchase your hosting plan.

Publishing Web Content

In the previous hour, you learned about the process of requesting web content via a web browser and how the web server responds to those requests. In this hour you'll learn where you, as the content creator, fit into making web content available online—you have to publish that content on a web server in order for other people to find it.

Creating the Sample File for this Hour

Before we begin, take a look at Listing 2.1. This listing represents a simple piece of web content—a few lines of HTML that print "Hello World! Welcome to My Web Server." in large, bold letters on two lines centered within the browser window.

Listing 2.1   Our Sample HTML File

```
<html>
<head>
<title>Hello World!</title>
</head>
<body>
<h1 align="center">Hello World!<br/>Welcome to My Web Server.</h1>
</body>
</html>
```

To make use of this content, open a text editor of your choice, such as Notepad (on Windows) or TextEdit (on a Mac). Do not use WordPad, Microsoft Word, or other full-featured word-processing software, as those create different sorts of files than the plain-text files we use for web content.

WHAT YOU'LL LEARN IN THIS HOUR:

▶ How to create a basic HTML file using a text editor

▶ How to transfer files to your web server using FTP

▶ Where files should be placed on a web server

▶ How to distribute web content without a web server

▶ How to use other publishing methods such as blogs

NOTE

You will learn more about text editors in Hour 3. Right now, we just want you to have a sample file that you can put on a web server!

Type the content that you see in Listing 2.1 and then save the file using **sample.html** as the file name. The .html extension tells the web server that your file is, indeed, full of HTML. When the file contents are sent to the web browser that requests it, the browser will also know that it is HTML and will render it appropriately.

Now that you have a sample HTML file to use—and hopefully somewhere to put it, such as a web hosting account—let's get to publishing your web content.

Using FTP to Transfer Files

As you've learned so far, you have to put your web content on a web server in order to make it accessible to others. This process typically occurs by using *File Transfer Protocol (FTP)*. To use FTP, you need an FTP client—a program used to transfer files from your computer to a web server.

FTP clients require three pieces of information in order to connect to your web server; this information will have been sent to you by your hosting provider after you set up your account:

- ▶ The hostname, or address, to which you will connect
- ▶ Your account username
- ▶ Your account password

Once you have this information, you are ready to use an FTP client to transfer content to your web server.

Selecting an FTP Client

Regardless of the FTP client you use, FTP clients generally use the same type of interface. Figure 2.1 shows an example of FireFTP, which is an FTP client used with the Firefox web browser. The directory listing of the local machine (your computer) appears on the left of your screen and the directory listing of the remote machine (the web server) appears on the right. Typically you will see right-arrow and left-arrow buttons—as shown in Figure 2.1. The right arrow sends selected files from your computer to your web server; the left arrow sends files from the web server to your computer. Many FTP clients also allow you to simply select files and then drag and drop those files to the target machines.

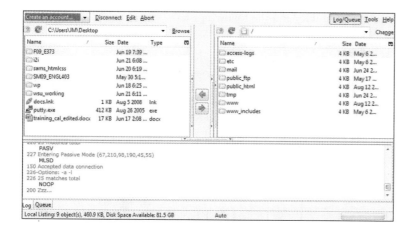

FIGURE 2.1
The FireFTP interface.

There are many FTP clients freely available to you, but you can also transfer files via the web-based File Manager tool that is likely part of your web server's control panel. However, that method of file transfer typically introduces more steps into the process and isn't nearly as streamlined (or simple) as installing an FTP client on your own machine.

Here are some popular free FTP clients:

▶ Classic FTP (http://www.nchsoftware.com/classic/) for Mac and Windows

▶ Cyberduck (http://cyberduck.ch/) for Mac

▶ Fetch (http://fetchsoftworks.com/) for Mac

▶ FileZilla (http://filezilla-project.org/) for all platforms

▶ FireFTP (http://fireftp.mozdev.org/) Firefox extension for all platforms

Once you have selected an FTP client and installed it on your computer, you are ready to upload and download files from your web server. In the next section, you'll see how this process works using the sample file created at the beginning of this hour.

Using an FTP Client

The following steps show how to use Classic FTP to connect to your web server and transfer a file. However, all FTP clients use similar, if not exact, interfaces. If you understand the following steps, you should be able to use any FTP client.

Remember, you first need the hostname, the account username, and the account password.

1. Start the Classic FTP program and click the Connect button. You will be prompted to fill out information for the site to which you wish to connect, as shown in Figure 2.2.

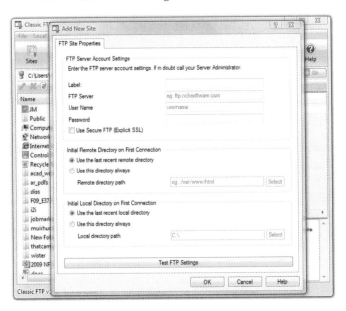

2. Fill in each of the items shown in Figure 2.2 as follows:

   ▶ The site Label is the name you'll use to refer to your own site. Nobody else will see this name, so enter whatever you want.

   ▶ The FTP Server is the FTP address of the web server to which you need to send your web pages. This address will have been given to you by your hosting provider. It will probably be yourdomain.com, but check the information you received when you signed up for service.

   ▶ The User Name field and the Password field should also be completed using information given to you by your hosting provider.

   ▶ Don't change the values for Initial Remote Directory on First Connection and Initial Local Directory on First Connection until you are used to using the client and have established a workflow.

3. When you're finished with the settings, click OK to save the settings and establish a connection with the web server.

   You will see a dialog box indicating that Classic FTP is attempting to connect to the web server. Upon successful connection, you will see an interface like that which is shown in Figure 2.3, showing the contents of the local directory on the left and the contents of your web server on the right.

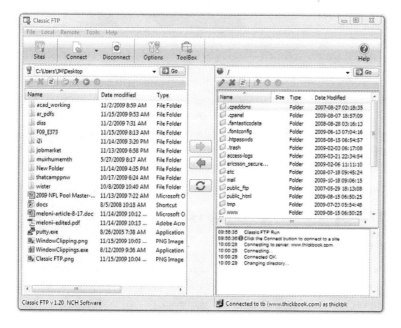

FIGURE 2.3
A successful connection to a remote web server via Classic FTP.

4. You are now *almost* ready to transfer files to your web server. All that remains is to change directories to what is called the *document root* of your web server. The document root of your web server is the directory that is designated as the top-level directory for your web content—the starting point of the directory structure, which you will learn more about later in this hour. Often, this directory will be named public_html (as shown in Figure 2.3), www (also shown in Figure 2.3, as www has been created as an alias for public_html) or htdocs. This is not a directory that you will have to create, as your hosting provider will have created it for you.

   Double-click the document root directory name to open it. The display shown on the right of the FTP client interface should change to show the contents of this directory (it will probably be empty at this point, unless your web hosting provider has put placeholder files in that directory on your behalf).

5. The goal is to transfer the sample.html file you created earlier from your computer to the web server. Find the file in the directory listing on the left of the FTP client interface (navigate around if you have to) and click it once to highlight the file name.

6. Click the right-arrow button in the middle of the client interface to send the file to the web server. Once the file transfer is completed, the right side of the client interface should refresh to show you that the file has made it to its destination.

7. Click the Disconnect button to close the connection, and then exit out of the Classic FTP program.

These steps are conceptually similar to the steps you will take anytime you want to send files to your web server via FTP. You can also use your FTP client to create subdirectories on the remote web server. To create a subdirectory using Classic FTP, click the Remote menu and then click New Folder. Different FTP clients will have different interface options to achieve the same goal.

Understanding Where to Place Files on the Web Server

An important aspect of maintaining web content is determining how you will organize that content—not only for the user to find, but also for you to maintain on your server. Putting files in directories will help you to manage those files.

Naming and organizing directories on your web server, and developing rules for file maintenance, is completely up to you. However, maintaining a well-organized server simply makes your management of its content more efficient in the long run.

Basic File Management

As you browse the web, you might have noticed that URLs change as you navigate through web sites. For instance, if you're looking at a company's web site and you click on graphical navigation leading to the company's products or services, the URL will probably change from

http://www.companyname.com/

to

http://www.companyname.com/products/

or

http://www.companyname.com/services/

In the previous section, I used the term *document root* without really explaining what that is all about. The document root of a web server is essentially the trailing "slash" in the full URL. For instance, if your domain is yourdomain.com and your URL is http://www.yourdomain.com/, then the document root is the directory represented by the trailing slash (/). The document root is the starting point of the directory structure you create on your web server; it is the place where the web server begins looking for files requested by the web browser.

If you put the sample.html file in your document root as previously directed, then you will be able to access it via a web browser at the following URL:

http://www.yourdomain.com/sample.html

If you were to enter this URL into your web browser, you would see the rendered sample.html file as shown in Figure 2.4.

FIGURE 2.4
The sample.html file accessed via a web browser.

However, if you created a new directory within the document root and put the sample.html file in that directory, then the file would be accessed at this URL:

http://www.yourdomain.com/newdirectory/sample.html

If you put the sample.html file in the directory you originally saw upon connecting to your server—that is, you did *not* change directories and place the file in the document root—then the sample.html file would not be accessible from your web server at any URL. The file will still be on the machine that you know as your web server, but since the file is not in the document root—where the server software knows to start looking for files—it will never be accessible to anyone via a web browser.

The bottom line? Always navigate to the document root of your web server before you start transferring files.

This is especially true with graphics and other multimedia files. A common directory on web servers is called "images," where, as you can imagine, all the image assets are placed for retrieval. Other popular directories include "css" for stylesheet files (if you are using more than one) and "js" for external JavaScript files. Or, if you know you will have an area on your web site where visitors can download many different types of files, you might simply call that directory "downloads."

Whether it's a ZIP file containing your art portfolio or an Excel spreadsheet with sales numbers, it's often useful to publish files on the Internet that aren't simply web pages. To make a file available on the Web that isn't an HTML file, just upload the file to your web site as if it *were* an HTML file, following the instructions earlier in this hour for uploading. After the file is uploaded to the web server, you can create a link to it (as you'll learn in later hours). In other words, your web server can "serve" much more than HTML.

Here's a sample of the HTML code that you will learn in that hour. The following code would be used for a file named artfolio.zip, located in the downloads directory of your web site, and link text that reads "Download my art portfolio!":

```
<a href="/downloads/artfolio.zip">Download my art portfolio!</a>
```

Using an Index Page

When you think of an index, you probably think of the section in the back of a book that tells you where to look for various keywords and topics. The index file in a web server directory can serve that purpose—if you design it that way. In fact, that's where the name originates.

The index.html file (or just *index file*, as it's usually referred to) is the name you give to the page you want people to see as the default file when they navigate to a specific directory in your web site. If you've created that page with usability in mind, your users will be able to get to all content in that section from the index page.

For example, Figure 2.5 shows the drop-down navigation and left-side navigation both contain links to three pages: Solutions Overview (the section index page itself), Connection Management, and Cost Management. The content of the page itself—called index.html and located within the solutions directory—also has links to those two additional pages in the solutions section. When users arrive at the index page of the solutions section in this particular web site, they can reach any other page in that section (and three different ways!).

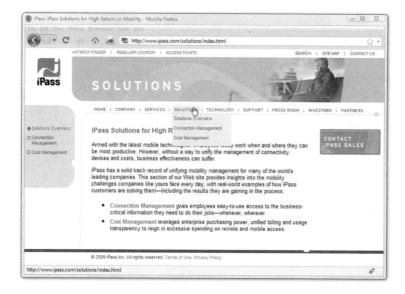

FIGURE 2.5
Showing a good section index page.

Another function of the index page is that when users visit a directory on your site that has an index page, but they do not specify that page, they will still land on the main page for that section of your site—or for the site itself.

For instance, in the previous example, a user could have typed either of the following URLs and landed on the main page of the solutions section of that web site:

http://www.ipass.com/solutions/

http://www.ipass.com/solutions/index.html

Had there been no index.html page in the solutions directory, the results would depend on the configuration of the web server. If the server is configured to disallow directory browsing, the user would have seen a "Directory Listing Denied" message when attempting to access the URL without a specified page name. However, if the server is configured to allow directory browsing, the user would have seen a list of the files in that directory.

These server configuration options will have already been determined for you by your hosting provider. If your hosting provider allows you to modify server settings via a control panel, then you can change these settings so that your server responds to requests based on your own requirements.

Not only is the index file used in subdirectories, it's used in the top-level directory (or document root) of your web site as well. The first page of your web site—or *home page* or *main page*, or however you wish to refer to the web content you want users to see when they first visit your domain—should be named index.html and placed in the document root of your web server. This will ensure that when users type http://www.yourdomain.com/ into their web browsers, the server will respond with content you intended them to see (rather than "Directory Listing Denied" or some other unintended consequence).

Distributing Content without a Web Server

Publishing HTML and multimedia files online is obviously the primary reason to learn HTML and create web content. However, there are also situations in which other forms of publishing simply aren't viable. For example, you might want to distribute CD-ROMs, DVD-ROMs, or USB drives at a trade show with marketing materials designed as web content—that is, hyperlinked text viewable through a web browser, but without a web server involved. You might also want to include HTML-based instructional manuals on removable media for students at a training seminar. These are just two examples of how HTML pages can be used in publishing scenarios that don't involve the Internet.

This process is also called creating *local* sites; even though there's no web server involved, these bundles of hypertext content are still called *sites*. The local term comes into play since your files are accessed locally and not remotely (via a web server).

Publishing Content Locally

Let's assume you need to create a local site that you want to distribute on a USB drive. Even the cheapest USB drives hold so much data these days—and basic hypertext files are quite small—that you can distribute an entire site *and a fully-functioning web browser* all on one little drive.

Simply think of the directory structure of your USB drive just as you would the directory structure of your web server. The top-level of the USB drive directory structure can be your document root. Or if you are distributing a web browser along with the content, you might have two directories—for example, one named browser and one named content. In that case, the content directory would be your document root. Within the document root, you could have additional subfolders in which you place content and other multimedia assets.

It's as important to maintain a good organization with a local site as it is with a remote web site, so that you avoid broken links in your HTML files. You will learn more about the specifics of linking together files in a later hour.

Publishing Content on a Blog

You might have a blog hosted by a third-party, such as Blogger or WordPress (among others), and thus have already published content without having a dedicated web server or even knowing any HTML. These services offer *visual editors* in addition to *source editors*, meaning that you can type your words and add visual formatting such as bold, italics, or font colors without knowing the HTML for these actions. But still, the content becomes actual HTML when you click the Publish button in these editors.

However, with the knowledge you will acquire throughout this book, your blogging will be enhanced because you will able to use the source editor for your blog post content and blog templates, thus affording you more control over the look and feel of that content. These actions occur differently than the process you learned for creating an HTML file and uploading it via FTP to your own dedicated web server, but I would be remiss if I did not note that blogging is, in fact, a form of web publishing.

NOTE

Distributing a web browser isn't required when creating and distributing a local site, although it's a nice touch. You can reasonably assume that users have their own web browsers and will open the index.html file in a directory to start browsing the hyperlinked content. However, if you would like to distribute a web browser on the USB drive, go to http://www.portableapps.com/ and look for Portable Firefox.

Testing Web Content

Whenever you transfer files to your web server or place them on removable media for local browsing, you should immediately test every page thoroughly. The following checklist will help ensure that your web content behaves the way you expected. Note that some of the terms might be unfamiliar to you at this point, but come back to this checklist as you progress through this book and create larger projects:

- ▶ Before you transfer your files, test them locally on your machine to ensure that the links work and the content reflects the visual design you intended. After you transfer the pages to a web server or removable device, test them all again.

- ▶ Perform these tests with as many browsers that you can—Chrome, Firefox, Internet Explorer, Opera, and Safari is a good list—and on both Mac and Windows platforms. If possible, check at low resolution (800x600) and high resolution (1600x1200).

- ▶ Turn off auto image loading in your web browser before you start testing so that you can see what each page looks like without the graphics. Check your alt tag messages and then turn image loading back on to load the graphics and review the page carefully again.

- ▶ Use your browser's font size settings to look at each page in various font sizes to ensure that your layout doesn't fall to pieces if users override your font specifications with their own.

- ▶ Wait for each page to completely finish loading and then scroll all the way down to make sure that all images appear where they should.

- ▶ Time how long it takes each page to load. Does it take more than a few seconds to load? If so, is the information on that page valuable enough to keep users from going elsewhere before the page finishes loading? Granted, broadband connections are common, but that doesn't mean you should load up your pages with 1 MB images.

If your pages pass all those tests, you can rest easy; your site is ready for public viewing.

Summary

You began this hour by creating a very simple HTML file to use as a test file for the process of transferring files to your web server. You learned how that file transfer process works and what type of software you need to perform those transfers (an FTP client). You also learned a little bit about web server directory structures and file management, as well as the very important purpose of the index.html file in a given web server directory. You also learned that you can distribute web content on removable media, and you learned how to go about structuring the files and directories to achieve the goal of viewing content without using a remote web server. Finally, you learned how to test your files before releasing your site for public consumption.

Q&A

Q All the tests you recommend would take longer than creating my pages! Can't I get away with less testing?

A If your pages aren't intended to make money or provide an important service, it's probably not a big deal if they look funny to some users or produce errors once in a while. In that case, just test each page with a couple of different browsers and call it a day. However, if you need to project a professional image, there is no substitute for rigorous testing.

Q Seriously, who cares how I organize my web content?

A Believe it or not, the organization of your web content does matter to search engines and potential visitors to your site—you'll learn more about this in Hour 24, "Helping People Find Your Web Pages." But overall, having an organized web server directory structure will help you keep track of content that you are likely to update frequently. For instance, if you have a dedicated directory for images or multimedia, you will know exactly where to look for a file you wish to update—no need to hunt through directories containing other content.

Workshop

The workshop contains quiz questions and exercises to help you solidify your understanding of the material covered. Try to answer all questions before looking at the "Quiz Answers" section that follows.

Quiz

1. What three pieces of information do you need to connect to your web server via FTP?

2. What is the purpose of the index.html file?

3. Does your web site have to include a directory structure?

Quiz Answers

1. The hostname, your account username, and your account password.

2. The index.html file is typically the default file for a directory within a web server. It allows users to access http://www.yourdomain.com/somedirectory/ without using a trailing file name and still end up in the appropriate place.

3. No. Using a directory structure for file organization is completely up to you, although it is highly recommended to use one because it simplifies content maintenance.

Exercises

▶ Using your FTP client, create a subdirectory within the document root of your web site. Paste the contents of the sample.html file into another file named index.html, change the text between the `<title>` and `</title>` tags to something new, and change the text between the `<h1>` and `</h1>` tags to something new. Save the file and upload it to the new subdirectory. Use your web browser to navigate to the new directory on your web server and see that the content in the index.html file appears. Then, using your FTP client, delete the index.html file from the remote subdirectory. Return to that URL with your web browser, reload the page, and see how the server responds without the index.html file in place.

▶ Using the same set of files created in the exercise above, place these files on a removable media device—a CD-ROM or a USB drive, for example. Use your browser to navigate this local version of your sample web site, and think about the instructions you would have to distribute with this removable media so that others could use it.

Understanding HTML and XHTML Connections

The first two hours gave you a basic idea of the process behind creating web content and viewing it online or locally, if you do not yet have a web hosting provider. In this hour, we'll get down to the business of explaining the various elements that must appear in an HTML file.

At the end of the hour, you'll learn how HTML differs from XHTML and why there are two different languages designed to do the same thing—create web content. In general, this hour provides a quick summary of HTML and XHTML basics and gives some practical tips to make the most of your time as a web page author and publisher. It's not all theory, however; you do get to see a real web page and the HTML code behind it.

Here's a review of what you need to do before you're ready to use the rest of this book:

1. Get a computer. I used a computer with Windows Vista to test the sample web content and capture the figures in this book, but you can use any Windows, Macintosh, or Linux/UNIX machine to create and view your web content.

2. Get a connection to the Internet. Whether you have a dial-up, wireless, or broadband connection doesn't matter for the creation and viewing of your web content, but the faster the connection, the better for the overall experience. The Internet Service Provider (ISP), school, or business that provides your Internet connection can help you with the details of setting it up properly. Additionally, many public spaces such as coffee shops, bookstores, and libraries offer free wireless Internet service that you can use if you have a laptop computer with Wi-Fi network support.

WHAT YOU'LL LEARN IN THIS HOUR:

▶ How to create a simple web page in HTML

▶ How to include all the HTML Tags that every web page must have

▶ How to organize a page with paragraphs and line breaks

▶ How to organize your content with headings

▶ How to validate your web content

▶ How to differentiate between HTML, XML, XHTML, and HTML 5

NOTE

Not sure how to find an ISP? The best way is to comparison-shop online (using a friend's computer or a public computer that's already connected to the Internet). You'll find a comprehensive list of national and regional ISPs at http://www.the-list.com/.

NOTE

Although all web browsers process and handle information in the same general way, there are some specific differences among them that result in things not always looking the same in different browsers. Be sure to check your web pages in multiple browsers to make sure that they look reasonably consistent.

NOTE

As discussed in Hour 1, if you plan to put your web content on the Internet (as opposed to publishing it on CD-ROM or a local intranet), you'll need to transfer it to a computer that is connected to the Internet 24 hours a day. The same company or school that provides you with Internet access might also provide web space; if not, you might need to pay a hosting provider for the service.

WARNING

Do not create your first HTML file with Microsoft Word or any other HTML-compatible word processor; most of these programs attempt to rewrite your HTML for you in strange ways, potentially leaving you totally confused. Additionally, I recommend that you *do not* use a graphical, what-you-see-is-what-you-get (WYSIWYG) editor, such as Microsoft FrontPage or Adobe Dreamweaver. You'll likely find it easier and more educational to start out with a simple text editor while you're just learning HTML. You can progress to visual tools (such as FrontPage and Dreamweaver) after you have a better understanding of what's going on "under the hood."

3. Get web browser software. This is the software your computer needs in order to retrieve and display web content. As you learned in the first hour, the most popular browser software (in alphabetical order) is Apple Safari, Google Chrome, Mozilla Firefox, Microsoft Internet Explorer, and Opera. It's a good idea to install several of these browsers so that you can experiment and make sure that your content looks consistent across them all; you can't make assumptions about the browsers other people are using.

4. Explore! Use a web browser to look around the Internet for web sites that are similar in content or appearance to those you'd like to create. Note what frustrates you about some pages, what attracts you and keeps you reading others, and what makes you come back to some pages over and over again. If there is a particular topic that interests you, consider searching for it using a popular search engine such as Google (`http://www.google.com/`) or Bing (http://www.bing.com/).

Getting Started with a Simple Web Page

In the first hour, you learned that a "web page" is just a text file that is "marked-up" by (or surrounded by) HTML codes that tell the browser how to display the text. To create these text files, use a *text editor* such as Notepad (on Windows) or TextEdit (on a Mac)—do not use WordPad, Microsoft Word, or other full-featured word-processing software, as those create different sorts of files than the plain-text files we use for web content.

Before you begin working, you should start with some text that you want to put on a web page:

1. Find (or write) a few paragraphs of text about yourself, your family, your company, your softball team, or some other subject in which you're interested.

2. Save this text as plain, standard ASCII text. Notepad and most simple text editors always save files as plain text, but if you're using another program, you might need to choose this file type as an option (after selecting File, Save As).

As you go through this hour, you will add HTML markup (called *tags*) to the text file, thus making it into web content.

When you save files containing HTML tags, always give them a name ending in .html. This is important: if you forget to type the .html at the end of the filename when you save the file, most text editors will give it some other extension (such as .txt). If that happens, you might not be able to find the file when you try to look at it with a web browser; if you find it, it certainly won't display properly. In other words, web browsers expect a web page file to have a file extension of .html.

You might also encounter a web page with a file extension of .htm, which is also acceptable. You might find other file extensions used on the Web, such as .jsp (Java Server Pages), .asp (Microsoft Active Server Pages), or .php (PHP: Hypertext Preprocessor), but these file types use server-side technologies that are beyond the scope of HTML.

Listing 3.1 shows an example of text you can type and save to create a simple HTML page. If you opened this file with Firefox, you would see the page shown in Figure 3.1. Every web page you create must include the `<html></html>`, `<head></head>`, `<title></title>`, and `<body></body>` tag pairs.

NOTE

If you're using TextEdit on a Macintosh computer, the steps for creating an HTML file are a little different than for using Notepad on a Windows computer—both are popular text editors, but with the latter you must first click on the Format menu and select Make Plain Text and then change the preferences under the Saving header by unchecking the box for Append '.txt' Extension to Plain Text Files. Also, the default preferences are set to show .html documents as they would appear in a browser, which won't allow you to edit them. To fix this, check Ignore Rich Text Commands in HTML Files under the Rich Text Processing header.

Listing 3.1   The `<html>`, `<head>`, `<title>`, and `<body>` Tags

```
<?xml version="1.0" encoding="UTF-8"?>
<!DOCTYPE html PUBLIC "-//W3C//DTD XHTML 1.1//EN"
  "http://www.w3.org/TR/xhtml11/DTD/xhtml11.dtd">

<html xmlns="http://www.w3.org/1999/xhtml" xml:lang="en">
  <head>
    <title>The First Web Page</title>
  </head>

  <body>
    <p>
      In the beginning, Tim created the HyperText Markup Language. The Internet
      was without form and void, and text was upon the face of the monitor and
      the Hands of Tim were moving over the face of the keyboard. And Tim said,
      Let there be links; and there were links. And Tim saw that the links were
      good; and Tim separated the links from the text. Tim called the links
      Anchors, and the text He called Other Stuff. And the whole thing together
      was the first Web Page.
    </p>
  </body>
</html>
```

In Listing 3.1, as in every HTML page, the words starting with < and ending with > are actually coded commands. These coded commands are called HTML tags because they "tag" pieces of text and tell the web browser what kind of text it is. This allows the web browser to display the text appropriately.

The first few lines of code in the web page serve as standard boilerplate code that you will include in all of your pages. This code actually identifies the page as an XHTML 1.1 document, which means that, technically, the web page is an XHTML page. All the pages developed throughout the book are XHTML 1.1 pages. Because XHTML is a more structured version of HTML, it's still okay to generally refer to all the pages in the book as HTML pages. By targeting XHTML 1.1 with your code, you are developing web pages that adhere to the very latest web standards. This is a good thing!

Before you learn the meaning of the HTML tags used in Listing 3.1, you might want to see exactly how I went about creating and viewing the document itself. Follow these steps:

1. Type all the text in Listing 3.1, including the HTML tags, in Windows Notepad (or use Macintosh TextEdit or another text editor of your choice).

2. Select File, Save As. Be sure to select plain text (or ASCII text) as the file type.

3. Name the file **firstpage.html**.

4. Choose the folder on your hard drive where you would like to keep your web pages—and remember which folder you choose! Click the Save or OK button to save the file.

5. Now start your favorite web browser. (Leave Notepad running, too, so you can easily switch between viewing and editing your page.)

In Internet Explorer, select File, Open and click Browse. If you're using Firefox, select File, Open File. Navigate to the appropriate folder and select the `firstpage.html` file. Some browsers and operating systems will also allow you to drag and drop the `firstpage.html` file onto the browser window in order to view it.

Voilà! You should see the page shown in Figure 3.1.

If you have obtained a web hosting account, you could use FTP at this point to transfer the firstpage.html file to the web server. In fact, from this hour forward, the instructions will assume you have a hosting provider and are comfortable sending files back and forth via FTP; if that is not the case, please review the first two hours before moving on. Or, if you are consciously choosing to work with files locally (without a web host), be prepared to adjust the instructions to suit your particular needs (such as ignoring "transfer the files" and "type in the URL").

NOTE

You don't need to be connected to the Internet to view a web page stored on your own computer. By default, your web browser tries to connect to the Internet every time you start it, which makes sense most of the time. However, this can be a hassle if you're developing pages locally on your hard drive (offline) and you keep getting errors about a page not being found. If you have a full-time web connection via a LAN, cable modem, or DSL, this is a moot point because the browser will never complain about being offline. Otherwise, the appropriate disciplinary action will depend on your breed of browser; check the options under your browser's "Tools" menu.

HTML Tags Every XHTML Web Page Must Have

NOTE

It isn't terribly important that you understand concepts such as character encoding at this point. What is important is that you include the appropriate boilerplate code in your pages so that they adhere to the latest web standards. As of this writing, XHTML 1.1 is a web standard. HTML 5 is not yet a web standard, but if you were creating an HTML 5 document, these lines at the beginning of your HTML file would not be necessary.

The time has come for the secret language of HTML tags to be revealed to you. When you understand this language, you will have creative powers far beyond those of other humans. Don't tell the other humans, but it's really pretty easy.

Before you get into the HTML tags, let's first address the messy-looking code at the top of Listing 3.1. The first line indicates that the HTML document is, in fact, an XML document:

```
<?xml version="1.0" encoding="UTF-8"?>
```

The version of XML is set to 1.0, which is fairly standard, as is the type of character encoding (UTF-8).

The second and third lines of code in Listing 3.1 are even more complicated looking:

```
<!DOCTYPE html PUBLIC "-//W3C//DTD XHTML 1.1//EN"
  "http://www.w3.org/TR/xhtml11/DTD/xhtml11.dtd">
```

NOTE

The XML/XHTML boilerplate code isn't strictly required in order for you to create web pages. You can delete the opening lines of code in the example so that the page starts with the `<html>` tag and it will still open fine in a web browser. The extra code is included to ensure your pages are up to date with the current web standards. Additionally, the extra code allows you to validate your web pages for accuracy, which you'll learn how to do a bit later in this lesson.

Again, the specifics of this code aren't terribly important as long as you remember to include the code at the start of your pages. This code identifies the document as being XHTML 1.1, which then allows web browsers to make sure the code meets all the requirements of XHTML 1.1.

Most HTML tags have two parts: an *opening tag*, which indicates where a piece of text begins, and a *closing tag*, which indicates where the piece of text ends. Closing tags start with a / (forward slash) just after the < symbol. Another type of tag is the *empty tag*, which is unique in that it doesn't include a pair of matching opening and closing tags. Instead, an empty tag consists of a single tag that starts with a < and ends with a / just before the > symbol. Following is a quick summary of these three tags just to make sure you understand the role each of them plays:

▶ An *opening tag* is an HTML tag that indicates the start of an HTML command; the text affected by the command appears after the opening tag. Opening tags always begin with < and end with >, as in `<html>`.

▶ A *closing tag* is an HTML tag that indicates the end of an HTML command; the text affected by the command appears before the closing tag. Closing tags always begin with </ and end with >, as in `</html>`.

▶ An *empty tag* is an HTML tag that issues an HTML command without enclosing any text in the page. Empty tags always begin with < and end with />, as in `<br />` and `<img />`.

For example, the `<body>` tag in Listing 3.1 tells the web browser where the actual body text of the page begins, and `</body>` indicates where it ends. Everything between the `<body>` and `</body>` tags will appear in the main display area of the web browser window, as shown in Figure 3.1.

The very top of the browser window (refer to Figure 3.1) shows title text, which is any text that is located between `<title>` and `</title>`. The title text is also used to identify the page on the browser's Bookmarks or Favorites menu, depending on which browser you use. It's important to provide titles for your pages so that visitors to the page can properly bookmark them for future reference.

You will use the `<body>` and `<title>` tag pairs in every HTML page you create because every web page needs a title and body text. You will also use `<html>` and `<head>`, which are he other two tags shown in Listing 3.1. Putting `<html>` at the very beginning of a document simply indicates that the document is a web page. The `</html>` at the end indicates that the web page is over.

Within a page, there is a head section and a body section. Each section is identified by `<head>` and `<body>` tags. The idea is that information in the head of the page somehow describes the page but isn't actually displayed by a web browser. Information placed in the body, however, is displayed by a web browser. The `<head>` tag always appears near the beginning of the HTML code for a page, just after the opening `<html>` tag.

The `<title>` tag pair used to identify the title of a page appears within the head of the page, which means it is placed after the opening `<head>` tag and before the closing `</head>` tag. (Upcoming hours reveal some other advanced header information that can go between `<head>` and `</head>`, such as style sheet rules that are used to format the page.)

The `<p>` tag used in Listing 3.1 encloses a paragraph of text. You should enclose your chunks of text in the appropriate container tags whenever possible.

NOTE

You no doubt noticed in Listing 3.1 that there is some extra code associated with the `<html>` tag. This code consists of two attributes (`xmlns` and `xml:lang`), which are used to specify additional information related to the tag. These two attributes are standard requirements of all XHTML web pages; the former defines the XML namespace, while the latter defines the language of the content. Throughout this book a standard namespace is defined, and the English language is used. If you are writing in a different language, replace the `"en"` (for English) with the language identifier relevant to you.

TIP

You might find it convenient to create and save a *bare-bones page* (also known as a *skeleton page*) with just the opening and closing `<html>`, `<head>`, `<title>`, and `<body>` tags, similar to the document used in Listing 3.1. You can then open that document as a starting point whenever you want to make a new web page and save yourself the trouble of typing all those obligatory tags every time.

Organizing a Page with Paragraphs and Line Breaks

When a web browser displays HTML pages, it pays no attention to line endings or the number of spaces between words. For example, the top version of the poem shown in Figure 3.2 appears with a single space between all words, even though that's not how it's entered in Listing 3.2. This is because extra whitespace in HTML code is automatically reduced to a single space. Additionally, when the text reaches the edge of the browser window, it automatically wraps to the next line, no matter where the line breaks were in the original HTML file.

Listing 3.2   HTML Containing Paragraph and Line Breaks

```
<?xml version="1.0" encoding="UTF-8"?>
<!DOCTYPE html PUBLIC "-//W3C//DTD XHTML 1.1//EN"
  "http://www.w3.org/TR/xhtml11/DTD/xhtml11.dtd">

<html xmlns="http://www.w3.org/1999/xhtml" xml:lang="en">
  <head>
    <title>The Advertising Agency Song</title>
  </head>

  <body>
    <p>
      When your client's    hopping mad,
      put his picture in the ad.

      If he still should    prove refractory,
      add a picture of his factory.

    </p>

    <hr />

    <p>
      When your client's hopping mad,<br />
      put his picture in the ad.
    </p>
    <p>
      If he still should prove refractory,<br />
      add a picture of his factory.
    </p>
  </body>
</html>
```

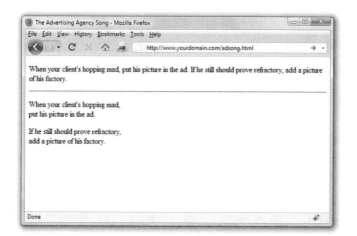

FIGURE 3.2
When the HTML in Listing 3.2 is viewed as a web page, line and paragraph breaks only appear where there are <br /> and <p> tags.

You must use HTML tags if you want to control where line and paragraph breaks actually appear. When text is enclosed within the <p></p> container tags, a line break will be assumed after the closing tag. In later hours, you will learn to control the height of the line break using CSS. The <br /> tag forces a line break within a paragraph. Unlike the other tags you've seen so far, <br /> doesn't require a closing </br> tag—this is one of those empty tags discussed earlier. Although HTML 4 does not require the / in empty tags, XHTML does and future standards will, so it's important for you to stick to the latest standards and create web pages that are coded properly. Always code empty tags so that they end with />.

The poem in Listing 3.2 and Figure 3.2 shows the <br /> and <p> tags being used to separate the lines and verses of an advertising agency song. You might have also noticed the <hr /> tag in the listing, which causes a horizontal rule line to appear on the page (see Figure 3.2). Inserting a horizontal rule with the <hr /> tag also causes a line break, even if you don't include a <br /> tag along with it. Like <br />, the <hr /> horizontal rule tag is an empty tag and therefore never gets a closing </hr> tag.

WARNING

You might find that a lot of web content that includes <br> instead of <br />. Or you might find that it does not include the closing </p> tag. Just remember there is a lot of antiquated web content floating around the Internet, and just because you see it in use doesn't mean it's correct. Save yourself a lot of future work and frustration by adhering to the standards you learn in this book. Developing clean HTML coding habits is a very important part of becoming a successful web designer.

Formatting Text in HTML

Take a passage of text and try your hand at formatting it as proper HTML:

1. Add `<html><head><title>My Title</title></head><body>` to the beginning of the text (using your own title for your page instead of **My Title**). Also include the boilerplate code at the top of the page that takes care of meeting the requirements of XHTML.

2. Add `</body></html>` to the very end of the text.

3. Add a `<p>` tag at the beginning of each paragraph and a `</p>` tag at the end of each paragraph.

4. Use `<br />` tags anywhere you want single-spaced line breaks.

5. Use `<hr />` to draw horizontal rules separating major sections of text, or wherever you'd like to see a line across the page.

6. Save the file as *mypage*.**html** (using your own filename instead of **mypage**).

7. Open the file in a web browser to see your web content. (Send the file via FTP to your web hosting account, if you have one.)

8. If something doesn't look right, go back to the text editor to make corrections and save the file again (and send it to your web hosting account, if applicable). You then need to click Reload/Refresh in the browser to see the changes you made.

WARNING

If you are using a word processor to create the web page, be sure to save the HTML file in plain-text or ASCII format.

Organizing Your Content with Headings

When you browse through web pages on the Internet, you'll notice that many of them have a heading at the top that appears larger and bolder than the rest of the text. Listing 3.3 is sample code and text for a simple web page containing an example of a heading as compared to normal paragraph text. Any text between `<h1>` and `</h1>` tags will appear as a large heading. Additionally, `<h2>` and `<h3>` make progressively smaller headings, and so on as far down as `<h6>`.

Listing 3.3   Heading Tags

```
<?xml version="1.0" encoding="UTF-8"?>
<!DOCTYPE html PUBLIC "-//W3C//DTD XHTML 1.1//EN"
  "http://www.w3.org/TR/xhtml11/DTD/xhtml11.dtd">

<html xmlns="http://www.w3.org/1999/xhtml" xml:lang="en">
  <head>
    <title>My Widgets</title>
  </head>

  <body>
    <h1>My Widgets</h1>
    <p>My widgets are the best in the land. Continue reading to
    learn more about my widgets.</p>

    <h2>Widget Features</h2>
    <p>If I had any features to discuss,  you can bet I'd do
    it here.</p>

    <h3>Pricing</h3>
    <p>Here, I would talk about my widget pricing.</p>

    <h3>Comparisons</h3>
    <p>Here, I would talk about how my widgets compare to my
    competitor's widgets.</p>

  </body>
</html>
```

NOTE

By now you've probably caught on to the fact that HTML code is often indented by its author to reveal the relationship between different parts of the HTML document. This indentation is entirely voluntary—you could just as easily run all the tags together with no spaces or line breaks and they would still look fine when viewed in a browser. The indentations are for you so that you can quickly look at a page full of code and understand how it fits together. Indenting your code is a very good web design habit and ultimately makes your pages easier to maintain.

As you can see in Figure 3.3, the HTML that creates headings couldn't be simpler. In this example, the phrase "My Widgets" is prominently displayed using the <h1> tag. To create the biggest (level-1) heading, just put an <h1> tag at the beginning and a </h1> tag at the end of the text you wish to use as a heading. For a slightly smaller (level-2) heading—for information that is of lesser importance than the title— use the <h2> and </h2> tags around your text. For content that should appear even less prominently than a level-2 heading, use the <h3> and </h3> tags around your text. Your headings should follow a content hierarchy; use only one level-1 heading, have one (or more) level-2 headings after the level-1 heading, use level-3 headings directly after level-2 headings, and so on.

Theoretically, you can also use <h4>, <h5>, and <h6> tags to make progres-

FIGURE 3.3
The use of three levels of headings shows the hierarchy of content on this sample product page.

On many web pages nowadays, graphical images of ornately rendered letters and logos are often used in place of the ordinary text headings discussed in this hour. However, using text headings is one of many search engine optimization (SEO) tips that you will learn about in Hour 24, "Helping People Find Your Web Pages." Search engines look at heading tags to see how you organize your content; they give higher preference to content that you have indicated is more important (for example, a level-1 heading) versus content that you indicate is of lesser importance (lower-level headings).

sively less important headings, but these aren't used very often. Web browsers seldom show a noticeable difference between these headings and the `<h3>` headings anyway, and content usually isn't displayed in such a manner as to need six levels of headings in order to show the content hierarchy.

It's important to remember the difference between a *title* and a *heading*. These two words are often interchangeable in day-to-day English, but when you're talking HTML, `<title>` gives the entire page an identifying name that isn't displayed on the page itself; it's displayed only on the browser window's title bar. The heading tags, on the other hand, cause some text on the page to be displayed with visual emphasis. There can be only one `<title>` per page and it must appear within the `<head>` and `</head>` tags, whereas you can have as many `<h1>`, `<h2>`, and `<h3>` headings as you want, in any order that suits your fancy. However, as I mentioned before, you should use the heading tags to keep tight control over content hierarchy; do not use headings as a way to achieve a particular "look," as that's what CSS is for.

You'll learn to take complete control over the appearance of text on your web pages in Part II of this book. Short of taking exacting control of the size, family, and color of fonts, headings provide the easiest and most popular way to draw extra attention to important text.

Peeking at Other Designers' Pages

Given the visual and sometimes audio pizzazz present in many popular web pages, you probably realize that the simple pages described in this hour are only the tip of the HTML iceberg. Now that you know the basics, you might surprise yourself with how much of the rest you can pick up just by looking at other people's pages on the Internet. You can see the HTML for any page by right-clicking and selecting View Source in any web browser.

Don't worry if you aren't yet able to decipher what some HTML tags do or exactly how to use them yourself. You'll find out about all those things in the next few hours. However, sneaking a preview now will show you the tags that you do know in action and give you a taste of what you'll soon be able to do with your web pages.

Validating Your Web Content

In Hour 2, I discussed ways to test your pages; one very important way to test your pages is to *validate* them. Think of it this way: it's one thing to design and draw a beautiful set of house plans, but it's quite another for an architect to stamp it as a safe structure suitable for construction. Validating your web pages is a similar process; in this case, however, the architect is an application—not a person.

In brief, validation is the process of testing your pages with a special application that searches for errors and makes sure your pages follow the strict XHTML standard. Validation is simple. In fact, the standards body responsible for developing web standards—the World Wide Web Consortium (W3C)—offers an online validation tool you can use. To validate a page, follow this URL: http://validator.w3.org/. The W3C Markup Validation Service is shown in Figure 3.4.

FIGURE 3.4
The W3C Markup Validation
Service allows you to validate an
HTML (XHTML) document to
ensure it has been coded
accurately.

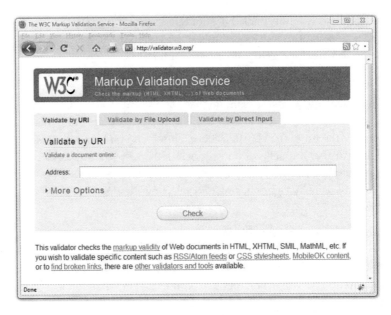

FIGURE 3.4
The W3C Markup Validation
Service allows you to validate an
HTML (XHTML) document to
ensure it has been coded
accurately.

If you've already published a page online, you can use the Validate by URI
tab. Use the Validate by File Upload tab to validate files stored on your
local computer file system. The Validate by Direct Input tab allows you to
paste the contents of a file from your text editor. If all goes well, your page
will get a passing report (see Figure 3.5).

FIGURE 3.5
If a page passes the W3C Markup
Validation Service, you know it is
ready for prime time.

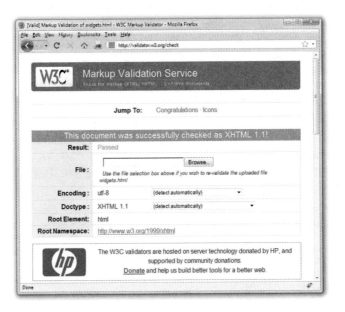

If the W3C Markup Validation Service encounters an error in your web page, it will provide specific details (including the line numbers of the offending code). This is a great way to hunt down problems and rid your pages of buggy code. Validation not only informs you whether your pages are constructed properly, it also assists you in finding and fixing problems before you post pages for the world to see.

The Scoop on HTML, XML, XHTML, and HTML 5

In its early days, HTML was great because it allowed scientists to share information over the Internet in an efficient and relatively structured manner. It wasn't until later that graphical web browsers were created and HTML started being used to code more than scientific papers. HTML quickly went from a tidy little markup language for researchers to an online publishing language. After it was established that HTML could be jazzed up for graphical browsing, the creators of web browsers went crazy by adding lots of nifty features to the language. Although these new features were neat at first, they compromised the original design of HTML and introduced inconsistencies when it came to how browsers displayed web pages; new features worked on only one browser or another, and you were out of luck if you happened to be running the wrong browser. HTML started to resemble a bad remodeling job on a —a job done by too many contractors and without proper planning. As it turns out, some of the browser-specific features created during this time have now been adopted as standards while others have been dropped completely.

As with most revolutions, the birth of the Web was very chaotic, and the modifications to HTML reflected that chaos. Over the years, a significant effort has been made to reel in the inconsistencies of HTML and restore some order to the language. The problem with disorder in HTML is that it results in web browsers having to guess at how a page is to be displayed, which is not a good thing. Ideally, a web page designer should be able to define exactly how a page is to look and have it look the same regardless of what kind of browser or operating system someone is using. Better still, a designer should be able to define exactly what a page *means* and have that page look consistent across different browsers and platforms. This utopia is still off in the future somewhere, but a markup language called XML (Extensible Markup Language) began to play a significant role in leading us toward it.

XML is a general language used to create specific languages, such as HTML. It might sound a little strange, but it really just means that XML

TIP

Some web development tools include built-in validation features you can use in lieu of the W3C Markup Validation Service. Some examples include browser extensions such as Firebug (http://getfirebug.com/) and HTML Validator (http://users.skynet.be/mgueury/mozilla/), but many other programs offer similar functionality—check your user documentation.

provides a basic structure and set of rules to which any markup language must adhere. Using XML, you can create a unique markup language to describe just about any kind of information, including web pages. Knowing that XML is a language for creating other markup languages, you could create your own version of HTML using XML. You could even create a markup language called BCCML (Bottle Cap Collection Markup Language), for example, which you could use to create and manage your extensive collection of rare bottle caps. The point is that XML lays the ground rules for organizing information in a consistent manner, and that information can be anything from web pages to bottle caps.

You might be thinking that bottle caps don't have anything to do with the Web, so why mention them? The reason is that XML is not entirely about web pages. XML is actually broader than the Web in that it can be used to represent any kind of information on any kind of computer. If you can visualize all the information whizzing around the globe among computers, mobile phones, handheld computers, televisions, and radios, you can start to understand why XML has much broader applications than just cleaning up web pages. However, one of the first applications of XML is to restore some order to the Web, which is why XML is relevant to learning HTML.

If XML describes data better than HTML, does it mean that XML is set to upstage HTML as the markup language of choice for the Web? No. XML is not a replacement for HTML; it's not even a competitor of HTML. XML's impact on HTML has to do with cleaning up HTML. HTML is a relatively unstructured language that benefits from the rules of XML. The natural merger of the two technologies resulted in HTML's adherence to the rules and structure of XML. To accomplish this merger, a new version of HTML was formulated that follows the stricter rules of XML. The new XML-compliant version of HTML is known as XHTML. Fortunately for you, you'll actually be learning XHTML throughout this book since it is really just a cleaner version of HTML.

You might have heard about HTML 5, which is touted as the next web standard. It will be, but not for several years. When it does become a web standard, it will not render XHTML useless—HTML 5 is not a replacement for XHTML, but is a major revision of HTML 4. In other words, XHTML and HTML 5 can coexist on the web, and web browsers that currently support XHTML will also (one day) support HTML 5 as well.

The goal of this book is to guide you through the basics of web publishing, using XHTML and CSS as the core languages of those pages. However, whenever possible I will note elements of the languages that are not present in HTML 5, should you want to design your content for even further sustainability. If you gain a solid understanding of web publishing and the ways in which CSS works with the overall markup language of the page (be it XHTML or HTML 5), you will be in a good position if, in a few years, you decide you want to move from XHTML to HTML 5.

Summary

This hour introduced the basics of what web pages are and how they work. You learned that coded HTML commands are included in a text file, and that typing HTML text yourself is better than using a graphical editor to create HTML commands for you—especially when you're learning HTML. You were introduced to the most basic and important HTML tags. By adding these coded commands to any plain-text document, you can quickly transform it into a bona fide web page. You learned that the first step in creating a web page is to put a few obligatory HTML tags at the beginning and end, including a title for the page. You then mark where paragraphs and lines end and add horizontal rules and headings if you want them. Table 3.1 summarizes all the tags introduced in this hour.

Table 3.1 HTML Tags Covered in Hour 3

Tag	Function
`<html>`...`</html>`	Encloses the entire HTML document.
`<head>`...`</head>`	Encloses the head of the HTML document. Used within the `<html>` tag pair.
`<title>`...`</title>`	Indicates the title of the document. Used within the `<head>` tag pair.
`<body>`...`</body>`	Encloses the body of the HTML document. Used within the `<html>` tag pair.
`<p>`...`</p>`	A paragraph; skips a line between paragraphs.
` `	A line break.
`<hr />`	A horizontal rule line.
`<h1>`...`</h1>`	A first-level heading.
`<h2>`...`</h2>`	A second-level heading.
`<h3>`...`</h3>`	A third-level heading.
`<h4>`...`</h4>`	A fourth-level heading (seldom used).
`<h5>`...`</h5>`	A fifth-level heading (seldom used).
`<h6>`...`</h6>`	A sixth-level heading (seldom used).

Finally, you learned about XML and XHTML, and how they relate to HTML, as well as what "HTML 5" means in relation to what it is you're learning here.

Q&A

Q I've created a web page, but when I open the file in my web browser, I see all the text including the HTML tags. Sometimes I even see weird gobbledygook characters at the top of the page! What did I do wrong?

A You didn't save the file as plain-text. Try saving the file again, being careful to save it as Text Only or ASCII Text. If you can't quite figure out how to get your word processor to do that, don't stress. Just type your HTML files in Notepad or TextEdit instead and everything should work just fine. (Also, always make sure that the filename of your web page ends in .html or .htm.)

Q I've seen web pages on the Internet that don't have `<html>` tags at the beginning. You said pages always have to start with `<html>`. What's the deal?

A Many web browsers will forgive you if you forget to include the `<html>` tag and will display the page correctly anyway. However, it's a very good idea to include it because some software does need it to identify the page as valid HTML. Besides, you want your pages to be bona fide XHTML pages so that they conform to the latest web standards.

Workshop

The workshop contains quiz questions and activities to help you solidify your understanding of the material covered. Try to answer all questions before looking at the "Answers" section that follows.

Quiz

1. What four tags are required in every HTML page?

2. What HTML tags and text would you use to produce the following web content:

   ▶ A small heading with the words **We are Proud to Present**

   ▶ A horizontal rule across the page

   ▶ A large heading with the one word **Orbit**

- ▸ A medium-sized heading with the words **The Geometric Juggler**

- ▸ Another horizontal rule

3. What code would you use to create a complete HTML web page with the title **Foo Bar**, a heading at the top that reads **Happy Hour at the Foo Bar**, followed by the words **Come on down!** in regular type?

Answers

1. `<html>`, `<head>`, `<title>`, and `<body>` (along with their closing tags, `</html>`, `</head>`, `</title>`, and `</body>`).

2. Your code would look like this:

```
<h3>We are Proud to Present</h3>
<hr />
<h1>Orbit</h1>
<h2>The Geometric Juggler</h2>
<hr />
```

3. Your code would look like this:

```
<?xml version="1.0" encoding="UTF-8"?>
<!DOCTYPE html PUBLIC "-//W3C//DTD XHTML 1.1//EN"
  "http://www.w3.org/TR/xhtml11/DTD/xhtml11.dtd">

<html xmlns="http://www.w3.org/1999/xhtml" xml:lang="en">
  <head>
    <title>Foo Bar</title>
  </head>

  <body>
    <h1>Happy Hour at the Foo Bar</h1>
    <p>Come on Down!</p>
  </body>
</html>
```

Exercises

▶ Even if your main goal in reading this book is to create web content for your business, you might want to make a personal web page just for practice. Type a few paragraphs to introduce yourself to the world and use the HTML tags you've learned in this hour to make them into a web page.

▶ Throughout the book you'll be following along with the code examples and making pages of your own. Take a moment now to set up a basic document template containing the XML declaration, doctype declaration, and tags for the core HTML document structure. That way, you can be ready to copy and paste that information whenever you need it.

HOUR 4
Understanding Cascading Style Sheets

In the previous hour, you learned the basics of HTML and XHTML, including how to set up a skeletal HTML template for all your web content. In this hour, you will learn how to fine-tune the display of your web content using *cascading style sheets(CSS)*. The concept behind style sheets is simple: You create a style sheet document that specifies the fonts, colors, spacing, and other characteristics that establish a unique look for a web site. You then link every page that should have that look to the style sheet, instead of specifying all those styles repeatedly in each separate document. Therefore, when you decide to change your official corporate typeface or color scheme, you can modify all your web pages at once just by changing one or two entries in your style sheet rather than changing them in all of your static web files. So a *style sheet* is a grouping of formatting instructions that control the appearance of several HTML pages at once.

Style sheets enable you to set a great number of formatting characteristics, including exacting typeface controls, letter and line spacing, and margins and page borders, just to name a few. Style sheets also enable sizes and other measurements to be specified in familiar units, such as inches, millimeters, points, and picas. You can also use style sheets to precisely position graphics and text anywhere on a web page, either at specific coordinates or relative to other items on the page.

In short, style sheets bring a sophisticated level of display to the Web. And they do so—you'll pardon the expression—with style.

WHAT YOU'LL LEARN IN THIS HOUR:

▶ How to create a basic style sheet

▶ How to use style classes

▶ How to use style IDs

▶ How to construct internal style sheets and inline styles

NOTE

If you have three or more web pages that share (or should share) similar formatting and fonts, you might want to create a style sheet for them as you read this hour. Even if you choose not to create a complete style sheet, you'll find it helpful to apply styles to individual HTML elements directly within a web page.

How CSS Works

The technology behind style sheets is called CSS, which stands for Cascading Style Sheets. CSS is a language that defines style constructs such as fonts, colors, and positioning, which are used to describe how information on a web page is formatted and displayed. CSS styles can be stored directly in an HTML web page or in a separate style sheet file. Either way, style sheets contain style rules that apply styles to elements of a given type. When used externally, style sheet rules are placed in an external style sheet document with the file extension `.css`.

A *style rule* is a formatting instruction that can be applied to an element on a web page, such as a paragraph of text or a link. Style rules consist of one or more *style properties* and their associated values. An *internal style sheet* is placed directly within a web page, whereas an *external style sheet* exists in a separate document and is simply linked to a web page via a special tag—more on this tag in a moment.

The "cascading" part of the name CSS refers to the manner in which style sheet rules are applied to elements in an HTML document. More specifically, styles in a CSS style sheet form a hierarchy in which more specific styles override more general styles. It is the responsibility of CSS to determine the precedence of style rules according to this hierarchy, which establishes a cascading effect. If that sounds a bit confusing, just think of the cascading mechanism in CSS as being similar to genetic inheritance, in which general traits are passed from parents to a child, but more specific traits are entirely unique to the child. Base style rules are applied throughout a style sheet but can be overridden by more specific style rules.

A quick example should clear things up. Take a look at the following code to see whether you can tell what's going on with the color of the text:

```
<div style="color:green">
  This text is green.
  <p style="color:blue">This text is blue.</p>
  <p>This text is still green.</p>
</div>
```

In the previous example, the color green is applied to the `<div>` tag via the `color` style property. Therefore, the text in the `<div>` tag is colored green. Because both `<p>` tags are children of the `<div>` tag, the green text style cascades down to them. However, the first `<p>` tag overrides the color style and changes it to blue. The end result is that the first line (not surrounded by a paragraph tag) is green, the first official paragraph is blue and the second official paragraph retains the cascaded green color.

Like many web technologies, CSS has evolved over the years. The original version of CSS, known as *Cascading Style Sheets Level 1 (CSS1)* was created in 1996. The later CSS 2 standard was created in 1998 and CSS 2 is still in use today. All modern web browsers support CSS 2, and you can safely use CSS 2 style sheets without too much concern. So when I talk about CSS throughout the book, I'm referring to CSS 2.

You'll find a complete reference guide to CSS at http://www.w3.org/Style/CSS/. The rest of this hour explains how to put CSS to good use.

A Basic Style Sheet

Despite their intimidating power, style sheets can be simple to create. Consider the web pages shown in Figure 4.1 and Figure 4.2. These pages share several visual properties that could be put into a common style sheet:

► They use a large, bold Verdana font for the headings and a normal size and weight Verdana font for the body text.

► They use an image named `logo.gif` floating within the content and on the right side of the page.

► All text is black except for subheadings, which are purple.

► They have margins on the left side and at the top.

► There is vertical space between lines of text.

► The footnotes are centered and in small print.

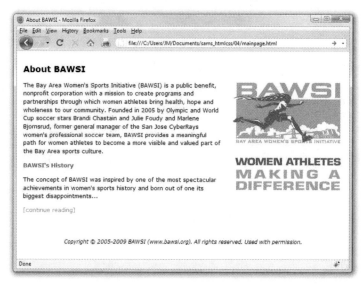

FIGURE 4.1
This page uses a style sheet to fine-tune the appearance and spacing of the text and images.

FIGURE 4.2
This page uses the same style
sheet as the one shown in Figure
4.1, thus maintaining a consistent
look and feel.

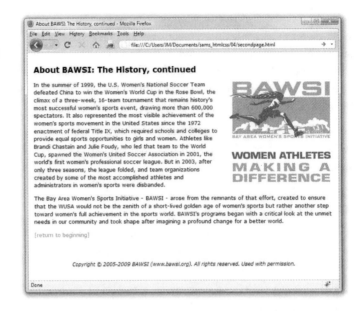

Listing 4.1 shows the code for style sheet specifying these properties.

Listing 4.1   A Single External Style Sheet

```
body {
  font-size: 10pt;
  font-family: Verdana, Geneva, Arial, Helvetica,sans-serif;
  color: black;
  line-height: 14pt;
  padding-left: 5pt;
  padding-right: 5pt;
  padding-top: 5pt;
}


h1 {
  font: 14pt Verdana, Geneva, Arial, Helvetica,sans-serif;
  font-weight: bold;
  line-height: 20pt;
}

p.subheader {
  font-weight: bold;
  color: #593d87;
}

img {
  padding: 3pt;
  float: right;
}
```

Listing 4.1   A Single External Style Sheet

```
a {
  text-decoration: none;
}

a:link, a:visited {
  color: #8094d6;
}

a:hover, a:active {
  color: #FF9933;
}

div.footer {
  font-size: 9pt;
  font-style: italic;
  line-height: 12pt;
  text-align: center;
  padding-top: 30pt;
}
```

This might initially appear to be a lot of code, but if you look closely, you'll see that there isn't a lot of information on each line of code. It's fairly standard to place individual style rules on their own line to help make style sheets more readable. Speaking of code readability, perhaps the first thing you noticed about this style sheet code is that it doesn't look anything like normal HTML code. CSS uses a language all its own to specify style sheets.

Of course, the listing includes some familiar HTML tags. As you might guess, body, h1, p, img, a, and div in the style sheet refer to the corresponding tags in the HTML documents to which the style sheet will be applied. The curly braces after each tag name contain the specifications for how all content within that tag should appear.

In this case, all body text should be rendered at a size of 10 points, in the Verdana font (if possible), and with the color black and 14 points between lines. If the user does not have the Verdana font installed, the list of fonts in the style sheet represents the order in which the browser should search for fonts to use: Geneva, then Arial, then Helvetica. If the user has none of those fonts, the browser will use whatever default sans-serif font is available. Additionally, the page should have left, right, and top margins of 5 points each.

Any text within an <h1> tag should be rendered in boldface Verdana at a size of 14 points. Moving on, any paragraph that uses only the <p> tag will inherit all the styles indicated by the body element. However, if the `<p>` tag uses a special class named `subheader`, the text will appear bold and in the color #593d87 (a purple color).

The `pt` after each measurement in Listing 4.1 means *points* (there are 72 points in an inch). If you prefer, you can specify any style sheet measurement in inches (`in`), centimeters (`cm`), pixels (`px`), or widths-of-a-letter-m, which are called ems (`em`).

NOTE

You can specify font sizes as large as you like with style sheets, although some display devices and printers will not correctly handle fonts larger than 200 points.

You might have noticed that each style rule in the listing ends with a semi-colon (`;`). Semicolons are used to separate style rules from each other. It is therefore customary to end each style rule with a semicolon so you can easily add another style rule after it.

To link this style sheet to HTML documents, include a `<link />` tag in the `<head>` section of each document. Listing 4.2 shows the HTML code for the page shown in Figure 4.1. It contains the following `<link />` tag:

```
<link rel="stylesheet" type="text/css" href="styles.css" />
```

This assumes that the style sheet is stored under the name `styles.css` in the same folder as the HTML document. As long as the web browser supports style sheets—and all modern browsers do support style sheets—the properties specified in the style sheet will apply to the content in the page without the need for any special HTML formatting code. This confirms the ultimate goal of XHTML, which is to provide a separation between the content in a web page and the specific formatting required to display that content.

Listing 4.2   HTML Code for the Page Shown in Figure 4.1

```
<?xml version="1.0" encoding="UTF-8"?>
<!DOCTYPE html PUBLIC "-//W3C//DTD XHTML 1.1//EN"
  "http://www.w3.org/TR/xhtml11/DTD/xhtml11.dtd">

<html xmlns="http://www.w3.org/1999/xhtml" xml:lang="en">
  <head>
    <title>About BAWSI</title>
    <link rel="stylesheet" type="text/css" href="styles.css" />
  </head>
  <body>
    <h1>About BAWSI</h1>
    <p><img src="logo.gif" alt="BAWSI logo"/>The Bay Area Women's
    Sports Initiative (BAWSI) is a public benefit, nonprofit
    corporation with a mission to create programs and partnerships
    through which women athletes bring health, hope and wholeness to
    our community. Founded in 2005 by Olympic and World Cup soccer
```

Listing 4.2   HTML Code for the Page Shown in Figure 4.1

```
    stars Brandi Chastain and Julie Foudy and Marlene Bjornsrud,
    former general manager of the San Jose CyberRays women's
    professional soccer team, BAWSI provides a meaningful path for
    women athletes to become a more visible and valued part of the
    Bay Area sports culture.</p>
    <p class="subheader">BAWSI's History</p>
    <p>The concept of BAWSI was inspired by one of the most
    spectacular achievements in women's sports history and born out
    of one its biggest disappointments... </p>
    <p><a href="secondpage.html">[continue reading]</a></p>
    <div class="footer">Copyright &copy; 2005-2009 BAWSI
    (www.bawsi.org). All rights reserved.  Used with permission.</div>
  </body>
</html>
```

The code in Listing 4.2 is interesting because it contains no formatting of any kind. In other words, there is nothing in the HTML code that dictates how the text and images are to be displayed—no colors, no fonts, nothing. Yet the page is carefully formatted and rendered to the screen, thanks to the link to the external style sheet, `styles.css`. The real benefit to this approach is that you can easily create a site with multiple pages that maintains a consistent look and feel. And you have the benefit of isolating the visual style of the page to a single document (the style sheet) so that one change impacts all pages.

Starting from scratch, create a new text document called mystyles.css and add some style rules for the following basic HTML tags: `<body>`, `<p>`, `<h1>`, and `<h2>`. Once your style sheet has been created, make a new HTML file that contains these basic tags. Play around with different style rules and see for yourself how simple it is to change entire blocks of text in paragraphs with one simple change in a style sheet file.

TIP

In most web browsers, you can view the style rules in a style sheet by opening the `.css` file and choosing Notepad or another text editor as the helper application to view the file. (To determine the name of the `.css` file, look at the HTML source of any web page that links to it.) To edit your own style sheets, just use a text editor.

NOTE

Although CSS is widely supported in all modern web browsers, it hasn't always enjoyed such wide support. Additionally, not every browser's support of CSS is flawless. To find out about how major browsers compare to each other in terms of CSS support, take a look at this web site: http://www.quirksmode.org/css/contents.html.

TRY IT YOURSELF ▼

Create a Style Sheet of Your Own

A CSS Style Primer

You now have a basic knowledge of CSS style sheets and how they are based on style rules that describe the appearance of information in web pages. The next few sections of this hour provide a quick overview of some of the most important style properties and allow you to get started using CSS in your own style sheets.

CSS includes various style properties that are used to control fonts, colors, alignment, and margins, to name just a few. The style properties in CSS can be generally grouped into two major categories:

▶ Layout properties, which consist of properties that impact the positioning of elements on a web page, such as margins, padding, alignment, and so on.

▶ Formatting properties, which consist of properties that affect the visual display of elements within a web site, such as the font type, size, color, and so on.

Layout Properties

CSS layout properties are used to determine how content is placed on a web page. One of the most important layout properties is the `display` property, which describes how an element is displayed with respect to other elements. There are four possible values for the `display` property:

▶ `block`—The element is displayed on a new line, as in a new paragraph.

▶ `list-item`—The element is displayed on a new line with a list-item mark (bullet) next to it.

▶ `inline`—The element is displayed inline with the current paragraph.

▶ `none`—The element is not displayed; it is hidden.

It's easier to understand the `display` property if you visualize each element on a web page occupying a rectangular area when displayed—the `display` property controls the manner in which this rectangular area is displayed. For example, the `block` value results in the element being placed on a new line by itself, whereas the `inline` value places the element next to the content just before it. The `display` property is one of the few style properties that can be applied in most style rules. Following is an example of how to set the `display` property:

```
display:block;
```

You control the size of the rectangular area for an element with the `width` and `height` properties. Like many size-related CSS properties, `width` and `height` property values can be specified in several different units of measurement:

- ▶ `in`—Inches
- ▶ `cm`—Centimeters
- ▶ `mm`—Millimeters
- ▶ `px`—Pixels
- ▶ `pt`—Points

You can mix and match units however you choose within a style sheet, but it's generally a good idea to be consistent across a set of similar style properties. For example, you might want to stick with points for font properties or pixels for dimensions. Following is an example of setting the width of an element using pixel units:

```
width: 200px;
```

Formatting Properties

CSS formatting properties are used to control the appearance of content on a web page, as opposed to controlling the physical positioning of the content. One of the most popular formatting properties is the `border` property, which is used to establish a visible boundary around an element with a box or partial box. The following `border` properties provide a means of describing the borders of an element:

- ▶ `border-width`—The width of the border edge.
- ▶ `border-color`—The color of the border edge.
- ▶ `border-style`—The style of the border edge.
- ▶ `border-left`—The left side of the border.
- ▶ `border-right`—The right side of the border.
- ▶ `border-top`—The top of the border.
- ▶ `border-bottom`—The bottom of the border.
- ▶ `border`—All the border sides.

The `border-width` property is used to establish the width of the border edge. It is often expressed in pixels, as the following code demonstrates:

```
border-width:5px;
```

Not surprisingly, the `border-color` and `border-style` properties are used to set the border color and style. Following is an example of how these two properties are set:

```
border-color:blue;
border-style:dotted;
```

The `border-style` property can be set to any of the following values:

- ▶ `solid`—A single-line border.
- ▶ `double`—A double-line border.
- ▶ `dashed`—A dashed border.
- ▶ `dotted`—A dotted border.
- ▶ `groove`—A border with a groove appearance.
- ▶ `ridge`—A border with a ridge appearance.
- ▶ `inset`—A border with an inset appearance.
- ▶ `outset`—A border with an outset appearance.
- ▶ `none`—No border.

The default value of the `border-style` property is `none`, which is why elements don't have a border unless you set the border property to a different style. The most common border styles are the `solid` and `double` styles.

The `border-left`, `border-right`, `border-top`, and `border-bottom` properties allow you to set the border for each side of an element individually. If you want a border to appear the same on all four sides, you can use the single `border` property by itself, which expects the following styles separated by a space: `border-width`, `border-style`, and `border-color`. Following is an example of using the `border` property to set a border that consists of two (double) red lines that are a total of 10 pixels in width:

```
border:10px double red;
```

Whereas the color of an element's border is set with the `border-color` property, the color of the inner region of an element is set using the `color` and `background-color` properties. The `color` property sets the color of text in an element (foreground) and the `background-color` property sets the color of the background behind the text. Following is an example of setting both color properties to predefined colors:

```
color:black;
background-color:orange;
```

You can also assign custom colors to these properties by specifying the colors in hexadecimal (covered in more detail in Hour 9, "Working with Colors") or as RGB (Red Green Blue) decimal values, just as you do in HTML:

```
background-color:#999999;
color:rgb(0,0,255);
```

You can also control the alignment and indentation of web page content without too much trouble. This is accomplished with the `text-align` and `text-indent` properties, as the following code demonstrates:

```
text-align:center;
text-indent:12px;
```

After you have an element properly aligned and indented, you might be interested in setting its font. The following font properties are used to set the various parameters associated with fonts:

- ▶ `font-family`—The family of the font.
- ▶ `font-size`—The size of the font.
- ▶ `font-style`—The style of the font (`normal` or `italic`).
- ▶ `font-weight`—The weight of the font (`light`, `medium`, `bold`, and so on).

The `font-family` property specifies a prioritized list of font family names. A prioritized list is used instead of a single value to provide alternatives in case a font isn't available on a given system. The `font-size` property specifies the size of the font using a unit of measurement, usually points. Finally, the `font-style` property sets the style of the font and the `font-weight` property sets the weight of the font. Following is an example of setting these font properties:

```
font-family: Arial, sans-serif;
font-size: 36pt;
font-style: italic;
font-weight: medium;
```

Now that you know a whole lot more about style properties and how they work, refer back at Listing 4.1 and see whether it makes a bit more sense. Here's a recap of the style properties used in that style sheet, which you can use as a guide for understanding how it works:

- ▶ font—Lets you set many font properties at once. You can specify a list of font names separated by commas; if the first is not available, the next is tried, and so on. You can also include the words bold and/or italic and a font size. Each of these font properties can be specified separately with font-family, font-size, font-weight, and font-style if you prefer.

- ▶ line-height—Also known in the publishing world as *leading*. This sets the height of each line of text, usually in points.

- ▶ color—Sets the text color using the standard color names or hexadecimal color codes (see Hour 9 for more details).

- ▶ text-decoration—Useful for turning link underlining off—simply set it to none. The values of underline, italic, and line-through are also supported. The application of styles to links is covered in more detail in Hour 8, "Using External and Internal Links."

- ▶ text-align—Aligns text to the left, right, or center, along with justifying the text with a value of justify.

- ▶ padding—Adds padding to the left, right, top, and bottom of an element; this padding can be in measurement units or a percentage of the page width. Use padding-left and padding-right if you want to add padding to the left and right of the element independently. Use padding-top or padding-bottom to add padding to the top or bottom of the element, as appropriate. You'll learn more about these style properties in Hours 14 and 15.

Using Style Classes

This is a "teach yourself" book, so you don't have to go to a single class to learn how to give your pages great style, although you do need to learn what a style class is. Whenever you want some of the text on your pages to look different from the other text, you can create what amounts to a custom-built HTML tag. Each type of specially formatted text you define is called a *style class*. A *style class* is a custom set of formatting specifications that can be applied to any element in a web page.

Before showing you a style class, I need to take a quick step back and clarify some CSS terminology. First off, a CSS *style property* is a specific style that can be assigned a value, such as `color` or `font-size`. You associate a style property and its respective value with elements on a web page by using a selector. A *selector* is used to identify tags on a page to which you apply styles. Following is an example of a selector, a property, and a value all included in a basic style rule:

```
h1 { font: 36pt Courier; }
```

In this code, `h1` is the selector, `font` is the style property, and `36pt Courier` is the value. The selector is important because it means that the font setting will be applied to all `h1` elements in the web page. But maybe you want to differentiate between some of the `h1` elements—what then? The answer lies in style classes.

Suppose you want two different kinds of `<h1>` headings for use in your documents. You would create a style class for each one by putting the following CSS code in a style sheet:

```
h1.silly { font: 36pt Comic Sans; }
h1.serious { font: 36pt Arial; }
```

Notice that these selectors include a period (.) after `h1`, followed by a descriptive class name. To choose between the two style classes, use the `class` attribute, like this:

```
<h1 class="silly">Marvin's Munchies Inc. </h1>
<p>Text about Marvin's Munchies goes here. </p>
```

Or you could use this:

```
<h1 class="serious">MMI Investor Information</h1>
<p>Text for business investors goes here.</p>
```

When referencing a style class in HTML code, simply specify the class name in the `class` attribute of an element. In the previous example, the words `Marvin's Munchies Inc.` would appear in a 36-point Comic Sans font, assuming that you included a `<link />` to the style sheet at the top of the web page and assuming that the user has the Comic Sans font installed. The words `MMI Investor Information` would appear in the 36-point Arial font instead. You can see another example of classes in action in Listing 4.2: look for the `subheader <p>` class and the `footer <div>` class.

What if you want to create a style class that could be applied to any element, rather than just headings or some other particular tag? You can associate a style class with the `<div>` tag, as in Listing 4.2, which is used to enclose any text in a block that is somewhat similar to a paragraph of text; the `<div>` tag is another useful container element.

You can essentially create your own custom HTML tag by using the `div` selector followed by a period (.) followed by any style class name you make up and any style specifications you choose. That tag can control any number of font, spacing, and margin settings all at once. Wherever you want to apply your custom tag in a page, use a `<div>` tag with the `class` attribute followed by the class name you created.

For example, the style sheet in Listing 4.1 includes the following style class specification:

```
div.footer {
  font-size: 9pt;
  font-style: italic;
  line-height: 12pt;
  text-align: center;
  padding-top: 30pt;
}
```

This style class is applied in Listing 4.2 with the following tag:

```
<div class="footer">
```

Everything between that tag and the closing `</div>` tag in Listing 4.2 appears in 9-point, centered, italic text with 12-point vertical line spacing and 30 points of padding at the top of the element.

What makes style classes so valuable is how they isolate style code from web pages, effectively allowing you to focus your HTML code on the actual content in a page, not how it is going to appear on the screen. Then you can focus on how the content is rendered to the screen by fine-tuning the style sheet. You might be surprised by how a relatively small amount of code in a style sheet can have significant effects across an entire web site. This makes your pages much easier to maintain and manipulate.

TIP

You might have noticed a change in the coding style when multiple properties are included in a style rule. For style rules with a single style, you'll commonly see the property placed on the same line as the rule, like this:

```
div.footer { font-size: 9pt; }
```

However, when a style rule contains multiple style properties, it's much easier to read and understand the code if you list the properties one-per-line, like this:

```
div.footer {
  font-size:9pt;
  font-style: italic;
  line-height:12pt;
  text-align: center;
  padding-top: 30pt;
}
```

TRY IT YOURSELF ▼

**Add Classes to
Your Style Sheet**

Using the style sheet you created earlier in this hour, add some style classes to your style sheet. To see the fruits of your labor, apply those classes to
the HTML page you created as well. Use classes with your <h1> and <p>
tags to get the feel for things.

Using Style IDs

When you create custom style classes, you can use those classes as many
times as you would like—they are not unique. However, there will be
some instances when you want to have precise control over unique elements for layout or formatting purposes (or both). In such instances, look
to IDs instead of classes.

A *style ID* is a custom set of formatting specifications that can be applied
only to one element in a web page. You can use IDs across a set of pages
but only once per time within each page.

For example, suppose you have a title within the body of all your pages.
Each page has only one title, but all of the pages themselves include one
instance of that title. Following is an example of a selector with an ID indicated, plus a property and a value:

```
p#title {font: 24pt Verdana, Geneva, Arial, sans-serif}
```

Notice that this selector includes a hash mark, or pound sign (#), after p,
followed by a descriptive ID name. When referencing a style ID in HTML
code, simply specify the ID name in the id attribute of an element, like so:

```
<p id="title">Some Title Goes Here</p>
```

Everything between the opening and closing <p> tags will appear in 24-
point Verdana text—but only once on any given page. You will often see
style IDs used to define specific parts of a page for layout purposes, such
as a header area, footer area, main body area, and so on. These types of
areas in a page will appear only once per page, so using an ID rather than
a class is the appropriate choice.

Internal Style Sheets and Inline Styles

In some situations, you might want to specify styles that will be used in only one web page, in which case you can enclose a style sheet between `<style>` and `</style>` tags and include it directly in an HTML document. Style sheets used in this manner must appear in the `<head>` of an HTML document. No `<link />` tag is needed and you cannot refer to that style sheet from any other page (unless you copy it into the beginning of that document, too). This kind of style sheet is known as an internal style sheet, as you learned earlier in the hour.

Listing 4.3 shows an example of how you might specify an internal style sheet.

Listing 4.3   A Web Page with an Internal Style Sheet

```
<?xml version="1.0" encoding="UTF-8"?>
<!DOCTYPE html PUBLIC "-//W3C//DTD XHTML 1.1//EN"
  "http://www.w3.org/TR/xhtml11/DTD/xhtml11.dtd">

<html xmlns="http://www.w3.org/1999/xhtml" xml:lang="en">
  <head>
    <title>Some Page</title>

    <style type="text/css">
      div.footer {
        font-size: 9pt;
        line-height: 12pt;
        text-align: center;
      }
    </style>
  </head>
  <body>
  ...
  <div class="footer">
  Copyright 2009 Acme Products, Inc.
  </div>
  </body>
</html>
```

In the listing code, the `div.footer` style class is specified in an internal style sheet that appears in the head of the page. The style class is now available for use within the body of this page. And, in fact, it is used in the body of the page to style the copyright notice.

Internal style sheets are handy if you want to create a style rule that is used multiple times within a single page. However, in some instances you might need to apply a unique style to one particular element. This calls for an inline style rule, which allows you to specify a style for only a small part of a page, such as an individual element. For example, you can create and apply a style rule within a `<p>`, `<div>`, or `<span>` tag via the `style` attribute. This type of style is known as an *inline style* because it is specified right there in the middle of the HTML code.

Here's how a sample `style` attribute might look:

```
<p style="color:green">
  This text is green, but <span style="color:red">this text is
  red.</span>
  Back to green again, but...
</p>
<p>
  ...now the green is over, and we're back to the default color
  for this page.
</p>
```

This code makes use of the `<span>` tag to show how to apply the color style property in an inline style rule. In fact, both the `<p>` tag and the `<span>` tag in this example use the color property as an inline style. What's important to understand is that the `color:red` style property overrides the `color:green` style property for the text appearing between the `<span>` and `</span>` tags. Then in the second paragraph, neither of the `color` styles applies because it is a completely new paragraph that adheres to the default color of the entire page.

NOTE

`<span>` and `</span>` are *dummy* tags that do nothing in and of themselves except specify a range of content to apply any `style` attributes that you add. The only difference between `<div>` and `<span>` is that `<div>` is a block element and therefore forces a line break, whereas `<span>` doesn't. Therefore, you should use `<span>` to modify the style of any portion of text that is to appear in the middle of a sentence or paragraph without any line break.

Validate Your Style Sheets

Just as it is important to validate your HTML or XHTML markup, it is important to validate your style sheet. A specific validation tool for CSS can be found at `http://jigsaw.w3.org/css-validator/`. Just like the validation tool discussed in Hour 3, you can point the tool to a web address, upload a file, or paste content into the form field provided. The ultimate goal is a result such as that shown in Figure 4.3: valid!

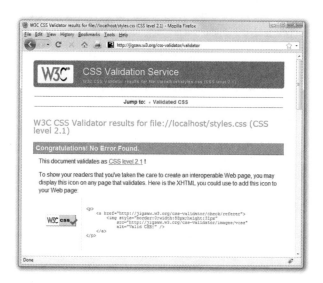

FIGURE 4.3
The W3C CSS Validator shows there are no errors in the style sheet contents of Listing 4.1.

Summary

In this hour, you learned that a style sheet can control the appearance of many HTML pages at once. It can also give you extremely precise control over the typography, spacing, and positioning of HTML elements. You also learned that by adding a `style` attribute to almost any HTML tag, you can control the style of any part of an HTML page without referring to a separate style sheet document.

You learned about three main approaches to including style sheets in your web site: a separate style sheet file with the extension .css that is linked to in the `<head>` of your documents, a collection of style rules placed in the head of the document within the `<style>` tag, and as rules placed directly in an HTML tag via the `style` attribute.

Table 4.1 summarizes the tags discussed in this hour. Refer to the CSS 2 style sheet standards at http://www.w3c.org for details on what options can be included after the `<style>` tag or the `style` attribute.

Table 4.1   HTML Tags and Attributes Covered in Hour 4

Tag/Attributes	Function
`<style>...</style>`	Allows an internal style sheet to be included within a document. Used between `<head>` and `</head>`.
Attribute	
`type="contenttype"`	The Internet content type. (Always `"text/css"` for a CSS style sheet.)
`<link />`	Links to an external style sheet (or other document type). Used in the `<head>` section of the document.
Attribute	
`href="url"`	The address of the style sheet.
`type="contenttype"`	The Internet content type. (Always `"text/css"` for a CSS style sheet.)
`rel="stylesheet"`	The link type. (Always `"stylesheet"` for style sheets.)
`<span>...</span>`	Does nothing but provide a place to put `style` or other attributes. (Similar to `<div>...</div>` but does not cause a line break.)
Attribute	
`style="style"`	Includes inline style specifications. (Can be used in `<span>`, `<div>`, `<body>`, and most other HTML tags.)

Q&A

Q Say I link a style sheet to my page that says all text should be blue, but there's a `<span style="font-color:red">` tag in the page somewhere. Will that text display as blue or will it display as red?

A Red. Local inline styles always take precedence over external style sheets. Any style specifications you put between `<style>` and `</style>` tags at the top of a page will also take precedence over external style sheets (but not over inline styles later in the same page). This is the cascading effect of style sheets that I mentioned earlier in the hour. So you can think of cascading style effects as starting with an external style sheet, which is overridden by an internal style sheet, which is overridden by inline styles.

Q Can I link more than one style sheet to a single page?

A Sure. For example, you might have a sheet for formatting (text, fonts, colors, and so on) and another one for layout (margins, padding, alignment, and so on)—just include a `<link />` for both. Technically speaking, the CSS standard requires web browsers to give the user the option to choose between style sheets when multiple sheets are presented via multiple `<link />` tags. However, in practice, all major web browsers simply include every style sheet. The preferred technique for linking in multiple style sheets involves using the special `@import` command. Following is an example of importing multiple style sheets with `@import`:

```
@import url(styles1.css);
@import url(styles2.css);
```

Similar to the `<link />` tag, the `@import` command must be placed in the head of a web page. You learn more about this handy little command in Hour 20, "Creating Print-Friendly Designs," when you learn how to create a style sheet specifically for printing web pages.

Workshop

The workshop contains quiz questions and activities to help you solidify your understanding of the material covered. Try to answer all questions before looking at the "Answers" section that follows.

Quiz

1. What code would you use to create a style sheet to specify 30-point blue Arial headings and all other text in double-spaced, 10-point blue Times Roman (or the default browser font)?

2. If you saved the style sheet you made for Question 1 as `corporate.css`, how would you apply it to a web page named `intro.html`?

3. How many different ways are there to ensure style rules can be applied to your content?

Answers

1. Your style sheet would include:

   ```
   h1 { font: 30pt blue Arial; }
   body { font: 10pt blue; }
   ```

2. Put the following tag between the `<head>` and `</head>` tags of the `intro.html` document:

   ```
   <link rel="stylesheet" type="text/css" href="corporate.css" />
   ```

3. Three: externally, internally, and inline.

Exercises

▶ Develop a standard style sheet for your web site and link it into all your pages. (Use internal style sheets and/or inline styles for pages that need to deviate from it.) If you work for a corporation, chances are it has already developed font and style specifications for printed materials. Get a copy of those specifications and follow them for company web pages, too.

▶ Be sure to explore the official style sheet specs at http://www.w3.org/Style/CSS/ and try some of the more esoteric style properties not covered in this hour.

Working with Text Blocks and Lists

In the early days of the Web, text was displayed in only one font and in one size. However, a combination of HTML and CSS now makes it possible to control the appearance of text and how it is aligned and displayed on a web page. This hour will show you the basics of text alignment and will guide you through some advanced text tips and tricks, such as the use of lists. Because lists are so common, HTML provides tags that automatically indent text and add numbers, bullets, or other symbols in front of each listed item. You'll learn how to format different types of lists, which are part of the many ways to display content in your web site.

WHAT YOU'LL LEARN IN THIS HOUR:

▸ How to align text on a page

▸ How to use the three types of HTML lists

▸ How to place lists within lists

You can make the most of learning how to style text throughout this hour if you have some sample text that could be indented, centered, or otherwise manipulated:

▸ Any type of outline, bullet points from a presentation, numbered steps, glossary, or list of textual information from a database will serve as good material to work with.

▸ Any text will do, but try to find (or type) some text you want to put onto a web page. The text from a company brochure or from your résumé might be a good choice.

▸ If the text you'll be using is from a word processing or database program, be sure to save it to a new file in plain-text or ASCII format. You can then add the appropriate HTML tags and style attributes to format it as you go through this lesson.

▸ Before you use the code introduced in this chapter to format the body text, add the set of skeleton HTML tags you've used in previous hours (the `<html>`, `<head>`, `<title>`, and `<body>` tags).

TRY IT YOURSELF

Preparing Sample Text

Aligning Text on a Page

It's easy to take for granted the fact that most paragraphs are automatically aligned to the left when you're reading information on the Web. However, there certainly are situations in which you might choose to align content to the right or even the center of a page. HTML gives you the option to align a single HTML block-level element, such as text contained within a `<p></p>` or `<div></div>` tag pair. Before we get into the details of aligning block elements, however, let's briefly note how attributes work.

Using Attributes

Attributes are used to provide additional information related to an HTML tag. *Attributes* are special code words used inside an HTML tag to control exactly what the tag does. They are very important in even the simplest bit of web content, so it's important that you are comfortable using them.

Attributes invoke the use of styles, classes, or IDs that are applied to particular tags. If you define a particular class or ID in a style sheet—as you learned in Hour 4—then you can invoke that class or ID using `class="someclass"` or `id="someid"` within the tag itself. When the browser renders the content for display, it will look to the style sheet to determine exactly how the content will appear according to the associated style definitions. Similarly, you can use the `style` attribute to include style information for a particular element without connecting the element to an actual style sheet. For example, when you begin a paragraph with the `<p>` tag, you can specify whether the text in that particular paragraph should be aligned to the left margin, the right margin, or to the center of the page by setting the `style` attribute. If you want to associate that particular paragraph with an existing class or ID, you set the `class` or `id` attribute.

In the following example, each paragraph could be left-aligned:

```
<p style="text-align: left;">Text goes here.</p>
<p class="leftAlignStyle">Text goes here.</p>
<p id="firstLeftAlign">Text goes here.</p>
```

In the first paragraph, the style appears directly in the style attribute. In the second paragraph, the paragraph will be left-aligned if the style sheet entry for the `leftAlignStyle` class includes the text-align statement. Similarly, the third paragraph will be left-aligned if the style sheet entry for the `firstLeftAlign` class includes the text-align statement.

In the previous example and in examples shown in previous hours, you might have noticed the use of lowercase for tags, attributes, and styles. The exacting XHTML standard requires tags and attributes to be lowercase; the XHTML standard also requires quotation marks around attribute values.

For example, the following code will be rendered by most popular web browsers:

```
<P STYLE=TEXT-ALIGN:CENTER>
```

However, this code does not conform to XHTML standards because the tag is uppercased, the `style` attribute and its value (`text-align:center`) is uppercased, and the value isn't in quotation marks. If you want to stay compatible with the latest standards and software, you should always use the following instead:

```
<p style="text-align:center">
```

Aligning Block-Level Elements

To align a block-level element such as `<p>` to the right margin without creating a separate class or ID in a style sheet, simply place `style="text-align:right"` inside the `<p>` tag at the beginning of the paragraph. Similarly, to center the element, use `<p style="text-align:center">`. To align a paragraph to the left, use `<p style="text-align:left">`.

The `text-align` part of the `style` attribute is referred to as a *style rule*, which means that it is setting a particular style aspect of an HTML element. There are many style rules you can use to carefully control the formatting of web content.

The `text-align` style rule is not reserved for just the `<p>` tag. In fact, you can use the `text-align` style rule with any block-level element, which includes `<h1>`, `<h2>`, the other heading tags, and the `<div>` tag, among others. The `<div>` tag is especially handy because it can encompass other block-level elements and thus allow you to control the alignment of large portions of your web content all at once. The div in the `<div>` tag is for *division*.

Listing 5.1 demonstrates the `style` attribute and `text-align` style rule with both the `<p>` and the `<div>` tags. The results are shown in Figure 5.1. You'll learn many more advanced uses of the `<div>` tag in Part III.

NOTE

Every attribute and style rule in HTML has a default value that is assumed when you don't set the attribute yourself. In the case of the `text-align` style rule of the `<p>` tag, the default value is `left`, so using the bare-bones `<p>` tag has the same effect as using `<p style="text-align:left">`. Learning the default values for common style rules is an important part of becoming a good web page developer.

Listing 5.1   The `text-align` Style Rule Used with the `style` Attribute

```
<?xml version="1.0" encoding="UTF-8"?>
<!DOCTYPE html PUBLIC "-//W3C//DTD XHTML 1.1//EN"
  "http://www.w3.org/TR/xhtml11/DTD/xhtml11.dtd">

<html xmlns="http://www.w3.org/1999/xhtml" xml:lang="en">
  <head>
    <title>Bohemia</title>
  </head>

  <body>
    <div style="text-align:center">
      <h1>Bohemia</h1>
      <h2>by Dorothy Parker</h2>
    </div>
    <p style="text-align:left">
      Authors and actors and artists and such<br />
      Never know nothing, and never know much.<br />
      Sculptors and singers and those of their kidney<br />
      Tell their affairs from Seattle to Sydney.
    </p>
    <p style="text-align:center">
      Playwrights and poets and such horses' necks<br />
      Start off from anywhere, end up at sex.<br />
      Diarists, critics, and similar roe<br />
      Never say nothing, and never say no.
    </p>
    <p style="text-align:right">
      People Who Do Things exceed my endurance;<br />
      God, for a man that solicits insurance!
    </p>
  </body>
</html>
```

FIGURE 5.1
The results of using the text alignment in Listing 5.1.

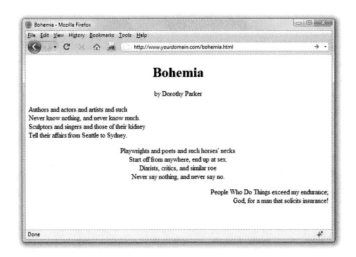

The use of `<div style="text-align:center">` ensures that the content area, including the two headings, are centered. However, the text alignment of the individual paragraphs within the `<div>` override the setting and ensure that the text of the first paragraph is left-aligned, the second paragraph is centered, and the third paragraph is right-aligned.

The Three Types of HTML Lists

For clarity, it's often useful to present information on a web page as a list of items. There are three basic types of HTML lists. All three are shown in Figure 5.2, and Listing 5.2 reveals the HTML used to construct them:

▶ **Ordered list**—An indented list that has numbers or letters before each list item. The ordered list begins with the `<ol>` tag and ends with a closing `</ol>` tag. List items are enclosed in the `<li></li>` tag pair and line breaks appear automatically at each opening `<li>` tag. The entire list is indented.

▶ **Unordered list**—An indented list that has a bullet or other symbol before each list item. The unordered list begins with the `<ul>` tag and closes with `</ul>`. Like the ordered list, its list items are enclosed in the `<li></li>` tag pair. A line break and symbol appear at each opening `<li>` tag and the entire list is indented.

▶ **Definition list**—A list of terms and their meanings. This type of list, which has no special number, letter, or symbol before each item, begins with `<dl>` and ends with `</dl>`. The `<dt></dt>` tag pair encloses each term and the `<dd></dd>` tag pair encloses each definition. Line breaks and indentations appear automatically.

Listing 5.2 Unordered Lists, Ordered Lists, and Definition Lists

```
<?xml version="1.0" encoding="UTF-8"?>
<!DOCTYPE html PUBLIC "-//W3C//DTD XHTML 1.1//EN"
  "http://www.w3.org/TR/xhtml11/DTD/xhtml11.dtd">

<html xmlns="http://www.w3.org/1999/xhtml" xml:lang="en">
  <head>
    <title>How to Be Proper</title>
  </head>

  <body>
    <h1>How to Be Proper</h1>
    <h2>Basic Etiquette for a Gentlemen Greeting a Lady Aquaintance</h2>
    <ul>
      <li>Wait for her acknowledging bow before tipping your hat.</li>
      <li>Use the hand farthest from her to raise the hat.</li>
```

Listing 5.2   Unordered Lists, Ordered Lists, and Definition Lists

```
    <li>Walk with her if she expresses a wish to converse; Never
    make a lady stand talking in the street.</li>
    <li>When walking, the lady must always have the wall.</li>
  </ul>
  <h2>Recourse for a Lady Toward Unpleasant Men Who Persist in Bowing</h2>
  <ol>
    <li>A simple stare of iciness should suffice in most instances.</li>
    <li>A cold bow discourages familiarity without offering insult.</li>
    <li>As a last resort: "Sir, I have not the honour of your
    aquaintance."</li>
  </ol>
  <h2>Proper Address of Royalty</h2>
  <dl>
    <dt>Your Majesty</dt>
    <dd>To the king or queen.</dd>
    <dt>Your Royal Highness</dt>
    <dd>To the monarch's spouse, children, and siblings.</dd>
    <dt>Your Highness</dt>
    <dd>To nephews, nieces, and cousins of the sovereign.</dd>
  </dl>
  </body>
</html>
```

FIGURE 5.2
The three basic types
of HTML lists.

NOTE

Remember that different web
browsers can display web content quite differently. The HTML
standard doesn't specify exactly
how web browsers should format lists, so users with older
web browsers might not see
exactly the same indentation
you see. You can use CSS to
gain precise control over list
items, which you will learn
about later in this hour.

Placing Lists Within Lists

Although definition lists are officially supposed to be used for defining terms, many web page authors use them anywhere they'd like to see some indentation. In practice, you can indent any text simply by putting `<dl><dd>` at the beginning of it and `</dd></dl>` at the end and skipping over the `<dt></dt>` tag pair. However, a better approach to indenting text is to use the `<blockquote></blockquote>` tag pair, which indents content without the presumption of a definition and allows for much more clear styling. With one set of attributes, you can set the width, height, background color, border type and color of your element area, and other visual effects.

Because of the level of control over the display of your items that you have when using CSS, there is no need to use *nested* lists to achieve the visual appearance of indentation. Reserve your use of nested lists for when the content warrants it. In other words, use nested lists to show a hierarchy of information, such as in Listing 5.3.

Ordered and unordered lists can be nested inside one another, down to as many levels as you want. In Listing 5.3, a complex indented outline is constructed from several unordered lists. You'll notice in Figure 5.3 that Firefox automatically uses a different type of bullet for each of the first three levels of indentation, making the list very easy to read. This is common in modern browsers.

NOTE

Nesting refers to a tag that appears entirely within another tag. Nested tags are also referred to as child tags of the (parent) tag that contains them. It is a common (but not required) coding practice to indent nested tags so that you can easily see their relationship to the parent tag.

Listing 5.3   Using Lists to Build Outlines

```
<?xml version="1.0" encoding="UTF-8"?>
<!DOCTYPE html PUBLIC "-//W3C//DTD XHTML 1.1//EN"
  "http://www.w3.org/TR/xhtml11/DTD/xhtml11.dtd">

<html xmlns="http://www.w3.org/1999/xhtml" xml:lang="en">
  <head>
    <title>Vertebrates</title>
  </head>

  <body>
    <h1>Vertebrates</h1>
    <ul>
      <li><span style="font-weight:bold">Fish</span>
        <ul>
          <li>Barramundi</li>
          <li>Kissing Gourami</li>
          <li>Mummichog</li>
        </ul>
      </li>
      <li><span style="font-weight:bold">Amphibians</span>
```

Listing 5.3   Using Lists to Build Outlines

```
<ul>
    <li>Anura
        <ul>
            <li>Goliath Frog</li>
            <li>Poison Dart Frog</li>
            <li>Purple Frog</li>
        </ul>
    </li>
    <li>Caudata
        <ul>
            <li>Hellbender</li>
            <li>Mudpuppy</li>
        </ul>
    </li>
        </ul>
    </li>
    <li><span style="font-weight:bold">Reptiles</span>
        <ul>
            <li>Nile Crocodile</li>
            <li>King Cobra</li>
            <li>Common Snapping Turtle</li>
        </ul>
    </li>
    </ul>
  </body>
</html>
```

FIGURE 5.3
In Firefox, multilevel unordered
lists are neatly indented and
bulleted for improved readability.

As shown in Figure 5.3, a web browser will normally use a solid disc for the first-level bullet, a hollow circle for the second-level bullet, and a solid square for all deeper levels. However, you can explicitly choose which type of bullet to use for any level by using `<ul style="list-style-type:disc">`, `<ul style="list-style-type:circle">`, or `<ul style="list-style-type:square">` instead of `<ul>`.

You can even change the bullet for any single point within an unordered list by using the `list-style-type` style rule in the `<li>` tag. For example, the following codes displays a hollow circle in front of the words extra and super and a solid square in front of the word special:

```
<ul style="list-style-type:circle">
  <li>extra</li>
  <li>super</li>
  <li style="list-style-type:square">special</li>
</ul>
```

The `list-style-type` style rule also works with ordered lists, but instead of choosing a type of bullet, you choose the type of numbers or letters to place in front of each item. Listing 5.4 shows how to use Roman numerals (`list-style-type:upper-roman`), capital letters (`list-style-type:upper-alpha`), lowercase letters (`list-style-type:lower-alpha`), and ordinary numbers in a multilevel list. Figure 5.4 shows the resulting outline, which is nicely formatted.

Although Listing 5.4 uses the `list-style-type` style rule only with the `<ol>` tag, you can also use it for specific `<li>` tags within a list (though it's hard to imagine a situation in which you would want to do this). You can also explicitly specify ordinary numbering with `list-style-type:decimal` and you can make lowercase Roman numerals with `list-style-type:lower-roman`.

Listing 5.4   Using the `list-style-type` Style Rule with the `style` Attribute in Multitiered Lists

```
<?xml version="1.0" encoding="UTF-8"?>
<!DOCTYPE html PUBLIC "-//W3C//DTD XHTML 1.1//EN"
  "http://www.w3.org/TR/xhtml11/DTD/xhtml11.dtd">

<html xmlns="http://www.w3.org/1999/xhtml" xml:lang="en">
  <head>
    <title>Advice from the Golf Guru</title>
  </head>

  <body>
    <h1>How to Win at Golf</h1>
```

Listing 5.4   Using the `list-style-type` **Style Rule with the** `style` **Attribute in Multitiered Lists**

```
<ol style="list-style-type:upper-roman">
  <li>Training
    <ol>
      <li>Mental prep
        <ol style="list-style-type:upper-alpha">
          <li>Watch golf on TV religiously</li>
          <li>Get that computer game with Tiger whatsisname</li>
          <li>Rent "personal victory" subliminal tapes</li>
        </ol>
      </li>
      <li>Equipment
        <ol style="list-style-type:upper-alpha">
          <li>Make sure your putter has a pro autograph on it</li>
          <li>Pick up a bargain bag of tees-n-balls at Costco</li>
        </ol>
      </li>
      <li>Diet
        <ol style="list-style-type:upper-alpha">
          <li>Avoid junk food
            <ol style="list-style-type:lower-alpha">
              <li>No hotdogs</li>
            </ol>
          </li>
          <li>Drink  wine and mixed drinks only, no beer</li>
        </ol>
      </li>
    </ol>
  </li>
  <li>Pre-game
    <ol>
      <li>Dress
        <ol style="list-style-type:upper-alpha">
          <li>Put on shorts, even if it's freezing</li>
          <li>Buy a new hat if you lost last time</li>
        </ol>
      </li>
      <li>Location and Scheduling
        <ol style="list-style-type:upper-alpha">
          <li>Select a course where your spouse or boss won't find you</li>
          <li>To save on fees, play where your buddy works</li>
        </ol>
      </li>
      <li>Opponent
        <ol style="list-style-type:upper-alpha">
          <li>Look for: overconfidence, inexperience</li>
          <li>Buy opponent as many pre-game drinks as possible</li>
        </ol>
      </li>
    </ol>
  </li>
</ol>
```

Listing 5.4 **Using the** `list-style-type` **Style Rule with the** `style` **Attribute in Multitiered Lists**

```
      </li>
      <li>On the Course
        <ol>
          <li>Tee off first, then develop severe hayfever</li>
          <li>Drive cart over opponent's ball to degrade aerodynamics</li>
          <li>Say "fore" just before ball makes contact with opponent</li>
          <li>Always replace divots when putting</li>
          <li>Water cooler holes are a good time to correct any errors in ball
          placement</li>
        </ol>
      </li>
    </ol>
  </body>
</html>
```

FIGURE 5.4
A well-formatted outline can make almost any plan look more plausible.

Summary

In this hour, you learned that attributes are used to specify options and special behavior of many HTML tags and you also learned to use the `style` attribute with CSS style rules to align text. You also learned how to create and combine three basic types of HTML lists: ordered lists, unordered lists, and definition lists. Lists can be placed within other lists to create outlines and other complex arrangements of text.

Table 5.1 summarizes the tags and attributes discussed in this hour. Don't feel like you have to memorize all these tags, by the way! That's why you have this book: You can look up the tags when you need them. Remember that all the HTML tags are listed in Appendix B, "Complete XHTML 1.1 and CSS 2 Quick Reference."

Table 5.1　HTML Tags and Attributes Covered in Hour 5

Tag/Attribute	Function
`<div>...</div>`	A region of text to be formatted.
`<dl>...</dl>`	A definition list.
`<dt>...</dt>`	A definition term, as part of a definition list.
`<dd>...</dd>`	The corresponding definition to a definition term, as part of a definition list.
`<ol>...</ol>`	An ordered (numbered) list.
`<ul>...</ul>`	An unordered (bulleted) list.
`<li>...</li>`	A list item for use with `<ol>` or `<ul>`.
Attributes	
`style="text-align:alignment"`	Align text to `center`, `left`, or `right`. (Can also be used with `<p>`, `<h1>`, `<h2>`, `<h3>`, and so on.)
`style="list-style-type:numtype"`	The type of numerals used to label the list. Possible values are `decimal`, `lower-roman`, `upper-roman`, `lower-alpha`, `upper-alpha`, and `none`.
`style="list-style-type:bullettype"`	The bullet dingbat used to mark list items. Possible values are `disc`, `circle`, `square`, and `none`.
`style="list-style-type:type"`	The type of bullet or number used to label this item. Possible values are `disc`, `circle`, `square`, `decimal`, `lower-roman`, `upper-roman`, `lower-alpha`, `upper-alpha`, and `none`.

Q&A

Q I've seen web pages that use three-dimensional little balls or other special graphics for bullets. How do they do that?

A That trick is a little bit beyond what this hour covers. You'll learn how to do it yourself in Hour 11.

Q How do I "full justify" text so that both the left and right margins are flush?

A You can use `text-align:justify` in your style declaration.

Workshop

The workshop contains quiz questions and activities to help you solidify your understanding of the material covered. Try to answer all questions before looking at the "Answers" section that follows.

Quiz

1. How would you center everything on an entire page?

2. How would you indent a single word and put a square bullet in front of it?

3. What would you use to create a definition list to show that the word "glunch" means "a look of disdain, anger, or displeasure" and that the word "glumpy" means "sullen, morose, or sulky"?

Answers

1. If you thought about putting a `<div style="text-align:center">` immediately after the `<body>` tag at the top of the page, and `</div>` just before the `</body>` tag at the end of the page, then you're correct. However, the `text-align` style is also supported directly in the `<body>` tag, which means you can forego the `<div>` tag and place the `style="text-align:center"` style directly in the `<body>` tag. Presto, the entire page is centered!

2. You would use:

```
<ul style="list-style-type:square">
  <li>supercalifragilisticexpealidocious</li>
</ul>
```

(Putting the `style="list-style-type:square"` in the `<li>` tag would give the same result because there's only one item in this list.)

3. You would use:

```
<dl>
<dt>glunch</dt><dd>a look of disdain, anger, or displeasure</dd>
<dt>glumpy</dt><dd>sullen, morose, or sulky</dd>
</dl>
```

Exercises

▶ Use the text alignment style attributes to place blocks of text in various places on your web page. Try nesting your paragraphs and divisions (`<p>` and `<div>`) to get a feel for how styles do or do not cascade through the content hierarchy.

▶ Try producing an ordered list outlining the information you'd like to put on your web pages. This will give you practice formatting HTML lists and also give you a head start on thinking about the issues covered in later hours of this book.

Working with Fonts

In the previous hour, you learned the basics of creating blocks of text and putting that text into list format. In this hour, you'll take a closer look at the bits of text themselves, and learn how to change the visual display of the font—it's font family, size, and weight, for example. You'll learn to incorporate boldface, italics, superscripts, subscripts, and strikethrough text into your pages. You will also learn how to change typefaces and font sizes.

WHAT YOU'LL LEARN IN THIS HOUR:

▶ How to use boldface, italics, and special text formatting

▶ How to tweak the font

▶ How to use special characters

NOTE

When viewing other designers' web content, you might notice methods of marking up text that are different than those taught in this book. The "old way" of formatting text includes the use of the `<b></b>` tag pair to indicate when a word should be bolded, the `<i></i>` tag pair to indicate when a word should be in italics, and the use of a `<font></font>` tag pair to specify font family, size, and other attributes. However, there is no reason to learn it because it is being phased out of HTML, and CSS is considerably more powerful.

TRY IT YOURSELF ▼

More Work with Sample Text

Just like you created a sample file to work with in the previous hour, create one for this hour so you can follow along and make the most of learning how to style text throughout this hour.

Since the information in this hour has to do with font-level styles, it doesn't really matter what type of text you use. There are so many different stylistic possibilities to try that they would never appear all on the same web page anyway (unless you wanted to drive your visitors batty). Take this opportunity to get a feel for how text-level changes can affect the appearance of your content.

Boldface, Italics, and Special Text Formatting

Way back in the age of the typewriter, we were content with plain-text and an occasional underline for emphasis. Today, **boldface** and *italic* text have become de rigueur in all paper communication. Naturally, you can add bold and italic text to your web content as well. There are several tags and style rules that make text formatting possible.

The "old school" approach to adding bold and italic formatting to text involves the `<b></b>` and `<i></i>` tag pairs. For boldface text, put the `<b>` tag at the beginning of the text and `</b>` at the end. Similarly, you can make any text italic by enclosing it between `<i>` and `</i>` tags. Although this approach still works fine in browsers and is supported by XHTML, it isn't as flexible or powerful as the CSS style rules for text formatting.

Although you'll learn much more about CSS style rules in Part III, it's worth a little foreshadowing just so you understand the text formatting options. The `font-weight` style rule allows you to set the weight, or boldness, of a font using a style rule. Standard settings for `font-weight` include `normal`, `bold`, `bolder`, and `lighter` (with `normal` being the default). Italic text is controlled via the `font-style` rule, which can be set to `normal`, `italic`, or `oblique`. Style rules can be specified together if you want to apply more than one, as the following example demonstrates:

```
<p style="font-weight:bold; font-style:italic">This paragraph is bold and
italic!</p>
```

In this example, both style rules are specified in the `style` attribute of the `<p>` tag. The key to using multiple style rules is that they must be separated by a semicolon (;).

You aren't limited to using font styles in paragraphs, however. The following code shows how to italicize text in a bulleted list:

```
<ul>
  <li style="font-style:italic">Important Stuff</li>
  <li style="font-style:italic">Critical Information</li>
  <li style="font-style:italic">Highly Sensitive Material</li>
  <li>Nothing All That Useful</li>
</ul>
```

You can also use the `font-weight` style rule within headings, but a heavier font usually doesn't have an effect on headings because they are already bold by default.

Although using CSS allows you to apply richer formatting, there are a few other HTML tags that are good for adding special formatting to text when you don't necessarily need to be as specific as CSS allows you to be. Following are some of these tags. Listing 6.1 and Figure 6.1 demonstrate each tag in action.

▶ `<small></small>`—Small text

▶ `<big></big>`—Big text; not present in HTML 5 because text size is better controlled by CSS.

▶ `<sup></sup>`—Superscript text

▶ `<sub></sub>`—Subscript text

▶ `<em></em>` or `<i></i>`—Emphasized (italic) text

▶ `<strong></strong>` or `<b></b>`—Strong (boldface) text

▶ `<tt></tt>`—Monospaced text (typewriter font) ; not present in HTML 5 because font appearance is better controlled by CSS.

▶ `<pre></pre>` —Monospaced text, preserving spaces and line breaks

WARNING

There used to be a `<u>` tag for creating underlined text, but there are a couple of reasons not to use it now. First off, users expect underlined text to be a link, so they might get confused if you underline text that isn't a link. Secondly, the `<u>` tag is *deprecated*, which means that it has been phased out of the HTML/XHTML language, as has the `<strike>` tag. Both tags are still supported in web browsers and likely will be for quite a while, but using CSS is the preferred approach to creating underlined and strikethrough text. In HTML 5, deleted text can be surrounded by the `<strike><strike>` tag pair, which will render as text with a strikethrough.

Listing 6.1   Special Formatting Tags

```
<?xml version="1.0" encoding="UTF-8"?>
<!DOCTYPE html PUBLIC "-//W3C//DTD XHTML 1.1//EN"
  "http://www.w3.org/TR/xhtml11/DTD/xhtml11.dtd">

<html xmlns="http://www.w3.org/1999/xhtml" xml:lang="en">
  <head>
    <title>The Miracle Product</title>
  </head>

  <body>
    <p>
      New <sup>Super</sup><strong>Strength</strong> H<sub>2</sub>O
      <em>plus</em> will knock out any stain, <big>big</big> or
      <small>small</small>.<br /> Look for new
      <sup>Super</sup><b>Strength</b> H<sub>2</sub>O <i>plus</i>
      in a stream near you.
    </p>
    <p>
      <tt>NUTRITION INFORMATION</tt> (void where prohibited)
    </p>
    <pre>
              Calories    Grams    USRDA
              /Serving    of Fat   Moisture
Regular          3          4        100%
Unleaded         3          2        100%
```

Listing 6.1   Special Formatting Tags

```
Organic            2        3        99%
Sugar Free         0        1        110%
        </pre>
    </body>
</html>
```

The `<tt>` tag usually changes the typeface to Courier New, a monospaced font. (*Monospaced* means that all the letters and spaces are the same width.) However, web browsers let users change the monospaced `<tt>` font to the typeface of their choice (look on the Options menu of your browser). The monospaced font might not even be monospaced for some users, though the vast majority of users stick with the standard fonts that their browsers show by default.

FIGURE 6.1
Here's what the character formatting from Listing 6.1 looks like.

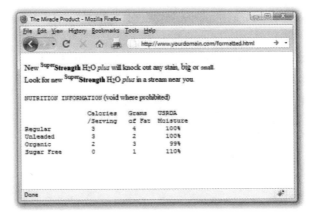

The `<pre>` tag causes text to appear in the monospaced font, but it also does something else unique and useful. As you learned in Hour 3, multiple spaces and line breaks are normally ignored in HTML files, but `<pre>` causes exact spacing and line breaks to be preserved. For example, without `<pre>`, the text at the end of Figure 6.1 would look like the following:

```
calories grams usrda /serving of fat moisture regular
3 4 100% unleaded 3 2 100% organic 2 3 99% sugar free 0 1 110%
```

Even if you added `<br />` tags at the end of every line, the columns wouldn't line up properly. However, when you put `<pre>` at the beginning and `</pre>` at the end, the columns line up properly because the exact spaces are kept—no `<br />` tags are needed. The `<pre>` tag gives you a quick and easy way to preserve the alignment of any monospaced text files you might want to transfer to a web page with minimum effort.

CSS provides you with more robust methods for lining up text (and doing anything with text, actually), and you'll learn more about them throughout Part III.

Tweaking the Font

The `<big>`, `<small>`, and `<tt>` tags give you some rudimentary control over the size and appearance of the text on your pages. However, there might be times when you'd just like a bit more control over the size and appearance of your text. Before I get into the appropriate way to tinker with the font in XHTML code, let's briefly take a look at how things were done prior to CSS because you might still find examples of this method when you look at the source code for other web sites. Remember, just because these older methods are in use doesn't mean you should follow suit.

Before style sheets entered the picture, the now phased-out `<font>` tag was used to control the fonts in web page text. For example, the following HTML will change the size and color of some text on a page:

```
<font size="5" color="purple">this text will be big and purple.</font>
```

As you can see, the `size` and `color` attributes of the `<font>` tag made it possible to alter the font of the text without too much effort. Although this approach worked fine, it was replaced with a far superior approach to font formatting, thanks to CSS style rules. Following are a few of the main style rules used to control fonts:

▶ `font-family`—Sets the family (typeface) of the font.

▶ `font-size`—Sets the size of the font.

▶ `color`—Sets the color of the font.

The `font-family` style rule allows you to set the typeface used to display text. You can and usually should specify more than one value for this style (separated by commas) so that if the first font isn't available on a user's system, the browser can try an alternative. You've already seen this in previous lessons. Providing alternative font families is important because each user potentially has a different set of fonts installed, at least beyond a core

NOTE

You'll learn more about controlling the color of the text on your pages in Hour 9, "Working with Colors." That hour also shows you how to create your own custom colors and how to control the color of text links.

set of common basic fonts (Arial, Times New Roman, and so forth). By providing a list of alternative fonts, you have a better chance of your pages gracefully falling back on a known font when your ideal font isn't found. Following is an example of the font-family style used to set the typeface for a paragraph of text:

```
<p style="font-family:arial, sans-serif, 'times roman'">
```

There are several interesting things about this example. First, arial is specified as the primary font. Capitalization does not affect the font family, so arial is no different from Arial or ARIAL. Another interesting thing about this code is how single quotes are used around the times roman font name because it has a space in it. However, since 'times roman' appears after the generic specification of sans-serif, it is unlikely that 'times roman' would be used. Because sans-serif is in the second position, it says to the browser "if Arial is not on this machine, use the default sans-serif font."

The font-size and color style rules are also commonly used to control the size and color of fonts. The font-size style can be set to a predefined size (such as small, medium, or large) or you can set it to a specific point size (such as 12pt or 14pt). The color style can be set to a predefined color (such as white, black, blue, red, or green) or you can set it to a specific hexadecimal color (such as #FFB499.) Following is the previous paragraph example with the font size and color specified:

```
<p style="font-family:arial, sans-serif, 'times roman'; font-size:14pt;
color:green">
```

The example web content in Listing 6.2 and shown in Figure 6.2 uses some font style rules to create the beginning of a basic online résumé.

Listing 6.2   Using Font Style Rules to Create a Basic Résumé

```
<?xml version="1.0" encoding="UTF-8"?>
<!DOCTYPE html PUBLIC "-//W3C//DTD XHTML 1.1//EN"
  "http://www.w3.org/TR/xhtml11/DTD/xhtml11.dtd">

<html xmlns="http://www.w3.org/1999/xhtml" xml:lang="en">
  <head>
    <title>R&eacute;sum&eacute; for Jane Doe</title>

    <style type="text/css">
      body {
        font-family: Verdana, sans-serif;
        font-size: 12px;
      }
```

Listing 6.2   Using Font Style Rules to Create a Basic Résumé

```
    h1 {
      font-family:Georgia, serif;
      font-size:28px;
      text-align:center;
    }

    p.contactinfo {
      font-size:14px;
      text-align:center;
    }

    p.categorylabel {
      font-size:12px;
      font-weight:bold;
      text-transform:uppercase;
    }

    div.indented {
      margin-left: 25px;
    }
  </style>
</head>
<body>
    <h1>Jane Doe</h1>
    <p class="contactinfo">1234 Main Street, Sometown,
    CA 93829<br/>
    tel: 555-555-1212, e-mail: jane@doe.com</p>

    <p class="categorylabel">Summary of Qualifications</p>
    <ul>
    <li>Highly skilled and dedicated professional offering a
    solid background in whatever it is you need.</li>
    <li>Provide comprehensive direction for whatever it is
    that will get me a job.</li>
    <li>Computer proficient in a wide range of industry-related
    computer programs and equipment. Any industry.</li>
    </ul>

    <p class="categorylabel">Professional Experience</p>
    <div class="indented">
        <p><span style="font-weight:bold;">Operations Manager,
        Super Awesome Company, Some City, CA [Sept 2002 –
        present]</span></p>
        <ul>
        <li>Direct all departmental operations</li>
        <li>Coordinate work with internal and external
        resources</li>
        <li>Generally in charge of everything</li>
        </ul>
      <p><span style="font-weight:bold;">Project Manager,
        Less Awesome Company, Some City, CA [May 2000 - Sept
```

Listing 6.2   Using Font Style Rules to Create a Basic Résumé

```
              2002]</span></p>
              <ul>
              <li>Direct all departmental operations</li>
              <li>Coordinate work with internal and external
              resources</li>
              <li>Generally in charge of everything</li>
              </ul>
        </div>

        <p class="categorylabel">Education</p>
        <ul>
        <li>MBA, MyState University, May 2002</li>
        <li>B.A, Business Administration, MyState University,
        May 2000</li>
        </ul>

        <p class="categorylabel">References</p>
        <ul>
        <li>Available upon request.</li>
        </ul>
    </body>
</html>
```

FIGURE 6.2
Here's what the code used in
Listing 6.2 looks like.

Using CSS, which organizes sets of styles into classes—as you learned in Hour 4—you can see how text formatting is applied to different areas of this content. If you look closely at the definition of the `div.indented` class, you will see the use of the `margin-left` style. This style, which you will learn more about in Part II, applies a certain amount of space (25 pixels, in this example) to the left of the element. That space accounts for the indentation shown in Figure 6.2.

Working with Special Characters

Most fonts now include special characters for European languages, such as the accented *é* in *Café*. There are also a few mathematical symbols and special punctuation marks, such as the circular ▸ bullet.

You can insert these special characters at any point in an HTML document using the appropriate codes shown in Table 6.1. You'll find an even more extensive list of codes for multiple character sets at http://www.webstandards.org/learn/reference/named_entities.html.

For example, the word *café* could be written using either of the following methods:

```
caf&eacute;
caf&#233;
```

Table 6.1   Commonly Used English Language Special Characters

Character	Numeric Code	Code Name	Description
"	&#34;	&quot;	Quotation mark
&	&#38;	&amp;	Ampersand
<	&#60;	&lt;	Less than
>	&#62;	&gt;	Greater than
¢	&#162;	&cent;	Cent sign
£	&#163;	&pound;	Pound sterling
¦	&#166;	¦ or &brkbar;	Broken vertical bar
§	&#167;	&sect;	Section sign
©	&#169;	&copy;	Copyright
®	&#174;	&reg;	Registered trademark
°	&#176;	&deg;	Degree sign
±	&#177;	&plusmn;	Plus or minus
^{2}	&#178;	&sup2;	Superscript two
^{3}	&#179;	&sup3;	Superscript three
·	&#183;	&middot;	Middle dot
^{1}	&#185;	&sup1;	Superscript one
¼	&#188;	&frac14;	Fraction one-fourth
½	&#189;	&frac12;	Fraction one-half
¾	&#190;	&frac34;	Fraction three-fourths
Æ	&#198;	&AElig;	Capital AE ligature

Table 6.1   Commonly Used English Language Special Characters

Character	Numeric Code	Code Name	Description
æ	`&#230;`	`&aelig;`	Small ae ligature
É	`&#201;`	`&Eacute;`	Accented capital E
é	`&#233;`	`&eacute;`	Accented small e
×	`&#215;`	`&times;`	Multiplication sign
÷	`&#247;`	`&divide;`	Division sign

Although you can specify character entities by number, each symbol also has a mnemonic name that is often easier to remember.

HTML/XHTML uses a special code known as a *character entity* to represent special characters such as © and ®. Character entities are always specified starting with & and ending with ;. Table 6.1 lists the most commonly used character entities, although HTML supports many more.

Table 6.1 includes codes for the angle brackets, quotation, and ampersand. You must use those codes if you want these symbols to appear on your pages; otherwise, the web browser interprets them as HTML commands.

In Listing 6.3 and Figure 6.3, several of the symbols from Table 6.1 are shown in use.

Listing 6.3   Special Character Codes

```
<?xml version="1.0" encoding="UTF-8"?>
<!DOCTYPE html PUBLIC "-//W3C//DTD XHTML 1.1//EN"
  "http://www.w3.org/TR/xhtml11/DTD/xhtml11.dtd">

<html xmlns="http://www.w3.org/1999/xhtml" xml:lang="en">
  <head>
    <title>Punctuation Lines</title>
  </head>

  <body>
    <p>
      Q: What should you do when a British banker picks a fight
      with you?<br />
      A: &pound; some &cent;&cent; into him.
      <hr />
      Q: What do you call it when a judge takes part of a law
      off the books?<br />
      A: &sect; violence.
      <hr />
      Q: What did the football coach get from the locker room
      vending machine in the middle of the game?<br />
      A: A &frac14; back at &frac12; time.
```

Listing 6.3   Special Character Codes

```
    <hr />
    Q: How hot did it get when the police detective interrogated
    the mathematician?<br />
    A: x&sup3;&deg;
    <hr />
    Q: What does a punctilious plagiarist do?<br />
    A: &copy;
    <hr />
  </p>
 </body>
</html>
```

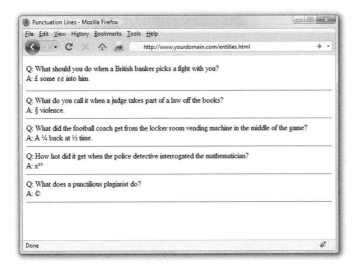

FIGURE 6.3
This is how the HTML page in Listing 6.3 looks in most web browsers.

Summary

In this hour you learned how to make text appear as boldface or italic and how to code superscripts, subscripts, special symbols, and accented letters. You saw how to make the text line up properly in preformatted passages of monospaced text and how to control the size, color, and typeface of any section of text on a web page.

Table 6.2 summarizes the tags and attributes discussed in this hour. Remember that all the HTML tags are listed in Appendix B, "XHTML 1.1 and CSS 2 Quick Reference."

Table 6.2   HTML Tags and Attributes Covered in Hour 6

Tag/Attribute	Function
`<em>...</em>`	Emphasis (usually italic).
`<strong>...</strong>`	Stronger emphasis (usually bold).
`<b>...</b>`	Boldface text.
`<i>...</i>`	Italic text.
`<tt>...</tt>`	Typewriter (monospaced) font.
`<pre>...</pre>`	Preformatted text (exact line endings and spacing will be preserved—usually rendered in a monospaced font).
`<big>...</big>`	Text is slightly larger than normal.
`<small>...</small>`	Text is slightly smaller than normal.
`<sub>...</sub>`	Subscript.
`<sup>...</sup>`	Superscript.
Attributes	
`style="font-family:typeface"`	The typeface (family) of the font, which is the name of a font, such as `Arial`. (Can also be used with `<p>`, `<h1>`, `<h2>`, `<h3>`, and so on.)
`style="font-size:size"`	The size of the font, which can be set to `small`, `medium`, or `large`, as well as `x-small`, `x-large`, and so on. Can also be set to a specific point size (such as `12pt`).
`style="color:color"`	Changes the color of the text.

Q&A

Q How do I find out the exact name for a font I have on my computer?

A On a Windows or Macintosh computer, open the Control Panel and click the `Fonts` folder—the fonts on your system are listed (Vista users might have to switch to "Classic View" in your Control Panel). When specifying fonts in the `font-family` style rule, use the exact spelling of font names. Font names are not case-sensitive, however.

Q How do I put Kanji, Arabic, Chinese, and other non-European characters on my pages?

A First of all, users who need to read these characters on your pages must have the appropriate language fonts installed. They must also have selected that language character set and its associated font for their web browsers. You can use the Character Map program in Windows (or a similar program in other operating systems) to get the numerical codes for each character in any language font. To find Character Map, click Start, All Programs, Accessories, and then System Tools. If the character you want has a code of 214, use Ö to place it on a web page. If you cannot find the Character Map program, use your operating system's built-in Help function to find the specific location.

The best way to include a short message in an Asian language (such as `We Speak Tamil—Call Us!`) is to include it as a graphics image. That way every user will see it, even if they use English as their primary language for web browsing. But even to use a language font in a graphic, you will likely have to download a specific language pack for your operating system. Again, check your system's Help function for specific instructions.

Workshop

The workshop contains quiz questions and activities to help you solidify your understanding of the material covered. Try to answer all questions before looking at the "Answers" section that follows.

Quiz

1. How would you create a paragraph in which the first three words are bold, using styles rather than the <b> or <strong> tags?

2. How would you represent the chemical formula for water?

3. How do you display "© 2009, Webwonks Inc." on a web page?

Answers

1. You would use:

```
<p><span style="font-weight: bold">First three words</span> are
bold.</p>
```

2. You would use H₂O.

```
<p><span style="font-weight: bold">First three words</span> are
bold.</p>
```

3. You would use either of the following:

```
&copy; 2004, Webwonks Inc.
&#169; 2004, Webwonks Inc.
```

Exercises

▶ Apply the font-level style attributes you learned about in this chapter to various block-level elements such as <p>, <div>, <ul>, and <li> items. Try nesting your elements to get a feel for how styles do or do not cascade through the content hierarchy.

HOUR 7
Using Tables to Display Information

In this hour, you learn how to build HTML tables you can use to control the spacing, layout, and appearance of tabular data in your web content. Although you can achieve similar results using CSS, there are definitely times when a table is the best way to present information and you'll find that tables are useful for arranging information into rows and columns. I will also explain how designers have used tables for page layout in the past, and how that isn't always the best idea. Before we begin, just remember a table is simply an orderly arrangement of content into vertical columns and horizontal rows.

As you read this hour, think about how arranging text into tables could benefit your web content. The following are some specific ideas to keep in mind:

▶ The most obvious application of tables is to organize tabular information, such as a multicolumn list of names and numbers.

▶ Whenever you need multiple columns of text or images, tables are the answer.

On your own, try adding a table modeled after the examples in this hour. The "Exercises" section at the end of this hour offers a couple of detailed suggestions along these lines as well.

WHAT YOU'LL LEARN IN THIS HOUR:

▶ How to create simple tables

▶ How to control the size of tables

▶ How to align content and span rows and columns within tables

TRY IT YOURSELF ▼

Putting Your Content into Tables

Creating a Simple Table

A table consists of rows of information with individual cells inside. To make tables, you have to start with a `<table>` tag. Of course, you end your tables with the `</table>` tag. If you want the table to have a border, use a border attribute to specify the width of the border in pixels. A border size of 0 or none (or leaving the border attribute out entirely) will make the border invisible, which is often handy when you are using a table as a page layout tool.

With the `<table>` tag in place, the next thing you need is the `<tr>` tag. The `<tr>` tag creates a table row, which contains one or more cells of information before the closing `</tr>`. To create these individual cells, use the `<td>` tag (`<td>` stands for table data). Place the table information between the `<td>` and `</td>` tags. A *cell* is a rectangular region that can contain any text, images, and HTML tags. Each row in a table is made up of at least one cell. Multiple cells within a row form columns in a table.

There is one more basic tag involved in building tables. The `<th>` tag works exactly like a `<td>` tag except `<th>` indicates that the cell is part of the heading of the table. Most web browsers render the text in `<th>` cells as centered and boldface.

You can create as many cells as you want, but each row in a table should have the same number of columns as the other rows. The HTML code shown in Listing 7.1 creates a simple table using only the four table tags I've mentioned thus far. Figure 7.1 shows the resulting page as viewed in a web browser.

Listing 7.1   Creating Tables with the `<table>`, `<tr>`, `<td>`, and `<th>` Tags

```
<?xml version="1.0" encoding="UTF-8"?>
<!DOCTYPE html PUBLIC "-//W3C//DTD XHTML 1.1//EN"
  "http://www.w3.org/TR/xhtml11/DTD/xhtml11.dtd">

<html xmlns="http://www.w3.org/1999/xhtml" xml:lang="en">
  <head>
    <title>Baseball Standings</title>
  </head>

  <body>
  <h1>Baseball Standings</h1>
    <table>
      <tr>
        <th>Team</th>
        <th>W</th>
```

Listing 7.1   Creating Tables with the `<table>`, `<tr>`, `<td>`, and `<th>` Tags

TIP

```
       <th>L</th>
          <th>GB</th>
       </tr>
       <tr>
          <td>Los Angeles Dodgers</td>
          <td>62</td>
          <td>38</td>
          <td>—</td>
       </tr>
       <tr>
          <td>San Francisco Giants</td>
          <td>54</td>
          <td>46</td>
          <td>8.0</td>
       </tr>
       <tr>
          <td>Colorado Rockies</td>
          <td>54</td>
          <td>46</td>
          <td>8.0</td>
       </tr>
       <tr>
          <td>Arizona Diamondbacks</td>
          <td>43</td>
          <td>58</td>
          <td>19.5</td>
       </tr>
       <tr>
          <td>San Diego Padres</td>
          <td>39</td>
          <td>62</td>
          <td>23.5</td>
       </tr>
    </table>
  </body>
</html>
```

TIP

HTML ignores extra spaces between words and tags. However, you might find your HTML tables easier to read (and less prone to time-wasting errors) if you use spaces to indent `<tr>` and `<td>` tags, as I did in Listing 7.1.

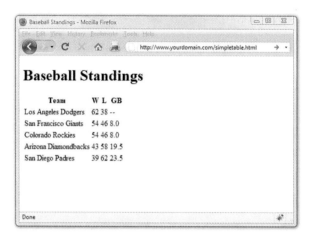

The table in the example contains baseball standings, which are perfect for arranging in rows and columns—if not a little plain. You'll learn to jazz things up a bit during this hour. The headings in the table show the Team, Wins (W), Losses (L), and Games Behind (GB) in the standings.

Although we did not apply any styles to the HTML in Listing 7.1, you can use any text style in a table cell. However, styles or HTML tags used in one cell don't carry over to other cells, and tags from outside the table don't apply within the table. For example, consider the following table:

```
<p style="font-weight:bold">
  <table>
    <tr>
      <td style="font-style:italic">hello</td>
      <td>there</td>
    </tr>
  </table>
</p>
```

In this example, the `<p>` tag is used around a table to demonstrate how tables are immune to outside tags. The word `there` would be neither bold-face nor italic because neither the `font-weight:bold` style outside the table nor the `font-style:italic` style from the previous cell affects it. In this example, the word `hello` is in italics, however.

To boldface the words `hello` and `there`, change the table code to this:

```
<table style="font-weight:bold">
  <tr>
    <td style="font-style:italic">hello</td>
    <td>there</td>
  </tr>
</table
```

In this example, both words are in bold and the word `hello` is italicized as well. Of course, you don't have to apply styles at the table level. The `font-weight:bold` style could just as easily be applied to each cell individually; you could repeat `style="font-weight:bold"` in each cell or create a class in your style sheet and use `class="classname"` in each cell—it's your choice.

Controlling Table Sizes

When a table width is not specified, the size of a table and its individual cells automatically expand to fit the data you place into it. However, you can choose to control the exact size of the entire table by using `width` and/or `height` styles in the `<table>` tag. You can also control the size of each cell by putting `width` and `height` styles in the individual `<td>` tags. The `width` and `height` styles can be specified as either pixels or percentages. For example, the following code creates a table 500 pixels wide and 400 pixels high:

```
<table style="width:500px; height:400px">
```

To make the first cell of the table 20% of the total table width and the second cell 80% of the table width, type the following:

```
<table style="width:100%">
  <tr>
    <td style="width:20%">skinny cell</td>
    <td style="width:80%">fat cell</td>
  </tr>
</table>
```

Notice that the table is sized to 100%, which ensures the table fills the entire width of the browser window. When you use percentages instead of fixed pixel sizes, the table will resize automatically to fit any size browser window while maintaining the aesthetic balance you're after. In this case, the two cells within the table are automatically resized to 20% and 80% of the total table width, respectively.

In Listing 7.2, the simple table from Listing 7.1 is expanded to show specific control over table cell widths.

NOTE

There are actually `width` and `height` HTML attributes that were deprecated in the move to XHTML, and you might still see them when you look at another designer's code. These attributes still work in web browsers but you should use the `width` and `height` style properties instead, because they represent the appropriate use of XHTML.

Listing 7.2   Specifying Table Cell Widths

```
<?xml version="1.0" encoding="UTF-8"?>
<!DOCTYPE html PUBLIC "-//W3C//DTD XHTML 1.1//EN"
  "http://www.w3.org/TR/xhtml11/DTD/xhtml11.dtd">

<html xmlns="http://www.w3.org/1999/xhtml" xml:lang="en">
  <head>
    <title>Baseball Standings</title>
  </head>

  <body>
  <h1>Baseball Standings</h1>
    <table>
      <tr>
        <th style="width:35px;"></th>
        <th style="width:175px;">Team</th>
        <th style="width:25px;">W</th>
        <th style="width:25px;">L</th>
        <th style="width:25px;">GB</th>
      </tr>
      <tr>
        <td><img src="losangeles.gif" alt="Los Angeles
          Dodgers" /></td>
        <td>Los Angeles Dodgers</td>
        <td>62</td>
        <td>38</td>
        <td>—</td>
      </tr>
      <tr>
        <td><img src="sanfrancisco.gif" alt="San Francisco
          Giants" /></td>
        <td>San Francisco Giants</td>
        <td>54</td>
        <td>46</td>
        <td>8.0</td>
      </tr>
      <tr>
        <td><img src="colorado.gif" alt="Colorado
          Rockies" /></td>
        <td>Colorado Rockies</td>
        <td>54</td>
        <td>46</td>
        <td>8.0</td>
      </tr>
      <tr>
        <td><img src="arizona.gif" alt="Arizona
          Diamondbacks" /></td>
        <td>Arizona Diamondbacks</td>
        <td>43</td>
        <td>58</td>
        <td>19.5</td>
      </tr>
```

Listing 7.2   Specifying Table Cell Widths

```
      <tr>
        <td><img src="sandiego.gif" alt="San Diego Padres" /></td>
        <td>San Diego Padres</td>
        <td>39</td>
        <td>62</td>
        <td>23.5</td>
      </tr>
    </table>
  </body>
</html>
```

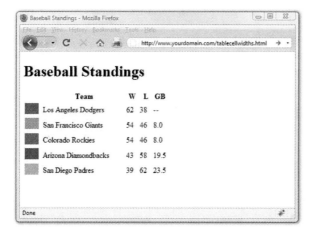

FIGURE 7.2
The HTML code in Listing 7.2 creates a table with six rows and five
columns, with specific widths used
for each column.

There are two differences between the code from Listing 7.1 and the code
used in Listing 7.2. First, an additional column has been added in Listing
7.2; this column does not have a heading, but the `<th></th>` tag pair is still
present in the first table row. In rows two through six, this additional column contains an image (the `<img />` tag). The second difference in Listing
7.2 is the addition of a specific width style for each `<th>` element in the first
row. The first column is defined as 35px wide, the second 175px wide, and
the third, fourth, and fifth columns are each 25px wide.

Also note that these widths are not repeated in the `<td>` elements in subsequent rows. Technically you must define only the widths in the first row;
the remaining rows will follow suit because they are all part of the same
table. However, if you used another formatting style (such as a style to
change font size or color), that style must be repeated for each element that
should have those display properties.

Alignment and Spanning Within Tables

By default, anything you place inside a table cell is aligned to the left and vertically centered. Figures 7.1 and 7.2 show this default alignment. However, you can align the contents of table cells both horizontally and vertically with the `text-align` and `vertical-align` style properties.

You can apply these alignment attributes to any `<tr>`, `<td>`, or `<th>` tag. Alignment attributes assigned to a `<tr>` tag apply to all cells in that row. Depending on the size of your table, you can save yourself a considerable amount of time and effort by applying these attributes at the `<tr>` level and not in each `<td>` or `<th>` tag.

The HTML code in Listing 7.3 uses a combination of text alignment styles to apply a default alignment to a row, but overridden in a few individual cells. Figure 7.3 shows the result of the code in Listing 7.3.

Following are some of the more commonly used `vertical-align` style property values: `top`, `middle`, `bottom`, `text-top`, `text-bottom`, and `baseline` (for text). These property values give you plenty of flexibility in aligning table data vertically.

Listing 7.3   Alignment, Cell Spacing, Borders, and Background Colors in Tables

```
<?xml version="1.0" encoding="UTF-8"?>
<!DOCTYPE html PUBLIC "-//W3C//DTD XHTML 1.1//EN"
  "http://www.w3.org/TR/xhtml11/DTD/xhtml11.dtd">

<html xmlns="http://www.w3.org/1999/xhtml" xml:lang="en">
  <head>
    <title>Things to Fear</title>
  </head>

  <body>
    <h1>Things to Fear</h1>
    <table border="2" cellpadding="4" cellspacing="2"
    width="100%">
      <tr style="background-color:red;color:white">
        <th colspan="2">Description</th>
        <th>Size</th>
        <th>Weight</th>
        <th>Speed</th>
      </tr>
      <tr style="vertical-align:top">
        <td><img src="handgun.gif" alt=".38 Special"/></td>
```

Listing 7.3   Alignment, Cell Spacing, Borders, and Background Colors in
                    Tables

```
<td style="font-size: 14px;font-weight:bold;
vertical-align:middle;text-align:center">.38 Special</td>
<td>Five-inch barrel.</td>
<td>Twenty ounces.</td>
<td>Six rounds in four seconds.</td>
</tr>
<tr style="vertical-align:top">
<td><img src="rhino.gif" alt="Rhinoceros" /></td>
<td style="font-size: 14px;font-weight:bold;
vertical-align:middle;text-align:center">Rhinoceros</td>
<td>Twelve feet, horn to tail.</td>
<td>Up to two tons.</td>
<td>Thirty-five miles per hour in bursts.</td>
</tr>
<tr style="vertical-align:top">
<td><img src="axeman.gif" alt="Broad Axe" /></td>
<td style="font-size: 14px;font-weight:bold;
vertical-align:middle;text-align:center">Broad Axe</td>
<td>Thirty-inch blade.</td>
<td>Twelve pounds.</td>
<td>Sixty miles per hour on impact.</td>
</tr>
</table>
</body>
</html>
```

FIGURE 7.3
The code in Listing 7.3 shows the
use of the colspan attribute and
alignment styles.

At the top of Figure 7.3, a single cell (Description) spans two columns. This is accomplished with the `colspan` attribute in the `<th>` tag for that cell. As you might guess, you can also use the `rowspan` attribute to create a cell that spans more than one row.

Spanning is the process of forcing a cell to stretch across more than one row or column of a table. The `colspan` attribute causes a cell to span across multiple columns; `rowspan` has the same effect on rows.

Additionally, text styles are used in the second cell within the Description column to create bold text that is both vertically aligned to the middle and horizontally aligned to the center of the cell.

There are a few tricks in Listing 7.3 that I haven't explained yet. You can give an entire table—and each individual row or cell in a table—its own background, distinct from any background you might use on the web page itself. You can do this by placing the `background-color` or `background-image` style in the `<table>`, `<tr>`, `<td>`, or `<th>` tag exactly as you would in the `<body>` tag (see Hour 9, "Working with Colors"). To give an entire table a yellow background, for example, you would use `<table style="background-color:yellow">` or the equivalent `<table style="background-color:#FFFF00">`. In Listing 7.3, only the top row has a background color; it uses `<tr style="background-color:red;color:white">` to apply a red background across the cells in that row. Additionally, the `color` style ensures that the text in that row is white.

Similar to the `background-color` style property is the `background-image` property (not shown in this example), which is used to set an image for a table background. If you wanted to set the image `leaves.gif` as the background for a table, you would use `<table style="background-image:url(leaves.gif)">`. Notice that the image file is placed within parentheses and preceded by the word `url`, which indicates that you are describing where the image file is located.

Tweaking tables goes beyond just using style properties. As shown in Listing 7.3, you can control the space around the borders of a table with the `cellpadding` and `cellspacing` attributes. The `cellspacing` attribute sets the amount of space (in pixels) between table borders and between table cells themselves. The `cellpadding` attribute sets the amount of space around the edges of information in the cells, also in pixels. Setting the `cellpadding` value to 0 causes all the information in the table to align as closely as possible to the table borders, possibly even touching the borders. The `cellpadding` and `cellspacing` attributes give you good overall control of the table's appearance.

TIP

Keeping the structure of rows and columns organized in your mind can be the most difficult part of creating tables with cells that span multiple columns or rows. The tiniest error can often throw the whole thing into disarray. You'll save yourself time and frustration by sketching your tables on paper before you start writing the HTML to implement them.

NOTE

You will often see alternating row colors in a table. For instance, one row might have a grey background and the next row might have a white background. Alternating row colors helps users read the content of your table more clearly, especially if the table is quite large.

NOTE

Although the `cellpadding` and `cellspacing` attributes are still allowed in XHTML, a CSS equivalent for them exists in the form of the `padding` and `border-spacing` style properties. Review the information in Appendix B, "XHTML 1.1 and CSS 2 Quick Reference," for information and examples.

Page Layout with Tables

At the beginning of this Hour, I indicated that designers have used tables for page layout as well as to display tabular information. You will still find many examples of table-based layouts if you peek at another designer's source code. This method of design grew out of the old (mid-1990s to early 2000s) inconsistencies in browser support for CSS. All browsers supported tables and in generally the same way, so web designers latched on to the table-based method of content creation to achieve the same visual page display across all browsers. However, now that support for CSS is relatively similar across all major browsers, designers can follow the long-standing standards-based recommendation *not* to use tables for page layout.

The World Wide Web Consortium (W3C), the standards body that oversees the future of the Web, promotes style sheets as the proper way to lay out pages (instead of using tables). Style sheets are ultimately much more powerful than tables, which is why the bulk of this book teaches you how to use style sheets for page layout.

The main reasons for avoiding using tables for layout include:

▶ Mixing Presentation with Content—One of the goals of CSS and standards-compliant web design is to separate the presentation layer from the content layer.

▶ Creating Unnecessarily Difficult Redesigns—To change a table-based layout, you would have to change the table-based layout on every single page of your site (unless it is part of a complicated, dynamically-driven site, in which case you would have to undo all the dynamic pieces and remake them).

▶ Accessibility Issues—Screen reading software looks to tables for content, and so will often try to read your layout table as a content table.

▶ Rendering on Mobile Devices—Table layouts are often not flexible enough to scale downward to small screens (see Hour 19, "Creating Fixed or Liquid Layouts").

These are but a few of the issues in table-based web design. For a closer look at some of these issues, see the popular presentation "Why Tables for Layout is Stupid" at http://www.hotdesign.com/seybold/everything.html.

Summary

In this hour, you learned to arrange text and images into organized arrangements of rows and columns called tables. You learned the three basic tags for creating tables and many optional attributes and styles for controlling the alignment, spacing, and appearance of tables. You also learned that tables can be used together and nested within one another for an even wider variety of layout options.

Table 7.1 summarizes the tags and attributes covered in this hour.

Table 7.1   HTML Tags and Attributes Covered in Hour 7

Tag/Attribute	Function
`<table>...</table>`	Creates a table that can contain any number of rows (`<tr>` tags).
Attributes	
`border="width"`	Indicates the width in pixels of the table borders. Using `border="0"` or omitting the `border` attribute makes borders invisible.
`cellspacing="spacing"`	The amount of space between the cells in the table, in pixels.
`cellpadding="padding"`	The amount of space between the edges of the cell and its contents, in pixels.
`style="width:width"`	The width of the table on the page, either in exact pixel values or as a percentage of the page width.
`style="height:height"`	The height of the table on the page, either in exact pixel values or as a percentage of the page height.
`style="background-color:color"`	Background color of the table and individual table cells that don't already have a background color.
`style="backgroundimage:url(imageurl)"`	A background image to display within the table and individual table cells that don't already have a background image (if a background color is also specified, the color will show through transparent areas of the image).

Table 7.1   HTML Tags and Attributes Covered in Hour 7

Attributes

`<tr>...</tr>`	Defines a table row containing one or more cells (`<td>` tags).

Attributes

`style="text-align:alignment"`	The horizontal alignment of the contents of the cells within this row. Possible values are `left`, `right`, and `center`.
`style="vertical-align:alignment"`	The vertical alignment of the contents of the cells within this row. Common used values include `top`, `middle`, and `bottom`.
`style="background-color:color"`	Background color of all cells in the row that do not already have a background color.
`style="backgroundimage:url(imageurl)"`	Background image to display within all cells in the row that do not already have their own background image.
`<td>...</td>`	Defines a table data cell.
`<th>...</th>`	Defines a table heading cell. (Accepts all the same attributes and styles as `<td>`.)

Attributes

`style="text-align:alignment"`	The horizontal alignment of the contents of the cell. Possible values are `left`, `right`, and `center`.
`style="vertical-align:alignment"`	The vertical alignment of the contents of the cell. Commonly used values are `top`, `middle`, and `bottom`.
`rowspan="numrows"`	The number of rows this cell will span.
`colspan="numcols"`	The number of columns this cell will span.
`style="width:width"`	The width of this column of cells, in exact pixel values or as a percentage of the table width.

Table 7.1   HTML Tags and Attributes Covered in Hour 7

Attributes

`style="height:height"`	The height of this row of cells, in exact pixel values or as a percentage of the table height.
`style="background-color:color"`	Background color of the cell.
`style="backgroundimage:url(imageurl)"`	Background image to display within the cell.

Q&A

Q I made a big table and when I load the page, nothing appears on the page for a long time. Why the wait?

A Complex tables can take a while to appear on the screen. The web browser has to figure out the size of everything in the table before it can display any part of it. You can speed things up a bit by always including `width` and `height` attributes for every graphics image within a table. Using `width` attributes in the `<table>` and `<td>` tags also helps.

Q Can I put a table within a table?

A Yes, you can nest tables within other table cells. However, nested tables—especially large ones—take time to load and render properly. Before you create a nested table, think about the content you are placing on the page and ask yourself if it could be displayed using CSS. You might not know all the answers until you finish this book, but here's a hint: In most cases, the answer will be "yes."

Workshop

The workshop contains quiz questions and activities to help you solidify your understanding of the material covered. Try to answer all questions before looking at the "Answers" section that follows.

Quiz

1. How would you create a simple two-row, two-column table with a standard border?

2. Expanding on Question 1, how would you add 30 pixels of space between the table border and the cells?

3. Continuing with the table you've built in Questions 1 and 2, how would you make the top-left cell green, the top-right cell red, the bottom-left cell yellow, and the bottom-right cell blue?

Answers

1. Use the following HTML:

```
<table border="1">
  <tr>
    <td>Top left...</td>
    <td>Top right...</td>
  </tr>
  <tr>
    <td>Bottom left...</td>
    <td>Bottom right...</td>
  </tr>
</table>
```

2. Add `cellspacing="30"` to the `<table>` tag.

3. Add `style="background-color:green"` to the top left `<td>` tag, add `style="background-color:red"` to the top right `<td>` tag, add `style="background-color:yellow"` to the bottom left `<td>` tag, and add `style="background-color:blue"` to the bottom right `<td>` tag.

Exercises

▶ Do you have any pages that have information visitors might be interested in viewing as lists or tables? Use a table to present some tabular information. Make sure each column has its own heading (or perhaps its own graphic). Play around with the various types of alignment and spacing that you have learned in this hour.

▶ You will often see alternating row colors in a table, with one row having a grey background and the next a white background. The goal of alternating colors in table rows is so that the individual rows are easier to discern when looking quickly at the table full of data. Create a table with alternating row colors and text colors (if necessary). Although the lesson on colors comes in Hour 9, you have enough information in this lesson to begin trying out the process.

Using External and Internal Links

So far, you have learned how to use HTML tags to create some basic web pages. However, at this point, those pieces of content are islands unto themselves, with no connection to anything else (although it is true that in Hour 4 I sneaked a few page links into the examples). To turn your work into "real" web content, you need to connect it to the rest of the Web—or at least to your other pages within your own personal or corporate sites.

This hour shows you how to create hypertext links to content within your own document and how to link to other external documents. Additionally, you will learn how to style hypertext links so that they display in the color and decoration that you desire—not necessarily the default blue underlined display.

Using Web Addresses

The simplest way to store web content for an individual web site is to place the files all in the same folder together. When files are stored together like this, you can link to them by simply providing the name of the file in the href attribute of the <a> tag.

An *attribute* is an extra piece of information associated with a tag that provides further details about the tag. For example, the href attribute of the <a> tag identifies the address of the page to which you are linking.

Once you have more than a few pages, or once you start to have an organization structure to the content in your site, you should put your files into directories (or "folders," if you will) whose names reflect the content within them. For example, all your images could be in an "images" directory, corporate information could be in an "about" directory, and so on.

WHAT YOU'LL LEARN IN THIS HOUR:

- ▶ How to use anchor links
- ▶ How to link between pages on your own site
- ▶ How to link to external content
- ▶ How to link to an e-mail address
- ▶ How to use window targeting with your links
- ▶ How to style your links with CSS

NOTE

Before we begin, you might want a refresher on the basics of where to put files on your server and how to manage files within a set of directories. This information is important to know when creating links in web content. Refer back to Hour 2, specifically the section entitled "Understanding Where to Place Files on the Web Server."

Regardless of how you organize your documents within your own web server, you can use relative addresses, which include only enough information to find one page from another.

A *relative address* describes the path from one web page to another, instead of a full (or *absolute*) Internet address.

If you recall from Hour 2, the document root of your web server is the directory designated as the top-level directory for your web content. In web addresses, that document root is represented by the forward slash (/). All subsequent levels of directories are separated by the same type of forward slash. For example:

```
/directory/subdirectory/subsubdirectory/
```

Suppose you are creating a page named zoo.html in your document root and you want to include a link to pages named african.html and asian.html in the elephants subdirectory. The links would look like the following:

```
<a href="/elephants/african.html">Learn about African elephants.</a>
<a href="/elephants/asian.html">Learn about Asian elephants.</a>
```

These specific addresses are actually called relative-root addresses in that they are relative addresses that lack the entire domain name, but they are specifically relative to the document root specified by the forward slash.

Using a regular relative address, you can skip the initial forward slash. This type of address allow the links to become relative to whatever directory they are in—it could be the document root or it could be another directory one or more levels down from the document root:

```
<a href="elephants/african.html">Learn about African elephants.</a>
<a href="elephants/asian.html">Learn about Asian elephants.</a>
```

Your african.html and asian.html documents in the elephants subdirectory could link back to the main zoo.html page in either of these ways:

```
<a href="http://www.yourdoman.com/zoo.html">Return to the zoo.</a>
<a href="/zoo.html">Return to the zoo.</a>
<a href="../zoo.html">Return to the zoo.</a>
```

The first link is an absolute link. With an absolute link there is *absolutely* no doubt where the link should go, because the full URL is provided—domain name included.

The second link is a relative-root link. It is relative to the domain you are currently browsing and therefore does not require the protocol type (for example, http://) and the domain name (for example, www.yourdomain.com), but the initial forward slash is provided to show that the address begins at the document root.

In the third link, the *double dot* (..) is a special command that indicates the folder that contains the current folder—in other words, the *parent folder*. Anytime you see the double dot, just think to yourself "go up a level" in the directory structure.

If you use relative addressing consistently throughout your web pages, you can move the pages to another folder, disk drive, or web server without changing the links.

Relative addresses can span quite complex directory structures if necessary. Hour 23, "Organizing and Managing a Web Site," offers more detailed advice for organizing and linking large numbers of web pages.

TIP

The general rule surrounding relative addressing (elephants/african.html) versus absolute addressing (http://www.takeme2thezoo.com /elephants/african.html) is that you should use relative addressing when linking to files that are stored together, such as files that are all part of the same web site. Absolute addressing should be used when you're linking to files somewhere else—another computer, another disk drive, or, more commonly, another web site on the Internet.

TRY IT YOURSELF ▼

Hopefully by now you've created a page or two of your own while working through the lessons. Follow these steps to add a few more pages and link them together:

1. Use a "home" page as a main entrance and as a central hub to which all of your other pages are connected. If you created a page about yourself or your business, use that page as your home page. You also might like to create a new page now for this purpose.

2. On the home page, put a list of links to the other HTML files you've created (or placeholders for the HTML files you plan to create soon). Be sure that the exact spelling of the filename, including any capitalization, is correct in every link.

3. On every other page besides the home page, include a link at the bottom (or top) leading back to your home page. That makes it simple and easy to navigate around your site.

4. You might also want to include a list of links to related or interesting sites, either on your home page or on a separate links page. People often include a list of their friends' personal pages on their own home page. Businesses, however, should be careful not to lead potential customers away to other sites too quickly—there's no guarantee they'll remember to use relative addressing for links between your own pages and absolute addressing for links to other sites.

Linking Within a Page Using Anchors

The `<a>` *tag*—the tag responsible for hyperlinks on the web—got its name from the word "anchor," which means a link serves as a designation for a spot in a web page. In examples shown throughout this book so far, you've learned how to use the `<a>` tag to link to somewhere else, but that's only half of its usefulness. Let's get started working with anchor links that link to content within the same page.

Identifying Locations in a Page with Anchors

The `<a>` tag can be used to mark a spot on a page as an anchor, allowing you to create a link that points to that exact spot. Listing 8.1, which is presented a bit later in the hour, demonstrates a link to an anchor within a page. To see how such links are made, let's take a quick peek ahead at the first `<a>` tag in the listing:

```
<a id="top"></a>
```

NOTE

Instead of using `id`, older versions of HTML used `name`. Newer versions of HTML and XHTML have done away with the `name` attribute and instead use `id`.

The `<a>` tag normally uses the `href` attribute to specify a hyperlinked target. The `<a href>` is what you click and `<a id>` is where you go when you click there. In this example, the `<a>` tag is still specifying a target but no actual link is created. Instead, the `<a>` tag gives a name to the specific point on the page where the tag occurs. The `</a>` tag must be included and a unique name must be assigned to the `id` attribute, but no text between `<a>` and `</a>` is necessary.

Linking to Anchor Locations

Listing 8.1 shows a site with various anchor points placed throughout a single page. Take a look at the last `<a>` tag in Listing 8.1 to see an example:

```
<a href="#top">Return to Index.</a>
```

The # symbol means that the word `top` refers to a named anchor point within the current document, rather than to a separate page. When a user clicks `Return to Index`, the web browser displays the part of the page starting with the `<a id="top">` tag.

Listing 8.1   Setting Anchor Points by Using the `<a>` Tag with an `id` Attribute

```
<?xml version="1.0" encoding="UTF-8"?>
<!DOCTYPE html PUBLIC "-//W3C//DTD XHTML 1.1//EN"
  "http://www.w3.org/TR/xhtml11/DTD/xhtml11.dtd">

<html xmlns="http://www.w3.org/1999/xhtml" xml:lang="en">
  <head>
    <title>Alphabetical Shakespeare</title>
  </head>

  <body>
    <h1><a id="top"></a>First Lines of Shakespearean Sonnets</h1>
    <p>Don't you just hate when you go a-courting, and you're down
      on one knee about to rattle off a totally romantic Shakespearean
      sonnet, and zap! You space it. <em>"Um... It was, uh... I think it
      started with a  B..."</em></p>
    <p>Well, appearest thou no longer the dork. Simply refer to this page,
      click on the first letter of the sonnet you want, and get an instant
      reminder of the first line to get you started. <em>"Beshrew that
      heart that makes my heart to groan..."</em></p>
    <h2 style="text-align:center">Alphabetical Index</h2>
    <h3 style="text-align:center">
    <a href="#A">A</a> <a href="#B">B</a> <a href="#C">C</a>
    <a href="#D">D</a> <a href="#E">E</a> <a href="#F">F</a>
    <a href="#G">G</a> <a href="#H">H</a> <a href="#I">I</a>
    <a href="#J">J</a> <a href="#K">K</a> <a href="#L">L</a>
    <a href="#M">M</a> <a href="#N">N</a> <a href="#O">O</a>
    <a href="#P">P</a> <a href="#Q">Q</a> <a href="#R">R</a>
    <a href="#S">S</a> <a href="#T">T</a> <a href="#U">U</a>
    <a href="#V">V</a> <a href="#W">W</a> <a href="#X">X</a>
    <a href="#Y">Y</a> <a href="#Z">Z</a>
    </h3>
    <hr />
    <h3><a id="A"></a>A</h3>
    <ul>
    <li>A woman's face with nature's own hand painted,</li>
    <li>Accuse me thus, that I have scanted all, </li>
    <li>Against my love shall be as I am now</li>
    <li>Against that time (if ever that time come) </li>
    <li>Ah wherefore with infection should he live, </li>
    <li>Alack what poverty my muse brings forth, </li>
    <li>Alas 'tis true, I have gone here and there, </li>
    <li>As a decrepit father takes delight, </li>
    <li>As an unperfect actor on the stage, </li>
    <li>As fast as thou shalt wane so fast thou grow'st, </li>
    </ul>
    <p><a href="#top"><em>Return to Index.</em></a></p>
    <hr />
    <!-- continue with the alphabet —>
    <h3><a id="Z"></a>Z</h3>
```

NOTE

Near the end of Listing 8.1 you will see a line that reads:

```
<!-- continue with the alpha-
bet -->
```

This text (an HTML comment) will appear in your source code but will not be displayed by the browser. You can learn more about commenting your code in Hour 23.

WARNING

Anchor names specified via the `id` attribute in the `<a>` tag must start with an alphanumeric character. So if you want to simply number the IDs of anchors, be sure to start them with text (as in photo1, photo2, and so on) instead of just 1, 2, and so on. Purely numeric anchor IDs will work in browsers but they don't qualify as valid XHTML code.

Listing 8.1   Setting Anchor Points by Using the `<a>` Tag with an `id` Attribute

```
   <p>(No sonnets start with Z.)</p>
   <p><a href="#top"><em>Return to Index.</em></a></p>
  </body>
</html>
```

Each of the `<a href>` links in Listing 8.1 makes an underlined link leading to a corresponding `<a id>` anchor—or it would if I had filled in all the text. Only A and Z will work in this example since only the A and Z links have corresponding text to link to, but feel free to fill in the rest on your own! Clicking the letter Z under Alphabetical Index in Figure 8.1, for example, takes you to the part of the page shown in Figure 8.2.

FIGURE 8.1
The `<a id>` tags in Listing 8.1 don't appear at all on the web page. The `<a href>` tags appear as underlined links.

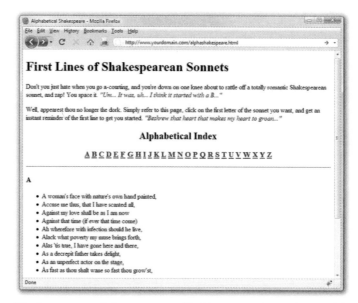

Having mastered the concept of linking to sections of text within a single page, you can now learn to link together other pieces of web content.

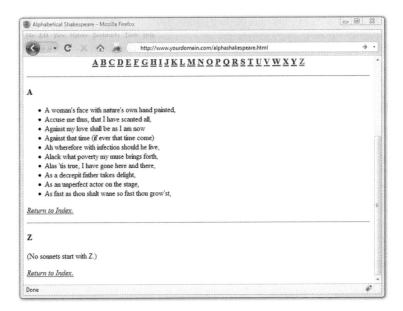

FIGURE 8.2
Clicking the letter Z on the page shown in Figure 8.1 takes you to the appropriate section of the same page.

Linking Between Your Own Web Content

As you learned earlier in this hour, you do not need to include `http://` before each address specified in the `href` attribute when linking to content within your domain (or on the same computer, if you are viewing your site locally). When you create a link from one file to another file within the same domain or on the same computer, you don't need to specify a complete Internet address. In fact, if the two files are stored in the same folder, you can simply use the name of the HTML file by itself:

```
<a href="pagetwo.html">Go to Page 2.</a>
```

As an example, Listing 8.2 and Figure 8.3 show a quiz page with a link to the answers page shown in Listing 8.3 and Figure 8.4. The answers page contains a link back to the quiz page. Because the page in Listing 8.2 links to another page in the same directory, the filename can be used in place of a complete address.

Listing 8.2   The `historyanswers.html` file

```
<?xml version="1.0" encoding="UTF-8"?>
<!DOCTYPE html PUBLIC "-//W3C//DTD XHTML 1.1//EN"
  "http://www.w3.org/TR/xhtml11/DTD/xhtml11.dtd">

<html xmlns="http://www.w3.org/1999/xhtml" xml:lang="en">
  <head>
    <title>History Quiz</title>
  </head>

  <body>
    <h1>History Quiz</h1>
    <p>Complete the following rhymes. (Example: William the Conqueror
    Played cruel tricks on the Saxons in... ten sixty-six.)</p>
    <ol>
    <li>Columbus sailed the ocean blue in...</li>
    <li>The Spanish Armada met its fate in...</li>
    <li>London burnt like rotten sticks in...</li>
    </ol>
    <p style="text-align: center;font-weight: bold;">
    <a href="historyanswers.html">Check Your Answers!</a>
    </p>
  </body>
</html>
```

Listing 8.3   The `historyanswers.html` file which `historyquiz.html`
Links To

```
<?xml version="1.0" encoding="UTF-8"?>
<!DOCTYPE html PUBLIC "-//W3C//DTD XHTML 1.1//EN"
  "http://www.w3.org/TR/xhtml11/DTD/xhtml11.dtd">

<html xmlns="http://www.w3.org/1999/xhtml" xml:lang="en">
  <head>
    <title>History Quiz Answers</title>
  </head>

  <body>
    <h1>History Quiz Answers</h1>
    <ol>
    <li>...fourteen hundred and ninety-two.</li>
    <li>...fifteen hundred and eighty eight.</li>
    <li>...sixteen hundred and sixty-six.</li>
    </ol>
    <p style="text-align: center;font-weight: bold;">
    <a href="historyquiz.html">Return to the Questions</a>
    </p>
  </body>
</html>
```

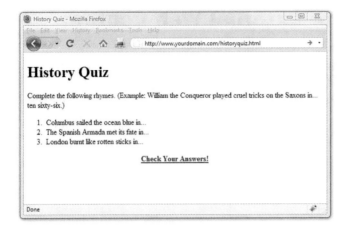

FIGURE 8.3
This is the `historyquiz.html` file listed in Listing 8.2 and referred to by the link in Listing 8.3.

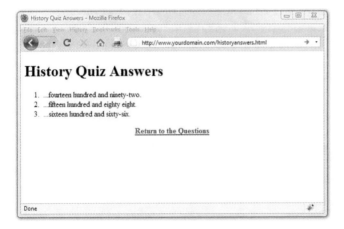

FIGURE 8.4
The `Check Your Answers!` link in Figure 8.3 takes you to this answers page. The `Return to the Questions` link takes you back to what's shown in Figure 8.3.

Using filenames instead of complete Internet addresses saves you a lot of typing. More important, the links between your pages will work properly no matter where the group of pages is stored. You can test the links while the files are still on your computer's hard drive. You can then move them to a web server, a CD-ROM, a DVD, or a memory card and all the links will still work correctly. There is nothing magic about this simplified approach to identifying web pages—it all has to do with web-page addressing, as you've already learned.

Linking to External Web Content

The only difference between linking to pages within your own site and linking to external web content is that when linking outside your site, you need to include the full address to that bit of content. The full address includes the `http://` before the domain name and then the full pathname to the file (for example, an HTML file, image file, multimedia file, and so on).

For example, to include a link to Google from within one of your own web pages, you would use this type of absolute addressing in your `<a>` link:

```
<a href="http://www.google.com/">Go to Google</a>
```

You can apply what you learned in previous sections to creating links to named anchors on other pages. Linked anchors are not limited to the same page. You can link to a named anchor on another page by including the address or file name followed by # and the anchor name. For example, the following link would take you to an anchor named `photos` within the `african.html` page inside the `elephants` directory on the domain `www.takeme2thezoo.com`.

```
<a href="http://www.takemetothezoo.com/elephants/african.html#photos">
Check out the African Elephant Photos!</a>
```

If you are linking from another page already on the www.takemetothezoo.com domain (because you are, in fact, the site maintainer), then your link might simply be:

```
<a href="/elephants/african.html#photos">Check out the African Elephant
Photos!</a>
```

The `http://` and the domain name would not be necessary in that instance, as you have already learned.

Linking to an Email Address

In addition to linking between pages and between parts of a single page, the `<a>` tag allows you to link to email addresses. This is the simplest way to enable your web page visitors to "talk back" to you. Of course, you could just provide visitors with your email address and trust them to type it into whatever email programs they use, but that increases the likelihood for errors. By providing a clickable link to your email address, you can make it almost completely effortless for them to send you messages and eliminate the chance for tyops.

An HTML link to an email address looks like the following:

```
<a href="mailto:yourusername@yourdomain.com">Send me an email
message.</a>
```

The words `Send me an email message` will appear just like any other `<a>` link.

If you want people to see your actual email address (so that they can make note of it or send a message using a different email program), include it both in the `href` attribute and as part of the message between the `<a>` and `</a>` tags, like this:

```
<a
href="mailto:yourusername@yourdomain.com">yourusername@yourdomain.com</a>
```

In most web browsers, when someone clicks the link, she gets a window into which she can type a message that is immediately sent to you—whatever email program the person uses to send and receive email will automatically be used. You can provide some additional information in the link so that the subject and body of the message also have default values. You do this by adding `subject` and `body` variables to the `mailto` link. You separate the variables from the email address with a question mark (?), the value from the variable with an equal sign (=), and then separate each of the variable and value pairs with an ampersand (&). You don't have to understand the variable/value terminology at this point. Here is an example of specifying a subject and body for the preceding email example:

```
<a href="mailto:author@somedomain.com?subject=Book Question&body=
When is the next edition coming out?">author@somedomain.com</a>
```

When a user clicks this link, an email message is created with author@somedomain.com as the recipient, `Book Question` as the subject of the message, and `When is the next edition coming out?` as the message body.

Before you run off and start plastering your email address all over your web pages, I have to give you a little warning and then let you in on a handy trick. You're no doubt familiar with spammers that build up databases of email addresses and then bombard them with junk mail advertisements. One way spammers "harvest" email addresses is by using programs that automatically search web pages for `mailto` links.

Fortunately, there is a little trick that will thwart the vast majority of spam-

TIP

If you want to specify only an email message subject and not the body, you can just leave off the ampersand and the body variable, equal sign, and value text string as follows:

```
<a
href="mailto:author@somedomai
n.com?subject=Book
Question>author@somedomain.co
m</a>
```

mers. This trick involves using character entities to encode your email address, which confuses "scraper" programs that attempt to "harvest" your email address from your web pages. As an example, take the email address, `jcmeloni@gmail.com`. If you replace the letters in the address with their character entity equivalents, most email harvesting programs will be thrown off. Lowercase ASCII character entities begin at `&#97;` for letter a and increase through the alphabet in order. For example, letter j is `&#106`, c is `&#99`, and so on. Replacing all the characters with their ASCII attributes produces the following:

```
<a
href="mailto:&#106;&#099;&#109;&#101;&#108;&#111;&#110;&#105;&#064;&#103;
&#109;&#097;&#105;&#108;&#046;&#099;&#111;&#109;">Send me an email
message.</a>
```

Since the browser interprets the character encoding as, well, characters, the end result is the same from the browser's perspective. However, automated email harvesting programs search the raw HTML code for pages, which in this case is showing a fairly jumbled-looking email address. If you don't want to figure out the character encoding for your own address, just type **email address encoder** in your search engine and you will find some services online that will produce an encoded string for you.

Opening a Link in a New Browser Window

Now that you have a handle on how to create addresses for links—both internal (within your site) and external (to other sites)—there is one additional method of linking: forcing the user to open links in new windows.

You've no doubt heard of *pop-up windows*, which are browser windows—typically advertising products or services—that are opened and displayed automatically without the user's approval. However, the concept of opening another window or targeting another location does serve a valid purpose in some instances. For example, you might want to present information in a smaller secondary browser window but allow the user to still see the information in the main window. This is often the case when clicking on a link to an animated demo, movie clip, or other multimedia element. You could also want to target a new browser window when you are linking to content off-site.

However, opening a new browser window on behalf of your user—especially when it's a full-size new window—goes against some principles of usability and accessibility. When people opened new windows, typically it happened through the use of the target attribute of the <a> tag. The target attribute has been removed from the <a> tag in the strict XHTML 1.1 specification.

There are valid ways to achieve the same result while still adhering to principles of usability and accessibility, but these methods require a little JavaScript and other advanced techniques. You will learn these methods in Hour 18, "Using Mouse Actions to Modify Text Display," which will also cover standards-compliant and accessible ways to invoke new windows with your external links.

Using CSS to Style Hyperlinks

The default display of a text-based hyperlink on a web page is underlined blue text. You might also have noticed that links you have previously visited appear as underlined purple text—that color is also a default. If you've spent any time at all on the web, you will also have noticed that not all links are blue or purple—and for that, I think, we are all thankful. Using a little CSS and knowledge of the various pseudoclasses for the <a> link, you can make your links look however you want.

A *pseudoclass* is a class that describes styles for elements that apply to certain circumstances, such as various states of user interaction with that element.

For example, the common pseudoclasses for the <a> tag are link, visited, hover, and active. You can remember them with the mnemonic "Love-Hate"—LV (love) HA (hate), if you wish.

> ▶ a:link describes the style of a hyperlink that has not been visited previously
>
> ▶ a:visited describes the style of a hyperlink that has been visited previously and is present in the browser's memory
>
> ▶ a:hover describes the style of a hyperlink as a user's mouse hovers over it (and before it has been clicked)
>
> ▶ a:active describes the style of a hyperlink that is in the act of being clicked but has not yet been released.

For example, let's say you want to produce a link with the following styles:

NOTE

You can use graphics as links (instead of using text as links) by putting an <img /> tag between the opening <a> and closing </a> tags. You'll learn how to use graphics as links in Hour 11, "Using Images in Your Web Site."

> ▶ A font that is bold and Verdana (and not underlined, meaning it has no text decoration)
>
> ▶ A base color that is light blue
>
> ▶ A color of red when users hover over it or when they are clicking it
>
> ▶ A color of grey after users have visited it.

Your style sheet entries might look like the following:

```
a {
    font-family: Verdana, sans-serif;
    font-weight: bold;
    text-decoration: none;
}
a:link {
    color: #6479A0;
}
a:visited {
    color: #CCCCCC;
}
a:hover {
    color: #E03A3E;
}
a:active {
    color: #E03A3E;
}
```

Since the example link will be Verdana bold (and not underlined) regardless of the state it is in, those three property and value pairs can reside in the rule for the a selector. However, since each pseudoclass must have a specific color associated with it, we use a rule for each pseudoclass as shown in the code example. The pseudoclass inherits the style of the parent rule, unless the rule for the pseudoclass specifically overrides that rule. In other words, all the pseudoclasses in the previous example will be Verdana bold, (and not underlined). If, however, we had used the following rule for the hover pseudoclass, the text would display in Comic Sans when users hovered over it (if, in fact, the user has the Comic Sans font installed):

```
a:hover {
    font-family: "Comic Sans MS";
    color: #E03A3E;
}
```

Additionally, since the active and hover pseudoclasses use the same font color, you can combine style rules for them:

```
a:hover, a:active {
    color: #E03A3E;
}
```

Listing 8.4 puts these code snippets together to produce a page using styled pseudoclasses; the results of this code can be seen in Figure 8.5.

Listing 8.4   Using Styles to Display Link Pseudoclasses

```
<?xml version="1.0" encoding="UTF-8"?>
<!DOCTYPE html PUBLIC "-//W3C//DTD XHTML 1.1//EN"
  "http://www.w3.org/TR/xhtml11/DTD/xhtml11.dtd">

<html xmlns="http://www.w3.org/1999/xhtml" xml:lang="en">
  <head>
    <title>Sample Link Style</title>

    <style type="text/css">
     a {
        font-family: Verdana, sans-serif;
        font-weight: bold;
        text-decoration: none;
     }
     a:link {
        color: #6479A0;
     }
     a:visited {
        color: #CCCCCC;
     }
     a:hover, a:active {
        color: #FF0000;
     }
    </style>
  </head>
  <body>
        <h1>Sample Link Style</h1>
        <p><a href="simplelinkstyle.html">The first time you see me, I should
        be a light blue, bold, non-underlined link in the Verdana font</a>.</p>
  </body>
</html>
```

If you view the example in your web browser, indeed the link should be a light blue, bold, non-underlined Verdana font. If you hover over the link, or click the link without releasing it, it should turn red. If you click and release the link, the page will simply reload because the link points to the file with the same name. However, at that point the link will be in your browser's memory and thus will be displayed as a visited link—and it will appear grey instead of blue.

You can use CSS to apply a wide range of text-related changes to your links. You can change fonts, sizes, weights, decoration, and so on. Sometimes you might want several different sets of link styles in your style sheet. In that case, you can create classes; you aren't limited to working with only one set of styles for the <a> tag. The following example is a set of style sheet rules for a `footerlink` class for links I might want to place in the footer area of my web site:

```
a.footerlink {
     font-family: Verdana, sans-serif;
     font-weight: bold;
     font-size: 75%;
     text-decoration: none;
}
a.footerlink:link, a.footerlink:visited {
     color: #6479A0;
}
a.footerlink:hover, a.footerlink:active {
     color: #E03A3E;
}
```

As you can see in the example that follows, the class name (`footerlink`) appears after the selector name (`a`), separated by a dot, and before the pseudoclass name (`hover`), separated by a colon:

```
selector.class:pseudoclass
a.footerlink:hover
```

Spend some time with Appendix B, "XHTML 1.1 and CSS 2 Quick Reference" for an idea of the styles you can apply to your links.

Summary

The <a> tag is what makes hypertext "hyper." With it, you can create links between pages as well as links to specific anchor points on any page. This hour focused on creating and styling simple links to other pages using either relative or absolute addressing to identify the pages.

You learned that when you're creating links to other people's pages, it's important to include the full Internet address of each page in an <a href> tag. For links between your own pages, include just the filenames and enough directory information to get from one page to another.

You also learned how to create named anchor points within a page and how to create links to a specific anchor. You also learned how to link to your email address so that users can easily send you messages. You even learned how to protect your email address from spammers. Finally, you learned methods for controlling the display of your links using CSS.

Table 8.1 summarizes the <a> tag discussed in this hour.

Table 8.1   HTML Tags and Attributes Covered in Hour 8

Tag/Attribute	Function
<a>...</a>	With the href attribute, creates a link to another document or anchor; with the id attribute, creates an anchor that can be linked to.
Attributes	
href="address"	The address of the document or anchor point to link to.
id="name"	The name for this anchor point in the document.

Q&A

Q **What happens if I link to a page on the Internet and then the person who owns that page deletes or moves it?**

A That depends on how the maintainer of that external page has set up his web server. Usually, you will see a page not found message or something to that effect when you click a link that has been moved or deleted. You can still click the Back button to return to your page. As a site maintainer, you can periodically run link-checking programs to ensure your internal and external links are valid. An example of this is the Link Checker service at http://validator.w3.org/checklink.

Q **One of the internal links on my web site works fine on my computer, but when I put the pages on the Internet, the link doesn't work anymore. What's up?**

A These are the most likely culprits:

 ▶ *Capitalization problems.* On Windows computers, linking to a file named `MyFile.html` with `<a href="myfile.html">` will work. On most web servers, the link must be `<a href="MyFile.html">` (or you must change the name of the file to `MyFile.html`). To make matters worse, some text editors and file transfer programs actually change the capitalization without telling you! The best solution is to stick with all-lowercase filenames for web pages.

 ▶ *Spaces in filenames.* Most web servers don't allow filenames with spaces. For example, you should never name a web page `my page.html`. Instead, name it `mypage.html` or even `my_page.html` (using an underscore instead of a space).

 ▶ *Local absolute addresses.* If, for some reason, you link to a file using a local absolute address, such as `C:\mywebsite\news.html`, the link won't work when you place the file on the Internet. You should never use local absolute addresses; when this occurs, it is usually an accident caused by a temporary link that was created to test part of a page. So, be careful to remove any test links before publishing a page on the Web.

Q **Can I put both `href` and `id` in the same `<a>` tag? Would I want to for any reason?**

A You can, and it might save you some typing if you have a named anchor point and a link right next to each other. It's generally better, however, to use `<a href>` and `<a id>` separately to avoid confusion because they play very different roles in an HTML document.

Q **What happens if I accidentally misspell the name of an anchor or forget to put the # in front of it?**

A If you link to an anchor name that doesn't exist within a page or misspell the anchor name, the link goes to the top of that page.

Workshop

The workshop contains quiz questions and exercises to help you solidify your understanding of the material covered. Try to answer all questions before looking at the "Answers" section that follows.

Quiz

1. Your best friend from elementary school finds you on the Internet and says he wants to trade home page links. How do you put a link to his site at www.supercheapsuits.com/~billybob/ on one of your pages?

2. What HTML would you use to make it possible for someone clicking the words "About the Authors" at the top of a page to skip down to a list of credits somewhere else on the page?

3. If your email address is bon@soir.com, how would you make the text "goodnight greeting" into a link that people can click to compose and send you an email message?

Answers

1. Put the following on your page:

```
<a href="http://www.supercheapsuits.com/~billybob/">Billy Bob's
site</a>
```

2. Type this at the top of the page:

```
<a href="#credits">About the Authors</a>
```

Type this at the beginning of the credits section:

```
<a id="credits"></a>
```

3. Type the following on your web page:

```
Send me a <a href="mailto:bon@soir.com">goodnight greeting</a>!
```

Exercises

▶ Create an HTML file consisting of a formatted list of your favorite web sites. You might already have these sites bookmarked in your web browser, in which case you can visit them to find the exact URL in the browser's address bar.

▶ If you have created any pages for a web site, look through them and consider whether there are any places in the text where you'd like to make it easy for people to contact you. Include a link in that place to your email address. You can never provide too many opportunities for people to contact you and tell you what they need or what they think about your products—especially if you're running a business.

HOUR 9
Working with Colors

All the sample pages shown in this book thus far have used a standard white background and black text. That's not a requirement, although some variation of dark text on a light background is the most common color combination you'll find online. After a brief overview of some best practices in color selection, you'll learn when you can use colors, how to pick colors, and how to specify colors when creating various elements of your web site.

Best Practices for Choosing Colors

I can't tell you exactly which colors to use in your web site, but I can help you understand the considerations you should make when selecting those colors on your own. The colors you use can greatly influence your visitors; if you are running an e-commerce site, you will want to use colors that entice your users to view your catalog and eventually purchase something. To that end, you want to make sure colors are used judiciously and with respect. You might wonder how "respect" enters into the mix when talking about colors, but remember the World Wide Web is an international community and interpretations differ; for instance, pink is a very popular color in Japan, but very unpopular in Eastern European countries. Similarly, green is "the color of money" in the United States, but the vast majority of other countries have multi-colored paper bills such that "the color of money" isn't a single color at all and thus the metaphor would be of no value to them.

WHAT YOU'LL LEARN IN THIS HOUR:

▶ How to choose colors for your website

▶ How colors work on the Web

▶ How to use hexadecimal values for color

▶ How to use CSS to set background, text, and border colors

Besides using colors that are culturally sensitive, other best practices include:

▶ Use a natural palette of colors. This doesn't mean you should use earth tones, but instead refers to using colors that one would naturally see on a casual stroll around town—avoid ultrabright colors that can cause eye strain.

▶ Use a small color palette. You don't need to use 15 different colors to achieve your goals. In fact, if your page includes text and images in 15 different colors, you might reevaluate the message you're attempting to send. Focus on three or four main colors with a few complimentary colors, at the most.

▶ Consider your demographics. You are likely not able to control your demographics and thus have to find a middle ground that accommodates everyone. The colors enjoyed by younger people are not necessarily those appreciated by older people, just as there are color biases between men and women and people from different geographic regions and cultures.

With just these few tips in mind, it might seem as if your color options are limited. Not so—it simply means you should think about the decisions you're making before you make them. A search for "color theory" in the search engine of your choice should give you more food for thought, as will the use of the color wheel.

The *color wheel* is a chart that shows the organization of colors in a circular manner. The method of display is an attempt to help you visualize the relationships between primary, secondary, and complementary colors. Color schemes are developed from working with the color wheel; understanding color schemes can help you determine the color palette to use consistently throughout your web site. For example, knowing something about color relationships will hopefully allow you to avoid using orange text on a light blue background, or bright blue text on a brown background.

Some common color schemes in web design are:

▶ **Analogous**—Colors that are adjacent to each other on the color wheel, such as yellow and green. One color is the dominant color and its analogous friend is used to enrich the display.

▶ **Complementary**—Colors that are opposite from each other on the color wheel, such as a warm color (red) and a cool color (green).

▶ **Triadic**—Three colors that are equally spaced around the color wheel. The triadic scheme provides balance while still allowing rich color use.

There are entire books and courses devoted to understanding color theory, so continuing the discussion in this book would indeed be a tangent. However, if you intend to work in web design and development, you will be served well by a solid understanding of the basics of color theory. Spend some time reading about it—an online search will provide a wealth of information.

Additionally, spend some hands-on time with the color wheel. The Color Scheme Generator at http://colorschemedesigner.com/ allows you to start with a base color and produce monochromatic, complementary, triadic, tetradic, analogic, and accented analogic color schemes.

Understanding Web Colors

Specifying a background color other than white for a web page is easier than you probably realize. For example, to specify blue as the background color for a page, put `style="background-color:blue"` inside the `<body>` tag or in the style sheet rule for the body element. Of course, you can use many colors other than blue. In fact, there are 16 colors listed in the W3C standards: aqua, black, blue, fuchsia, gray, green, lime, maroon, navy, olive, purple, red, silver, teal, white, and yellow.

Obviously there are many more colors displayed on the Web than just those 16. In fact, there are 140 color names that you can use with assurance that all browsers will display these colors similarly. Here's a partial list of the 140 descriptive color names: azure, bisque, cornflowerblue, darksalmon, firebrick, honeydew, lemonchiffon, papayawhip, peachpuff, saddlebrown, thistle, tomato, wheat, and whitesmoke.

But names are subjective—for instance, if you look at the color chart of 140 cross-browser color names, you will not be able to distinguish between fuchsia and magenta. You will then realize that the associated hexadecimal color values for those two terms, fuchsia and magenta, are exactly the same: #FF00FF. You'll learn about hexadecimal color values in the next section, but for now, know that if you want to be standards-compliant and use more than the 16 color names the W3C standards dictate, you should use the hexadecimal color codes whenever possible.

There are, in fact, 16 million colors made possible with hexadecimal color codes. However, most modern computer displays can display "only" 16,384. But 16,384 is still a lot more than 140, or 16.

NOTE

For a complete list of the 140 descriptive color names, as well as their hexadecimal codes and an example of the color as displayed by your browser, visit http://www.w3schools.com/HTML/html_colornames.asp.

TIP

It's worth pointing out that color names are not case-sensitive. So, Black, black, and BLACK are all black, although most web designers stick with lowercase or mixed case (if they use color names at all, as most designers will use the hexadecimal notation for a more nuanced approach to color use).

You should be aware that not all computer monitors display colors in the same hues. What might appear as a beautiful light blue background color on your monitor might be more of a purple hue on another user's monitor. Neutral, earth-tone colors (such as medium gray, tan, and ivory) can produce even more unpredictable results on many computer monitors. These colors might even seem to change color on one monitor depending on lighting conditions in the room or the time of day.

In addition to changing the background of your pages to a color other than white, you can change the color of text links, including various properties of links (such as the color for when a user hovers over a link versus when the user clicks a link—as you learned in the previous hours). You can also set the background color of container elements (such as paragraphs, divs, blockquotes, and table cells) and you can use colors to specify the borders around those elements. You'll see some examples of colors and container elements later in this hour.

There are plenty of very bad websites, some created by earnest people with no trace of irony whatsoever. However, "The World's Worst Website" shown in Figure 9.1 was purposefully created to show some of the more egregious sins of web site design, especially with its use of colors. A screenshot does not do it justice—visit and experience the site for yourself at http://www.angelfire.com/super/badwebs/main.htm.

FIGURE 9.1
A partial screenshot of "The World's Worst Website."

If you search for **bad web site examples** in your search engine, you will find many sites that collect examples of bad design and explain just why such a site should be in a Hall of Shame rather than a Hall of Fame. Many sites are considered "bad" because of their visual displays, and that display begins with color selection. Therefore, understanding colors, as well as the nuances of their specification and use, is a crucial step to creating a good web site.

Using Hexadecimal Values for Colors

To remain standards-compliant, as well as to retain precise control over the colors in your web site, you can reference colors by their hexadecimal value. The hexadecimal value of a color is an indication of how much red, green, and blue light should be mixed into each color. It works a little bit like Play-Doh—just mix in the amounts of red, blue, and green you want to get the appropriate color.

The hexadecimal color format is *#rrggbb*, in which *rr*, *gg*, and *bb* are two-digit hexadecimal values for the red (rr), green (gg), and blue (bb) components of the color. If you're not familiar with hexadecimal numbers, don't sweat it. Just remember that FF is the maximum and 00 is the minimum. Use one of the following codes for each component:

- ▶ FF means full brightness.
- ▶ CC means 80 percent brightness.
- ▶ 99 means 60 percent brightness.
- ▶ 66 means 40 percent brightness.
- ▶ 33 means 20 percent brightness.
- ▶ 00 means none of this color component.

For example, bright red is #FF0000, dark green is #003300, bluish-purple is #660099, and medium-gray is #999999. To make a page with a red background and dark green text, the HTML code would look like the following:

```
<body style="background-color:#FF0000; color:#003300">
```

Although only six examples of two-digit hexadecimal values are shown here, there are actually 225 combinations of two-digit hexadecimal values—0 through 9 and A through F, paired up. For example, F0 is a possible hex value (decimal value 240), 62 is a possible hex value (decimal value 98), and so on.

As previously discussed, the rr, gg, and bb in the #rrggbb hexadecimal color code format stand for the red, green, and blue components of the color. Each of those components has a decimal value ranging from 0 (no color) to 255 (full color).

So, white (or #FFFFFF) translates to a red value of 255, a green value of 255, and a blue value of 255. Similarly, black (#000000) translates to a red value of 0, a green value of 0, and a blue value of 0. True red is #FF0000 (all red, no green, and no blue), true green is #00FF00 (no red, all green, no blue), and true blue is #0000FF (no red, no green, and all blue). All other hexadecimal notations translate to some variation of the 255 possible values for each of the three colors. The cross-browser compatible color name CornflowerBlue is associated with the hexadecimal notation #6495ED—a red value of 40, a green value of 149, and a blue value of 237 (almost all of the available blue values).

When picking colors, either through a graphics program or by finding something online that you like, you might see the color notion in hexadecimal or decimal. If you type **hexadecimal color converter** in your search engine, you will find numerous options to help you convert color values into something you can use in your style sheets.

Using CSS to Set Background, Text, and Border Colors

When using CSS, there are three instances in which color values can be used: when specifying the background color, the text color, or the border color of elements. Previous hours contained examples of specifying colors without going in great detail about color notion or color theory. For example, in Hour 8, you learned about using colors for various link states. In Hour 7, one of the quiz questions asked how to fill table cells with colors.

Figure 9.2 shows an example of color usage that could very easily go into a web design Hall of Shame. I can't imagine ever using these combinations of colors and styles in a serious web site, but it serves here as an example of how color style *could* be applied to various elements.

Listing 9.1 shows the XHTML and CSS styles used to produce Figure 9.2.

Listing 9.1   Using Styles to Produce Background, Text, and Border Colors

```
<?xml version="1.0" encoding="UTF-8"?>
<!DOCTYPE html PUBLIC "-//W3C//DTD XHTML 1.1//EN"
  "http://www.w3.org/TR/xhtml11/DTD/xhtml11.dtd">

<html xmlns="http://www.w3.org/1999/xhtml" xml:lang="en">
  <head>
    <title>Background, Text, and Border Colors</title>
  </head>

  <body>
      <h1>Background, Text, and Border Colors</h1>

      <p style="background-color:#CCCCCC;
      border:1px solid #000000; color:#FF0000">
      Grey paragraph, black border, red text with a
      <span style="color:#FFA500">orange span</span>.</p>

      <div style="width:300px; height:75px; margin-bottom: 12px;
      background-color:#000000; border:2px dashed #FF0000;color:
        #FFFFFF">
      Black div, red border, white text. </div>

      <table border="1">
      <tr>
      <td style="background-color: #00FF00">Green Table Cell</td>
      <td style="background-color: #FF0000">Red Table Cell</td>
      </tr>
      <tr>
      <td style="background-color: #FFFF00">Blue Table Cell</td>
      <td style="background-color: #0000FF">Yellow Table Cell</td>
      </tr>
      </table>

      <blockquote style="background-color:#0000FF;
      border:4px dotted #FFFF00; color:#FFFFFF"><p>Blue blockquote,
      yellow border, white text.</p></blockquote>
  </body>
</html>
```

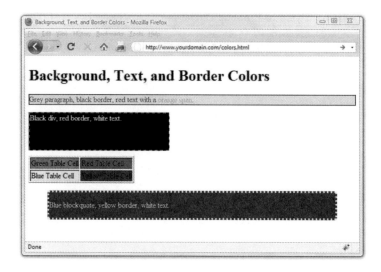

You can do quite a lot with borders, specifying different widths, types, and colors for all four borders of an element: top, right, bottom, and left. See Appendix B, "XHTML 1.1 and CSS 2 Quick Reference" for more information.

Looking at the styles used in Listing 9.1, you should be able to figure out almost everything except some of the border styles. In CSS, borders can't be designated as a color without also having a width and type; in the first example shown in Listing 9.1, the border width is 1px and the border type is solid. In the second example shown in Listing 9.2, the border width is 2px and the border type is dashed. In the fourth example shown in Listing 9.2, the border width is 4px and the border type is dotted.

When picking colors for your web site, remember that a little bit goes a long way—if you really like a bright and spectacular color, use it as an accent color and not throughout the primary design elements. For readability, remember that light backgrounds with dark text are much easier to read than dark backgrounds with light text.

Finally, consider the not-insignificant portion of your audience that might be color blind. For accessibility, you might consider using the Colorblind Web Page Filter tool at http://colorfilter.wickline.org/ to see what your site will look like to a person with color blindness.

Summary

In this hour, you learned a few best practices for thinking about color use, and how to use the color wheel to help you find colors that will complement your text. Additionally, you learned about hexadecimal notion for colors—that all colors are expressed in notations related to the amount of red, green, and blue in them—and how hexadecimal notation allows you to apply nuanced colors to your elements. More importantly, you learned about the three color-related style properties that can be used to apply color to container backgrounds, borders, and text using CSS.

Table 9.1 summarizes these style properties.

Table 9.1   Style Properties Covered in Hour 9

Attribute/Style	Function
`style="background-color:color"`	Sets the background color of an element (such as `<body>`, `<p>`, `<div>`, `<blockquote>`, and other containers).
`style="color:color"`	Sets the color of text within an element.
`style="border:size type color "`	Sets the color of the four borders around an element. Border colors cannot be used without also specifying the width and type of the border.

Q&A

Q **Don't web browsers let people choose their own background and text colors?**

A Yes, web browsers allow users to override the colors that you, as a web page author, specify. Some might see your white-on-blue page as green-on-white or their own favorite colors instead, but very few people actually use this option. The colors specified in the `<body>` tag will usually be seen.

Q **I've heard that there are 231 "browser-safe colors" that I can use on web pages and that I shouldn't use any other colors. Is that true?**

A Here's the real story: There are 231 colors that will appear less "fuzzy" to users who operate their computers in a 256-color (8-bit) video mode. Some web page authors try to stick to those colors. However, true-color or high-color computer displays are all but standard these days, and they show all colors with equal clarity. So if your graphics program can provide color values to you in hexadecimal format, feel free to plug that value straight into your style sheet to display custom color schemes.

Workshop

The workshop contains quiz questions and activities to help you solidify your understanding of the material covered. Try to answer all questions before looking at the "Answers" section that follows.

Quiz

1. How would you give a web page a black background and make all text bright green? Would you want to?

2. When selecting a color scheme for your web site, which of the following types of color relationships would give you more color options: analogous, complementary, or triadic?

3. If you specify `background-color` `#FFFFFF` for the body element in your style sheet, then use `background-color` `#FF0000` for the first `<div>` that you use on your page, will the background of that `<div>` be red or white?

Answers

1. Put the following at the beginning of the web page or use a style rule for the body element:

   ```
   <body style="background-color:#000000; color:#00FF00">
   ```

2. Triadic. It refers to three colors evenly spaced around the color wheel.

3. The background of your `<div>` will be red, because the background-color specification of a container element will override the specification in the `<body>` tag or body entry in the style sheet.

Exercises

▶ Select a base color that you like—perhaps a lovely blue or an earthy tone—and use the Color Scheme Generator at http://colorschemedesigner.com/ to come up with a set of colors that you can use in a web site. I recommend the tetrad or accented analogic scheme types.

▶ Once you have a set of colors—or a few options for sets of colors— create a basic HTML page with a <h1> element, a paragraph of text, and perhaps some list items. Use the color-related styles you've learned about in this hour to change the background color of the page, and the text of the various block-level elements, in order to see how these sets of colors might work together. See how they interact and determine which colors are best used for containers and which are best used for plain text, header text, and link text.

HOUR 10
Creating Images for Use on the Web

Although paying attention to color schemes and producing a visually appealing web site is important, you don't have to be an artist by trade to put high-impact graphics on your web pages. More importantly, you don't need to spend hundreds or thousands of dollars on software, either. This hour will help you get started with creating some of the images you can use in your web site. Although the sample figures in this chapter use a popular and free graphics program for Windows, Mac, and Linux users (GNU Image Manipulation Program, or GIMP), you can apply the knowledge learned in this hour to any major Windows or Macintosh graphics application—although the menus and options might be slightly different.

In this hour, you learn only how to create the graphics themselves, including different types of graphic uses. In Hour 11, "Using Images in Your Web Site," you'll learn how to integrate your graphics using HTML and CSS.

Choosing Graphics Software

You can use almost any graphics program to create images for your web site, from the simple paint program that typically comes free with your computer's operating system to an expensive professional program such as Adobe Photoshop. Similarly, if you have a digital camera or scanner attached to your computer, it probably came with some graphics software capable of creating web page graphics. There are also several free image editors available for download—or even online as a web application—that deal just with the manipulation of photographic elements.

WHAT YOU'LL LEARN IN THIS HOUR:

▶ How to choose graphics software

▶ How to prepare photographs for use online

▶ How to create banners and buttons

▶ How to reduce the number of colors in an image

▶ How to create transparent images

▶ How to create tiled backgrounds

▶ How to create animated web graphics

NOTE

Adobe Photoshop is without a doubt the cream of the crop when it comes to image-editing programs. However, it is expensive and quite complex if you don't have experience working with computer graphics. For more information on Adobe's products, visit the Adobe web site at http://www.adobe.com/. If you are in the market for one of their products, you can download a free evaluation version from their site.

Using Another Site's Material

One of the best ways to save time creating the graphics and media files for web pages is, of course, to avoid creating them altogether. Grabbing a graphic from any web page is as simple as right-clicking it (or clicking and holding the button on a Macintosh mouse) and selecting Save Image As or Save Picture As (depending on your browser). Extracting a background image from a page is just as easy: Right-click it and select Save Background As.

However, you should never use images without the explicit permission of the owner, either by asking them or by looking for a Creative Commons license. To take images without explicit permission is a copyright violation (and is also distasteful). To learn more about copyrights, visit http://www.utsystem.edu/OGC/IntellectualProperty/cprtindx.htm.

You might also want to consider royalty-free clip art, which doesn't require you to get copyright permission. A good source of clip art online is Microsoft's Office Online Clip Art and Media web site, which is located at http://office.microsoft.com/clipart/. Barry's Clipart Server is another popular clip art destination, and it's located at http://www.barrysclipart.com/.

If you already have software you think might be good for creating web graphics, try using it to do everything described in this hour. If it can't do some of the tasks covered here, it probably won't be a good tool for web graphics. In that case, download and install GIMP from http://www.gimp.org. This fully-functional graphics program is completely free:

1. Go to http://www.gimp.org/ and click the Downloads link.

2. You should see a link leading to a download for your operating system. You can also click the **Show other downloads** link, which will lead you to all the available options. Once you see the link to the software specifically made for your operating system, click that link to begin the download.

3. Once the download is complete, double-click the installer to install the program.

The examples in this hour use GIMP to illustrate several key web graphics techniques you'll need to know. Of course, there are so many ways to produce images, and so many different types of software you can use, I can't even begin to explain them all. However, all of the major software programs for creating graphics will include detailed help functions, documentation, and online user tutorials. Use the power of your search engine to learn what I simply cannot explain in just one hour.

If GIMP doesn't suit you, consider downloading the evaluation version of Adobe Photoshop or Corel DRAW. For photo manipulation only, there are many free options, all with helpful features. Google's Picasa, which is available free at http://picasa.google.com/, is one such option. Picnik (http://www.picnik.com/) is another. Both of these programs are suited for editing images rather than creating them from scratch, and Picasa is also oriented toward organizing your digital photograph collection. As such, these types of programs are not necessarily going to help you design a banner or button image for your site. However, these programs can help you work with some supplementary images and they are powerful enough that they are worth checking out.

The Least You Need to Know About Graphics

Two forces are always at odds when you post graphics and multimedia on the Internet. The users' eyes and ears want all your content to be as detailed and accurate as possible and they also want that information displayed immediately. Intricate, colorful graphics mean big file sizes, which increase the transfer time even over a fast connection. How do you maximize the quality of your presentation while minimizing file size? To make these choices, you need to understand how color and resolution work together to create a subjective sense of quality.

The resolution of an image is the number of individual dots, or pixels, that make up an image. Large, high-resolution images generally take longer to transfer and display than small, low-resolution images. Resolution is usually specified as the width times the height of the image, expressed in pixels; a 300×200 image, for example, is 300 pixels wide and 200 pixels high.

You might be surprised to find that resolution isn't the most significant factor determining an image file's storage size (and transfer time). This is because images used on web pages are always stored and transferred in compressed form. Image compression is the mathematical manipulation that images are put through to squeeze out repetitive patterns. The mathematics of image compression is complex, but the basic idea is that repeating patterns or large areas of the same color can be squeezed out when the image is stored on a disk. This makes the image file much smaller and allows it to be transferred faster over the Internet. The web browser then restores the original appearance of the image when the image is displayed.

In the rest of this hour, you'll learn exactly how to create graphics with big visual impact and small file sizes. The techniques you'll use to accomplish this depend on the contents and purpose of each image. There are as many uses for web graphics as there are web pages, but four types of graphics are by far the most common:

▶ Photos of people, products, or places

▶ Graphical banners and logos

▶ Buttons or icons to indicate actions and provide links

▶ Background textures for container elements

Preparing Photographic Images

To put photos on your web pages, you need to convert your print-based photos to digital images or create photos digitally by using a digital camera. You might need to use the custom software that comes with your scanner or camera to save pictures onto your hard drive, or you can just drag and

NOTE

There are several types of image resolution, including pixel, spatial, spectral, temporal, and radiometric. You could spend hours just learning about each type; and if you were taking a graphics design class, you might do just that. For now, however, all you need to remember is that large images take longer to download and also use a lot of space in your display. Display size and storage or transfer size are factors you should take into consideration when designing your web site.

TIP

If you don't have a scanner or digital camera, almost all film developers offer a service that transfers photos from 35mm film to a CD-ROM or DVD-ROM for a modest fee. You can then copy the files from the CD-ROM or DVD-ROM to your hard drive and then use your graphics program to open and modify the image files.

drop files from your camera to your hard drive. If you are using a scanner to create digital versions of your print photos, you can control just about any scanner directly from the graphics program of your choice—see the software documentation for details.

After you transfer the digital image files to your computer, you can use your graphics program to crop, resize, color-correct, and compress to get them ready for use in your web site.

Cropping an Image

Since you want web page graphics to be as compact as possible, you'll usually need to crop your digital photos. When you *crop* a photo, you select the area you want to display and you crop away the rest. .

▼ TRY IT YOURSELF

Cropping in GIMP

The GIMP toolbox offers quick access to the crop tool and its possible attributes. Find an image file—either a digital image you have taken with your camera and stored on your hard drive, or an image you have found online. After opening the image in GIMP, perform the following steps to crop it in GIMP:

1. In the GIMP toolbox, click the crop tool (see Figure 10.1). Depending on the tool you select, there might be additional attributes you can select. For example, Figure 10.1 shows the attributes for the cropping tool (such as the aspect ratio, position, size, and so on).

FIGURE 10.1
Select the crop tool from the toolbox.

2. In the image you want to crop, draw a box around the selection by clicking the upper-left corner of the portion of the image you want to keep and holding the left mouse button while you drag down to the lower-right corner. See Figure 10.2.

3. Click one of the corners of the selection to apply the cropping.

Your graphics program will likely have a different method than the one shown, but the concept is the same: select the area to keep and then crop out the rest.

TRY IT YOURSELF ▼

Cropping in GIMP

FIGURE 10.2
Select the area of the image that you wish to display.

Even after your image has been cropped, it might be larger than it needs to be for a web page. Depending on the design of a specific web page, you might want to limit large images to no more than 800×600 pixels (if it is shown on a page by itself, such as an item catalog) or even 640×480 pixels or smaller. When shown alongside text, images tend to be in the 250 to 350 pixel range for width, so there's just enough room for the text as well. In some cases, you might want to also provide a thumbnail version of the image that links to a larger version, in which case you'll probably stick closer to 100 pixels in the larger dimension for the thumbnail.

TIP
Your graphics software will likely have an omnipresent size display somewhere in the image window itself. In GIMP, the current image size can be seen in the top of the window. Other programs might show it in the lower-right or lower-left corner. You might also see the magnification ratio in the window, as well as the ability to change it (by zooming in or zooming out).

Resizing an Image

The exact tool necessary to change an image's size will depend on the program you are using. In GIMP, go to the Image menu and click Scale Image to open the Scale Image dialog box (see Figure 10.3).

FIGURE 10.3
Use the Scale Image dialog box to change the size of an image.

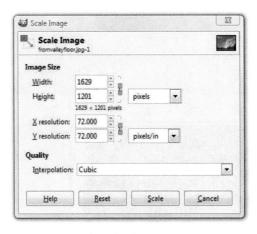

NOTE

As with many of the features in GIMP, the Scale Image dialog box appears in front of the window containing the image being resized. This placement allows you to make changes in the dialog box, apply them, and see the results immediately.

You'll almost always want to resize using the existing aspect ratio, meaning that when you enter the width you'd like the image to be, the height will be calculated automatically (and vice versa) to keep the image from squishing out of shape. In GIMP, the aspect ratio is locked by default, as indicated by the chain link displayed next to the Width and Height options shown in Figure 10.3. Clicking once on the chain will unlock it, enabling you to specify pixel widths and heights of your own choosing—squished or not.

In most, if not all, graphics programs, you can also resize the image based on percentages instead of providing specific pixel dimensions. For example, if my image started out as 1629 x 1487 and I didn't want to do the math to determine the values necessary to show it as half that width, I could simply select Percent (in this instance from the drop-down next to the pixel display shown in Figure 10.3) and change the default setting (100) to 50. The image width would then become 815 pixels wide by 744 high — and no math was necessary on my part.

Tweaking Image Colors

If you are editing photographic images rather than creating your own graphics, you might need to use some color-correction tools to get the photo just right. Like many image editing programs, GIMP offers several options for adjusting an image's brightness, contrast, and color balance, as well as a filter to reduce the dreaded red-eye. To remove red-eye using GIMP, go to Filters, click Enhance, and then click Red Eye Removal.

Most of these options are pretty intuitive. If you want the image to be brighter, adjust the brightness. If you want more red in your image, adjust the color balance. In GIMP, the Colors menu gives you access to numerous tools. As with the Scale Image dialog box described in the previous section, each tool displays a dialog box in the foreground of your workspace. As you adjust the colors, the image reflects those changes. This preview function is a feature included in most image editing software.

Figure 10.4 shows the Adjust Hue/Lightness/Saturation tool, one of the many tools provided on the Colors menu. As shown in the figure, many color-related changes occur by using various sliders in dialog boxes to adjust the values you are working with. The Preview feature allows you to see what you are doing as you are doing it. The Reset Color button returns the image to its original state without any changes applied.

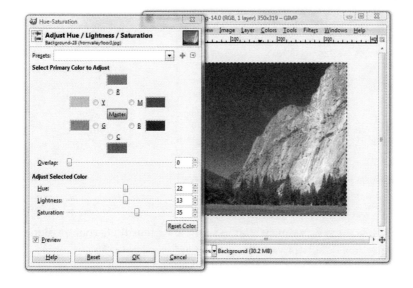

FIGURE 10.4
The Adjust Hue/Lightness/Saturation tool is one of many slider-based color modification tools available in GIMP.

Because of the numerous tools available to you, and the preview function available with each tool, a little playful experimentation is the best way to find out what each tool does.

Controlling JPEG Compression

Photographic images on the web work best when saved in the JPEG file format rather than GIF; JPG allows you to retain the number of colors in the file while still keeping the overall file size to a manageable level. When you're finished adjusting the size and appearance of your photo, select File, Save As and choose JPEG as the file type. Your graphics program will likely provide you with another dialog box through which you can control various JPEG options, such as compression.

Figure 10.5 shows the Save as JPEG dialog box you'll see when you save a JPEG in GIMP. You can see here that you can control the compression ratio for saving JPEG files by adjusting the Quality slider between 1 (low quality, small file size) and 100 (high quality, large file size).

FIGURE 10.5
GIMP allows you reduce file size while still retaining image quality by saving in the JPEG format.

You might want to experiment a bit to see how various JPEG compression levels affect the quality of your images, but 85% quality (or 15% compression) is generally a good compromise between file size (and therefore download speed) and quality for most photographic images.

Creating Banners and Buttons

Graphics that you create from scratch, such as banners and buttons, require you to make considerations uniquely different from photographs.

The first decision you need to make when you produce a banner or button is how big it should be. Most people accessing the web now have a computer with a screen that is at least 1024×768 pixels in resolution, if not considerably larger. For example, my screen is currently set at 1440×900 pixels. You should generally plan your graphics so that they will always fit within smaller screens (1024×768), with room to spare for scrollbars and margins. The crucial size constraint is the horizontal width of your pages because scrolling a page horizontally is a huge hassle and a source of confusion for web users. Vertically scrolling a page is much more acceptable, so it's okay if your pages are taller than the minimum screen sizes.

Assuming that you target a minimum resolution of 800×600 pixels, full-sized banners and title graphics should be no more than 770 pixels wide by 430 pixels tall, which is the maximum viewable area of the page after you've accounted for scrollbars, toolbars, and other parts of the browser window. Within a page, normal photos and artwork should be from 100 to 300 pixels in each dimension, and smaller buttons and icons should be 20 to 100 pixels tall and wide. Obviously, if you design for the 1024×768 resolution, you have more screen "real estate" to work with, but the size guidelines for banners, buttons, and other supplementary graphics are still in effect.

To create a new image in GIMP, go to File and choose New. The Create a New Image dialog box displays (see Figure 10.6). If you aren't sure how big the image needs to be, just accept the default size of a 640×480. Or you can choose one of the other pre-determined sizes in the Template drop-down, such as Web banner common 468×60 or Web banner huge 728×90. Those two settings are indeed considered "common" and "huge" for web site banners. Otherwise, enter the width and height of the new image.

TIP

For many years, designing for 800×600 screen resolution has been the norm. Still keep that low number in mind, as many people do not open applications in full-screen mode. However, designing for a baseline 1,024×768 screen resolution is not a bad idea.

FIGURE 10.6
You need to decide on the size of
an image before you start working
on it.

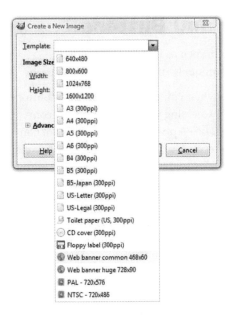

For the image's background color, you should usually choose white to
match the background that most web browsers use for web pages
(although as you learned in the previous hour, that color can be
changed).When you know that you'll be creating a page with a background other than white, you can choose a different background color for
your image. Or you might want to create an image with no background at
all, in which case you'll select Transparency as the background color. When
an image's background is transparent, the web page behind the image is
allowed to show through those areas of the image. In GIMP, select the
background color for your new image by opening the Advanced Options
in the Create a New Image dialog box.

When you enter the width and height of the image in pixels and click OK,
you are faced with a blank canvas—an intimidating sight if you're as art-
phobic as most of us! However, there are so many image creation tutorials
(not to mention entire books) available to lead you through the process, I
am comfortable leaving you to your own creative devices. This hour is all
about introducing you to the things you want to keep in mind when creating graphics for use in your sites. This hour does not necessarily teach you
exactly how to do it, because being comfortable with the tool *you* choose is
the first step to mastering them.

Reducing the Number of Colors in an Image

One of the most effective ways to reduce the size of, and therefore the download time for, an image is to reduce the number of colors used in the image. This can drastically reduce the visual quality of some photographic images, but it works great for most banners, buttons, and other icons.

You'll be glad to know that there is a special file format for images with a limited number of colors; it's called the Graphics Interchange Format (GIF). When you save an image as a GIF, you might be prompted to flatten layers or reduce the number of colors by converting to an indexed image, as those are requirements for GIFs, as shown in Figure 10.7. The dialog box will simply ask you to confirm these changes that the save process will do for you—do not concern yourself with understanding these options at this time, but read your software's help file regarding layers and indexed colors for a full understanding.

Remember, the GIF image format is designed for images that contain areas of solid colors, such as web page titles and other illustrated graphics; the GIF format is not ideal for photographs.

> **TIP**
>
> *Dithering* is a technique used by image-editing programs to simulate a color that isn't in the color palette with alternating pixels of two similar colors. For example, a dithered pink color would consist of alternating pixels of red and white pixels, which would give the general impression of pink. Dithering can make images look better in some cases, but it should usually be avoided for web page graphics. Why? It substantially increases the information complexity of an image, and that usually results in much larger file sizes and slower downloads.

FIGURE 10.7
When saving an image as a GIF, you might be prompted to convert it to an indexed color palette.

PNG (pronounced "ping") is another useful file format that is supported in all major web browsers. While the GIF image format allows you to specify a single transparent color, which means that the background of the web page will show through those areas of an image, the PNG format takes things a step further by allowing you to specify varying degrees of transparency.

Working with Transparent Images

You might have seen web sites that use background colors or images in their container elements, but also have images present in the foreground that allow the background to show through parts of the foreground graphics. In these cases, the images in the foreground have portions which are transparent, so that the images themselves—which are always on a rectangular canvas—do not show the areas of the canvas in which the design does not occur. You'll often want to use these types of partially transparent images to make graphics look good over any background color or background image you might have in place.

To make part of an image transparent, the image must be saved in the GIF or PNG file format. As mentioned previously in this lesson, most graphics programs that support the GIF format allow you to specify one color to be transparent, whereas PNG images allow for a range of transparency. Largely because of this transparency range, the PNG format is superior to GIF. All the latest web browsers already support PNG images. For more information on the PNG image format, visit http://www.libpng.org/pub/png/pngintro.html.

The process of creating a transparent image depends on the type of image you are creating (GIF or PNG) and the graphics software you are using to create it. For instructions, look in your graphics program's help files or type **transparent images with [your program here]** into your search engine.

Creating Tiled Backgrounds

Any GIF or JPEG image can be used as a background tile within a container element. However, before you go off and create a tiled background, especially a highly patterned tiled background, ask yourself what that tiled background adds to the overall look and feel of your web site, and—more importantly—ask yourself if the text of the site can be read easily when placed over that pattern?

Think about the web sites you frequent every day and consider the fact that few use tiled, patterned backgrounds on their entire pages. If you restrict your browsing to web sites for companies, products, sports teams, or other sites in which information (primarily text) is privileged, the number of sites with tiled, patterned backgrounds will decrease even further. While the web affords everyone the right of individuality in design, if you are creating a site for your business, you might want to avoid a highly patterned background with contrasting colored text.

If you do use a tiled, patterned background image for your entire site, remember that tiled images look best when you can't tell they're tiled images. In other words, you know you have a good image when the top edge of a background tile matches seamlessly with the bottom edge, and the left edge matches with the right.

Figures 10.8 and 10.9 show background tiles in use, both with seamless background, but with varying degrees of effectiveness.

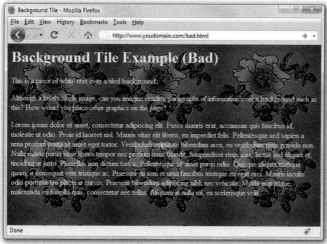

FIGURE 10.8
This is an example of a seamless background image whereby you can tell the background is tiled because you can see six identical shapes.

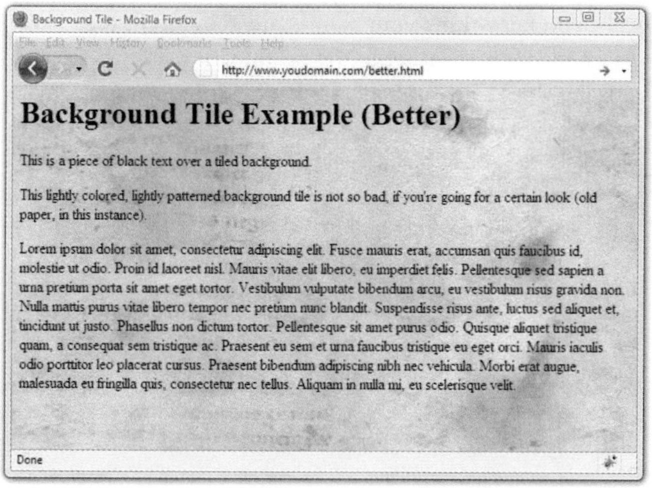

FIGURE 10.9
This is also an example of a seamless background image, only you can't tell that it is tiled.

In Hour 11, you'll learn how to place background images within your container elements. Despite my warnings in this section, there are actually times when background images can be powerful weapons in your design arsenal—just not when used as entire page backgrounds.

Creating Animated Web Graphics

The GIF image format allows you to create animated images that can be used to add some motion that will spice up any web page. Animated GIF images also transfer much faster than most of the video or multimedia files that are often used for similar effect. With GIMP, you can create animated GIFs by creating multiple layers within an image and then modifying the Animated GIF options when saving the file. Additionally, if you have a series of images you want to animate, you can use the free, web-based GIF animation service at Gickr (http://www.gickr.com/).

The first step in creating a GIF animation is to create a series of images to be displayed one after the other—or a series of layers, depending on your particular software program. Each of these images is called a *frame*. By the way, this use of the word *frame* has nothing whatsoever to do with the *frames* you'll learn about in Hour 13, "Working with Frames." Instead, think of the frames like how movies or cartoons are put together—the images that you see on the screen are made up of many individual frames with slight differences in their appearance. Once you have your frames in mind, the process of tying them together is relatively simple—it's the planning stage that's the most difficult. Take some time to sketch out the frames in storyboard fashion, especially if you plan to have more than just a few frames. After you know how your frames are going to fit together, use the Gickr service mentioned earlier in this section, or read the documentation for your graphics software to learn its particular process for pulling it all together.

Summary

In this hour, you learned the basics of preparing graphics for use on web pages. If nothing else, you learned that this is a very complex topic, and you learned just enough in this hour to whet your appetite. The examples in this hour used the popular (and free!) GIMP software package, but feel free to use the graphics software that best suits your needs.

You learned how to crop, resize, and tweak image colors, and you learned about the different file formats. There are many considerations you must keep in mind when including graphics in your site, including graphic size and resolution and how to use transparency, animated GIFs, and tiled backgrounds.

Q&A

Q Instead of learning all this stuff myself, shouldn't I just hire a graphics artist to design my pages?

A This is a difficult question to answer, and it's not because I have a conflict of interest here—I work for a web development and design agency, so it's in my best interest to recommend agencies. But an agency isn't always the best solution. Hiring a graphic designer takes time and money. Additionally, there are many graphics artists who do not produce work suitable for the web—they are specifically print-based artists, and the print world is quite different than the online world. Also, hiring an individual who deems himself a graphics designer to create a web site might not play to the strengths of that particular graphics designer. In other words, he might be good at designing the graphical elements of a web site, but he might *not* be good as a content architect or at working with HTML and CSS. If your site is simply a personal site, a professional design might not be where you want to spend your money. But if your site is intended to promote a business, a product, a school, or anything else whereby your image is integral to your success, it's worth your while (and money) to consult with web design professional.

Q I've produced graphics for printing on paper. Are web page graphics any different?

A Yes. In fact, many of the rules for print graphics are reversed on the Web. Web page graphics have to be low-resolution, while print graphics should be as high-resolution as possible. White washes out black on computer screens, while black bleeds into white on paper. Also, someone might stop a web page from loading when only half the graphics have been downloaded. Try to avoid falling into old habits if you've done a lot of print graphics design.

Q I have a Windows AVI video clip. Can I turn it into a GIF animation?

A Yes. Simply open the AVI file with software such as Animation Shop to convert it to a GIF animation. The software will give you the option to reduce the number of frames; it's usually a good idea to sample every third frame or so to keep the file size down to reasonable proportions. You can also embed AVI files directly into web pages, as discussed in Hour 12, "Using Multimedia in Your Web Site."

Workshop

The workshop contains quiz questions and activities to help you solidify your understanding of the material covered. Try to answer all questions before looking at the "Answers" section that follows.

Quiz

1. You have a scanned picture of a horse that you need to put on a web page. How big should you make it? In what file format should you save it?

2. Your company logo is a black letter Z with a red circle behind it. What size should you draw or scan it? What file format should you save it for use on your web page?

3. Your business partner comes to you with a richly detailed background graphic of dark forest foliage and wants you to use it as the background on your corporate site—with bold white text. What do you do?

Answers

1. Depending on how important the image is to your page, you should make it as small as 100×40 pixels or as large as 300×120 pixels. The JPEG format, with about 85% compression, would be best. Of course, you could also provide a thumbnail link to a larger image that is viewed by itself. You'll learn how to use images as links in the next hour.

2. About 100×100 pixels is generally good for a square logo, but a simple graphic like that will compress very well. You could make it up to 300×300 pixels or more (and have the space in your template to position it appropriately—but that's a pretty big square). Save it as an indexed GIF file since it contains very few colors.

3. You tell him no and you refuse to allow him to have any input on design decisions in the future.

Exercises

▶ If you have an archive of company (or personal) photo prints, look through it to find a few that might enhance your web site. Scan them (or send them out to be scanned), so that you'll have a library of digital photos, ready to use on your pages. If you have digital files of photos taken on a digital camera, you can obviously skip the scanning step and jump straight into prepping the images for your web pages.

▶ Before you start designing graphics for an important business site, try spicing up your own personal home page. This will give you a chance to learn GIMP (or give you a chance to use your graphics software) so that you'll know what you're doing when you tackle the task at work.

Using Images in Your Web Site

In Hour 10, "Creating Images for Use on the Web," you learned how to find and create digital images for use in your web site. This hour shows you how easy it is to place those images in your web site. In this hour you'll learn the HTML for placing and describing images in your site, how to align images, and how to use images as links or "maps" to other content.

WHAT YOU'LL LEARN IN THIS HOUR:

▶ How to place an image on a web page

▶ How to describe images with text

▶ How to specify image height and width

▶ How to align images

▶ How to turn images into links

▶ How to use background images

▶ How to use image maps

You should get two or three images ready now so that you can try putting them on your own pages as you follow along with this hour. If you have some image files already saved in the GIF, PNG, or JPEG format (the filenames will end in `.gif`, `.png`, or `.jpg`), use those. It's also fine to use any graphics you created while reading the preceding lesson.

Search engines (such as Google) can become a gold mine of images by leading you to sites related to your own theme. Search engines can also help you discover the oodles of sites specifically dedicated to providing free and cheap access to reusable media collections. Also, don't forget Microsoft's massive clip art library at the Office

TRY IT YOURSELF ▼

Prepare Images for Use in Your Web Site

Online Clip Art and Media web site, located at http://office.microsoft.com/clipart/. Other valuable sources include Google Images (http://images.google.com/) and Flickr (http://www.flickr.com)—look for images using Creative Commons licenses that allow for free use with attribution.

Placing Images on a Web Page

To put an image on a web page, first move the image file into the same folder as the HTML file or in a directory named Images for easy organization.

Insert the following HTML tag at the point in the text where you want the image to appear. Use the name of your image file instead of myimage.gif:

```
<img src="myimage.gif" alt="My Image" />
```

If your image file were in the images directory below the document root, you would use:

```
<img src="/images/myimage.gif" alt="My Image" />
```

Both the src and the alt attributes of the <img /> tag are required in XHTML web pages. The src attribute identifies the image file and the alt attribute allows you to specify descriptive text about the image, the latter of which is intended to serve as an alternative to the image in the event that a user is unable to view the image. You'll read more on the alt attribute later, in the section "Describing Images with Text."

As an example of how to use the <img /> tag, Listing 11.1 inserts an image at the top of the page, before a paragraph of text. Whenever a web browser displays the HTML file in Listing 11.1, it automatically retrieves and displays the image file as shown in Figure 11.1.

Listing 11.1   Using the <img /> Tag to Place Images on a Web Page

```
<?xml version="1.0" encoding="UTF-8"?>
<!DOCTYPE html PUBLIC "-//W3C//DTD XHTML 1.1//EN"
  "http://www.w3.org/TR/xhtml11/DTD/xhtml11.dtd">

<html xmlns="http://www.w3.org/1999/xhtml" xml:lang="en">
  <head>
    <title>A Spectacular Yosemite View</title>
  </head>

  <body>
    <h1>A Spectacular Yosemite View</h1>
    <p><img src="hd.jpg" alt="Half Dome" /></p>
    <p><strong>Half Dome</strong> is a granite dome in Yosemite National Park,
      located in northeastern Mariposa County, California, at the eastern
      end of Yosemite Valley. The granite crest rises more than 4,737 ft
      (1,444 m) above the valley floor.</p>
    <p>This particular view is of Half Dome as seen from Washburn Point.</p>
  </body>
</html>
```

FIGURE 11.1
When a web browser displays the HTML code shown in Listing 11.1, it renders the hd.jpg image.

NOTE

Theoretically, you can include an image from any web site within your own pages. In those cases, the image is retrieved from the other page's web server whenever your page is displayed. You could do this, but you shouldn't! Not only is it bad manners, because you are using the other person's bandwidth for your own personal gain, it also can make your pages display more slowly. You also have no way of controlling when the image might be changed or deleted.

If you are granted permission to republish an image from another web page, always transfer a copy of that image to your computer and use a local file reference, such as <img src="myimage.jpg" /> instead of <img src="http://www.otherserver.com/theirimage.jpg" />. This advice is not applicable, however, when you host your images—such as photographs—at a service specifically meant as an image repository, such as Flickr (http://www.flickr.com/). Services like Flickr provide you with a URL for each image, and each URL includes Flickr's domain in the address.

If you guessed that img stands for *image*, you're right. And src stands for *source*, which is a reference to the location of the image file. As discussed earlier in the book, an image is always stored in a file separate from the text, even though it appears to be part of the same page when viewed in a browser.

Just as with the <a href> tag used for hyperlinks, you can specify any complete Internet address in the src attribute of the <img /> tag. Alternatively, if an image is located in the same folder as the HTML file, you can specify just the filename. You can also use relative addresses, such as /images/birdy.jpg or ../smiley.gif.

Describing Images with Text

Each <img /> tag in Listing 11.1 includes a short text message, such as alt="Half Dome". The alt stands for *alternate text*, which is the message that appears in place of the image itself if it does not load. An image might not load if its address is incorrect, if the user has turned off automatic image downloading in her web browser preferences, or if the Internet connection is very slow and the data has yet to transfer. Figure 11.2 shows an example of alt text used in place of an image.

FIGURE 11.2
Users will see alt messages
when images do not appear.

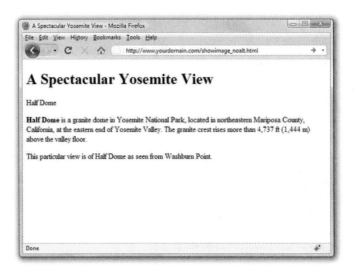

Even when graphics have fully loaded and are visible in the web browser, the alt message typically appears in a little box (known as a *tool tip*) whenever the mouse pointer passes over an image. The alt message also helps any user who is visually impaired (or is using a voice-based interface to read the web page).

You must include a suitable alt attribute in every <img /> tag on your web pages, keeping in mind the variety of situations in which people might see that message. A very brief description of the image is usually best, but web page authors sometimes put short advertising messages or subtle humor in their alt messages; too much humor and not enough information is frowned upon, however. For small or unimportant images, it's tempting to omit the alt message altogether, but it is a required attribute of the <img /> tag. This doesn't mean your page won't display properly, but it does mean you'll be in violation of the latest XHTML standards. I recommend assigning an empty text message to alt if you absolutely don't need it (alt=""), which is sometimes the case with small or decorative images.

The title attribute is not required by the <img /> tag, but it functions similarly to the alt attribute; in fact, the title attribute supersedes the alt attribute for tool tips if both attributes are present. Knowing this, the best approach for describing images via text is to use both the alt attribute and the title attribute to provide relevant notation or helpful hints about the image that you think might be useful when viewed as a tool tip or via screen reader software.

Specifying Image Height and Width

Because text moves over the Internet much faster than graphics, most web browsers display the text on a page before they display images. This gives users something to read while they're waiting to see the pictures, which makes the whole page seem to load faster.

You can make sure that everything on your page appears as quickly as possible and in the right places by explicitly stating each image's height and width. That way, a web browser can immediately and accurately make room for each image as it lays out the page and while it waits for the images to finish transferring.

For each image you want to include in your site, you can use your graphics program to determine its exact height and width in pixels. You might also be able to find these image properties by using system tools. For example, in Windows, you can see an image's height and width by right-clicking on the image, selecting Properties, and then selecting Details. Once you know the height and width of an image, you can include its dimensions in the `<img />` tag, like this:

```
<img src="myimage.gif" alt="Fancy Picture" width="200" height="100" />
```

TIP

The height and width specified for an image don't have to match the image's actual height and width. A web browser will try to squish or stretch the image to display whatever size you specify. However, this is generally a bad idea because browsers aren't particularly good at resizing images. If you want an image to display smaller, you're definitely better off resizing it in an image editor.

Aligning Images

Just as you can align text on a page, you can align images on the page using special attributes. Not only can you align images horizontally, you also can align them vertically with respect to text and other images that surround them.

Horizontal Image Alignment

As discussed in Hour 5, "Working with Text Blocks and Lists," you can use `<div style="text-align:center">`, `<div style="text-align:right">`, and `<div style="text-align:left">` to align an element to the center, to the right margin, or to the left margin. These style settings affect both text and images and can be used within the `<p>` tag as well.

Like text, images are normally lined up with the left margin unless a `style="text-align:center"` or `style="text-align:right"` setting indicates that they should be centered or right-justified. In other words, `left` is the default value of the `text-align` style property.

You can also wrap text around images by using the float style property directly within the <img /> tag.

In Listing 11.2, <img style="float:left" /> aligns the first image to the left and wraps text around the right side of it, as you might expect. Similarly, <img style="float:right" /> aligns the second image to the right and wraps text around the left side of it. Figure 11.3 shows how these images align on a web page. There is no concept of floating an image to the center because there would be no way to determine how to wrap text on each side of it.

NOTE

The float style property is actually more powerful than described here and, in fact, applies to more than just images. You can use the float style property creatively to arrive at some interesting page layouts, as you'll learn later in the book.

Listing 11.2   Using text-align Styles to Align Images on a Web Page

```
<?xml version="1.0" encoding="UTF-8"?>
<!DOCTYPE html PUBLIC "-//W3C//DTD XHTML 1.1//EN"
  "http://www.w3.org/TR/xhtml11/DTD/xhtml11.dtd">

<html xmlns="http://www.w3.org/1999/xhtml" xml:lang="en">
  <head>
    <title>More Spectacular Yosemite Views</title>
  </head>

  <body>
    <h1>More Spectacular Yosemite Views</h1>
    <p><img src="elcap_sm.jpg" alt="El Capitan" width="100"
    height="75" style="float:left; padding: 6px;"/><strong>El
    Capitan</strong> is a 3,000-foot (910 m) vertical rock formation
    in Yosemite National Park, located on the north side of Yosemite
    Valley, near its western end. The granite monolith is one of the
    world's favorite challenges for rock climbers.  The formation was
    named "El Capitan" by the Mariposa Battalion when it explored the
    valley in 1851.</p>
    <p><img src="tunnelview_sm.jpg" alt="Tunnel View" width="100"
    height="80" style="float:right; padding: 6px;"/><strong>Tunnel
    View</strong> is a viewpoint on State Route 41 located directly east
    of the Wawona Tunnel as one enters Yosemite Valley from the south.
    The view looks east into Yosemite Valley including the southwest face
    of El Capitan, Half Dome, and Bridalveil Falls. This is, to many, the
    first views of the popular attractions in Yosemite.</p>
  </body>
</html>
```

FIGURE 11.3
Showing the image alignment from Listing 11.2.

NOTE

Notice the addition of padding in the style attribute for both `<img/>` tags used in Listing 11.2. This padding provides some "breathing room" between the image and the text—6 pixels on all four sides of the image. You will learn more about padding in Hour 13.

Vertical Image Alignment

Sometimes, you might want to insert a small image in the middle of a line of text; or you might like to put a single line of text next to an image as a caption. In either case, it would be handy to have some control over how the text and images line up vertically. Should the bottom of the image line up with the bottom of the letters, or should the text and images all be arranged so that their middles line up? You can choose between these and several other options:

▶ To line up the top of an image with the top of the tallest image or letter on the same line, use `<img style="vertical-align:text-top" />`.

▶ To line up the bottom of an image with the bottom of the text, use `<img style="vertical-align:text-bottom" />`.

▶ To line up the middle of an image with the overall vertical center of everything on the line, use `<img style="vertical-align:middle" />`.

▶ To line up the bottom of an image with the baseline of the text, use `<img style="vertical-align:baseline" />`.

NOTE

The `vertical-align` style property also supports values of `top` and `bottom`, which can be used to align images with the overall top or bottom of a line of elements regardless of any text on the line.

All four of these options are used in Listing 11.3 and displayed in Figure 11.4. Four thumbnail images are now listed vertically down the page, along with descriptive text next to each image. Various settings for the `vertical-align` style property are used to align each image and its relevant text.

TIP

If you don't include any `align` attribute in an `<img />` tag, the bottom of the image will line up with the baseline of any text next to it. That means you never actually have to type `style="vertical-align:baseline"` because it is assumed by default. However, if you specify a margin for an image and intend for the alignment to be a bit more exacting with the text, you might want to explicitly set the `vertical-align` attribute to `text-bottom`. Take a look at the last image shown in Figure 11.4 to see an example of the text appearing slightly below the image due to the image margin—this is a result of the `baseline` setting for `vertical-align`.

Listing 11.3   Using `vertical-align` Styles to Align Text with Images

```
<?xml version="1.0" encoding="UTF-8"?>
<!DOCTYPE html PUBLIC "-//W3C//DTD XHTML 1.1//EN"
  "http://www.w3.org/TR/xhtml11/DTD/xhtml11.dtd">

<html xmlns="http://www.w3.org/1999/xhtml" xml:lang="en">
  <head>
    <title>Small But Mighty Spectacular Yosemite Views</title>
  </head>

  <body>
    <h1>Small But Mighty Yosemite Views</h1>
    <p><img src="elcap_sm.jpg" alt="El Capitan" width="100"
    height="75" style="vertical-align:text-top;"/><strong>El
    Capitan</strong> is a 3,000-foot (910 m) vertical rock formation
    in Yosemite National Park.</p>
    <p><img src="tunnelview_sm.jpg" alt="Tunnel View" width="100"
    height="80" style="vertical-align:text-bottom;"/><strong>Tunnel
    View</strong> looks east into Yosemite Valley.</p>
    <p><img src="upperyosefalls_sm.jpg" alt="Upper Yosemite Falls"
    width="87" height="100" style="vertical-align:middle;"/><strong>Upper
    Yosemite Falls</strong> are 1,430 ft and are among the twenty highest
    waterfalls in the world. </p>
    <p><img src="hangingrock_sm.jpg" alt="Hanging Rock" width="100"
    height="75" style="vertical-align:baseline;"/><strong>Hanging
    Rock</strong>, off Glacier Point, used to be a popular spot for people
    to, well, hang from.  Crazy people.</p>
  </body>
</html>
```

FIGURE 11.4
Showing the vertical image alignment options used in Listing 11.3.

Try adding some images to your web pages now and experiment with different values of `text-align`, `vertical-align`, and `float`. To get you started, here's a quick review of how to add a hypothetical fish image (`fish.jpg`) to any web page.

1. Copy the fish.jpg image file to the same directory as the HTML file (or leave the image in its current location and make sure you remember where it is located).

2. With a text editor, choose where you want the image to appear in the text and add `<img src="fish.jpg" alt="Bright Orange Goldfish with Bulging Eyes" />`to that location.

3. If you want the image to be centered, put `<div style="text-align:center">` before the `<img />` tag and `</div>` after it. To wrap text around the image, add `style="float:right"` or `style="float:left"` to the `<img />` tag. And, finally, use the `vertical-align` style property directly within the `<img />` tag to control the vertical alignment of the image with respect to other images and text next to it.

4. If you have time for a little more experimentation, try combining multiple images of various sizes using various vertical alignment settings.

Turning Images into Links

You probably noticed in Figure 11.1 that the image on the page is quite large, which fine in this particular example but isn't ideal when you're trying to present multiple images. It makes more sense in this case to create smaller image thumbnails that link to larger versions of each image. Then you can arrange the thumbnails on the page so that visitors can easily see all the content, even if they see only a smaller version of the actual (larger) image. Thumbnails are one of the many ways you can use image links to spice up your pages.

To turn any image into a clickable link to another page or image, you can use the `<a href>` tag that you used previously to make text links . Listing 11.4 contains the code for a modification of Listing 11.2—which already used thumbnails—to provide links to larger versions of the images. To ensure that the user knows to click the thumbnails, the image and some helper text is enclosed in a `<div>`, as shown in Figure 11.5.

Listing 11.4   Using Tumbnails for Effective Image Links

```
<?xml version="1.0" encoding="UTF-8"?>
<!DOCTYPE html PUBLIC "-//W3C//DTD XHTML 1.1//EN"
  "http://www.w3.org/TR/xhtml11/DTD/xhtml11.dtd">

<html xmlns="http://www.w3.org/1999/xhtml" xml:lang="en">
  <head>
    <title>More Spectacular Yosemite Views</title>
      <style type="text/css">
      div.imageleft {
        float:left;
        clear: all;
        text-align:center;
        font-size:9px;
        font-style:italic;
      }
      div.imageright {
        float:right;
        clear: all;
        text-align:center;
        font-size:9px;
        font-style:italic;
      }
      img {
        padding: 6px;
        border: none;
      }
      </style>
  </head>
  <body>
    <h1>More Spectacular Yosemite Views</h1>
    <p><div class="imageleft">
    <a href="http://www.flickr.com/photos/nofancyname/614253439/"><img
    src="elcap_sm.jpg" alt="El Capitan" width="100" height="75"/></a>
    <br/>click image to enlarge</div><strong>El Capitan</strong>
    is a 3,000-foot (910 m) vertical rock formation in Yosemite National
    Park, located on the north side of Yosemite Valley, near its western
    end. The granite monolith is one of the world's favorite challenges
    for rock climbers.  The formation was named "El Capitan" by the
    Mariposa Battalion when it explored the valley in 1851.</p>
    <p><div class="imageright">
    <a href="http://www.flickr.com/photos/nofancyname/614287355/"><img
    src="tunnelview_sm.jpg" alt="Tunnel View" width="100"
      height="80"/></a>
    <br/>click image to enlarge</div><strong>Tunnel View</strong> is a
    viewpoint on State Route 41 located directly east of the Wawona Tunnel
    as one enters Yosemite Valley from the south. The view looks east into
    Yosemite Valley including the southwest face of El Capitan, Half Dome,
    and Bridalveil Falls. This is, to many, the first views of the popular
    attractions in Yosemite.</p>
  </body>
</html>
```

FIGURE 11.5
Using thumbnails as links
improves the layout of a page that
uses large images.

The code in Listing 11.4 uses additional styles that will be explained in more detail in Hours 14 and 15, but you should be able to figure out the basics:

▶ The <a> tags link these particular images to larger versions, which in this case are stored on an external server (at Flickr).

▶ The <div> tags, and their styles, are used to align those sets of graphics and caption text (and also include some padding).

Unless instructed otherwise, web browsers display a colored rectangle around the edge of each image link. Like text links, the rectangle usually appears blue for links that haven't been visited recently or purple for links that have been visited recently—unless you specify different colored links in your style sheet. Because you seldom, if ever, want this unsightly line around your linked images, you should usually include style="border:none" in any <img /> tag within a link. In this instance, the border:none style is made part of the style sheet entry for the img element because we use the same styles twice.

When you click one of the thumbnail images on the sample page shown, the link is opened in the browser, as shown in Figure 11.6.

FIGURE 11.6
Clicking a linked thumbnail image opens the target of the link.

Using Background Images

As you learned in the previous hour, you can use background images to act as a sort of "wallpaper" in a container element, so that the text or other images appear on top of this underlying design.

The basic style properties that work together to create a background are:

▶ `background-color`: specifies the background color of the element. While not image-related, it is part of the set of background-related properties.

▶ `background-image`: specifies the image to use as the background of the element using the following syntax: `url('imagename.gif')`.

▶ `background-repeat`: specifies how the image should repeat, both horizontally and vertically. By default (without specifying anything), background images will repeat both horizontally and vertically. Other options are: `repeat` (same as default), `repeat-x` (horizontal), `repeat-y` (vertical), and `no-repeat` (only one appearance of the graphic).

▶ `background-position`: specifies where the image should be initially placed relative to its container. Options include: `top-left`, `top-center`, `top-right`, `center-left`, `center-center`, `center-right`, `bottom-left`, `bottom-center`, `bottom-right`, and specific pixel and percentage placements.

When specifying a background image, you can put all of these specifications together into one property, like so:

```
body {
    background: #ffffff url('imagename.gif') no-repeat top right;
}
```

In the previous style sheet entry, the body element of the web page will be white and include a graphic named `imagename.gif` on the top right. Another use for the `background` property is the creation of custom bullets for your unordered lists. To use images as bullets, first define the style for the `<ul>` tag as follows:

```
ul {
    list-style-type: none;
    padding-left: 0;
    margin-left: 0;
}
```

Next, change the declaration for the `<li>` tag to:

```
li {
    background: url(mybullet.gif) left center no-repeat
}
```

Make sure that `mybullet.gif` (or whatever you name your graphic) is on the web server and accessible; in that case, all unordered list items will show your custom image rather than the standard filled disc bullet.

We will return to the specific use of background properties in later lessons when using CSS for overall page layouts.

Using Imagemaps

Sometimes you might want to use an image as navigation, but beyond the simple button-based or link-based navigation that you often see in web sites. For example, perhaps you have a web site with medical information and you want to show an image of the human body that links to pages that provide information about various body parts. Or you have a web site that provides a world map users can click to access information about countries. You can divide an image into regions that link to different documents, depending on where users click within that image. This is called an *imagemap*, and any image can be made into an imagemap.

Why Imagemaps Aren't Always Necessary

The first thing you should know about imagemaps is that you probably won't need to use them except in very special cases. It's almost always easier and more efficient to use several ordinary images that are placed directly next to one another and provide a separate link for each image.

For example, see Figure 11.7. This is a web page that shows 12 different corporate logos; this example is a common type of web page in the business world, one in which you give a little free advertisement to your partners. You *could* present these logos as one large image and create an imagemap that provides links to each of the 12 companies. Users could click each logo in the image to visit each company's site. Or you could display the images on the page as in this example, and use 12 separate images—one for each company—with each image including a link to that particular company.

FIGURE 11.7
Web page with 12 different logos; this could be presented as a single imagemap or divided into 12 separate pieces.

An imagemap is the best choice for an image that has numerous parts, is oddly arranged, or the design of the image itself might be too complicated to divide into separate images. Figure 11.8 shows an image that is best suited as an imagemap.

FIGURE 11.8
An image that wouldn't take well to being sliced up—better make it an imagemap.

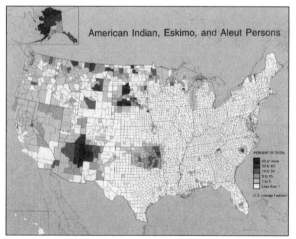

Mapping Regions Within an Image

To create any type of imagemap, you need to figure out the numerical pixel coordinates of each region within the image that you want to turn into a clickable link. These clickable links are also known as *areas*. Your graphics program might provide you with an easy way to find these coordinates. Or you might want to use a standalone imagemapping tool such as Mapedit (http://www.boutell.com/mapedit/) or the online imagemap maker at http://www.image-maps.com/. In addition to helping you map the coordinates, these tools also provide the HTML code necessary to make the maps work.

Using an image mapping tool is often as simple as using your mouse to draw a rectangle (or a custom shape) around the area you wish to be a link. Figure 11.9 shows the result of one of these rectangular selections as well as the interface for adding the URL and the title or alternate text for this link. Several pieces of information are necessary to creating the HTML for your imagemap: coordinates, target URL, title of link, and alternative text for the link.

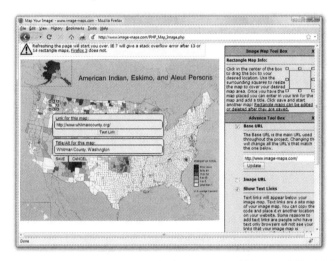

FIGURE 11.9
Using an imagemapping tool to create linked areas of a single graphic.

TRY IT YOURSELF ▼

Create Your Own Imagemap

You're more likely to remember how to make imagemaps if you get an image of your own and turn it into an imagemap as you continue with this hour:

▶ For starters, it's easiest to choose a fairly large image that is visually divided into roughly rectangular regions.

▶ If you don't have a suitable image handy, use your favorite graphics program to make one. Perhaps use a single photograph showing several people and use each person as an area of the imagemap.

▶ Try a few different imagemapping tools to determine which you like best. Start with standalone software such as MapEdit (http://www.boutell.com/mapedit/) and move to the online imagemap maker at http://www.image-maps.com/. There are others; use the search engine of your choice to find variations on the "imagemap software" theme.

Creating the HTML for an Imagemap

If you use an imagemap generator, you will already have the HTML necessary for creating the imagemap. However, it is a good idea to understand the parts of the code so that you can check it for accuracy. The following HTML code is required to start any imagemap:

```
<map name="mapname">
```

Keep in mind that you can use whatever name you want for the `name` of the `<map>` tag, although it helps if you make it as descriptive as possible. Next, you'll need an `<area />` tag for each region of the image. Following is an example of a single `<area />` tag that is used in the mapping-a-map imagemap example:

```
<area shape="rect" coords="100,136,116,152"
    href="http://www.whitmancounty.org/"
    alt="Whitman County, WA"
     title="Whitman County, WA" />
```

This `<area />` tag has five attributes, which you will use with every area you describe in an imagemap:

- ▶ `shape` indicates whether the region is a rectangle (`shape="rect"`), a circle (`shape="circle"`), or an irregular polygon (`shape="poly"`).

- ▶ `coords` gives the exact pixel coordinates for the region. For rectangles, give the x,y coordinates of the upper-left corner followed by the x,y coordinates of the lower-right corner. For circles, give the x,y center point followed by the radius in pixels. For polygons, list the x,y coordinates of all the corners in a connect-the-dots order.

- ▶ `href` specifies the page to which the region links. You can use any address or filename that you would use in an ordinary `<a href>` link tag.

- ▶ `alt` allows you to provide a piece of text that is associated with the shape. Most browsers (Firefox excluded) display this text in a small box when a user hovers his mouse over the shape. This text adds a subtle but important visual cue to users who might not otherwise realize that they are looking at an imagemap. Firefox correctly uses the `title` attribute in addition to the `alt` attribute to provide a visual cue, which is why, as noted previously in this hour, you should use both attributes.

Each distinct clickable region in an imagemap must be described as a single area, which means a typical imagemap consists of a list of areas. After coding the `<area />` tags, you are done defining the imagemap, so wrap things up with a closing `</map>` tag.

The last step in creating an imagemap is wiring it to the actual map image. The map image is placed on the page using an ordinary `<img />` tag. However, there is an extra `usemap` attribute that is coded like this:

```
<img src="map.png" usemap="#countymap"
    style="border:none; width:650px; height:509px"
    alt="Native Peoples Census Map" />
```

When specifying the value of the `usemap` attribute, use the name you put in the `id` of the `<map>` tag (and don't forget the # symbol). Also include the `style` attribute to specify the height and width of the image and to turn off the border around the imagemap, which you might or might not elect to keep in imagemaps of your own.

Listing 11.5 shows the complete code for a sample web page containing the map graphic, its imagemap and a few mapped areas.

Listing 11.5   Defining the Regions of an Imagemap with `<map>` and `<area />` Tags

```
<?xml version="1.0" encoding="UTF-8"?>
<!DOCTYPE html PUBLIC "-//W3C//DTD XHTML 1.0 Transitional//EN"
    "http://www.w3.org/TR/xhtml1/DTD/xhtml1-transitional.dtd">

<html xmlns="http://www.w3.org/1999/xhtml" xml:lang="en">
  <head>
    <title>Testing an Imagemap</title>
  </head>

  <body>
    <h1>Testing an Imagemap</h1>
        <p style="text-align:center">Click on a logo to go to the
        county's web site.<br/>
        <img src="map.png" usemap="#countymap"
        style="border:none; width:650px;height:509px"
        alt="Native Peoples Census Map" /></p>

        <map name="countymap" id="countymap">
        <area shape="rect" coords="100,136,116,152"
          href="http://www.whitmancounty.org/"
          alt="Whitman County, WA" title="Whitman County, WA" />
        <area shape="rect" coords="29,271,42,283"
          href="http://www.sccgov.org/" alt="Santa Clara County, CA"
          title="Santa Clara County, CA" />
        <area shape="rect" coords="535,216,548,228"
          href="http://visitingmifflincounty.com/"
          alt="Mifflin County, PA" title="Mifflin County, PA" />
    </map>
  </body>
</html>
```

NOTE

If you're a stickler for details, you might have noticed—check out the first few lines of code—that this web page is coded as an XHTML 1.0 document, as opposed to the XHTML 1.1 used with most of the other examples in the book. This is done because some browsers (Internet Explorer, for one) are lagging in their support of a single XHTML 1.1 change in how imagemaps are used. This change is specific to the `usemap` attribute, which in XHTML 1.1 doesn't require the # symbol in front of the map name. In fact, the # symbol isn't allowed at all in XHTML 1.1. The # symbol is, however, allowed in XHTML 1.0, so to satisfy current web browsers and still provide you with a valid web page, this particular example uses XHTML 1.0.

Figure 11.10 shows the imagemap in action. Notice in the bottom of your browser window that your browser (in this example, Firefox) displays the link address for whatever area the mouse is hovering over. Additionally, when you hover the mouse over an area, the `alt` or `title` text for that area—in this example, Whitman County—is displayed on the imagemap.

FIGURE 11.10
The imagemap defined in Listing 11.5 as it displays on the web page.

NOTE

There is a method of producing mapped images that relies solely on CSS and not the HTML `<map>` tag. You will learn more about this in Hour 16, "Using CSS to Do More With Lists."

Summary

This hour has shown you how to use the `<img />` tag to place images on your web pages. You learned how to include a short text message that appears in place of the image as it loads and also appears whenever users move the mouse pointer over the image. You also learned how to control the horizontal and vertical alignment of each image and how to wrap text around the left or right of an image.

You also learned how to use images as links—either by using the `<a>` tag around the images or by creating imagemaps. You also learned a little bit about how to use images in the background of container elements.

Table 11.1 summarizes the attributes of the `<img />` tag covered in this hour, along with relevant style properties.

Table 11.1   HTML Tags and Attributes Covered in Hour 11

Tag/Attribute	Function
`<img />`	Places an image file within the page.
`<map>...</map>`	A client-side imagemap referenced by `<img usemap="..." />`. Includes one or more `<area />` tags.
`<area />`	Defines a clickable link within a client-side imagemap.
Attributes	
`src="address"`	The address or filename of the image.
`alt="altdescription"`	An alternative description of the image that is displayed in place of the image, primarily for users who can't view the image itself.
`title="title"`	A text message that is displayed as an image title, typically in a small pop-up box (tool tip) over the image.
`width="width"`	The width of the image (in pixels).
`height="height"`	The height of the image (in pixels).
`style="border:attributes"`	Gets rid of the border around the image if the image is serving as a link.
`style="vertical-align:alignment"`	Aligns the image vertically to `text-top`, `top`, `text-bottom`, `bottom`, `middle`, or `baseline`.

Table 11.1   HTML Tags and Attributes Covered in Hour 11

Tag/Attribute	Function
`style="float:float"`	Floats the image to one side so text can wrap around it. Possible values are `left`, `right`, and `none` (default).
`usemap="name"`	The name of an imagemap specification for client-side image mapping. Used with `<map>` and `<area />`.
`shape="value"`	Within the `<area />` tag, specifies the shape of the clickable area. Valid options for this attribute are `rect`, `poly`, and `circle`.
`coords="values"`	Within the `<area />` tag, specifies the coordinates of the clickable region within an image. Its meaning and setting vary according to the type of area.
`href="linkurl"`	Within the `<area />` tag, specifies the URL that should be loaded when the area is clicked.

Q&A

Q How long can I make a message that I put after `alt=` in an `<img />` tag?

A Theoretically, as long as you want. For practicality, you should keep the message short enough that it fits in a smaller space than the image itself. For big images, 10 words might be fine; in some cases, I've even seen web page authors include a small paragraph of text. For small images, a single word is best.

Q I used the `<img />` tag just as you advised, but when I view the page, all I see is a little box with an × or some shapes in it. What's wrong?

A The broken image icon you're seeing can mean one of two things: Either the web browser couldn't find the image file or the image isn't saved in a format the browser recognizes. To solve these problems, first check to make sure that the image is where it is supposed to be. If it is, then open the image in your graphics editor and save it again as a GIF, JPG, or PNG format.

Q What happens if I overlap areas on an imagemap?

A You are allowed to overlap areas on an imagemap. Just keep in mind that when determining which link to follow, one area will have precedence over the other area. Precedence is assigned according to which areas are listed first in the imagemap. For example, the first area in the map has precedence over the second area, which means that a click in the overlapping portion of the areas will link to the first area. If you have an area within an imagemap that doesn't link to anything (known as a "dead" area), you can use this overlap trick to deliberately prevent this area from linking to anything. To do this, just place the dead area before other areas so that the dead area overlaps them, and then set its href attribute to "".

Workshop

The workshop contains quiz questions and activities to help you solidify your understanding of the material covered. Try to answer all questions before looking at the "Answers" section that follows.

Quiz

1. How would you insert an `elephant.jpg` image file at the very top of a web page?

2. How would you make the word `Elephant` display whenever the actual `elephant.jpg` image couldn't be displayed by a web browser?

3. You want to create an imagemap of a 200×200-pixel image named `quarters.gif`. When viewers click the upper-left quarter of the image, you want them to get a page named `topleft.html`. When they click the upper-right quarter, you want them to get `topright.html`. Clicking the lower-left quarter should bring up `bottomleft.html`, and the lower-right panel should lead to `bottomright.html`. What HTML would you use to implement this as an imagemap?

Answers

1. Copy the image file into the same directory folder as the HTML text file. Immediately after the `<body>` tag in the HTML text file, type
   `<p><img src="elephant.jpg" alt="" /></p>`.

2. Use the following HTML:
   ```
   <img src="elephant.jpg" alt="elephant" />
   ```

3. Create the following imagemap:

```
<map name="quartersmap" id="quartersmap">
  <area shape="rect" coords="0,0,99,99" href="topleft.html"
     alt="top left" />
   <area shape="rect" coords="100,0,199,99" href="topright.html"
     alt="top right" />
   <area shape="rect" coords="0,100,99,199" href="bottomleft.html"
     alt="bottom left" />
   <area shape="rect" coords="100,100,199,199"
href="bottomright.html"
     alt="bottom right" />
</map>
<img src="quarters.gif" width="200" height="200"
     usemap="#quartersmap"
     alt="quarters" title="quarters" />
```

Exercises

▶ Practicing any of the image placement methods in this lesson will go a long way toward helping you determine the role that images can, and will, play in the web sites you design. Using a few sample images, practice using the float style to place images and text in relation to one another. Remember the possible values for float are left, right, and none (default).

▶ Image alignment is also an important aspect of good visual web design. Using a few sample images, practice using the vertical-align style to place images and text in relation to one another. Remember the possible values for image-align are text-top, top, text-bottom, bottom, middle, and baseline.

HOUR 12
Using Multimedia in Your Web Site

The term *multimedia* encompasses everything we see and hear on a web page: audio, video, and animation, as well as static images and text. In previous hours, you learned how to use images and text, so in this hour, you'll learn about including the other types of multimedia in your web sites. You won't learn how to create any particular audio, video, or animation, but you will learn how to include such files in your site, through either linking or embedding the content.

Before even thinking about including multimedia in your site, remember that not every user has devices that will play your media type, nor do all users have broadband Internet connections which allow these large files to transfer quickly. Always warn your visitors that the links they click will take them to multimedia files, and offer them the choice to view or listen to the content—don't force the files upon them.

WHAT YOU'LL LEARN IN THIS HOUR:

▶ How to link to multimedia files

▶ How to embed multimedia files

▶ Additional tips for using multimedia

Before you learn how to place multimedia on your web pages, you need to have some multimedia content to start with.

Creating multimedia of any kind can be a challenging and complicated task. If you're planning to create your own content from scratch, you'll need far more than this book to become the next crackerjack multimedia developer. After you have some content, however, this hour will show you how to place your new creations into your web pages.

For those of us who are artistically challenged, several alternative ways to obtain useful multimedia assets are available. Aside from the obvious (such as hiring an artist), here are a few suggestions:

▶ Much of the material on the Internet is free. Of course, it's still a good idea to double-check with the author or current owner of the

TRY IT YOURSELF ▼

Create or Find some Multimedia to Use in Your Web Site

Create or Find some Multimedia to Use in Your Web Site

content; you don't want to be sued for copyright infringement. In addition, various offices of the U.S. government generate content which, by law, belongs to all Americans. (For example, any NASA footage found online is free for your use.)

▶ Many search engines (google.com, yahoo.com, lycos.com, and so on) have specific search capabilities for finding multimedia files. As long as you are careful about copyright issues, this can be an easy way to find multimedia related to a specific topic. A simple search for **sample Flash animations**, **sample QuickTime movie**, or **sample audio files** will produce more results than you can handle.

▶ If you are creatively inclined, determine the medium you like most— for some of you it might be video production, others may enjoy audio production, and still others might want to dabble in animation. Once you have determined a starting point, look into the various types of software which will enable you to create such artistic masterpieces. Many companies provide multimedia software, such as Adobe (http://www.adobe.com/) and Apple (http://www.apple.com/) to name but two.

Linking to Multimedia Files

Regardless of the specific media types shown in this hour, the procedures shown for incorporating multimedia into your web pages will be similar no matter which media format you choose.

The simplest and most reliable option for incorporating a video or audio file into your web site is to simply link it in with `<a href>`, exactly as you would link to another HTML file.

For example, the following line could be used to offer a MOV video of a hockey game:

```
<a href="hockey.mov">View the hockey video clip.</a>
```

When the user clicks the words `View the hockey video clip.`, the `hockey.mov` QuickTime video file is transferred to her computer from your web server. Whichever helper application or plug-in she has installed automatically starts as soon as the file has finished downloading. If no compatible helper or plug-in can be found, the web browser will offer her a chance to download the appropriate plug-in or save the video on her hard drive for later viewing.

Listing 12.1 contains the code for a web page that uses a simple image link to play a video in Windows Media file format. In addition to the image link, a link is also placed within the text to provide context for the user.

Listing 12.1   Using the `<a>` to Link an Image to a Windows Media Video

```
<?xml version="1.0" encoding="UTF-8"?>
<!DOCTYPE html PUBLIC "-//W3C//DTD XHTML 1.1//EN"
  "http://www.w3.org/TR/xhtml11/DTD/xhtml11.dtd">

<html xmlns="http://www.w3.org/1999/xhtml" xml:lang="en">
  <head>
    <title>Fun in the Pond</title>
  </head>

  <body>
    <h1>Fun in the Pond</h1>
    <p><a href="pond.wmv"><img src="projector.gif" alt="Pond Video"
    style="border-style:none; float:left; padding:12px" /></a>
    Michael's backyard pond is not only a fun hobby but also an
    ongoing home improvement project that is both creative and
    relaxing. He has numerous fish in the pond, all Koi from various
    places as far as Japan, Israel, and Australia. Although they
    don't bark, purr, or fetch anything other than food, these fish
    are his pets, and good ones at that. You can <a href="pond.wmv">
    click here</a> or on the animated graphic on the left
    to see a movie clip of some fish in the pond.</p>
  </body>
</html>
```

This code simply uses the `projector.gif` animated GIF image as a link to the `pond.wmv` video clip. Figure 12.1 shows the pond sample page with the projector image in view. When the image is clicked, the Windows Media Player is invoked and begins to play the movie.

FIGURE 12.1
The projector.gif animated GIF image is used as an image link to a Windows Media file that launches an external helper application.

To view the video, you need only to click the animated projector (or the text link in the paragraph). This action results in the browser either playing the video with the help of a plug-in (if one is found that can play the clip) or deferring to a suitable helper application.

If you change the link from pond.wmv (Windows Media) to pond.mov (QuickTime), your browser handles the link differently. Instead of launching another program, the QuickTime plug-in allows you to view the movie clip directly in the browser window (see Figure 12.2).

FIGURE 12.2
When you follow the image link, the pond.mov QuickTime movie is played using the QuickTime browser plug-in.

As you might have guessed, this approach of using a simple link to play multimedia files offers the best backward compatibility because the browser bears all the responsibility of figuring out how to play a multimedia clip. The downside to this is that you don't have much control over how a clip is played, and you definitely can't play a clip directly in the context of a page.

Embedding Multimedia Files

XHTML contains a standard `<object>` tag that is the preferred way to embed multimedia of any kind in a web page. This tag is used instead of the old `<embed />` tag that you might still see in some HTML source code.

Embedding a multimedia file into a page produces a set of software controls that allow the file to be played directly—no secondary window is necessary, and there's no need to navigate away from the page you are on. Following is code to embed the pond video, which you saw earlier, using the `<object>` tag by itself:

```
<object classid="CLSID:6BF52A52-394A-11d3-B153-00C04F79FAA6"
  width="320" height="305">
  <param name="type" value="video/x-ms-wmv" />
  <param name="URL" value="pond.wmv" />
  <param name="uiMode" value="full" />
  <param name="autoStart" value="false" />
</object>
```

This code isn't too terribly complicated when you consider that it literally embeds a video directly into your web page (see Figure 11.3). The messiest part of the code is the `classid` attribute of the `<object>` tag, which is set to a long alphanumeric code. This code is the "global ID" for Windows Media Player, which means that you're telling the `<object>` tag to embed Windows Media Player on the page to play the video clip. You can just copy and paste this code into your own web pages.

NOTE

If your browser has no support for QuickTime, you can download the QuickTime player free from Apple at http://www.apple.com/quicktime/. Even if you do have QuickTime installed, some browsers might still play QuickTime movies differently based on whether a plug-in is installed. For example, on my Windows computer, Internet Explorer and Firefox both play QuickTime movies directly in the browser window via a plug-in, whereas Opera launches QuickTime as a helper application.

NOTE

It's important to note that Windows Media Player is a sophisticated enough media player that it automatically *streams* multimedia files, which means that it begins playing them after loading only the first few seconds of content. The idea is that the rest of the content is loaded in the background while you're watching or listening to earlier portions. The result is that visitors don't have to wait through long download times when viewing or listening to your multimedia clips.

The width and height attributes of the <object> tag determine the size of the embedded Windows Media Player window. Some browsers will automatically size the embedded player to fit the content if you leave these attributes off, whereas others won't show anything at all. Play it safe by setting them to a size that suits the multimedia content being played.

There are four <param> tags within the <object> tag that are responsible for additional details about how the clip is to be played. Each tag has two attributes, name and value, which are responsible for associating data (value) with a particular setting (name). In this example, the URL for the media clip is set to pond.wmv. The third parameter, uiMode, determines which buttons and user interface options are made available by Windows Media Player—full indicates that all user interface features are enabled, such as the control buttons and volume slider. Finally, the autoStart parameter is set to false so that the video clip does not automatically start playing when the page is opened in a browser.

The type parameter is perhaps the trickiest. It identifies the type of media being displayed, which in this case is a Windows Media Video (WMV) file. This media type must be specified as one of the standard Internet MIME types.

A *MIME type* is an identifier for uniquely identifying different types of media objects on the Internet. MIME stands for Multipurpose Internet Mail Extensions, and this name comes from the fact that MIME types were originally used to identify email attachments. These MIME types should be used in the `type` attribute of the `<object>` tag to identify what kind of multimedia object is being referenced in the `data` attribute.

Following are the MIME types for several popular sound and video formats you might want to use in your web pages:

- ▶ WAV Audio—`audio/x-wav`
- ▶ AU Audio—`audio/basic`
- ▶ MP3 Audio—`audio/mpeg`
- ▶ MIDI Audio—`audio/midi`
- ▶ WMA Audio—`audio/x-ms-wma`
- ▶ RealAudio—`audio/x-pn-realaudio-plugin`
- ▶ AVI—`video/x-msvideo`
- ▶ WMV—`video/x-ms-wmv`
- ▶ MPEG Video—`video/mpeg`
- ▶ QuickTime—`video/quicktime`

Listing 12.2 shows the relevant code for the pond web page, where you can see the `<object>` tag as it appears in context.

Listing 12.2 Using an `<object>` Tag to Directly Embed a WMV Video Clip

```
<?xml version="1.0" encoding="UTF-8"?>
<!DOCTYPE html PUBLIC "-//W3C//DTD XHTML 1.1//EN"
  "http://www.w3.org/TR/xhtml11/DTD/xhtml11.dtd">

<html xmlns="http://www.w3.org/1999/xhtml" xml:lang="en">
  <head>
    <title>Fun in the Pond</title>
  </head>

  <body>
    <h1>Fun in the Pond</h1>
    <div style="float:left; padding:3px">
      <object classid="CLSID:6BF52A52-394A-11d3-B153-00C04F79FAA6"
        width="320" height="305">
        <param name="type" value="video/x-ms-wmv" />
        <param name="URL" value="pond.wmv" />
```

NOTE

Because the `<embed />` tag is not supported in XHTML, it will prevent your pages from validating. Unfortunately, there really is no workaround for this problem—we'll just have to wait for browsers to fully support the `<object>` tag by itself or move to the `<embed />` element of HTML 5.

Listing 12.2   Using an `<object>` Tag to Directly Embed a WMV Video Clip

```
                <param name="uiMode" value="full" />
                <param name="autoStart" value="false" />
                <embed width="320" height="305" type="video/x-ms-wmv"
                src="pond.wmv" controls="All" loop="false" autostart="false"
                pluginspage="http://www.microsoft.com/windows/windowsmedia/" />
        </object>
        </div>
        <p>Michael's backyard pond is not only a fun hobby but also
        an ongoing home improvement project that is both creative and
        relaxing.</p>
        <p>He has numerous fish in the pond, all Koi from various places
        as far as Japan, Israel, and Australia. Although they don't bark,
        purr, or fetch anything other than food, these fish are his pets,
        and good ones at that.</p>
    </body>
</html>
```

You might notice that there's some extra code that didn't appear in the earlier `<object>` tag example. Unfortunately, as discussed earlier in the hour, not all web browsers are entirely consistent in their support of the `<object>` tag. For this reason, it is necessary to include an `<embed />` tag within the `<object>` tag to account for browser inconsistencies. This isn't an ideal solution, but it's all we have while browser vendors continue to lag behind prevailing standards. If you pay close attention, you'll notice that the `<embed />` tag contains all the same information as the `<object>` tag.

NOTE

Video files aren't the only media files you can include within your web site using the `<object>` and `<embed />` tags. Adding any multimedia file will follow the same process. To determine exactly which classid and codebase attributes to use, as well as additional parameters (in the `<param />` tags), use your search engine to look up something like **object embed** *mediatype* where *mediatype* is Real Audio, QuickTime, Flash, or whatever you want.

The `<object>` tag is a bit more complex than what is revealed here. However, you don't need to know how to use the more advanced facets of the `<object>` tag just to play multimedia content. In other words, it isn't important for you to become a multimedia guru in order to share some multimedia clips on your web pages.

Additional Tips for Using Multimedia

Before you add video, audio, or animations to your web site, first ask yourself if you really should. When you use these types of multimedia, be sure to do so for a reason. Gratuitous sound and video, just like gratuitous images, can detract from your overall message. Then again, if your message is "Look at the videos I have made" or "Listen to my music and download some songs," then multimedia absolutely must play a role in your web site.

Here are a few additional tips to keep in mind:

▶ Don't include multimedia in a page and set it to automatically play when the page loads. Always give users the option to start (and stop) your sound or video.

▶ When possible, give users a choice of multimedia players. Don't limit yourself to multimedia content playable by only one type of player on only one operating system.

▶ Multimedia files are larger than the typical graphics and text files, which means you need to have the space on your web server to store them, as well as the bandwidth allotment to transfer them to whomever requests them via your web site.

▶ If your site is entirely audio or video and offers very little by way of text or graphics, understand that a certain segment of your audience won't see or hear what you want to present because of the limitations of their system or bandwidth. Provide these users with additional options to get your information.

▶ Leverage free online video hosting services, such as YouTube (http://www.youtube.com/). Not only does YouTube provide storage for your video clips, it will provide you with the code necessary to embed the video in your own web page. For example, Figure 12.4 shows the YouTube page for the cutest puppy in the world. If you copy and paste the text from the "Embed" area shown in the figure, you would get the following:

```
<object width="425" height="344">
<param name="movie"
value="http://www.youtube.com/v/yPxiHd2BOpo&rel=0&color1=0xb1b1b1
&color2=0xcfcfcf&feature=player_profilepage&fs=1"></param>
<param name="allowFullScreen" value="true"></param>
<param name="allowScriptAccess" value="always"></param>
<embed
src="http://www.youtube.com/v/yPxiHd2BOpo&rel=0&color1=0xb1b1b1&c
olor2=0xcfcfcf&feature=player_profilepage&fs=1"
type="application/x-shockwave-flash" allowfullscreen="true"
allowScriptAccess="always" width="425" height="344"></embed>
</object>
```

You could then insert the code into your web page.

FIGURE 12.4
YouTube provides storage of your
video files as well as links and
<object> code for use in your own
pages.

Summary

In this hour, you've learned how to embed video and sound into a web page. You learned how to use a simple link to a multimedia file, which is the most broadly supported but least flexible option for playing media content. You then learned how to use the <object> tag to embed a media player directly in a web page. Not only that, you learned that for maximum browser compatibility, it helps to assist the <object> tag with the <embed /> tag. The <object> and <embed /> tags can be used to include a vast array of media types, including WAV, MP3, RealAudio, and MIDI files—not to mention AVI, WMV, and QuickTime videos, to name just a few.

Table 12.1 summarizes the tags discussed in this hour.

Table 12.1   HTML Tags and Attributes Covered in Hour 12

Tag/Attribute	Function
`<object>...</object>`	Inserts images, videos, Java applets, ActiveX controls, or other objects into a document.
`<param>...</param>`	Runtime settings for an object, such as the width and height of the area it occupies on a page.
Attributes	
`name="name"`	A named parameter property.
`value="value"`	The value associated with a named parameter property.
`<embed />`	Embeds a multimedia file to be read or displayed by a plug-in application; this tag is technically deprecated but still useful due to browsers not fully supporting the `<object>` tag yet.
Attributes	
`width="width"`	The width of the embedded object in pixels.
`height="height"`	The height of the embedded object in pixels.
`type="mimetype"`	The MIME type of the multimedia content.
`src="mediaurl"`	The URL of the file to embed.
`controls="controls"`	The configuration of the user input controls for the media player; use `all` to enable all controls.
`loop="loop"`	Play the media clip once or loop it repeatedly; set to `true` or `false`.
`autostart="autostart"`	Play the media clip upon opening the page; set to `true` or `false`.
`pluginspage="pluginurl"`	The URL of the plug-in required to play the media clip.

Q&A

Q I hear a lot about streaming video and audio. What does that mean?

A In the past, video and audio files took minutes and sometimes hours to retrieve through most modems, which severely limited the inclusion of video and audio on web pages. The goal that everyone is moving toward is streaming video or audio, which plays while the data is being received. In other words, you don't have to completely download the clip before you can start to watch it or listen to it.

Streaming playback is now widely supported through most media players, in both standalone versions and plug-ins. When you embed a media object using the `<object>` tag, the underlying media player automatically streams the media clip if streaming is supported in the player.

Q How do I choose an audiovisual file format among QuickTime, Windows AVI/WAV, RealVideo/RealAudio, and MPEG? Is there any significant difference among them?

A QuickTime is the most popular video format among Macintosh users, though QuickTime players are available for Windows as well. Similarly, AVI/WMV and WAV/WMA are the video and audio formats for Windows users, but you can get players for the Macintosh that support these formats. MPEG is another popular audio and video standard. MPEG-3 (MP3 is already extremely popular as the high-fidelity audio standard of choice). One other audio format that is based on MPEG is Apple's AAC format, which might be more familiar to you as the native iTunes music format.

If most of your audience uses Windows, use AVI/WMV for video and WAV/WMA or MP3 for audio. If your audience includes a significant number of Macintosh users, use QuickTime or RealVideo/RealAudio, or at least offer some alternative. MP3 is also a viable option for Mac audio. If cross-platform compatibility is essential, consider going specifically with MP3 for audio or RealVideo/RealAudio—although only those who download special software from http://www.real.com/player/ will be able to see RealVideo/RealAudio clips.

Workshop

The workshop contains quiz questions and activities to help you solidify
your understanding of the material covered. Try to answer all questions
before looking at the "Answers" section that follows.

Quiz

1. What's the simplest method to provide access to a video on your
   web site for the widest possible audience?

2. What HTML would you use to embed a video file named `myvideo.avi`
   into a web page so that the users of all major web browsers will be
   able to see it? The video requires an area on the page that is
   320[ts]305 pixels in size.

3. How would you code a `<param>` tag within an `<object>` tag so that a
   media clip is played repeatedly?

Answers

1. Just link to it:

   ```
   <a href="myvideo.avi">my video</a>
   ```

2. Because the video clip is in a Microsoft format (AVI), you should
   embed a Windows Media player object using the following HTML
   code:

   ```
   <object classid="CLSID:6BF52A52-394A-11d3-B153-00C04F79FAA6"
   width="320" height="305">
     <param name="type" value="video/x-ms-avi" />
     <param name="URL" value="myvideo.avi" />
     <param name="uiMode" value="full" />
     <param name="autoStart" value="false" />
     <embed width="320" height="305" type="video/x-ms-avi"
     src="myvideo.avi" controls="All" loop="false" autostart="false"
     pluginspage="http://www.microsoft.com/windows/windowsmedia/">
   </embed>
   </object>
   ```

3. `<param name="loop" value="true" />`

Exercises

▶ Try your hand at creating your own video clip and embedding it in a web page, or find some freely available clips from the web and practice placement within your text.

▶ The techniques and tags covered in this hour for embedding media also work with Flash files. To find out how you can use Flash to put interactive animations in your web pages, check out the Flash home page at http://www.adobe.com/products/flash/.

Working with Frames

You might have visited web sites in which the browser window seemingly allowed you to move between several different pages. The truth is that the browser really was allowing you to view several pages at once by separating the browser window into regions that contain separate web pages; each region is known as a frame. Of course, from the user's perspective, everything comes together to form a single window of web content, but there are separate pages at work.

What Are Frames?

A *frame* is a rectangular region within the browser window that displays a web page alongside other pages in other frames. At first glance, Figure 13.1 might look like an ordinary web page, but it is actually two separate HTML pages, both displayed in the same web browser window. Each page is displayed in its own frame, arranged horizontally and separated by the horizontal bar.

WHAT YOU'LL LEARN IN THIS HOUR:

▶ How to build a frameset
▶ How to link between frames and windows
▶ How to use inline frames

FIGURE 13.1
Frames allow more than one web page to be displayed at once.

If frames are used, typically they are used to create a framed site that takes advantage of a static set of navigational links; you can see these links in the top frame of Figure 13.1. When one of the links in this example is clicked, the top frame will not change; a new page will be loaded and displayed in the bottom frame (see Figure 13.2).

FIGURE 13.2
Clicking Products brings up a new bottom page but leaves the top frame the same.

You should be aware that frames have long been a vexed issue in web design. The advantages have never really outweighed the disadvantages, yet due to differences in browser support for HTML and CSS standards, frames were seen as a way to achieve certain goals despite their shortcomings. As a web developer, I do not recommend the use of frames for the following reasons:

▶ Frames go against the fundamental concept of the Web, which is the hypertextual connection between individual instances of web content that can be accessed via a single web address (URL).

▶ Printing parts of a framed site are very difficult; unless you have clicked on the specific frame you wish to print, and select "Print this Frame" from a context menu (if one is available), all that will print is the frameset itself, which will have no content in it.

▶ If a frame lacks proper coding, or if it has proper coding but the code is used for nefarious purposes, a user could get stuck inside a framed site unable to view external content outside of the frame.

▶ Frames have been used historically in lieu of standard, professional, accessible methods of web development and design. There is no reason to choose the lesser option when the better option of CSS layout is available.

▶ For these (and other) reasons, frames have been removed from the HTML 5 standard. The antiquated `<frame />`, `<frameset>`, and `<noframes>` tags will simply not be available in the future.

Despite these shortcomings, you will learn in this hour how to create a very simple framed site. It is quite likely that you will still encounter framed sites, and you might need to know how to re-create the "look and feel" of the site but without using frames. In that case, it is important to understand how frames are constructed so you can successfully deconstruct them.

Additionally, you will learn about a type of frame—the `<iframe>`—that does serve an important purpose and will still be present in HTML 5.

Later in this book, you will learn how to use XHTML and CSS to produce the same functionality only without using the frames. For now, follow along the construction of this simple framed site so that you can learn the process should you ever have to *undo* one and re-create it a different way.

Building a Frameset

This section shows you how to create the simple framed site shown in Figures 13.1 and 13.2. The contents of each frame were created as ordinary HTML pages. The pages are top.html (for the navigation), home.html, products.html, services.html, and contact.html. These pages don't contain any tags you haven't already seen in other hours. A special page known as a frameset document was used to put the pages together; in this case, that document is index.html.

Creating a Frameset Document

A *frameset document* is an HTML page that instructs the web browser to split its window into multiple frames and specifies which web page should be displayed in each frame.

A frameset document actually has no content. It only tells the browser which other pages to load and how to arrange them in the browser window. Listing 13.1 shows the frameset document for the sample framed site shown in Figure 13.1 and Figure 13.2.

Listing 13.1   Frameset Document for the Site Shown in Figure 13.1

```
<?xml version="1.0" encoding="UTF-8"?>
<!DOCTYPE html PUBLIC "-//W3C//DTD XHTML 1.0 Frameset//EN"
  "http://www.w3.org/TR/xhtml1/DTD/xhtml1-frameset.dtd">

<html xmlns="http://www.w3.org/1999/xhtml" xml:lang="en">
  <head>
    <title>Sample Framed Site</title>
  </head>

  <frameset rows="50,*">
    <frame src="top.html" name="top" />
    <frame src="home.html" name="main" />
    <noframes>
     <body>
       <h1>Sample Framed Site</h1>
       Your browser does not support frames. Sorry!
     </body>
    </noframes>
  </frameset>
</html>
```

NOTE

It's important to notice that the DTD used in this sample page is not the familiar XHTML 1.1 DTD that you've been using throughout the book. This is because frames are not supported in the standard XHTML 1.1 DTD. Therefore, to validate a page with frames, you must instead use the XHTML 1.0 Frameset DTD, which is a special DTD designed just for pages that use frames.

Listing 13.1 uses a `<frameset>` tag instead of a `<body>` tag. No tags that would normally be contained in a `<body>` tag can be within the `<frameset>` tag. The `<frameset>` tag in this example includes a `rows` attribute, meaning that the frames should be arranged on top of each other like the horizontal rows of a table. If you want your frames to be side by side, use a `cols` attribute (instead of a `rows` attribute).

You must specify the sizes of the `rows` or `cols`, either as precise pixel values or as percentages of the total size of the browser window. You can also use an asterisk (*) to indicate that a frame should fill whatever space is available in the window. If more than one frame has an * value, the remaining space will be divided equally between them.

In Listing 13.1, `<frameset rows="50,*">` splits the window vertically into two frames. The top frame will be exactly 50 pixels tall and the bottom frame will take up all the remaining space in the window. The top frame contains the document `top.html` (see Listing 13.2) and the bottom frame contains `home.html` (see Listing 13.3).

Listing 13.2   The `top.html` Navigation Bar for the Sample Framed Site

```
<?xml version="1.0" encoding="UTF-8"?>
<!DOCTYPE html PUBLIC "-//W3C//DTD XHTML 1.0 Transitional//EN"
  "http://www.w3.org/TR/xhtml1/DTD/xhtml1-transitional.dtd">

<html xmlns="http://www.w3.org/1999/xhtml" xml:lang="en">
  <head>
    <title>Sample Framed Site</title>
  </head>

  <body style="background-color:#0000FF;">
    <div style="text-align:center;color:#FFFFFF;font-weight:bold;
        font-size:16pt">
      <a style="color:#FFFFFF;" href="home.html"
        target="main">HOME</a> ::
      <a style="color:#FFFFFF;" href="products.html"
        target="main">PRODUCTS</a> ::
      <a style="color:#FFFFFF;" href="services.html"
        target="main">SERVICES</a> ::
      <a style="color:#FFFFFF;" href="contact.html"
        target="main">CONTACT</a>
    </div>
  </body>
</html>
```

Listing 13.3   The `home.html` Single Content Frame Within the Sample
            Framed Site

```
<?xml version="1.0" encoding="UTF-8"?>
<!DOCTYPE html PUBLIC "-//W3C//DTD XHTML 1.0 Transitional//EN"
  "http://www.w3.org/TR/xhtml1/DTD/xhtml1-transitional.dtd">

<html xmlns="http://www.w3.org/1999/xhtml" xml:lang="en">
  <head>
    <title>Sample Framed Site</title>
  </head>

  <body style="background-color:#FFFFFF">
    <h1 style="text-align:center">Sample Framed Site: Home</h1>
    <p style="text-align:center">This is an example of the "home"
page.</p>
  </body>
</html>
```

In this example, the top navigation frame has a fixed height of 50 pixels.
But because you can't predict the size of the window in which users will

TIP

After the framesets in Listing 13.1, there is a complete web page between the `<body>` and `</body>` tags. Notice that this doesn't appear at all in Figure 13.1 or Figure 13.2. All web browsers that support frames will ignore anything between the `<noframes>` and `</noframes>` tags.

All major browsers these days support frames, so the issue of frames compatibility is much less significant now than in years past. Even so, it's easy enough to include the `<noframes>` tag and cover the few users who might still use ancient browsers—if you use frames at all, that is.

NOTE

The pages in Listing 13.2 and Listing 13.3 use the XHTML 1.0 Transitional DTD. XHTML 1.1 DTD is newer and much stricter, but frames require you to stick with XHTML 1.0 for validation purposes, so it made sense to also use XHTML 1.0 for the pages that appear within the frames.

view your web page, it is often convenient to use percentages rather than exact pixel values to dictate the size of the rows and columns. For example, to make a left frame 20% of the width of the browser window with a right frame taking up the remaining 80%, you would type the following :

```
<frameset cols="20%,80%">
```

Whenever you specify any frame size in pixels, it's a good idea to include at least one frame in the same frameset with a variable (*) width so that the document can grow to fill a window of any size.

Adding Individual Frames

Within the `<frameset>` and `</frameset>` tags, you should have a `<frame />` tag indicating which HTML document to display in each frame. Note that if you have fewer `<frame />` tags than the number of frames defined in the `<frameset>` tag, any remaining frames will be left blank.

Include an `src` attribute in each `<frame>` tag with the address of the web page to load in that frame. You can put the address of an image file, instead of a web page, if you just want a frame with a single image in it.

Linking Between Frames and Windows

NOTE

Technically speaking, the `name` tag is outdated and has been replaced by the `id` tag. However, current web browsers still rely on `name` instead of `id` when it comes to identifying frames as targets and the use of `name` is still valid XHTML. So, for now, you need to stick with the `name` attribute when identifying frames. Of course, it wouldn't hurt to use both attributes.

The real power of frames begins to emerge when you give a frame a unique name with the `name` attribute in the `<frame />` tag. You can then make any link on the page change the contents of that frame by using the `target` attribute in an `<a>` tag. For example, Listing 13.1 includes the following tag:

```
<frame src="home.html" name="main" />
```

This code displays the `home.html` page in that frame when the page loads and names the frame `"main"`.

In the code for the top frame, which is shown in Listing 13.2, you will see the following link:

```
<a style="color:#FFFFFF;" href="services.html"
    target="main">SERVICES</a>
```

When the user clicks this link, `services.html` is displayed in the frame named `main` (the lower frame). If the `target="main"` attribute had been left out, the `services.html` page would be displayed in the current (top) frame instead.

To save space, I haven't provided a listing of the services.html page; it's just a regular web page with no special frame-related features. You can see what it looks like within the frameset in Figure 13.2.

There are HTML attributes that you can use with your frame code to get rid of the frame dividers, make more space in small frames by reducing the size of the margins, and force frames not to have scrollbars. Listing 13.4 shows a modified version of the code in Listing 13.1. The two changes made to the code are the addition of the following attributes to the <frame> tags: scrolling="no" and frameborder="0".

Listing 13.4   Frameset Document for the Site Shown in Figure 13.3

```
<?xml version="1.0" encoding="UTF-8"?>
<!DOCTYPE html PUBLIC "-//W3C//DTD XHTML 1.0 Frameset//EN"
  "http://www.w3.org/TR/xhtml1/DTD/xhtml1-frameset.dtd">

<html xmlns="http://www.w3.org/1999/xhtml" xml:lang="en">
  <head>
    <title>Sample Framed Site</title>
  </head>

  <frameset rows="50,*">
    <frame src="top.html" name="top" scrolling="no" frameborder="0" />
    <frame src="home.html" name="main" scrolling="no" frameborder="0" />
    <noframes>
     <body>
       <h1>Sample Framed Site</h1>
       Your browser does not support frames. Sorry!
     </body>
    </noframes>
  </frameset>
</html>
```

FIGURE 13.3
This is the page whose code is shown in Listing 13.4 after attributes were added to the <frame /> tags.

Using Inline Frames

Inline frames do not have the same usability issues that regular frames do, but inline frames are used for different reasons. Instead of being a pure layout trick, the `<iframe>` is used much like an `<object>` tag—to place a chunk of something within an existing document. In the case of the `<object>` tag, that "something" is usually multimedia. You can use an `<iframe>` to embed an entirely separate HTML document, image, or other source. Listing 13.5 and Listing 13.6 show the code to produce the inline frame shown in Figure 13.4.

Listing 13.5   XHTML code to call an `<iframe>`

```
<?xml version="1.0" encoding="UTF-8"?>
<!DOCTYPE html PUBLIC "-//W3C//DTD XHTML 1.0 Frameset//EN"
  "http://www.w3.org/TR/xhtml1/DTD/xhtml1-frameset.dtd">

<html xmlns="http://www.w3.org/1999/xhtml" xml:lang="en">
  <head>
    <title>Using an iframe</title>
  </head>
  <body style="background-color:#CCCCCC">
     <h1 style="text-align:center">Inline Frame Example</h1>
        <div style="text-align:center">
           <iframe src="iframe_src.html"
           style="width:500px;height:100px;border:1px solid black;
           background-color:#FFFFFF">
           <p>Uh oh...your browser does not support iframes.</p>
           </iframe>
        </div>
  </body>
</html>
```

The only XHTML code you haven't yet encountered in Listing 13.5 is the `<iframe>` itself. You can see that it requires a value for the src attribute—the source—and that you can use styles to define a width, height, border type, and background color (among other things). Listing 13.6 shows the source of the `<iframe>`, which is just a regular file with some text and styles in it.

Listing 13.6   The Source of the `<iframe>` Called in Listing 13.5

```
<?xml version="1.0" encoding="UTF-8"?>
<!DOCTYPE html PUBLIC "-//W3C//DTD XHTML 1.0 Frameset//EN"
  "http://www.w3.org/TR/xhtml1/DTD/xhtml1-frameset.dtd">

<html xmlns="http://www.w3.org/1999/xhtml" xml:lang="en">
  <head>
    <title>iframe source</title>
  </head>
  <body>
        <p style="color:#FF0000;font-weight:bold">I AM A
```

Listing 13.6   The Source of the `<iframe>` Called in Listing 13.5

```
        SOURCE DOCUMENT...inside an iframe.</p>
  </body>
</html>
```

FIGURE 13.4
Listing 13.5 calls the inline frame
whose code is shown in Listing
13.6.

Inline frames are often used to bring in content from other web sites.
Common uses include serving ads to users from third-party advertising
services and using Google's Site Search to display search results to your
users (leveraging Google's search technology). Figure 13.5 shows an instance
of an `<iframe>` used to pull search results into a custom site template.

FIGURE 13.5
Using an `<iframe>` to display
Google Custom Search results.

In Figure 13.5, everything in the white area is actually content in an <iframe>, with the source being a script on Google's web site that runs and then displays content within the template at the Digital Inspiration web site. If you look closely at Figure 13.5—and I do not believe you can see it in the figure—you can see a faint grey border around the actual <iframe> itself.

Unlike the <frame /> you learned about earlier in this hour, the <iframe> is here to stay and is still a part of HTML 5.

Summary

In this hour, you learned how to display more than one page simultaneously by splitting the web browser window into frames. You learned how to use a frameset document to define the size and arrangement of the frames and you learned which web content will be loaded into each frame. You learned how to create links that change the contents of any frame you choose while leaving the other frames unchanged. You also learned about a few optional settings that control the appearance of resizable borders and scrollbars in frames. Finally, you learned how to use the inline frame to display content from your site or other web sites.

Table 13.1 summarizes the tags and attributes covered in this hour.

Table 13.1   HTML Tags and Attributes Covered in Hour 13

Tag/Attribute	Function
<frame />	Defines a single frame within a <frameset>.
Attributes	
src="url"	The URL of the document to be displayed in this frame.
id="name"	A name to be used for targeting this frame with the target attribute in <a href> links; compliant with XHTML.
name="name"	A name to be used for targeting this frame with the target attribute in <a href> links. Will eventually be replaced by id but for the time being is still useful because it works in current web browsers.
scrolling="yes/no/auto"	Determines whether a frame has scrollbars. Possible values are yes, no, and auto.

Table 13.1   HTML Tags and Attributes Covered in Hour 13

Attributes

`noresize="noresize"`	Prevents the user from resizing this frame (and possibly adjacent frames) with the mouse.
`<frameset>...</frameset>`	Divides the main window into a set of frames that can each display a separate document.

Attributes

`rows="numrows"`	Splits the window or frameset vertically into a number of rows specified by a number (such as 7), a percentage of the total window width (such as 25%), or an asterisk (*) indicating that a frame should take up all the remaining space or divide the space evenly between frames (if multiple * frames are specified).
`cols="numcols"`	Works similar to `rows`, except that the window or frameset is split horizontally into columns.
`frameborder="yes/no"`	Specifies whether to display a border for a frame. Options are 1 (yes) and 0 (no).
`<noframes>...</noframes>`	Provides an alternative document body in `<frameset>` documents for browsers that do not support frames (usually encloses `<body>...</body>`).
`<iframe>...</iframe>`	Creates an inline frame; accepts all the same attributes as does `<frame />` and can be styled with CSS.

Q&A

Q Can I display other users' web pages in one frame and my own pages in another frame at the same time? What if those other sites use frames, too?

A You can load any document from anywhere on the Internet (or an intranet) into a frame. If the document is a frameset, its frames are sized to fit within the existing frame into which you load it.

For example, you could put a list of your favorite links in one frame and use a separate frame to display the pages that those links refer to. This makes it easy to provide links to other sites without risking that someone will get lost and never come back to your own site.

You should also be aware that framing somebody else's pages so that they appear to be part of your own site might get you in legal trouble, so be sure to get explicit written permission from anyone whose pages you plan to put within one of your frames (just as you would if you were putting images or text from their site on your own pages).

Q **Do I need to put a** `<title>` **in all my frames? If I do, which title will be displayed at the top of the window?**

A The title of the frameset document is the only one that will be displayed. `<head>` and `<title>` tags are not required in framed documents, but it's a good idea to give all your pages titles just in case a user opens one by itself outside any frame.

Workshop

The workshop contains quiz questions and activities to help you solidify your understanding of the material covered. Try to answer all questions before looking at the "Answers" section that follows.

Quiz

1. Write the HTML code to list the names Mickey, Minnie, and Donald in a frame taking up the left 25% of the browser window. Make it so that clicking each name brings up a corresponding web page in the right 75% of the browser window.

2. What `<iframe>` code would produce a borderless `<iframe>` with a white background that encompasses 98% of the width of the page and is 250 pixels high?

Answers

1. You need five separate HTML documents. The first document is the frameset:

```
<html>
  <head>
    <title>Our Friends</title>
  </head>

  <frameset cols="25%,75%">
    <frame src="index.html" />
    <frame src="mickey.html" name="mainframe" />
  </frameset>
</html>
```

Next, you need the `index.html` document for the left frame:

```html
<html>
  <head>
    <title>Our Friends Index</title>
  </head>

  <body>
    <p>Pick a friend:</p>
    <p><a href="mickey.html" target="mainframe">Mickey</a><br />
      <a href="minnie.html" target="mainframe">Minnie</a><br />
      <a href="donald.html" target="mainframe">Donald</a></p>
  </body>
</html>
```

Finally, you need the three HTML pages named `mickey.html`, `minnie.html`, and `donald.html`. They contain the information about each friend.

2. Use the following code:

```html
<iframe src="some_source.html"
style="width:98%;height:250px;border:none;
  background-color:#FFFFFF">
 <p>Put message here for people not able to see the inline frame.</p>
</iframe>
```

Exercises

▶ Consider the reasons you might want to use a framed layout, and then sketch this layout on a piece of paper. Save this sketch for the upcoming lessons when you will learn to design layouts using XHTML and CSS, as these technologies offer you standards-compliant and user-friendly ways to achieve similar displays and functionality.

▶ Think of some ways you can use an `<iframe>` or two in your site—perhaps for an ad, or perhaps to leverage the free Google Site Search that you can offer to your users. Leave room in your design for that element.

Working with Margins, Padding, Alignment, and Floating

Now that you've learned some of the basics of creating web content, you'll spend this hour learning the nitty-gritty of using CSS to enhance that content. Throughout the previous hours, you have learned how to use basic CSS for display purposes (such as font sizes and colors). In the hours that follow, you'll dive in to using CSS to control aspects of your entire web "page" and not just individual pieces of text or graphics.

Before tackling page layout, however, it is important to understand four particular CSS properties individually before putting them all together:

▶ The `margin` and `padding` properties—for adding space around elements.

▶ The `align` and `float` properties—used to place your elements in relation to others.

The examples provided during this hour are not the most stylish examples of web content ever created, but they are not intended to be. Instead, the examples clearly show just how XHTML and CSS are working together. Once you master CSS through this and other hours, you'll be able to create web-based masterpieces such as the one shown in Figure 14.1, an example at CSS Zen Garden.

The sites at CSS Zen Garden probably do not look like the typical e-commerce or social networking sites that you visit on a regular basis. Instead, these sites showcase the artistic possibilities that can unfold using CSS. Make no mistake, these sites take careful thought and planning, but the potential designs are limitless.

WHAT YOU'LL LEARN IN THIS HOUR:

▶ How to add margins around elements
▶ How to add padding within elements
▶ How to keep everything aligned
▶ How to use the `float` property

FIGURE 14.1
This is one of many examples in
the CSS Zen Garden of XHTML
and CSS at work.

NOTE

Sites in the CSS Zen Garden
(http://www.csszengarden.
com/) show the types of design
that can be accomplished
through using standards-
compliant CSS. All of the user-
submitted entries in the Garden
use exactly the same HTML file,
but artists are free to modify
the CSS file to create their own
visual display. The example
shown in Figure 14.1 is by Andy
Clarke of Stuff and Nonsense
(http://www.stuffandnon-
sense.co.uk/).

Using Margins

Style sheet *margins* allow you to add empty space around the *outside* of the rectangular area for an element on a web page. It is important to remember that the `margin` property works with space outside of the element.

Following are the style properties for setting margins:

▶ `margin-top`—Sets the top margin.

▶ `margin-right`—Sets the right margin.

▶ `margin-bottom`—Sets the bottom margin.

▶ `margin-left`—Sets the left margin.

▶ `margin`—Sets the top, right, bottom, and left margins as a single property.

You can specify margins using any of the individual margin properties or using the single `margin` property. Margins can be specified as auto, meaning the browser itself sets the margin in specific lengths (pixels, points, ems) or in percentages. If you decide to set a margin as a percentage, keep in mind that the percentage is calculated based on the size of the entire page, not the size of the element. So if you set the `margin-left` property to 25%, the left margin of the element will end up being 25% of the width of the entire page.

The code in Listing 14.1 produces four rectangles on the page, each 250 pixels wide, 100 pixels high, and with a 5 pixel solid black border (see Figure 13.2). Each rectangle—or `<div>`, in this case—has a different background color. We want the margin around each `<div>` to be 15 pixels on all sides, so we can use:

```
margin-top:15px;
margin-right:15px;
margin-bottom:15px;
margin-left:15px;
```

You could also write that in shorthand, using the margin property:

```
margin:15px 15px 15px 15px;
```

When you use the margin property (or padding, or border) and you want all four values to be the same, you can simplify this even further and use:

```
margin:15px;
```

When using shorthand for setting margins, padding or borders, there are actually three approaches, which vary based on how many values you use when setting the property:

▶ One value—The size of all the margins.

▶ Two values—The size of the top/bottom margins and the left/right margins (in that order).

▶ Four values—The size of the top, right, bottom, and left margins (in that order).

You might find it easier to stick to either using one value or all four values, but that's certainly not a requirement.

Listing 14.1   Simple Code to Produce Four Colored `<div>`s with Borders and Margins

```
<?xml version="1.0" encoding="UTF-8"?>
<!DOCTYPE html PUBLIC "-//W3C//DTD XHTML 1.1//EN"
   "http://www.w3.org/TR/xhtml11/DTD/xhtml11.dtd">

<html xmlns="http://www.w3.org/1999/xhtml" xml:lang="en">
  <head>
  <title>Color Blocks</title>
```

NOTE

You can remember the shorthand order at least two different ways. First, if you think of an element as a rectangle, start at the top and work your way clockwise around the sides: top side, right side, bottom side, left side. Or you can use a first-letter mnemonic device and remember "TRBL," pronounced "trouble," which also represents a possible state of being should you forget the order of the margin properties.

Also note that the TRBL order is valid for padding properties and border properties as well.

Listing 14.1   Simple Code to Produce Four Colored `<div>`s with Borders and Margins

```
<style type="text/css">
    div {
        width:250px;
        height:100px;
        border:5px solid #000000;
        color:black;
        font-weight:bold;
        text-align:center;
    }

    div#d1 {
        background-color:red;
        margin:15px;
    }

    div#d2 {
        background-color:green;
        margin:15px;
    }

    div#d3 {
        background-color:blue;
    }

    div#d4 {
        background-color:yellow;
        margin:15px;
    }
    </style>
  </head>

  <body>
    <div id="d1">DIV #1</div>
    <div id="d2">DIV #2</div>
    <div id="d3">DIV #3</div>
    <div id="d4">DIV #4</div>
  </body>
</html>
```

Next, working with just the `margin` property in the style sheet entries in Listing 14.1, let's shift the margins around. In this example, you can't really see the right-side margin on any of these `<div>` elements because there's nothing to the right of them and they are not aligned to the right. With that

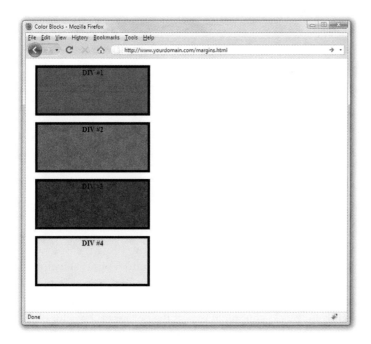

FIGURE 14.2
The basic color blocks sample
page shows four color blocks,
each with equal margins.

in mind, let's set `margin-right` to `0px` in all of these. Beyond that, the next
set of goals is to produce the following:

▶ No margin around the first color block.

▶ A left-side margin of 15 pixels, a top margin of 5 pixels, and no bottom margin around the second color block.

▶ A left-side margin of 75 pixels and no top margin or bottom margins
around the third color block.

▶ A left-side margin of 250 pixels and a top margin of 25 pixels around
the fourth color block.

This seems like it would be straightforward—no margin is being set
around the first block. Except we want a margin at the top of the second
block, so really there will be a visible margin between the first and second
blocks even if we are not specifying a margin for the first block.

The new style sheet entries for the four named `<div>`s would now look like
this:

```
div#d1 {
  background-color:red;
```

```
   margin:0px;
}

div#d2 {
   background-color:green;
   margin:5px 0px 0px 15px;
}

div#d3 {
   background-color:blue;
   margin:0px 0px 0px 75px;
}

div#d4 {
   background-color:yellow;
   margin:25px 0px 0px 250px;
}
```

The result of Listing 14.2 (see Figure 14.3) seems random but is actually quite useful for pointing out a few other important points. For example, when you recall that one of the goals was to produce no margin at all around the first color block, you might expect the border of the color block to be flush with the browser window. But as shown in Figure 14.3, there is a clear space between the content of the page and the frame of the browser window.

FIGURE 14.3
Modifications to the color blocks sample page display some different margins.

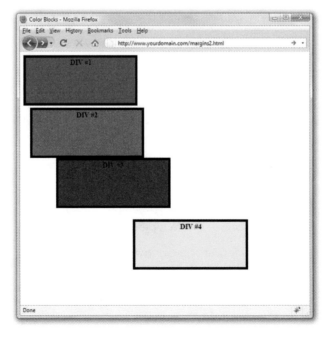

If we were working on element placement—which we will get to in the next hour—this would cause a problem in your layout. To ensure that your placements and margins are counted from a position flush with the browser, you will need to address the margin of the <body> element itself. In this case, you would add the following to your style sheet:

```
body {
  margin:0px;
}
```

Another "gotcha" to remember is that if you have two bordered elements stacked on top of each other but with no margin between them, the point at which they touch will appear to have a double border. You might then consider making the top element's border-bottom half the width, and also make the bottom element's border-top half the width. If you do this, the borders will appear to be the same width as the other sides when stacked on top of each other.

Also, you might have thought that by using a left-side margin of 250 pixels—the width of the <div>s—the fourth color block would begin where the third color block ended. That is not the case, however, because the third color block has a margin-left of 75 pixels. In order for them to even be close to lining up, the margin-left value for the fourth div would have to be 325 pixels.

Changing the styles to those shown in the code that follows produces the spacing shown in Figure 14.4. This gives the <body> element a zero margin, thus ensuring that a margin-left value of 25 pixels truly is 25 pixels from the edge of the browser frame. It also shows the second and third color blocks stacked on top of each other but with modifications to the border element so that a double border does not appear. Additionally, the fourth color block begins where the third color block ends.

```
body {
  margin:0px;
}
div {
  width:250px;
  height:100px;
  color:black;
  font-weight:bold;
  text-align:center;
}
div#d1 {
  border:5px solid #000000;
  background-color:red;
```

```
    margin:0px;
}
div#d2 {
  border-width:6px 6px 3px 6px;
  border-style:solid;
  border-color:#000000;
  background-color:green;
  margin:10px 0px 0px 15px;
}
div#d3 {
  border-width:3px 6px 6px 6px;
  border-style:solid;
  border-color:#000000;
  background-color:blue;
  margin:0px 0px 0px 15px;
}
div#d4 {
  border:5px solid #000000;
  background-color:yellow;
  margin:0px 0px 0px 265px;
}
```

FIGURE 14.4
A third modification to the color blocks pulls items into closer relation with each other.

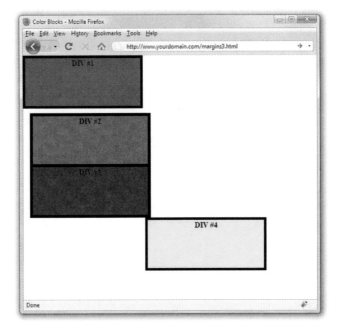

Figure 14.4 shows some overlap between the right edge of the third color block and the left edge of the fourth color block. Why is that the case, if the color blocks are 250 pixels wide, the third color block has a `margin-left` value of 15 pixels, and the fourth color block is supposed to have a 265 pixel margin to its left? Well, it does have that 265 pixel margin, but that margin size is not enough because we also have to factor in the 6 pixels of border. If we change the `margin` property for the fourth color block to reflect the following code, the third and fourth blocks line up according to plan (see Figure 14.5):

```
margin:0px 0px 0px 276px;
```

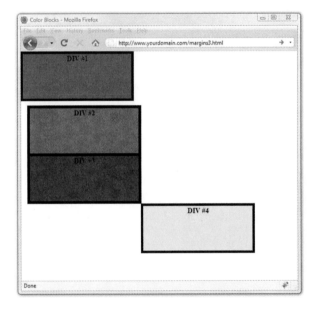

FIGURE 14.5
Changing the margin to allow for 11 pixels of border width.

As shown in these examples, margin specifications are incredibly useful for element placement but you must use caution when setting these specifications.

Padding Elements

Padding is similar to margins in that it adds extra space to elements, but the big difference is where that space is located. If you recall, margins are added to the outside of elements. On the other hand, padding adds space *inside* the rectangular area of an element. As an example, if you create a style rule for an element that establishes a width of 50 pixels and a height of 30 pixels, and then sets the padding of the rule to 5 pixels, the remaining content area will be 40 pixels by 20 pixels. Also, because the padding of an element appears within the element's content area, it will assume the same style as the content of the element, including the background color.

You specify the padding of a style rule using one of the `padding` properties, which work very much like the `margin` properties. The following padding properties are available for use in setting the padding of style rules:

- ▶ `padding-top`—Sets the top padding.
- ▶ `padding-right`—Sets the right padding.
- ▶ `padding-bottom`—Sets the bottom padding.
- ▶ `padding-left`—Sets the left padding.
- ▶ `padding`—Sets the top, right, bottom, and left padding as a single property.

As with margins, you can set the padding of style rules using individual padding properties or the single `padding` property. Padding can also be expressed using either a unit of measurement or a percentage.

Following is an example of how you might set the left and right padding for a style rule so that there are 10 pixels of padding on each side of an element's content:

```
padding-left:10px;
padding-right:10px;
```

As with margins, you can set all the padding for an element with a single property (the `padding` property). To set the padding property, you can use the same three approaches available for the `margin` property. Following is an example of how you would set the vertical padding (top/bottom) to 12 pixels and the horizontal padding (left/right) to 8 pixels for a style rule:

```
padding:12px 8px;
```

Following is more explicit code that performs the same task by specifying all the padding values:

```
padding:12px 8px 12px 8px;
```

In all of the previous figures, you'll note that the text DIV #1, DIV #2, and so on appears at the top of the colored block, with just a little space between the border and the text. That amount of space hasn't been specified by any padding value, but it appears as a sort of default within the element. But if you want specific control over your element padding, Listing 14.2 shows some examples. All of the color blocks are 250 pixels wide, 100 pixels high, have a 5 pixel solid black border, and 25 pixels of margin (see Figure 14.6). The fun stuff happens within the padding values for each individual <div>.

Listing 14.2   Simple Code to Produce Four Colored <div>s with Borders, Margins, and Padding

```
<?xml version="1.0" encoding="UTF-8"?>
<!DOCTYPE html PUBLIC "-//W3C//DTD XHTML 1.1//EN"
  "http://www.w3.org/TR/xhtml11/DTD/xhtml11.dtd">

<html xmlns="http://www.w3.org/1999/xhtml" xml:lang="en">
  <head>
    <title>Color Blocks</title>
    <style type="text/css">
      body {
        margin:0px;
      }
      div {
        width:250px;
        height:100px;
        border:5px solid #000000;
        color:black;
        font-weight:bold;
        margin:25px;
      }

      div#d1 {
        background-color:red;
        text-align:center;
        padding:15px;
      }

      div#d2 {
        background-color:green;
        text-align:right;
        padding:25px 50px 6px 6px;
      }

      div#d3 {
        background-color:blue;
        text-align:left;
        padding:6px 6px 6px 50px;
      }
```

Listing 14.2   Simple Code to Produce Four Colored <div>s with Borders, Margins, and Padding

```
div#d4 {
    background-color:yellow;
    text-align:center;
    padding:50px;
}
</style>
</head>

<body>
    <div id="d1">DIV #1</div>
    <div id="d2">DIV #2</div>
    <div id="d3">DIV #3</div>
    <div id="d4">DIV #4</div>
</body>
</html>
```

FIGURE 14.6
The basic color blocks sample page shows four color blocks with variable padding.

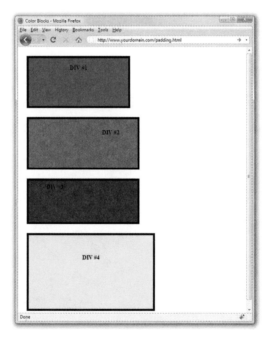

You should immediately recognize that something is amiss in this example. The color blocks are all supposed to be 250 pixels wide and 100 pixels high. The color blocks in Figure 14.6 are not uniform because despite our efforts to control the size of the <div>, the padding applied later overrides that initial size declaration.

If you place the text in a `<p>` element and give that element a white background (see Figure 14.7), you can see where the padding is in relation to the text. When there just isn't room to use all the padding that is defined, the surrounding element has to make adjustments. You will learn about this effect in detail in Hour 15, "Understanding the CSS Box Model and Positioning."

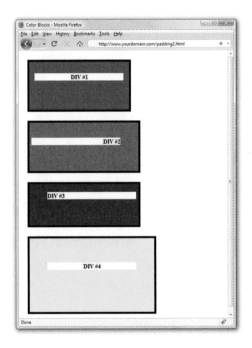

FIGURE 14.7
Showing the padding in relation to the text.

The greatest number of "tweaks" or "nudges" you make in your web design with CSS will have to do with margins and padding. Just remember: margins outside the element, padding inside it.

Keeping Everything Aligned

Knowing that content on a web page doesn't always fill the entire width of the rectangular area in which it is displayed, it is often helpful to control the alignment of the content. Even if text within a rectangular area extends to multiple lines, alignment still enters the picture because you might want the text left-justified, right-justified, or centered. There are two style properties that allow you to control the alignment of elements: `text-align` and `vertical-align`.

You saw examples of these style properties in action—aligning images—in Hour 11, but it doesn't hurt to mention these properties again here because alignment plays a role in overall page design as well.

As a refresher, using `text-align` aligns an element horizontally within its bounding area and it can be set to `left`, `right`, `center`, or `justify`.

The `vertical-align` property is similar to `text-align` except that it is used to align elements vertically. The `vertical-align` property specifies how an element is aligned with its parent, or in some cases, the current line of elements on the page. Current line refers to the vertical placement of elements that appear within the same parent element—in other words, inline elements. If several inline elements appear on the same line, you can set their vertical alignments the same to align them vertically. A good example would be a row of images that appear one after the next—the `vertical-align` property allows you to align them vertically.

Following are common values for use with the `vertical-align` property:

- ▶ `top`—Aligns the top of an element with the current line.
- ▶ `middle`—Aligns the middle of an element with the middle of its parent.
- ▶ `bottom`—Aligns the bottom of an element with the current line.
- ▶ `text-top`—Aligns the top of an element with the top of its parent.
- ▶ `baseline`—Aligns the baseline of an element with the baseline of its parent.
- ▶ `text-bottom`—Aligns the bottom of an element with the bottom of its parent.

Alignment works in conjunction with margins, padding, and—as you will learn in the next section—the `float` property to allow you to maintain control over your design.

Understanding the Float Property

Understanding the `float` property is fundamental to understanding CSS-based layout and design; it is one of the last pieces in the puzzle of how all these elements fit together. Briefly stated, the `float` property allows elements to be moved around in the design such that other elements can wrap around them. You will often find `float` used in conjunction with images (as you saw in Hour 11), but you can—and many designers do—float all sorts of elements in their layout.

Elements float horizontally, not vertically, so all you have to concern yourself with are two possible values: right and left. When used, an element that floats will float as far right or as far left (depending on the value of float) as the containing element will allow it. For example, if you have three <div>s float values of left, they will all line up to the left of the containing body element. If you have your <div>s within another <div>, they will line up to the left of *that* element, even if that element itself is floated to the right.

Floating is best understood by seeing a few examples, so let's move on to Listing 14.3. This listing simply defines three rectangular <div>s and floats them next to each other (floating to the left).

Listing 14.3   Using float to Place <div>s

```
<?xml version="1.0" encoding="UTF-8"?>
<!DOCTYPE html PUBLIC "-//W3C//DTD XHTML 1.1//EN"
  "http://www.w3.org/TR/xhtml11/DTD/xhtml11.dtd">

<html xmlns="http://www.w3.org/1999/xhtml" xml:lang="en">
  <head>
    <title>Color Blocks</title>
    <style type="text/css">
      body {
        margin:0px;
      }
      div {
        width:250px;
        height:100px;
        border:5px solid #000000;
        color:black;
        font-weight:bold;
        margin:25px;
      }

      div#d1 {
        background-color:red;
        float:left;
      }

      div#d2 {
        background-color:green;
        float:left;
      }

      div#d3 {
        background-color:blue;
        float:left;
      }
    </style>
```

Listing 14.3   Using `float` to Place `<div>`s

```
  </head>

  <body>
    <div id="d1">DIV #1</div>
    <div id="d2">DIV #2</div>
    <div id="d3">DIV #3</div>
  </body>
</html>
```

The resulting page is shown in Figure 14.8, and already you can see a problem—these three color blocks were supposed to be floated next to each other. Well, actually they are floated next to each other, except the browser window is not wide enough to display these three 250 pixel wide blocks with 25 pixels of margin between them. Since they are floating, the third one simply floats to the next line.

FIGURE 14.8
Using float to place the color blocks.

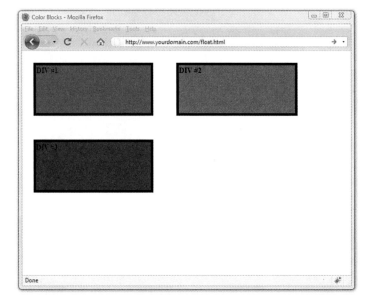

You can imagine this could be a problem in a specifically designed visual layout, so pay attention to your margins, padding, alignment, and floating while also testing within a target browser window size. Granted, the browser window shown in Figure 14.8 is a small one, to make this point about floating elements moving to the next line when there is no room for them to fit where they should. In other words, if you open the same HTML file with a larger browser window you might not see the issue—this is why you should also check your sites at different resolutions to see if a fix is needed. The "fix" here is to adjust the margins and other size-related properties of your <div>s.

Figure 14.9 shows another interesting possibility when using the float property. The only changes made to the code from Listing 14.3 involved making the color blocks only 100 pixels wide, reducing the margins to 10px, and changing the float alignment of the second color block to right (instead of left).

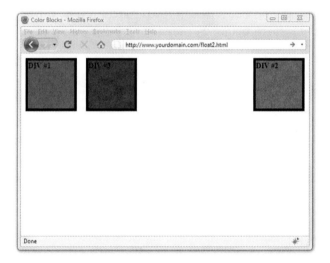

FIGURE 14.9
Using float to place the color blocks.

However, something very interesting happened. The second color block now appears visually as the third color block, as it is flush right. The second color block has a float value of right, so it has floated all the way to the right. The first and third color blocks are floating as left as possible, regardless of the way in which the <div> code appears in the HTML, which is:

```
<div id="d1">DIV #1</div>
<div id="d2">DIV #2</div>
<div id="d3">DIV #3</div>
```

Floating takes a lot of practice to get used to, especially when there are additional elements in your page and not just a few colored blocks. For example, what happens when you add a basic paragraph into the mix? All elements placed after the floating element will float around that element. To avoid that, use the clear property.

The `clear` property has five possible values: `left`, `right`, `both`, `none`, and inherit. The most common values are `left`, `right`, and `both`. Specifying `clear:left` will ensure there are no other floating elements allowed to the left, `clear:right` ensures there are no other floating elements to the right, and so on. Floating and clearing is a learn-by-doing process, so look for more situations in the workshop later in this hour.

Summary

This hour introduced you to some of the most fundamental style properties in CSS-based design: `margin`, `padding`, and `float`. You learned how the `margin` property controls space around the outside of elements and you learned how the `padding` property works with space within the elements.

After a refresher on the `text-align` and `vertical-align` properties you learned about in a previous lesson, you learned about the `float` property. The `float` property allows for specific placement of elements and additional content around those elements.

Q&A

Q The examples of margins and padding all had to do with boxes and text. Can I apply margins and padding to images as well?

A Yes, you can apply margins and padding to any block-level element, such as a `<p>`, a `<div>`, an `<img/>`, and lists such as `<ul>` and `<ol>` as well as list items (`<li>`)—just to name a few.

Workshop

The workshop contains quiz questions and activities to help you solidify your understanding of the material covered. Try to answer all questions before looking at the "Answers" section that follows.

Quiz

1. To place two `<div>` elements next to each other, but with a 30 pixel margin between them, what entry or entries can you use in the style sheet?

2. Which CSS style property and value is used to ensure that content does not appear to the left of a floating element?

3. What style sheet entry is used to place text within a `<div>` to appear 12 pixels from the top of the element?

Answers

1. You can use several. The first `<div>` uses a style property of `margin-right:15px` and the second `<div>` uses a style property of `margin-left:15px`. Or you can assign the full 30 pixels to either `<div>` using margin-right or margin-left as appropriate.

2. In this instance, use `clear:left`.

3. `padding-top:12px`

Exercises

▶ Fully understanding margins, padding, alignment, and floating takes practice. Using the color blocks code or `<div>`s of your own, practice all manner and sorts of spacing and floating before moving on to the next hour. The next hour discusses the CSS "box model" as a whole, which encompasses the individual items discussed in this hour.

▶ While you're at it, practice applying margins and padding to every block-level element you've learned so far. Get used to putting images within blocks of text and putting margins around the images so that the text does not run right up to the edge of the graphic.

Understanding the CSS Box Model and Positioning

In the previous hour, I mentioned the CSS Box Model a few times—this hour begins with a discussion of the box model and explains how the information you learned in the previous hour helps you understand this model. By learning the box model, you won't tear your hair out when you create a design and then realize the elements don't line up or that they seem a little "off." You'll know that in almost all cases, something—the margin, the padding, the border—just needs a little tweaking for it to work out.

You'll also learn more about CSS positioning, including stacking elements on top of each in a three-dimensional way (rather than a vertical way). Finally, you'll learn about controlling the flow of text around elements using the `float` property.

The CSS Box Model

Every element in HTML is considered a "box," whether it is a paragraph, a `<div>`, an image, or so on. Boxes have consistent properties, whether we see them or not, and whether they are specified at all in the style sheet or not. They're always present, and as designers, we have to keep their presence in mind when creating a layout.

Figure 15.1 is a diagram of the box model. The box model describes the way in which every HTML block-level element has the potential for a border, padding, and margin, and how the border, padding, and margin are applied. In other words, all elements have some padding between the content and the border of the element. Additionally, the border might or might not be visible, but space for it is here, just as there is a margin between the border of the element and any other content outside of the element.

WHAT YOU'LL LEARN IN THIS HOUR:

▶ How to conceptualize the CSS box model

▶ How to position your elements

▶ How to control the way elements stack up

▶ How to manage the flow of text

FIGURE 15.1
Every element in HTML is represented by the CSS Box Model.

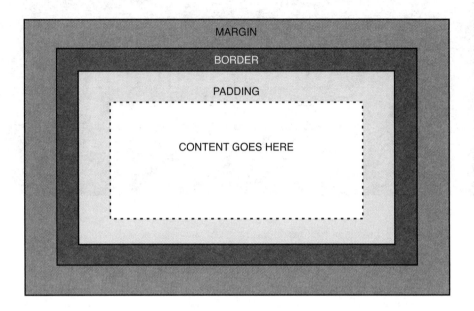

Here's yet another explanation of the box model, going from the outside inward:

▶ The *margin* is the area outside of the element. It never has color; it is always transparent.

▶ The *border* extends around the element, on the outer edge of any padding. The border can be of several types, widths, and colors.

▶ The *padding* exists around the content and inherits the background color of the content area.

▶ The *content* is surrounded by padding.

Here's where the tricky part comes in: to know the true height and width of an element, you have to take all the elements of the box model into account. If you remember the example from the previous hour when, despite specifically indicating a <div> should be 250 pixels wide and 100 pixels high, that <div> had to grow larger to accommodate the padding in use.

You already know how to set the width and height of an element using the width and height properties. The following example shows how to define a <div> that is 250 pixels wide, 100 pixels high, and has a red background, and has a black single pixel border:

```
div {
    width: 250px;
    height: 100px;
    background-color: #ff0000;
    border: 1px solid #000000;
}
```

This simple <div> is shown in Figure 15.2.

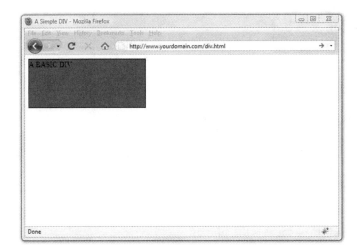

FIGURE 15.2
This is a simple <div>.

If we define a second element with these same properties, but also add
margin and padding properties of a certain size, we begin to see how the size
of the element changes. This is because of the box model.

The second <div> will be defined as follows, just adding 10 pixels of margin and 10 pixels of padding to the element:

```
div#d2 {
    width: 250px;
    height: 100px;
    background-color: #ff0000;
    border: 5px solid #000000;
    margin: 10px;
    padding: 10px;
}
```

The second <div>, shown in Figure 15.3, is defined as the same height and
width as the first one, but the overall height and width of the entire box
surrounding the element itself is much larger when margins and padding
are put in play.

FIGURE 15.3
This is supposed to be another simple <div> but the box model affects the size of the second <div>.

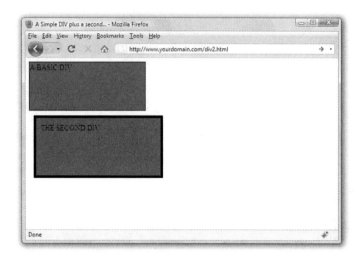

The total *width* of an element is the sum of:

```
width + padding-left + padding-right + border-left + border-right +
margin-left + margin-right
```

The total *height* of an element is the sum of:

```
height + padding-top + padding-bottom + border-top + border-bottom +
margin-top + margin-bottom
```

Therefore, the second <div> has an actual width of 300 (250 + 10 + 10 + 5 + 5 + 10 + 10) and an actual height of 150 (100 + 10 + 10 + 5 + 5 + 10 + 10).

By now you can begin to see how the box model will affect your design. Let's say you have only 250 pixels of horizontal space but you like 10 pixels of margin, 10 pixels of padding, and 5 pixels of border on all sides. To accommodate what you like with what you have room to display, you must specify the width of your <div> as only 200 pixels, so that 200 + 10 + 10 + 5 + 5 + 10 + 10 would add up to that 250 pixels of available horizontal space.

Now that you've been schooled in the way of the box model, keep it in mind throughout the rest of the work you do in this book and in your web design. Among other things, it will affect element positioning and content flow, which are the two topics we will tackle next.

NOTE

Throughout this book you've been drilled in the use of the DOCTYPE declaration—all sample code includes a DOCTYPE. Continue this practice not only so that your code validates, but because there is a very specific issue with Internet Explorer and the CSS Box Model: if a DOCTYPE is not defined, Internet Explorer manipulates the height and width of your elements in a way you did not intend. This causes browser incompatibility issues with your layout, so just remember to include a DOCTYPE.

The Whole Scoop on Positioning

Relative positioning is the default type of positioning used by HTML. You can think of relative positioning as being akin to laying out checkers on a checkerboard: The checkers are arranged from left to right, and when you get to the edge of the board, you move on to the next row. Elements that are styled with the `block` value for the `display` style property are automatically placed on a new row, whereas `inline` elements are placed on the same row immediately next to the element preceding them. As an example, `<p>` and `<div>` tags are considered block elements, whereas the `<span>` tag is considered an inline element.

The other type of positioning supported by CSS is known as *absolute positioning* because it allows you to set the exact position of HTML content on a page. Although absolute positioning gives you the freedom to spell out exactly where an element is to appear, the position is still relative to any parent elements that appear on the page. In other words, absolute positioning allows you to specify the exact location of an element's rectangular area with respect to its parent's area, which is very different from relative positioning.

With the freedom of placing elements anywhere you want on a page, you can run into the problem of overlap, which is when an element takes up space used by another element. There is nothing stopping you from specifying the absolute locations of elements such that they overlap. In this case, CSS relies on the z-index of each element to determine which element is on the top and which is on the bottom. You'll learn more about the z-index of elements later in the hour. For now, let's take a look at exactly how you control whether a style rule uses relative or absolute positioning.

The type of positioning (relative or absolute) used by a particular style rule is determined by the `position` property, which is capable of having one of the following two values: `relative` or `absolute`. After specifying the type of positioning, you then provide the specific position using the following properties:

- ▶ `left`—The left position offset.
- ▶ `right`—The right position offset.
- ▶ `top`—The top position offset.
- ▶ `bottom`—The bottom position offset.

You might think that these position properties make sense only for absolute positioning, but they actually apply to both types of positioning. Under relative positioning, the position of an element is specified as an off-set relative to the original position of the element. So if you set the `left` property of an element to 25px, the left side of the element will be shifted over 25 pixels from its original (relative) position. An absolute position, on the other hand, is specified relative to the parent of the element to which the style is applied. So if you set the `left` property of an element to 25px under absolute positioning, the left side of the element will appear 25 pixels to the right of the parent element's left edge. On the other hand, using the `right` property with the same value would position the element so that its *right* side is 25 pixels to the right of the parent's *right* edge.

Let's return to the color blocks example to show how positioning works. In Listing 15.1, the four color blocks have relative positioning specified. As you can see in Figure 15.4, the blocks are positioned vertically.

Listing 15.1   Showing Relative Positioning with Four Color Blocks

```
<?xml version="1.0" encoding="UTF-8"?>
<!DOCTYPE html PUBLIC "-//W3C//DTD XHTML 1.1//EN"
  "http://www.w3.org/TR/xhtml11/DTD/xhtml11.dtd">

<html xmlns="http://www.w3.org/1999/xhtml" xml:lang="en">
  <head>
    <title>Positioning the Color Blocks</title>
     <style type="text/css">
     div {
         position:relative;
         width:250px;
         height:100px;
         border:5px solid #000;
         color:black;
         font-weight:bold;
         text-align:center;
     }
     div#d1 {
       background-color:red;
     }

     div#d2 {
       background-color:green;
     }

     div#d3 {
       background-color:blue;
     }
```

Listing 15.1   Showing Relative Positioning with Four Color Blocks

```
      div#d4 {
        background-color:yellow;
      }
    </style>

  </head>
  <body>
    <div id="d1">DIV #1</div>
    <div id="d2">DIV #2</div>
    <div id="d3">DIV #3</div>
    <div id="d4">DIV #4</div>
  </body>
</html>
```

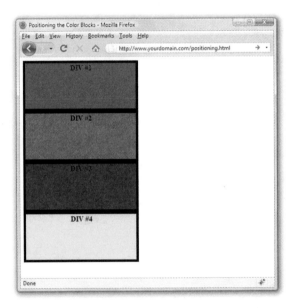

FIGURE 15.4
The color blocks are positioned vertically with one on top of the other.

The style sheet entry for the `<div>` element itself sets the `position` style property for the `<div>` element to `relative`. Because the remaining style rules are inherited from the `<div>` style rule, they inherit its relative positioning. In fact, the only difference between the other style rules is that they have different background colors.

Notice in Figure 15.4 that the `<div>` elements are displayed one after the next, which is what you would expect with relative positioning. But to make things more interesting, which is what we're here to do, you can change the positioning to absolute and explicitly specify the placement of the colors. In Listing 15.2, the style sheet entries are changed to use absolute positioning to arrange the color blocks.

Listing 15.2   Using Absolute Positioning of the Color Blocks

```
<?xml version="1.0" encoding="UTF-8"?>
<!DOCTYPE html PUBLIC "-//W3C//DTD XHTML 1.1//EN"
  "http://www.w3.org/TR/xhtml11/DTD/xhtml11.dtd">

<html xmlns="http://www.w3.org/1999/xhtml" xml:lang="en">
  <head>
    <title>Positioning the Color Blocks</title>
      <style type="text/css">
      div {
         position:absolute;
         width:250px;
         height:100px;
         border:5px solid #000;
         color:black;
         font-weight:bold;
         text-align:center;
      }
      div#d1 {
         background-color:red;
         left:0px;
         top:0px;
      }
      div#d2 {
         background-color:green;
         left:75px;
         top:25px;
      }
      div#d3 {
         background-color:blue;
         left:150px;
         top:50px;
      }
      div#d4 {
         background-color:yellow;
         left:225px;
         top:75px;
      }
      </style>
  </head>
  <body>
    <div id="d1">DIV #1</div>
    <div id="d2">DIV #2</div>
    <div id="d3">DIV #3</div>
    <div id="d4">DIV #4</div>
  </body>
</html>
```

This style sheet sets the position property to absolute, which is necessary in order for the style sheet to use absolute positioning. Additionally, the left and top properties are set for each of the inherited <div> style rules. However, the position of each of these rules is set so that the elements are displayed overlapping each other, as shown in Figure 15.5.

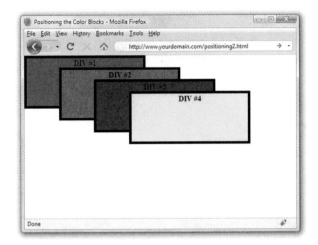

FIGURE 15.5
The color blocks are displayed using absolute positioning.

Now we're talking layout! Figure 15.5 shows how absolute positioning allows you to place elements exactly where you want them. It also reveals how easy it is to arrange elements so that they overlap each other. You might be curious as to how a web browser knows which elements to draw on top when they overlap. The next section covers how you can control stacking order.

Controlling the Way Things Stack Up

There are situations in which you'd like to carefully control the manner in which elements overlap each other on a web page. The z-index style property allows you to set the order of elements with respect to how they stack on top of each other. Although the name *z-index* might sound a little strange, it refers to the notion of a third dimension (Z) that points into the computer screen, in addition to the two dimensions that go across (X) and down (Y) the screen. Another way to think of the z-index is the relative position of a single magazine within a stack of magazines. A magazine nearer the top of the stack has a higher z-index than a magazine lower in the stack. Similarly, an overlapped element with a higher z-index is displayed on top of an element with a lower z-index.

The z-index property is used to set a numeric value that indicates the relative z-index of a style rule. The number assigned to z-index has meaning only with respect to other style rules in a style sheet, which means that setting the z-index property for a single rule doesn't mean much. On the other hand, if you set z-index for several style rules that apply to overlapped elements, the elements with higher z-index values will appear on top of elements with lower z-index values.

Listing 15.3 contains another version of the color blocks style sheet and HTML that uses z-index settings to alter the natural overlap of elements.

Listing 15.3   Using z-index to Alter the Display of Elements in the Color Blocks Sample

```
<?xml version="1.0" encoding="UTF-8"?>
<!DOCTYPE html PUBLIC "-//W3C//DTD XHTML 1.1//EN"
  "http://www.w3.org/TR/xhtml11/DTD/xhtml11.dtd">

<html xmlns="http://www.w3.org/1999/xhtml" xml:lang="en">
  <head>
    <title>Positioning the Color Blocks</title>
      <style type="text/css">
      div {
          position:absolute;
          width:250px;
          height:100px;
          border:5px solid #000;
          color:black;
          font-weight:bold;
          text-align:center;
      }
      div#d1 {
          background-color:red;
          left:0px;
          top:0px;
          z-index:0;
      }
      div#d2 {
          background-color:green;
          left:75px;
          top:25px;
          z-index:3;
      }
      div#d3 {
          background-color:blue;
          left:150px;
          top:50px;
          z-index:2;
      }
      div#d4 {
```

Listing 15.3   Using z-index to Alter the Display of Elements in the Color
                Blocks Sample

```
        background-color:yellow;
        left:225px;
        top:75px;
        z-index:1;
      }
    </style>
  </head>
  <body>
    <div id="d1">DIV #1</div>
    <div id="d2">DIV #2</div>
    <div id="d3">DIV #3</div>
    <div id="d4">DIV #4</div>
  </body>
</html>
```

The only change in this code from what you saw in Listing 15.3 is the addition of the z-index property in each of the numbered div style classes. Notice that the first numbered div has a z-index setting of 0, which should make it the lowest element in terms of the z-index, whereas the second div has the highest z-index. Figure 15.6 shows the color blocks page as displayed with this style sheet, which clearly shows how the z-index affects the displayed content and makes it possible to carefully control the overlap of elements.

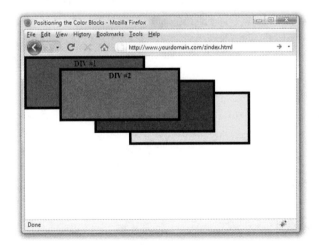

FIGURE 15.6
Using z-index to alter the display of the color blocks.

Although the examples show color blocks that are simple `<div>` elements, the `z-index` style property can impact any HTML content, including images.

Managing the Flow of Text

Now that you've seen some examples of placing elements relative to other elements or placing them absolutely, it's time to revisit the flow of content around elements. The conceptual *current line* is an invisible line used to place elements on a page. This line has to do with the flow of elements on a page; it comes into play as elements are arranged next to each other across and down the page. Part of the flow of elements is the flow of text on a page. When you mix text with other elements (such as images), it's important to control how the text flows around those other elements.

You've already seen two of these style properties in Hour 14. Following are some style properties that provide you with control over text flow:

▶ `float`—Determines how text flows around an element.

▶ `clear`—Stops the flow of text around an element.

▶ `overflow`—Controls the overflow of text when an element is too small to contain all the text.

The `float` property is used to control how text flows around an element. It can be set to either `left` or `right`. These values determine where to position an element with respect to flowing text. So setting an image's `float` property to `left` positions the image to the left of flowing text.

As you learned in the previous hour, you can prevent text from flowing next to an element by using the `clear` property, which can be set to `none`, `left`, `right`, or `both`. The default value for the clear property is `none`, indicating that text is to flow with no special considerations for the element. The `left` value causes text to stop flowing around an element until the left side of the page is free of the element. Likewise, the `right` value means that text is not to flow around the right side of the element. The `both` value indicates that text isn't to flow around either side of the element.

The `overflow` property handles overflow text, which is text that doesn't fit within its rectangular area; this can happen if you set the `width` and `height` of an element too small. The `overflow` property can be set to `visible`, `hidden`, or `scroll`. The `visible` setting automatically enlarges the element so that the overflow text will fit within it; this is the default setting for the property.

The `hidden` value leaves the element the same size, allowing the overflow text to remain hidden from view. Perhaps the most interesting value is `scroll`, which adds scrollbars to the element so that you can move around and see the text.

Summary

This hour began with the very important discussion about the CSS Box Model and how to calculate the width and height of elements when taking margins, padding, and borders into consideration. The hour continued by tackling absolute positioning of elements, and then you learned about positioning using `z-index`. You then learned about a few nifty little style properties that allow you to control the flow of text on a page.

Q&A

Q How would I determine when to use relative positioning and when to use absolute positioning?

A Although there are no set guidelines regarding the usage of relative versus absolute positioning, the general idea is that absolute positioning is required only when you want to exert a finer degree of control over how content is positioned. This has to do with the fact that absolute positioning allows you to position content down to the exact pixel, whereas relative positioning is much less predictable in terms of how it positions content. This isn't to say that relative positioning can't do a good job of positioning elements on a page; it just means that absolute positioning is more exact. Of course, this also makes absolute positioning potentially more susceptible to changes in screen size, which you can't really control.

Q If you don't specify the z-index of two elements that overlap each other, how do I know which element will appear on top?

A If the `z-index` property isn't set for overlapping elements, the element appearing later in the web page will appear on top. The easy way to remember this is to think of a web browser drawing each element on a page as it reads it from the HTML document; elements read later in the document are drawn on top of those which were read earlier.

Workshop

The workshop contains quiz questions and activities to help you solidify your understanding of the material covered. Try to answer all questions before looking at the "Answers" section that follows.

Quiz

1. What's the difference between relative positioning and absolute positioning?

2. Which CSS style property controls the manner in which elements overlap each other?

3. What HTML code could you use to display the words `"Where would you like to"` starting exactly at the upper-left corner of the browser window and displays the words `"GO TODAY?"` in large type exactly 80 pixels down and 20 pixels to the left of the corner?

Answers

1. In relative positioning, content is displayed according to the flow of a page, with each element physically appearing after the element preceding it in the HTML code. Absolute positioning, on the other hand, allows you to set the exact position of content on a page.

2. The `z-index` style property is used to control the manner in which elements overlap each other.

3. You could use:

```
<span style="position:absolute;left:0px;top:0px">
Where would you like to</span>
<h1 style="position:absolute;left:80px;top:20px">GO TODAY?</h1>
```

Exercises

▶ Practice working with the intricacies of the CSS Box Model by creating a series of elements with different margins, padding, and borders and see how these properties affect their height and width.

▶ Find a group of images that you like and use absolute positioning and maybe even some `z-index` values to arrange them in a sort of gallery. Try to place your images such that they form a design (such as a square, triangle, or circle).

Using CSS to Do More with Lists

In Hour 5, you were introduced to three types of HTML lists, and in Hour 14 you learned about margins, padding, and alignment of elements. In this hour, you will learn of how margins, padding, and alignment styles can be applied to different types of HTML lists, helping you produce some powerful design elements purely in HTML and CSS.

Specifically, you will learn how to modify the appearance of list elements—beyond the use of the `list-style-type` property that you learned in Hour 5—and how to use a CSS-styled list to replace the client-side image maps you learned about in Hour 11. You will put into practice many of the CSS styles you've learned thus far, and the knowledge you will gain in this hour will lead directly into the projects you will tackle in Hour 17, "Using CSS to Design Navigation."

HTML List Refresher

As you learned in Hour 5, there are three basic types of HTML lists. Each presents content in a slightly different way based on its type and the context:

▶ The *ordered list* is an indented list that displays numbers or letters before each list item. The ordered list is surrounded by `<ol>` and `</ol>` tags and list items are enclosed in the `<li></li>` tag pair. This list type is often used to display numbered steps or levels of content.

▶ The *unordered list* is an indented list that displays a bullet or other symbol before each list item. The unordered list is surrounded by `<ul>` and `</ul>` tags and list items are enclosed in the `<li></li>` tag pair. This list type is often used to provide a visual cue that brief, yet specific, bits of information will follow.

WHAT YOU'LL LEARN IN THIS HOUR:

▶ How the CSS Box Model affects lists

▶ How to customize the list item indicator

▶ How to use list items and CSS to create an image map

▶ A *definition list* is often used to display terms and their meanings, thereby providing information hierarchy within the context of the list itself—much like the ordered list but without the numbering. The definition list is surrounded by `<dl>` and `</dl>` tags with `<dt>` and `</dt>` tags enclosing the term and `<dd>` and `</dd>` tags enclosing the definitions.

When the content warrants it, you can nest your ordered and unordered — or place lists within other lists. Nested lists produce a content hierarchy, so reserve their use for when your content actually has a hierarchy you wish to display (such as content outlines or tables of content). Or, as you will learn in Hour 17, you can use nested lists when your site navigation contains sub-navigational elements.

How the CSS Box Model Affects Lists

NOTE

Some older browsers handle margins and padding differently, especially around lists and list items. However, at the time of writing, the HTML and CSS in this and other chapters in this book are displayed identically in current versions of the major web browsers (Apple Safari, Google Chrome, Microsoft Internet Explorer, Mozilla Firefox, and Opera). Of course, you should still review your web content in all browsers before you publish it online, but the need for "hacking" style sheets to accommodate the rendering idiosyncrasies of browsers is fading away.

Specific list-related styles include `list-style-image` (for placement of an image as a list-item marker), `list-style-position` (indicating where to place the list-item marker), and `list-style-type` (the type of list-item marker itself). But while these styles control the structure of the list and list items, you can use `margin`, `padding`, `color`, and `background-color` styles to achieve even more specific displays with your lists.

In Hour 14, you learned that every element has some padding between the content and the border of the element; you also learned there is a margin between the border of the element and any other content. This is true for lists, and when you are styling lists, you must remember that a "list" is actually made up of two elements: the parent list element type (`<ul>` or `<ol>`) and the individual list items themselves. Each of these elements has margins and padding that can be affected by a style sheet.

The examples in this hour show you how different CSS styles affect the visual display of HTML lists and list items. With these basic differences in mind, you will be able to fully control lists and, as you will practice in Hour 17, you will be able to use lists to achieve advanced visual effects within site navigation.

Listing 16.1 creates a basic list containing three items. In this listing, the unordered list itself (the `<ul>`) is given a blue background, a black border, and a specific width of 100 pixels, as shown in Figure 16.1. The list items (the individual `<li>`) have a grey background and a yellow border. The list item text and indicators (the bullet) are black.

Listing 16.1   Creating a Basic List with Color and Border Styles

```
<?xml version="1.0" encoding="UTF-8"?>
<!DOCTYPE html PUBLIC "-//W3C//DTD XHTML 1.1//EN"
  "http://www.w3.org/TR/xhtml11/DTD/xhtml11.dtd">

<html xmlns="http://www.w3.org/1999/xhtml" xml:lang="en">
  <head>
    <title>List Test</title>
    <style type="text/css">
      ul {
         background-color: #6666ff;
         border: 1px solid #000000;
         width:100px;
      }
      li {
         background-color: #cccccc;
         border: 1px solid #ffff00;
      }
    </style>
  </head>

  <body>
    <h1>List Test</h1>
    <ul>
      <li>Item #1</li>
      <li>Item #2</li>
      <li>Item #3</li>
    </ul>
  </body>
</html>
```

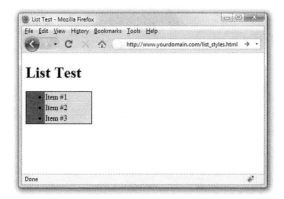

FIGURE 16.1
Styling the list and list items with colors and borders.

NOTE

You can test the default padding-left value as displayed by different browsers by creating a simple test file such as that shown in Listing 16.1, then adding `padding-left: 40px;` to the declaration for the ul selector in the style sheet. If you reload the page and the display does not change, then you know that your test browser uses 40 pixels as a default value for `padding-left`.

As shown in Figure 16.1, the `<ul>` creates a box in which the individual list items are placed. In this example, the entirety of the box has a blue background. But also note that the individual list items—in this example, they use a grey background and a yellow border—do not extend to the left edge of the box created by the `<ul>`.

This is because browsers automatically add a certain amount of padding to the left side of the `<ul>`. Browsers don't add padding to the margin, as that would appear around the outside of the box. They add padding inside the box and only on the left side. That padding value is approximately 40 pixels.

The default left-side padding value remains the same regardless of the type of list. If you add the following line to the style sheet, creating a list with no item indicators, you will find the padding remains the same (see Figure 16.2):

```
list-style-type: none;
```

FIGURE 16.2
The default left-side padding remains the same with or without list item indicators.

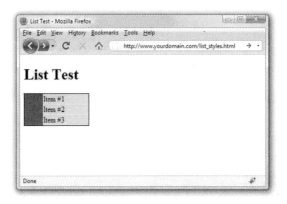

When you are creating a page layout that includes lists of any type, play around with padding to place the items "just so" on the page. Similarly, just because there is no default margin associated with lists doesn't mean you can't assign some to the display; adding margin values to the declaration for the ul selector will provide additional layout control.

But remember, so far we've worked with only the list definition itself; we haven't worked with the application of styles to the individual list items. In Figures 16.1 and 16.2, the grey background and yellow border of the list item shows no default padding or margin. Figure 16.3 shows the different effects created by applying padding or margin values to list items rather than the overall list "box" itself.

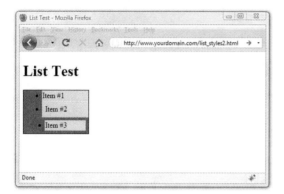

FIGURE 16.3
Different values affect the padding and margins on list items.

The first list item is the base item with no padding or margin applied to it. However, the second list item uses `style="padding: 6px;"` and you can see the six pixels of padding on all sides (between the content and the yellow border surrounding the element). Note that the placement of the bullet remains the same as the first list item. The third list item uses `style="margin: 6px;"` to apply six pixels of margin around the list item; this margin allows the blue background of the `<ul>` to show through.

Placing List Item Indicators

All this talk of margins and padding raises another issue: the control of list item indicators (when used) and how text should wrap around them (or not). The default value of the `list-style-position` property is "outside"—this placement means the bullets, numbers, or other indicators are kept to the left of the text, outside of the box created by the `<li></li>` tag pair. When text wraps within the list item, it wraps within that box and remains flush left with the left border of element.

But when the value of `list-style-position` is "inside," the indicators are inside the box created by the `<li></li>` tag pair. Not only are the list item indicators then indented further (they essentially become part of the text), the text wraps beneath each item indicator.

An example of both outside and inside list-style-positions is shown in Figure 16.4. The only changes between Listing 16.1 and the code used to produce the example shown in Figure 16.4 (not including the filler text added to "Item #2" and "Item #3") is that the second list item contains `style="list-style-position: outside;"` and the third list item contains `style="list-style-position: inside;"`.

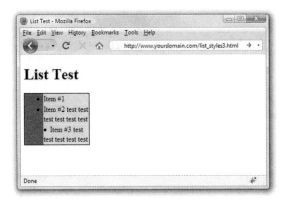

The additional filler text used for the second list item shows how the text wraps when the width of the list is defined as a value that is too narrow to display all on one line. The same result would have been achieved without using `style="list-style-position: outside;"` because that is the default value of `list-style-position` without any explicit statement in the code.

However, you can clearly see the difference when the "inside" position is used. In the third list item, the bullet and the text are both within the grey area bordered by yellow—the list item itself. Margins and padding affect list items differently when the value of `list-style-position` is `inside` (see Figure 16.5).

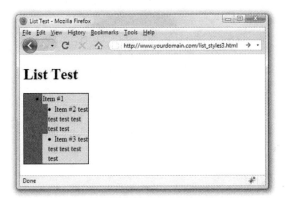

In Figure 16.5, both the second and third list items have a `list-style-position` value of `inside`. However, the second list item has a `margin-left` value of 12 pixels and the third list item has a `padding-left` value of 12 pixels. While both content blocks (list indicator plus the text) show text wrapped around the bullet, and the placement of these blocks within the grey area defining the list item is the same, the affected area is the list item within the list itself.

As you would expect, the list item with the `margin-left` value of 12 pixels displays 12 pixels of red showing through the transparent margin surrounding the list item. Similarly, the list item with the `padding-left` value of 12 pixels displays 12 pixels of grey background (of the list item) before the content begins. Padding is within the element; margin is outside the element.

By understanding the way margins and padding affect both list items and the list in which they appear, be able to create navigation elements in your web site that are pure CSS and do not rely on external images. In Hour 17, you will learn how to create both vertical and horizontal navigation menus as well as menu drop-downs.

Creating Image Maps with List Items and CSS

In Hour 11, you learned how to create client-side image maps using the `<map/>` tag in HTML. Image maps allow you to define an area of an image and assign a link to that area (rather than having to slice an image into pieces, apply links to individual pieces, and stitch the image back together in HTML). However, you can also create an image map purely out of valid XHTML and CSS.

The code in Listing 16.2 produces an image map similar to the one shown in Figure 16.6. (The code in Listing 16.2 does not produce the red borders shown in the figure. The borders were added to the figure to highlight the defined areas.) When the code is rendered in a web browser, it simply looks like a web page with an image placed in it. The actions happen when your mouse hovers over a "hot" area.

NOTE

For links to several tutorials geared toward creating XHTML and CSS image maps, visit http://designreviver.com/tutorials/css-image-map-techniques-and-tutorials/. The levels of interactivity in these tutorials differ, and some might introduce client-side coding outside of the scope of this book, but the explanations are thorough.

Listing 16.2   Creating an Image Map Using CSS

```
<?xml version="1.0" encoding="UTF-8"?>
<!DOCTYPE html PUBLIC "-//W3C//DTD XHTML 1.1//EN"
  "http://www.w3.org/TR/xhtml11/DTD/xhtml11.dtd">

<html xmlns="http://www.w3.org/1999/xhtml" xml:lang="en">
  <head>
    <title>CSS Image Map Example</title>
    <style type="text/css">
    #theImg {
       width:500px;
       height:375px;
       background:url(tea_shipment.jpg) no-repeat;
       position:relative;
       border: 1px solid #000000;
    }
    #theImg ul {
       margin:0px;
       padding:0px;
       list-style:none;
    }
    #theImg a {
       position:absolute;
       text-indent: -1000em;
    }
    #theImg a:hover {
       border: 1px solid #ffffff;
    }
    #ss a {
       top:0px;
       left:5px;
       width:80px;
       height:225px;
    }
    #gn a {
       top:226px;
       left:15px;
       width:70px;
       height:110px;
    }
    #ib a {
       top:225px;
       left:85px;
       width:60px;
       height:90px;
    }
    #iTEA1 a {
       top:100px;
       left:320px;
       width:178px;
       height:125px;
    }
```

Listing 16.2   Creating an Image Map Using CSS

```
#iTEA2 a {
    top:225px;
    left:375px;
    width:123px;
    height:115px;
}
</style>
</head>
<body>
    <div id="theImg">
    <ul>
    <li id="ss"><a href="[some URL]"
        title="Sugarshots">Sugarshots</a></li>
    <li id="gn"><a href="[some URL]"
        title="Golden Needle">Golden Needle</a></li>
    <li id="ib"><a href="[some URL]"
        title="Irish Breakfast">Irish Breakfast</a></li>
    <li id="iTEA1"><a href="[some URL]"
        title="IngenuiTEA">IngenuiTEA</a></li>
    <li id="iTEA2"><a href="[some URL]"
        title="IngenuiTEA">IngenuiTEA</a></li>
    </ul>
    </div>
    </body>
</html>
```

FIGURE 16.6
CSS allows you to define hotspots
in an image map.

As shown in Listing 16.2, the style sheet has quite a few entries but the actual HTML is quite short. List items are used to create five distinct clickable areas; those "areas" are list items given a specific height and width and placed over an image that sits in the background. If the image is removed from the background of the <div> that surrounds the list, the list items still exist and are still clickable.

Let's walk through the style sheet so that you understand the pieces that make up this XHTML and CSS image map, which is—at its most basic level—just a list of links.

The list of links is enclosed in a <div> named "theImg". In the style sheet, this <div> is defined as block element that is 500 pixels wide, 375 pixels high, and with a 1 pixel solid black border. The background of this element is an image named tea_shipment.jpg that is placed in one position and does not repeat. The next bit of HTML that you see is the beginning of the unordered list (<ul>). In the style sheet, this unordered list is given margin and padding values of zero pixels all around and a list-style of none—list items will not be preceded by any icon.

The list item text itself never appears to the user because of this trick in the style sheet entry for all <a> tags within the <div>:

```
text-indent: -1000em;
```

By indenting the text *negative* 1000 ems, you can be assured that the text will never appear. It does exist, but it exists in a non-viewable area 1000 ems to the left of the browser window. In other words, if you raise your left hand and place it to the side of your computer monitor, text-indent: -1000em places the text somewhere to the left of your pinky finger. But that's what we want because we don't need to see the text link. We just need an area to be defined as a link so that the user's cursor will change as it does when rolling over any link in a web site.

When the user's cursor hovers over a list item containing a link, that list item shows a one-pixel border that is solid white, thanks to this entry in the style sheet:

```
#theImg a:hover {
   border: 1px solid #ffffff;
}
```

The list items themselves are then defined and placed in specific positions based on the areas of the image that are supposed to be the clickable areas.

For example, the list item with the `"ss"` id, for `"Sugarshots"`—the name of the item shown in the figure—has its top-left corner placed zero pixels from the top of the `<div>` and five pixels in from the left edge of the `<div>`. This list item is 80 pixels wide and 225 pixels high. Similar style declarations are made for the `"#gn"`, `"#ib"`, `"#iTEA1"`, and `"#iTEA2"` list items, such that the linked areas associated with those ids appear in certain positions relative to the image.

Summary

This hour began with examples of how lists and list elements are affected by padding and margin styles. You first learned about the default padding associated with lists and how to control that padding. Next you learned how to modify padding and margin values and how to place the list item indicator either inside the list item or outside it, so you could begin to think about how styles and lists can affect your overall site design. Finally, you learned how to leverage lists and list elements to create a pure XHTML and CSS image map, thus reducing the need for slicing-up linked images or using the `<map/>` tag.

All of the examples in this hour were geared toward having you "think outside the (list) box," if you will, so that in the next hour you can embrace the use of unordered lists to produce horizontal or vertical navigation within your web site.

Q&A

Q There are an awful lot of web pages that talk about the "Box Model hack" regarding margins and padding, especially around lists and list elements. Are you sure I don't have to use a hack?

A At the beginning of this hour, you learned that the HTML and CSS in this hour (and others) all look the same in the current versions of the major web browsers. This is the product of several years of web developers having to do code hacks and other tricks before modern browsers began handling things according to CSS specifications rather than their own idiosyncrasies. Additionally, there is a growing movement to rid Internet users of the *very* old web browsers that necessitated most of these hacks in the first place. So, while I wouldn't necessarily advise you to design *only* for the current versions of the major web browsers, I also wouldn't recommend that you spend a ton of time implementing hacks for the older versions of browsers—which are used by less than five percent of the Internet population. You should continue to write solid code that validates and adheres to design principles, test your pages in a suite of browsers that best reflects your audience, and release your site to the world.

Q **The CSS Image Map seems like a lot of work. Is the `<map/>` tag so bad?**

A The `<map/>` tag isn't at all bad, and is valid in both XHTML and HTML 5. The determination of coordinates used in client-side image maps can be difficult, however, especially without graphics software or software intended for the creation of client-side image maps. The CSS version gives you more options for defining and displaying clickable areas, only one of which you've seen here.

Workshop

The workshop contains quiz questions and activities to help you solidify your understanding of the material covered. Try to answer all questions before looking at the "Answers" section that follows.

Quiz

1. What is the difference between the "inside" and "outside" `list-style-position` values? Which is the default value?

2. Does a `list-style` with a value of "none" still produce a structured list, either ordered or unordered?

3. What HTML code creates a list item that is 350 pixels wide, 100 pixels high, with a green background, a two-pixel dashed black border, and the list item indicator placed inside the container?

Answers

1. The `list-style-position` value of "inside" places the list item indicator inside the block created by the list item. A value of "outside" places the list item indicator outside the block. When "inside," content wraps beneath the list item indicator. The default value is "outside."

2. Yes. The only difference is that no list item indicator is present before the content within the list item.

3. Use the following code:

```
<ul>
<li style="width:350px; height:100px; background-color:#00ff00;
border:2px dashed #000000; list-style-position:inside;">text goes
here</li>
</ul>
```

Exercises

▶ Find an image and try your hand at mapping areas using the technique shown in this hour. Select an image that has areas you could use "hot spots" or clickable areas leading to other web pages on your site or to someone else's site. Then create the HTML and CSS to define the clickable areas and the URLs to which they should lead.

▶ In preparation for using lists as navigational elements in the next hour, think about your site structure and sketch out some top-level navigation as well as some secondary navigation links in those main sections. Think about whether your omnipresent navigational method will be horizontal or vertical navigation.

Using CSS to Design Navigation

WHAT YOU'LL LEARN IN
THIS HOUR

▶ How navigation lists differ
  from regular lists
▶ How to create vertical
  navigation with CSS
▶ How to create horizontal
  navigation with CSS

In the previous hour, you learned how to manipulate the appearance of lists and how to use a list for more than just simply presenting a bulleted or numbered set of items. In this lesson, you will learn a few of the many ways to use lists as vertical or horizontal navigation, including how to use lists to create drop-down menus.

The methods explained in this hour represent a very small subset of the numerous and varied navigation methods you can create using lists. However, the concepts are all similar; different results come from your own creativity and application of these basic concepts. To help you get your creative juices flowing, I will provide pointers to other examples of CSS-based navigation at the end of this hour.

How Navigation Lists Differ from Regular Lists

When we talk about using lists to create navigation elements, we really mean using CSS to display content in the way web site visitors expect navigation to look—in short, *different* from simple bulleted or numbered lists. While it is true that a set of navigation elements is essentially a list of links, those links are typically displayed in a way that makes it clear that users should interact with the content:

▶ The user's mouse cursor will change to indicate that the element is clickable.

▶ The area around the element changes appearance when the mouse hovers over it.

▶ The content area is visually set apart from regular text.

Older methods of creating navigation tended to rely on images—such as graphics with beveled edges and the use of contrasting colors for backgrounds and text—plus client-side programming with JavaScript to handle image-swapping based on mouse actions. But using pure CSS to create navigation from list elements produces a more usable, flexible, and search-engine friendly display that is accessible by users using all manner and sorts of devices.

Regardless of the layout of your navigational elements—horizontal or vertical—this hour discusses two levels of navigation: primary and secondary. *Primary navigation* takes users to the introductory pages of main sections of your site; *secondary navigation* reflects those pages within a certain section.

▼ TRY IT YOURSELF

Create Site-Wide Navigation

In the exercise at the end of the previous hour, you were asked to think about a navigational structure you might use within your own web site. If you have the information architecture in mind—the sections of information and, when necessary, the sub-sections—that's a good start. You can use that outline throughout this hour to create both vertical and horizontal navigation using that structure as a base.

Creating Vertical Navigation with CSS

Depending on your site architecture—both the display template you have created and the manner in which you have categorized the information in the site—you might find yourself using vertical navigation for either primary navigation or secondary navigation.

For example, suppose you have created a web site for your company and the primary sections are About Us, Products, Support, and Press. Within the primary About Us section, you might have several other pages, such as Mission, History, Executive Team, and Contact Us—these other pages are the secondary navigation within the primary About Us section.

Listing 17.1 sets up a basic secondary page with vertical navigation in the side of the page and content in the middle of the page. The links in the side and the links in the content area of the page are basic HTML list elements.

This listing and the example shown in Figure 17.1 provides a starting point for showing you how CSS enables you to transform two similar HTML structures into two different visual displays (and thus two different contexts).

Listing 17.1   Basic Page with Vertical Navigation in a List

```
<?xml version="1.0" encoding="UTF-8"?>
<!DOCTYPE html PUBLIC "-//W3C//DTD XHTML 1.1//EN"
  "http://www.w3.org/TR/xhtml11/DTD/xhtml11.dtd">

<html xmlns="http://www.w3.org/1999/xhtml" xml:lang="en">
  <head>
    <title>About Us</title>
    <style type="text/css">
      body {
          font: 12pt Verdana, Arial, Georgia, sans-serif;
      }
      #nav {
          width:150px;
          float:left;
          margin-top:12px;
          margin-right:18px;
      }
      #content {
          width:550px;
          float:left;
      }
    </style>
  </head>

  <body>
    <div id="nav">
    <ul>
      <li><a href="#">Mission</a></li>
      <li><a href="#">History</a></li>
      <li><a href="#">Executive Team</a></li>
      <li><a href="#">Contact Us</a></li>
    </ul>
    </div>
    <div id="content">
      <h1>About Us</h1>
      <p>On the introductory pages of main sections, it can be useful
      to repeat the secondary navigation and provide more context,
      such as:</p>
      <ul>
      <li><a href="#">Mission</a>: Learn more about our corporate
      mission and philanthropic efforts.</li>
      <li><a href="#">History</a>: Read about our corporate history
      and learn how we grew to become the largest widget maker
      in the country.</li>
      <li><a href="#">Executive Team</a>: Our team of executives makes
      the company run like a well-oiled machine (also useful for
      making widgets).</li>
      <li><a href="#">Contact Us</a>: Here you can find multiple
      methods for contacting us (and we really do care what you
      have to say).</li>
      </ul>
    </div>
  </body>
</html>
```

FIGURE 17.1
The starting point: unstyled list
navigation.

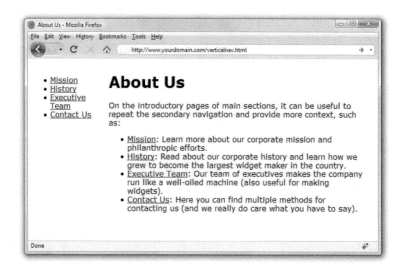

The contents of this page are set up in two `<div>` elements that sit next to each other: one is given an `id` value of `nav` and the other is given an `id` value of `content`. The only styles assigned to anything in this basic page are the width, margin, and float values associated with each `<div>`. No styles have been applied to the list elements.

To differentiate between the links present in the list in the content area and the links present in the list in the side navigation, add the following styles to the style sheet:

```
#nav a {
   text-decoration: none;
}
#content a {
   text-decoration: none;
   font-weight: bold;
 }
```

These styles simply say that all `<a>` links in the `<div>` with the `id` of `nav` have no underline and all `<a>` links in the `<div>` with the `id` of `content` have no underline and are bold. The difference is shown in Figure 17.2.

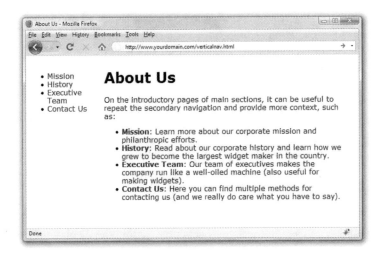

FIGURE 17.2
Differentiating the list elements using CSS.

But to really make the side navigation list look like something special, you have to dig deeper into the style sheet.

Styling the Single-Level Vertical Navigation

The goal with this particular set of navigation elements is simply to present them as a block of links without bullets and with background and text colors that change depending on their link state (regular link, visited link, hovering over the link, or activated link). The first step in the process is already complete: separating the navigation from the content. We have done that by putting the navigation in a `<div>` with an `id` of `nav`.

Next, you need to modify the `<ul>` that defines the link within the `nav` `<div>`. Let's take away the list indicator and ensure that there is no extra margin or padding hanging around besides the top margin. That top margin is used to line up the top of the navigation with the top of the "About Us" header text in the content area of the page:

```
#nav ul {
   list-style: none;
   margin: 12px 0px 0px 0px;;
   padding: 0px;
}
```

Since the navigation list items themselves appear as colored areas, give each list item a bottom border so that some visual separation of the content can occur:

```
#nav li {
   border-bottom: 1px solid #ffffff;
}
```

Now on to building the rest of the list items. The idea is that when the list items simply sit there acting as links, they are a special shade of blue with bold white text (although they are a smaller font size than the body text itself). To achieve that, add the following:

```
#nav li a:link, #nav li a:visited {
    font-size: 10pt;
    font-weight: bold;
    display: block;
    padding: 3px 0px 3px 3px;
    background-color: #628794;
    color: #ffffff;
}
```

All of the styles used previously should be familiar to you, except perhaps the use of `display: block;` in the style sheet entry. Setting the display property to block ensures that the entire `<li>` element is in play when a user hovers his mouse over it. Figure 17.3 shows the vertical list menu with these new styles applied to it.

FIGURE 17.3
The vertical list is starting to look like a navigation menu.

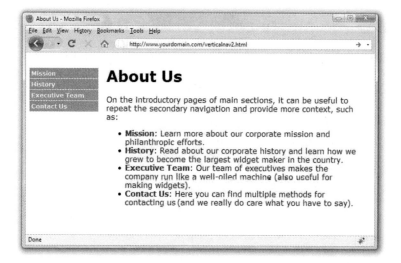

When the user's mouse hovers over a navigational list element, the idea is that some visual change takes place so the user knows the element is clickable. This is akin to how most software menus change color when a user's cursor hovers over the menu items. In this case, we'll change the background color of the list item and we'll change the text color of the list item; they'll be different from the blue and white shown previously.

```
#nav li a:hover, #nav li a:active {
    font-size: 10pt;
    font-weight: bold;
    display: block;
    padding: 3px 0px 3px 3px;
    background-color: #6cac46;
    color: #000000;
}
```

Figure 17.4 shows the results of all the stylistic work so far. By using a few entries in a style sheet, the simple list has been transformed into a visually differentiated menu.

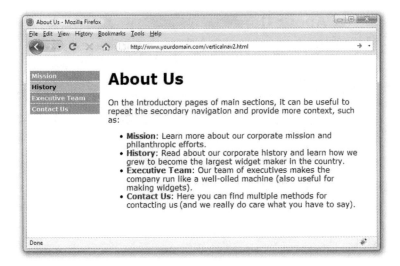

FIGURE 17.4
The list items now change color when the mouse hovers over them.

Styling the Multi-Level Vertical Navigation

What if your site architecture calls for another level of navigation that you want your users to see at all times? That is represented by nested lists (which you learned about in previous hours) and more style sheet entries. In this case, assume that there are four navigation elements under the Executive Team link. In the HTML, modify the list as follows:

```
<ul>
  <li><a href="#">Mission</a></li>
  <li><a href="#">History</a></li>
  <li><a href="#">Executive Team</a>
    <ul>
```

```
    <li><a href="#">&raquo; CEO</a>
    <li><a href="#">&raquo; CFO</a>
    <li><a href="#">&raquo; COO</a>
    <li><a href="#">&raquo; Other Minions</a>
    </ul>
  </li>
  <li><a href="#">Contact Us</a></li>
</ul>
```

This code produces a nested list under the Executive Team link (see Figure 17.5). The » HTML entity produces the right-pointing arrows that are displayed before the text in the new links.

FIGURE 17.5
Creating a nested navigation list (but one that is not yet styled well).

The new items appear as block elements within the list, but the hierarchy of information is not visually represented. To add some sort of visual element that identifies these items as sub-navigational elements attached to the Executive Team link, modify the style sheet again to add some indentation.

But before doing that, modify some of the other style sheet entries as well. In the previous section, we added selectors such as #nav ul and #nav li, which indicate "all <ul> in the <div> called nav" and "all <li> in the <div> called nav," respectively. However, we now have two instances of <ul> and another set of <li> elements with the <div> called nav, all of which we want to appear different from the original set.

To ensure both sets of list items are styled appropriately, make sure that the style sheet selectors clearly indicate the hierarchy of the lists. To do that, use entries such as #nav ul and #nav ul li for the first level of lists and #nav ul ul and #nav ul ul li for the second level of lists. Listing 17.2

shows the new version of style sheet entries and HTML that produces the menu shown in Figure 17.6.

Listing 17.2   Muli-Level Vertical Navigation in a List

```
<?xml version="1.0" encoding="UTF-8"?>
<!DOCTYPE html PUBLIC "-//W3C//DTD XHTML 1.1//EN"
  "http://www.w3.org/TR/xhtml11/DTD/xhtml11.dtd">

<html xmlns="http://www.w3.org/1999/xhtml" xml:lang="en">
  <head>
    <title>About Us</title>
    <style type="text/css">
      body {
          font: 12pt Verdana, Arial, Georgia, sans-serif;
      }
      #nav {
          width:150px;
          float:left;
          margin-top:12px;
          margin-right:18px;
      }
      #content {
          width:550px;
          float:left;
      }
      #nav a {
          text-decoration: none;
      }
      #content a {
          text-decoration: none;
          font-weight: bold;
      }
      #nav ul {
          list-style: none;
          margin: 12px 0px 0px 0px;
          padding: 0px;
      }
      #nav ul li {
          border-bottom: 1px solid #ffffff;
      }
      #nav ul li a:link, #nav ul li a:visited {
          font-size: 10pt;
          font-weight: bold;
          display: block;
          padding: 3px 0px 3px 3px;
          background-color: #628794;
          color: #ffffff;
      }
      #nav ul li a:hover, #nav ul li a:active {
          font-size: 10pt;
          font-weight: bold;
```

Listing 17.2   Muli-Level Vertical Navigation in a List

```
      display: block;
      padding: 3px 0px 3px 3px;
      background-color: #c6a648;
      color: #000000;
    }
    #nav ul ul {
      margin: 0px;
      padding: 0px;
    }
    #nav ul ul li {
      border-bottom: none;
    }
    #nav ul ul li a:link, #nav ul ul li a:visited {
      font-size: 8pt;
      font-weight: bold;
      display: block;
      padding: 3px 0px 3px 18px;
      background-color: #628794;
      color: #ffffff;
    }
    #nav ul ul li a:hover, #nav ul ul li a:active {
      font-size: 8pt;
      font-weight: bold;
      display: block;
      padding: 3px 0px 3px 18px;
      background-color: #c6a648;
      color: #000000;
    }
  </style>
</head>

<body>
  <div id="nav">
  <ul>
    <li><a href="#">Mission</a></li>
    <li><a href="#">History</a></li>
    <li><a href="#">Executive Team</a>
      <ul>
      <li><a href="#">&raquo; CEO</a>
      <li><a href="#">&raquo; CFO</a>
      <li><a href="#">&raquo; COO</a>
      <li><a href="#">&raquo; Other Minions</a>
      </ul>
    </li>
    <li><a href="#">Contact Us</a></li>
  </ul>
  </div>
  <div id="content">
    <h1>About Us</h1>
    <p>On the introductory pages of main sections, it can be useful
    to repeat the secondary navigation and provide more context,
```

Listing 17.2   Muli-Level Vertical Navigation in a List

```
such as:</p>
<ul>
<li><a href="#">Mission</a>: Learn more about our corporate
mission and philanthropic efforts.</li>
<li><a href="#">History</a>: Read about our corporate history
and learn how we grew to become the largest widget maker
in the country.</li>
<li><a href="#">Executive Team</a>: Our team of executives makes
the company run like a well-oiled machine (also useful for
making widgets).</li>
<li><a href="#">Contact Us</a>: Here you can find multiple
methods for contacting us (and we really do care what you
have to say.</li>
</ul>
</div>
</body>
</html>
```

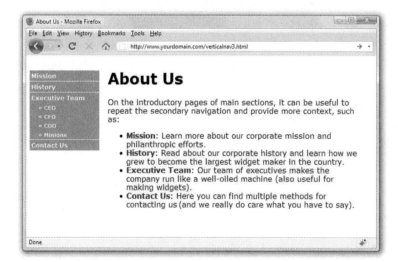

FIGURE 17.6
Creating two levels of vertical navigation using CSS.

The different ways of styling vertical navigation are limited only by your own creativity. You can use colors, margins, padding, background images, and any other valid CSS to produce vertical navigation that is quite flexible and easily modified. If you type **CSS vertical navigation** in your search engine, you will find thousands of examples—and they are all based on the simple principles you've learned in this hour.

Creating Horizontal Navigation with CSS

This hour began with vertical navigation because the concept of converting a list into navigation is easier to grasp when the navigation still looks like a list of items that you might write vertically on a piece of paper, like a grocery list. When creating horizontal navigation, you still use HTML list elements but instead of a vertical display achieved by using the inline value of the display property for both the <ul> and the <li>, use the block value of the display property instead. It really is as simple as that.

Listing 17.3 shows a starting point for a page featuring horizontal navigation. The page contains two main <div> elements: one for the header and one for the content. The header <div> contains a logo <div> and a navigation <div> floated next to each other. The list that appears in the navigation <div> has a display property value of inline for both the list and the list items. You can see these elements and their placement in Figure 17.7.

Listing 17.3   Basic Horizontal Navigation from a List

```
<?xml version="1.0" encoding="UTF-8"?>
<!DOCTYPE html PUBLIC "-//W3C//DTD XHTML 1.1//EN"
  "http://www.w3.org/TR/xhtml11/DTD/xhtml11.dtd">

<html xmlns="http://www.w3.org/1999/xhtml" xml:lang="en">
  <head>
    <title>ACME Widgets LLC</title>
    <style type="text/css">
      body {
         font: 12pt Verdana, Arial, Georgia, sans-serif;
      }
      #header {
         width: auto;
      }
      #logo {
         float:left;
      }
      #nav {
         float:left;
      }
      #nav ul {
         list-style: none;
         display: inline;
      }
      #nav li {
         display: inline;
      }
      #content {
```

Listing 17.3   Basic Horizontal Navigation from a List

```
          width: auto;
          float: left;
          clear: left;
      }
      #content a {
          text-decoration: none;
          font-weight: bold;
      }
    </style>
  </head>
  <body>
    <div id="header">
      <div id="logo">
        <img src="acmewidgets.jpg" alt="ACME Widgets LLC" />
      </div>
      <div id="nav">
        <ul>
        <li><a href="#">About Us</a></li>
        <li><a href="#">Products</a></li>
        <li><a href="#">Support</a></li>
        <li><a href="#">Press</a></li>
        </ul>
      </div>
    </div>
    <div id="content">
      <p><strong>ACME Widgets LLC</strong> is the greatest widget-maker
      in all the land.</p>
      <p>Don't believe us? Read on...</p>
      <ul>
      <li><a href="#">About Us</a>: We are pretty great.</li>
      <li><a href="#">Products</a>: Our products are the best.</li>
      <li><a href="#">Support</a>: It is unlikely you will need support,
      but we provide it anyway.</li>
      <li><a href="#">Press</a>: Read what others are saying (about how
      great we are).</li>
      </ul>
    </div>
  </body>
</html>
```

FIGURE 17.7
Creating functional—but not necessarily beautiful—horizontal navigation using inline list elements.

Modifying the display of this list occurs purely through CSS; the structure of the content within the HTML itself is already set. To achieve the desired display, use the following CSS. First, the `<div>` with the `id` of `nav` is modified to be a particular width, display a background color and border, and use a top margin of 85 pixels (so that it displays near the bottom of the logo).

```
#nav {
    float:left;
    margin: 85px 0px 0px 0px;
    width: 400px;
    background-color: #628794;
    border: 1px solid black;
}
```

The definition for the `<ul>` remains the same as in Listing 17.3 except for the changes in margin and padding:

```
#nav ul {
    margin: 0px;
    padding: 0px;
    list-style: none;
    display: inline;
}
```

The definition for the `<li>` remains the same as in Listing 17.3 except it has been given a `line-height` value of `1.8em`:

```
#nav li {
    display: inline;
    line-height: 1.8em;
}
```

The link styles are similar to those used in the vertical navigation; these entries have different padding values, but the colors and font sizes remain the same:

```
#nav ul li a:link, #nav ul li a:visited {
    font-size: 10pt;
    font-weight: bold;
    text-decoration: none;
    padding: 7px 10px 7px 10px;
    background-color: #628794;
    color: #ffffff;
}
#nav ul li a:hover, #nav ul li a:active {
    font-size: 10pt;
    font-weight: bold;
    text-decoration: none;
    padding: px 10px 7px 10px;
    background-color: #c6a648;
    color: #000000;
}
```

Putting these styles together, you produce the display shown in Figure 17.8.

FIGURE 17.8
Creating horizontal navigation with some style.

When the user rolls over the navigation elements, the background and text colors change in the same way they did when the user hovered her mouse over the vertical navigation menu. Also, just as you did with the vertical navigation menu, you can use nested lists to produce drop-down functionality in your horizontal menu. Try it yourself!

Summary

In this hour you learned how to use CSS to turn simple HTML unordered lists into horizontal and vertical navigation. By using CSS instead of graphics or JavaScript or other technologies, you will have more flexibility in both the display and maintenance of your site. Throughout this hour you learned that with a few entries in your style sheet, you can turn plain underlined text links into areas with borders and background colors and other text styles. Additionally, you learned how to present nested lists within menus.

Q&A

Q **Can I use graphics in the navigation menus as a custom list indicator?**

A Yes. You can use graphics within the HTML text of the list item or as background images within the `<li>` element. You can style your navigation elements just as you style any other list element. The only differences between an HTML unordered list and a CSS-based horizontal or vertical navigation list is that you are calling it that and you are using the unordered list for a specific purpose outside of the body of the text. Along with that, you then style the list to show the user that it is indeed something different—and you can do that with small graphics to accentuate your lists.

Q **Where can I find more examples of what I can do with lists?**

A The last time I checked, typing **CSS navigation** in a search engine returned approximately 44 million results. Here are a few starting places:

▶ A List Apart's CSS articles at http://www.alistapart.com/topics/code/

▶ Maxdesign's CSS Listamatic at http://css.maxdesign.com.au/listamatic/

▶ Vitaly Friedman's CSS Showcase at `http://www.alvit.de/css-showcase/`

Workshop

The workshop contains quiz questions and activities to help you solidify your understanding of the material covered. Try to answer all questions before looking at the "Answers" section that follows.

Quiz

1. When creating list-based navigation, how many levels of nested lists can you use?

2. True or False: using an `inline` value for the `display` property produces a horizontal list.

3. When creating a navigation list of any type, can the four pseudo-classes for the `a` selector have the same values?

Answers

1. Technically, you can nest your lists as deep as you want to. But from a usability standpoint, there is a limit to the number of levels that you would *want* to use to nest your lists. Three levels is typically the limit—more than that and you run the risk of creating a poorly organized site or simply giving the user more options than they need to see at all times.

2. True, if the `display` property is provided for the `ul` and `li` selectors in the style sheet.

3. Sure, but then you run the risk of users not realizing that your beautiful menus are indeed menus (since no visual display would occur for a mouse action).

Exercises

▶ Using the techniques shown for a multi-level vertical list, add sub-navigation items to the vertical list created at the end of the chapter.

▶ Look at the numerous examples of CSS-based navigation used in web sites and find some tricky-looking actions. Using the "view source" function of your web browser, look at the CSS used by these sites and try to implement something similar for yourself.

Using Mouse Actions to Modify Text Display

Throughout this book, you have seen examples of how mouse actions can affect the display of text. The simplest example is when the hover pseudo-class of the <a> link is defined in the style sheet to display text in a different color when a user's mouse hovers over it. In the previous hour, you learned how the hover pseudoclass changed both the text color and the background color of an <li> element.

In this hour, you'll learn how to achieve two specific actions that combine CSS and mouse actions—displaying additional text when an item is rolled over with the mouse, and using a mouse click to change the color of a container element. These two actions are useful in some circumstances to be sure; but, more importantly, they provide an entry point into more advanced work you might want to tackle later on in your web development.

Creating a Tool Tip with CSS

A *tooltip* is an element within a graphical user interface—could be a software program, could be a web site—that provides additional information when a cursor hovers over a specific item. Figure 18.1 shows a tooltip in action: the mouse rolls over the linked text "HTML" and the tooltip displays "HTML" in a small box. In this case, the text displayed in the tooltip comes from the title attribute of the <a> tag.

FIGURE 18.1
A standard tooltip in action.

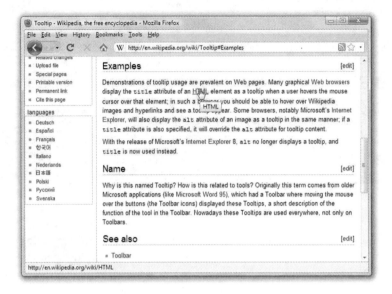

The display of the tooltip shown in Figure 18.1 is controlled by the soft-ware itself. That is, its display and appearance is not something you (as web developer) can control. However, you can create your own tooltips with a little CSS by applying concepts you've already practiced in previous hours.

Listing 18.1 contains the style sheet entries and HTML for a page that con-tains images and links, but with one link that also displays a custom tool tip.

Listing 18.1   Creating a Simple Tool Tip with CSS

```
<?xml version="1.0" encoding="UTF-8"?>
<!DOCTYPE html PUBLIC "-//W3C//DTD XHTML 1.1//EN"
  "http://www.w3.org/TR/xhtml11/DTD/xhtml11.dtd">

<html xmlns="http://www.w3.org/1999/xhtml" xml:lang="en">
  <head>
    <title>Steptoe Butte</title>
    <style type="text/css">
    a {
       text-decoration: none;
       font-weight: bold;
    }
    a.tip {
       position:relative;
       z-index:24;
    }
```

Listing 18.1   Creating a Simple Tool Tip with CSS

```
    a.tip:hover {
       z-index:25;
    }
    a.tip span {
       display: none;
    }
    a.tip:hover span {
       font-weight: normal;
       display: block;
       position: absolute;
       top: 20px;
       left: 25px;
       width: 150px;
       padding: 3px;
       border:1px solid #000;
       background-color:#ddd;
       color:#000;
    }
    </style>
  </head>
  <body>
    <h1>Steptoe Butte</h1>
    <p><img src="steptoebutte.jpg" alt="View from Steptoe Butte"
    style="float:left;margin-right:12px;margin-bottom:6px;border:1px
    solid #000" />Steptoe Butte is a quartzite island jutting out of the
    silty loess of the <a class="tip"
    href="http://en.wikipedia.org/wiki/Palouse">Palouse <span>Learn more
    about the Palouse!</span></a> hills in Whitman County, Washington. The
    rock that forms the butte is over 400 million years old, in contrast
    with the 15-7 million year old
    <a href="http://en.wikipedia.org/wiki/Columbia_River">Columbia River</a>
    basalts that underlie the rest of the Palouse (such "islands" of ancient
    rock have come to be called buttes, a butte being defined as a small hill
    with a flat top, whose width at top does not exceed its height).</p>
    <p>A hotel built by Cashup Davis stood atop Steptoe Butte from 1888 to
    1908, burning down several years after it closed. In 1946, Virgil McCroskey
    donated 120 acres (0.49 km2) of land to form Steptoe Butte State Park,
    which was later increased to over 150 acres (0.61 km2). Steptoe Butte is
    currently recognized as a National Natural Landmark because of its unique
    geological value. It is named in honor of
    <a href="http://en.wikipedia.org/wiki/Colonel_Edward_Steptoe">Colonel Edward
    Steptoe</a>.</p>
    <p>Elevation: 3,612 feet (1,101 m), approximately 1,000 feet (300 m) above
the
    surrounding countryside.</p>
    <p><em>Text from
    <a href="http://en.wikipedia.org/wiki/Steptoe_Butte">Wikipedia</a>, photo by
    the author.</em></p>
  </body>
</html>
```

Note that the first link in the text has a class associated with it. That `class` is called `tip`—that name differentiates it from other links that do not contain tooltips. However, because this is a `class` and not an `id`, it could be used for all of the other links in the page as well.

Note that the `tip` class itself has a defined `position` and `z-index`. The `position` values (`relative`) ensures that it remains presented as it naturally occurs in the text; the `z-index`, when compared to the `z-index` used by other related styles, ensures that the text of the link remains below other text with higher `z-index` values. The hover state of links using the `tip` class has a higher `z-index` value, for example.

The next two styles relate to the `<span>` tag in use. Text within the `<span>` tag within the `<a>` tag will not be displayed unless the tooltip is invoked by hovering the mouse over the visible link. For example, the link text looks like this:

```
<a class="tip" href="http://en.wikipedia.org/wiki/Palouse">Palouse
<span>Learn more about the Palouse!</span></a>
```

When you look at this bit of HTML, it looks like the words "Palouse Learn more about the Palouse!" should all be a link. However, since "Learn more about the Palouse!" is enclosed in the `<span>` tag, and a specific style is applied to that `<span>` in the style sheet, the words do not appear until the user's mouse hovers over the actual link (the word "Palouse"). Figure 18.2 displays this result.

The text "Learn more about the Palouse!" is placed in a `<span>` tag in the HTML but is styled within the style sheet. Namely, the `a.tip:hover span` selector creates a box that is 150 pixels wide with a grey background and black border. This box appears 20 pixels from the top of the element and 25 pixels in from the left of the parent element. This creates the tooltip.

FIGURE 18.2
A custom tooltip appears when the mouse hovers over the first link in the page.

Displaying Additional Rollover Text with CSS

A tooltip serves a specific purpose: to show a textual "tip" attached to a link. But you can use the same concept to show hidden text somewhere else in your layout, based on a mouse action. Take, for example, the ACME Widgets LLC main page from Hour 17—the version with horizontal navigation. By using the same concepts as those used in Listing 17.1, you can show additional text above the menu when users roll over one of the main section links. Figure 18.3 shows one of these in action; I recaptured some of that white space above the navigation and to the right of the logo.

FIGURE 18.3
Custom text above another element, visible only on rollover.

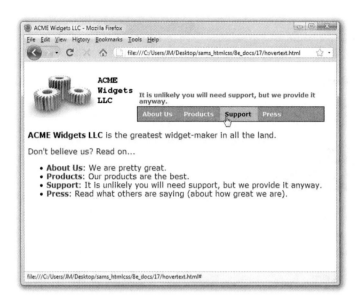

The only change made to the CSS from Listing 18.3 is the addition of the
following four styles. They perform the same tasks as the `tip` class styles
used in Listing 18.1 but the display is slightly different than the display in
Listing 18.1.

```
a.more {
    position:relative;
    z-index:24;
}
a.more:hover {
    z-index:25;
}
a.more span {
    display: none;
}
a.more:hover span {
    font-weight: bold;
    display: block;
    position: absolute;
    top: -35px;
    width: 400px;
    padding: 3px;
    color:#ff0000;
    line-height: 1em;
}
```

The value of -25px for the `top` property places the text enclosed in the
`<span>` tag 25 pixels above the top-left corner of the parent tag, as opposed

to the previous example, which placed it 20 pixels below the top-left corner of the parent tag. The changes to the HTML are similar to the changes in the previous section in that the text that is hidden until rollover appears in a `<span>` tag within an `<a>` link:

```
<ul>
  <li><a class="more" href="#">About Us <span>We are pretty
  great.</span></a></li>
 <li><a class="more" href="#">Products <span>Our products are
  the best.</span></a></li>
 <li><a class="more" href="#">Support <span>It is unlikely you
  will need support, but we provide it anyway.</span></a></li>
  <li><a class="more" href="#">Press <span>Read what others are
  saying (about how great we are).</span></a></li>
</ul>
```

Using these basic concepts, you can make any text appear anywhere you wish based on the user's mouse actions when hovering over an `<a>` link. In the next section, you'll learn how to use event attributes plus a little JavaScript to do even more with mouse actions and CSS.

Accessing Events

A user interaction such as a mouse click or key press is known as an *event*. The process of a script taking action based on an event is known as *event handling*. You use special attributes to associate event-handling script code with elements on a web page.

Following are some of the commonly used event attributes that come in handy in JavaScript, along with a description of when they occur with respect to a web page element:

- ▶ onload—Browser loads the element.

- ▶ onkeydown—User presses a key.

- ▶ onkeyup—User releases a key.

- ▶ onclick—User clicks the element with the left mouse button.

- ▶ ondblclick—User double-clicks the element with the left mouse button.

- ▶ onmousedown—User presses either mouse button while the mouse pointer is over the element.

- ▶ onmouseup—User releases either mouse button while the mouse pointer is over the element.

▶ onmouseover—User moves the mouse pointer into the boundaries of the element.

▶ onmousemove—User moves the mouse pointer while the pointer is over the element.

▶ onmouseout—User moves the mouse pointer out of the boundaries of the element.

As you can see, event attributes are used to responding to common user input events such as mouse clicks and key presses. You can associate JavaScript with an event by assigning the code to the event attribute, like this:

```
<h1 onclick="this.style.color = 'red';">I turn red when clicked.</h1>
```

In the code example above, a JavaScript snippet is assigned to the onclick event attribute of an <h1> tag, which means that the code runs in response to users clicking the left mouse button on the text. The script code responds by setting the color of the text to red. In this way, interactivity is added to normally bland text by changing the color of the text in response to a mouse click. This is the basis for how client-side scripts work in conjunction with your web browser.

In the next section, you'll see an example of how to use event handling to change the appearance of a <div>. Specifically, the contents of a <div> appear or disappear based on a mouse click.

Using onclick **to Change** <div> Appearance

The onclick event can be used to invoke all sorts of action; you might think of a mouse click as a way to submit a form by clicking on a button, but you can capture this event and use it to provide interactivity within your pages as well. In this example, you will see how you can use the onclick event to show or hide information contained in a <div>. Using the same text and image from in Listing 18.1 you will see how to add interactivity to your page by allowing the user to show previously hidden information when users click on a piece of text. This is referred to as a "piece of text" because, strictly speaking, the text is not a link. That is to say, it will look like a link and act like a link, but it will not be marked up within an <a> tag.

Listing 18.2 provides the complete code for this example, shown initially in Figure 18.4.

Listing 18.2   Using onclick to Show or Hide Content

```
<?xml version="1.0" encoding="UTF-8"?>
<!DOCTYPE html PUBLIC "-//W3C//DTD XHTML 1.1//EN"
  "http://www.w3.org/TR/xhtml11/DTD/xhtml11.dtd">

<html xmlns="http://www.w3.org/1999/xhtml" xml:lang="en">
  <head>
    <title>Steptoe Butte</title>
    <style type="text/css">
    a {
       text-decoration: none;
       font-weight: bold;
       color: #7a7abf;
    }
    #hide_e {
       display: none;
    }
    #elevation {
       display: none;
    }
    #hide_p {
       display: none;
    }
    #photos {
       display: none;
    }
    #show_e {
       display: block;
    }
    #show_p {
       display: block;
    }
    .fakelink {
       cursor:pointer;
       text-decoration: none;
       font-weight: bold;
       color: #E03A3E;
    }
    </style>
  </head>
  <body>
    <h1>Steptoe Butte</h1>
    <p><img src="steptoebutte.jpg" alt="View from Steptoe Butte"
    style="float:left;margin-right:12px;margin-bottom:6px;border:1px
    solid #000" />Steptoe Butte is a quartzite island jutting out of the
    silty loess of the <a class="tip"
    href="http://en.wikipedia.org/wiki/Palouse">Palouse <span>Learn more
    about the Palouse!</span></a> hills in Whitman County, Washington. The
    rock that forms the butte is over 400 million years old, in contrast
    with the 15-7 million year old
    <a href="http://en.wikipedia.org/wiki/Columbia_River">Columbia
```

Listing 18.2   Using `onclick` to Show or Hide Content

```
River</a>
    basalts that underlie the rest of the Palouse (such "islands" of ancient
    rock have come to be called buttes, a butte being defined as a small hill
    with a flat top, whose width at top does not exceed its height).</p>
    <p>A hotel built by Cashup Davis stood atop Steptoe Butte from 1888 to
    1908, burning down several years after it closed. In 1946, Virgil McCroskey
    donated 120 acres (0.49 km2) of land to form Steptoe Butte State Park,
    which was later increased to over 150 acres (0.61 km2). Steptoe Butte is
    currently recognized as a National Natural Landmark because of its unique
    geological value. It is named in honor of
    <a href="http://en.wikipedia.org/wiki/Colonel_Edward_Steptoe">Colonel Edward
    Steptoe</a>.</p>
    <div class="fakelink"
        id="show_e"
        onclick="this.style.display='none';
        document.getElementById('hide_e').style.display='block';
        document.getElementById('elevation').style.display='inline';
    ">&raquo; Show Elevation</div>

    <div class="fakelink"
        id="hide_e"
        onclick="this.style.display='none';
        document.getElementById('show_e').style.display='block';
        document.getElementById('elevation').style.display='none';
    ">&raquo; Hide Elevation</div>

    <div id="elevation">3,612 feet (1,101 m), approximately 1,000 feet (300 m)
    above the surrounding countryside.</div>

    <div class="fakelink"
        id="show_p"
        onclick="this.style.display='none';
        document.getElementById('hide_p').style.display='block';
        document.getElementById('photos').style.display='inline';
    ">&raquo; Show Photos from the Top of Steptoe Butte</div>

    <div class="fakelink"
        id="hide_p"
        onclick="this.style.display='none';
        document.getElementById('show_p').style.display='block';
        document.getElementById('photos').style.display='none';
    ">&raquo; Hide Photos from the Top of Steptoe Butte</div>
```

Listing 18.2   Using onclick to Show or Hide Content

```
<div id="photos"><img src="steptoe_sm1.jpg" alt="View from Steptoe Butte"
style="margin-right: 12px; border: 1px solid #000" /><img
src="steptoe_sm2.jpg" alt="View from Steptoe Butte"
style="margin-right: 12px; border: 1px solid #000" /><img
src="steptoe_sm3.jpg" alt="View from Steptoe Butte" style="margin-right:
12px; border: 1px solid #000" /></div>

<p><em>Text from
<a href="http://en.wikipedia.org/wiki/Steptoe_Butte">Wikipedia</a>, photos
by the author.</em></p>
</body>
</html>
```

FIGURE 18.4
The initial display of Listing 18.2.
Note the mouse pointer changes
to a hand when hovering over the
red text despite the fact it is not
an <a> link.

To begin, look at the six entries in the style sheet. The first entry simply
styles links that are surrounded by the <a></a> tag pair; these links display
as non-underlined, bold, blue links. You can see these regular links in the
two paragraphs of text in Figure 18.4 (and in the line at the bottom of the
page).

The next four entries are for specific IDs, and those IDs are all set to be invisible (display: none) when the page initially loads. The two IDs that follow are set to display as block elements when the page initially loads. Again, strictly speaking, these two IDs would not have to be defined as such because it is the default display. The style sheet includes these entries for the purpose of illustrating the differences. If you count the number of <div> elements in Listing 18.1, you will find six in the code: four invisible and two that are visible upon page load.

The goal in this example is to change the display value of two IDs when another ID is clicked. But first you have to make sure users realize a piece of text is clickable, and that typically happens when users see their mouse pointers change to reflect a link is present. Note in Figure 18.4 that the mouse pointer changes to a hand with a finger pointing at a particular link.

This functionality is achieved by defining a class for this particular text; the class is called fakelink, as you can see in this snippet of code:

```
<div class="fakelink"
    id="show_e"
    onclick="this.style.display='none';
    document.getElementById('hide_e').style.display='block';
    document.getElementById('elevation').style.display='inline';
">&raquo; Show Elevation</div>
```

The fakelink class ensures that the text is rendered as non-underlined, bold, and red; cursor: pointer causes the mouse pointer to change in such a way that users think the text is a link of the type that would normally be enclosed in an <a></a> tag. But the really interesting stuff happens when we associate an onclick attribute with a <div>. In the example snippet just shown, the value of the onclick attribute is a series of commands that change the current value of CSS elements.

Let's look at them separately:

```
this.style.display='none';
document.getElementById('hide_e').style.display='block';
document.getElementById('elevation').style.display='inline';
```

What you are looking at are different JavaScript methods meant to change particular elements. You will learn a little bit more about JavaScript in Hour 21. In general, JavaScript is well beyond the scope of this book, but I think you can follow along with what is happening here.

In the first line, the this keyword refers to the element itself. In other words, this refers to the <div> ID called show_e. The keyword style refers to the style object; the style object contains all the CSS styles that you assign to the element. In this case, we are most interested in the display style. Therefore, this.style.display means "the display style of the show_e ID," and what we are doing here is setting the value of the display style to none when the text itself is clicked.

But that is not all we are doing, as there are three actions that occur within the onclick attribute. The other two actions begin with document.getElementByID() and include a specific ID name within the parentheses. We use document.getElementByID() instead of this because the second and third actions set CSS style properties for elements that are not the parent element. As you can see in the snippet, in the second and third actions, we are setting the display property values for the element IDs hide_e and elevation. All told, when users click the currently-visible <div> called show_e:

▶ The show_e <div> becomes invisible.

▶ The hide_e <div> becomes visible and is displayed as a block.

▶ The elevation <div> becomes visible and is displayed inline.

The result of these actions is shown in Figure 18.5.

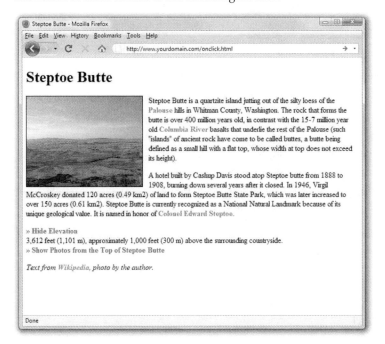

FIGURE 18.5
After clicking "Show Elevation," the visibility of it and other <div> elements change based on the commands in the onclick attribute.

There is another set of `<div>` elements in the code in Listing 18.2, the ones that control the visibility of the additional photos. These elements are not affected by the `onclick` actions in the elevation-related elements. That is to say, when you click on either "Show Elevation" or "Hide Elevation," the photos-related `<div>` elements do not change at all. You could show the elevation and not the photos (as seen in Figure 18.5), the photos and not the elevation, or both the elevation and photos at the same time (see Figure 18.6).

FIGURE 18.6
The page after clicking both "Show Elevation" and "Show Photos from the Top of Steptoe Butte."

This brief example has shown you the very beginning of the layout and interaction possibilities that await you when you master CSS in conjunction with events. For example, you can code your pages so that your users can change elements of the stylesheet or change to an entirely different stylesheet, move blocks of text to other places in the layout, take quizzes or submit forms, and much, much more.

Summary

In this hour, you learned how mouse actions can affect the display of text. In the first two sections, these actions were based on styles associated with the hover pseudoclass of the <a> tag, while later in the hour you were introduced to actions associated with specific user interaction events. The specific event in the example was the onclick event, but you also saw a list of other possible events, such as onload and onmouseover just to name a few.

The only new code introduced in the code itself was the use of the cursor property. Assigning a cursor property of pointer allowed you to indicate to users that particular text was acting as a link even though it was not enclosed in <a></a> tags as you are used to seeing.

Q&A

Q Some of the events covered in this hour sound a lot like the pseudo-classes for the <a> tag. What's the difference?

A It is true that the onmousedown event is like the active state and onmouseup and onmouseover are much like the hover state. There isn't a specific rule about when to use events instead of using the pseudo-classes, but it stands to reason that if you have no other reason to use an <a> tag, you shouldn't just to use the pseudoclasses.

Q Can you capture mouse or keyboard events on elements other than text, such as images?

A Yes, these types of events can be applied to actions related to clicking on or rolling over images as well as text. However, other multimedia objects, such as embedded YouTube videos or Flash files, are not inter-acted with in the same way, as those objects are played via additional software for which other mouse or keyboard actions are applicable. For instance, if you click on a YouTube video that is embedded in your web page, you are interacting with the YouTube player and no longer your actual web page—that action cannot be captured in the same way.

Workshop

The workshop contains quiz questions and activities to help you solidify your understanding of the material covered. Try to answer all questions before looking at the "Answers" section that follows.

Quiz

1. What happens when you use a negative value for the `top` property?

2. Which event is used to change something about the page when the user moves the mouse out of the boundaries of a particular element?

3. If you saw the `cursor: crosshair` style in a style sheet, what would you assume it did?

Answers

1. Using a negative value for `top` places content above the top-left corner of the parent element (rather than below it).

2. The `onmouseout` event is used.

3. Turn the user's mouse pointer into a large plus sign (or crosshair). It is unclear why you would do that, though, because this is an atypical presentation of the cursor. In other words, users will wonder why you did that to their interfaces; they won't appreciate it as a design decision on your part.

Exercises

▶ Create your own page with rollover tooltip texts, using colors and other styles that work with your own display template.

▶ Add commands to the `onclick` attributes in Listing 18.2 such that only one of the `<div>` elements (the elevation or photos) is visible at a time.

HOUR 19
Creating Fixed or Liquid Layouts

The bulk of this book has taught you all about styling web content, from font sizes and colors to images, block elements, lists, and more. But what has yet to be discussed is a high-level overview of page layout. In general, there are two types of layouts—fixed and liquid—but also a layout that is a combination of the two, wherein some elements are fixed while others are liquid.

In this hour, you'll first learn about the characteristics of these two types of layouts and see a few examples of web sites that use them. At the end of the hour, you will see a basic template that combines elements of both types of layouts. Ultimately, the type of layout you decide is up to you—it's hard to go wrong as long as your sites follow HTML and CSS standards.

WHAT YOU'LL LEARN IN THIS HOUR:

▶ How fixed layouts work
▶ How liquid layouts work
▶ How to create a fixed/liquid hybrid layout

TRY IT YOURSELF ▼
Find Examples of Layouts You Like

A good place for examples of liquid layouts is the WordPress Theme Gallery at http://wordpress.org/extend/themes/. WordPress is a blogging platform that is seeing increasing use as a non-blog site management tool. The theme gallery shows hundreds of examples of both fixed-width and liquid layouts which give you an idea, if not all of the code, for what you could create. Even though you are not working with a WordPress blog as part of the exercises in this book, the template gallery is a place where you can see and interact with many variations on designs.

Spend some time looking at the WordPress examples and perhaps the CSS Zen Garden as well at http://www.csszengarden.com/. This will help you get a feel for the types of layouts you like without being swayed one way or the other by the content within the layout.

Understanding Fixed Layouts

A fixed layout, or fixed-width layout, is just that—a layout in which the body of the page is set to a specific width. That width is typically controlled by a master "wrapper" <div> in which all content is contained. The width property of that <div> would be set in the style attribute or in a style sheet entry if the <div> was given an ID value such as "main" or "wrapper" (although the name is up to you).

When creating a fixed-width layout, the most important decision is determining the minimum screen resolution you want to accommodate. For many years, 800x600 has been the "lowest common denominator" for web designers, resulting in a typical fixed width of approximately 760 pixels. However, since 2007, the number of people using 800x600 screen resolution has been less than eight percent (and is currently approximately four percent). Given that, many web designers consider 1024x768 the current minimum screen resolution, leading to fixed-width designs anywhere between 800 and 1000 pixels wide.

A main reason for creating a fixed-width layout is so that you can have precise control over the appearance of the content area. However, if users visit your fixed-width site with smaller or much larger screen resolutions than the resolution you had in mind while you designed it, they might encounter scroll bars (if their resolution is smaller) or a large amount of empty space (if their resolution is greater).

The current ESPN.com home page provides a visual example of this issue; it has a content area fixed at 964 pixels wide. In Figure 19.1, the browser window is 800 pixels wide. On the right side of the image, important content is cut off (and at the bottom of the figure, a horizontal scroll bar displays in the browser).

However, Figure 19.2 shows how this site looks when the browser window is more than 1300 pixels wide: there is a lot of empty space (or "real estate") on both sides of the main body content.

There is another consideration when creating a fixed-width layout: whether to place the content flush-left or whether to center it. Placing the content flush-left produces extra space on the right side only; centering the content area creates extra space on both sides.

FIGURE 19.1
A fixed-width example with a smaller screen size.

FIGURE 19.2
A fixed-width example with a larger screen size.

Understanding Liquid Layouts

A liquid layout—also called a fluid layout—is one in which the body of the page does not use a specified width in pixels, although it might be enclosed in a master "wrapper" <div> that uses a percentage width. The idea behind the liquid layout is that it can be perfectly usable and still retain the overall design aesthetic even if the user has a very small or very wide screen.

Three examples of a liquid layout in action are shown in Figures 19.3, 19.4, and 19.5.

In Figure 19.3, the browser window is approximately 770 pixels wide. This example shows a reasonable minimum screen width before a horizontal scrollbar appears. In fact, the scrollbar does not appear until the browser is 735 pixels wide. On the other hand, Figure 19.4 shows a very small browser window (545 pixels wide).

FIGURE 19.3
A liquid layout as viewed in a
relatively small screen.

In Figure 19.4, you can see a horizontal scroll bar; in the header area of the page content, the logo graphic is beginning to take over the text and appear on top of it. But the bulk of the page is still quite usable. The informational content on the left side of the page is still legible and it is sharing the available space with the input form on the right side.

Figure 19.5 shows how this same page looks in a very wide screen.

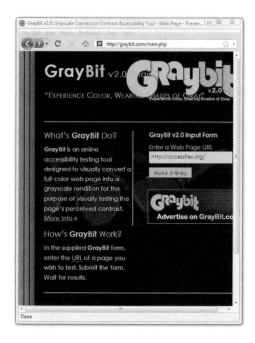

FIGURE 19.4
A liquid layout as viewed in a very small screen.

FIGURE 19.5
A liquid layout as viewed in a wide screen.

In Figure 19.5, the browser window is approximately 1330 pixels wide. There is plenty of room for all of the content on the page to spread out. This liquid layout is achieved because all of the design elements have a percentage width specified (instead of a fixed width). In doing so, the layout makes use of all the available browser real estate.

The liquid layout approach might seem like the best approach at first glance—after all, who wouldn't want to take advantage of all the screen real estate available to them? There is a fine line between taking advantage of space and not allowing the content to "breathe," as it were. Too much content is overwhelming; not enough content in an open space is underwhelming.

The pure liquid layout can be quite impressive, but it requires a significant amount of testing to ensure that it is usable in a wide range of browsers at varying screen resolutions. You might not have the time and effort to produce such a design; in that case, a reasonable compromise is the fixed/liquid hybrid layout.

Creating a Fixed/Liquid Hybrid Layout

A fixed/liquid hybrid layout is one that contains elements of both types of layouts. For example, you could have a fluid layout that includes fixed-width content areas either within the body area or as anchor elements (such as a left-side column or as a top navigation strip). You can even create a fixed content area that acts like a frame, as alluded to in Hour 13, "Working with Frames," in which the fixed content area remains fixed even as users scroll through the content.

Starting with a Basic Layout Structure

In this example, you'll learn to create a template that is liquid but with two fixed-width columns on either side of the main body area (which is a third column, if you think about it, only much wider than the others). The template will also have a delineated header and footer area. Listing 19.1 shows the basic HTML structure for this layout.

Listing 19.1   Basic Fixed/Liquid Hybrid Layout Structure

```
<?xml version="1.0" encoding="UTF-8"?>
<!DOCTYPE html PUBLIC "-//W3C//DTD XHTML 1.1//EN"
  "http://www.w3.org/TR/xhtml11/DTD/xhtml11.dtd">

<html xmlns="http://www.w3.org/1999/xhtml" xml:lang="en">
  <head>
    <title>Sample Layout</title>
    <link href="layout.css" rel="stylesheet" type="text/css" />
  </head>
```

Listing 19.1   Basic Fixed/Liquid Hybrid Layout Structure

```
<body>
  <div id="header">HEADER</div>
  <div id="wrapper">
      <div id="content_area">CONTENT</div>
      <div id="left_side">LEFT SIDE</div>
      <div id="right_side">RIGHT SIDE</div>
  </div>
  <div id="footer">FOOTER</div>
</body>
</html>
```

First, note that the style sheet for this layout is linked to with the `<link>` tag rather than included in the template. As a template is used for more than one page, you want to be able to control the display elements of the template in the most organized way possible. This means you need only to change the definitions of those elements in one place—the style sheet.

Next, you'll notice that the basic HTML is just that: extremely basic. And, truth be told, this basic HTML structure can be used for a fixed layout, a liquid layout, or the fix/liquid hybrid you'll see here, because all of the actual styling that makes a layout fixed, liquid, or hybrid happens in the style sheet.

What you actually have with the HTML structure in Listing 19.1 is an identification of the content areas you want to include in your site. This planning is crucial to any development; you have to know what you want to include before you even think about the type of layout you are going to use, let alone the specific styles that will be applied to that layout.

At this stage, the layout.css file includes only this entry:

```
body {
   margin:0;
   padding:0;
}
```

If you look at the HTML in Listing 19.1 and say to yourself "but those `<div>` elements will just stack on top of each other without any styles," you are correct. As shown in Figure 19.6, there is no layout to speak of.

FIGURE 19.6
A basic HTML template with no
styles applied to the <div>
elements.

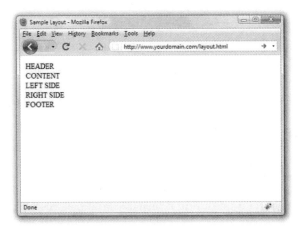

Defining Two Columns in a Fixed/Liquid Hybrid Layout

We can start with the easy things first. Since this layout is supposed to be liquid, we know that whatever we put in the header and footer areas will extend the width of the browser window regardless of how narrow or wide the window might be.

Adding the following code to the style sheet gives the header and footer area each a width of 100 percent as well as the same background color:

```
#header {
  float: left;
  width: 100%;
  background-color: #7152F4;
}
#footer {
  float: left;
  width: 100%;
  background-color: #7152F4;
}
```

Now things get a little trickier. We have to define the two fixed columns on either side of the page, plus the column in the middle. In the HTML, note that there is a <div> that surrounds all three and it is called "wrapper." This element is defined as follows:

```
#wrapper {
  float: left;
  padding-left: 200px;
  padding-right: 125px;
}
```

The use of the two padding definitions is to essentially reserve space for the two fixed-width columns on the left and right of the page. The column on the left will be 200 pixels wide, the column on the right will be 125 pixels wide, and each will have a different background color. But we also have to position the items relative to where they would be placed if the HTML remained unstyled (see Figure 19.6). This means adding position: relative to the style sheet entries for each of these columns. Additionally, we indicate that the <div> elements should float to the left.

But in the case of the left_side <div>, we also indicate that we want the right-most margin edge to be 200 pixels in from the edge (this is in addition to the column being defined as 200 pixels wide). We also want the margin on the left side to be a full negative margin; this will pull it into place (as you will soon see). The right_side <div> does not include a value for right but it does include a negative margin on the right side:

```
#left_side {
  position: relative;
  float: left;
  width: 200px;
  background-color: #52f471;
  right: 200px;
  margin-left: -100%;
}
#right_side {
  position: relative;
  float: left;
  width: 125px;
  background-color: #f452d5;
  margin-right: -125px;
}
```

At this point let's also define the content area so that it has a white background, takes up 100% of the available area, and floats to the left relative to its position:

```
#content_area {
  position: relative;
  float: left;
  background-color: #ffffff;
  width: 100%;
}
```

At this point, the basic layout will look something like that which is shown in Figure 19.7, with the areas clearly delineated.

FIGURE 19.7
A basic HTML template after some styles have been put in place.

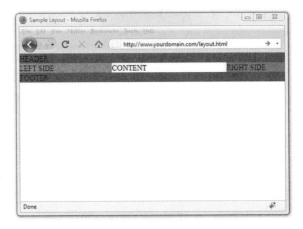

However, there's a problem with this template if the window is resized below a certain width. Since the left column is 200 pixels wide and the right column is 125 pixels wide, and you want at least *some* text in the content area, you can imagine this page will "break" if the window is only 350 to 400 pixels wide. Figure 19.8 shows what happens when the window is resized just under 400 pixels wide (390, to be exact).

FIGURE 19.8
A basic HTML template resized under 400 pixels: bad!

Setting the Minimum Width of a Layout

Although it is unlikely that users will visit your site with a browser less than 400 pixels wide, the example serves its purpose within the confines of this book's pages. You can extrapolate and apply this information broadly:

even in fixed/liquid hybrid sites, there will be a point at which your layout breaks down, unless you do something about it.

That "something" is to use the `min-width` property. The `min-width` property sets the minimum width of an element, not including padding, borders, or margins. Figure 19.9 shows what happens when `min-width` is applied to the `<body>` element.

FIGURE 19.9
A basic HTML template resized under 400 pixels: better!

Figure 19.9 shows a wee bit of the right column after scrolling to the right, but the point is that the layout does not break when resized below a minimum width. In this case, the minimum width is 525 pixels:

```
body {
  margin: 0;
  padding: 0;
  min-width: 525px;

}
```

The horizontal scrollbar appears in this example because the browser window itself is less than 500 pixels wide. The scrollbar disappears when the window is slightly larger than 525 pixels wide, and it's definitely out of the picture entirely when the browser is approximately 875 pixels wide (see Figure 19.10).

Handling Column Height in a Fixed/Liquid Hybrid Layout

This example is all well and good except for one problem: it has no content. When content is added to the various elements, more problems arise. As shown in Figure 19.11, the columns become as tall as necessary for the content they contain.

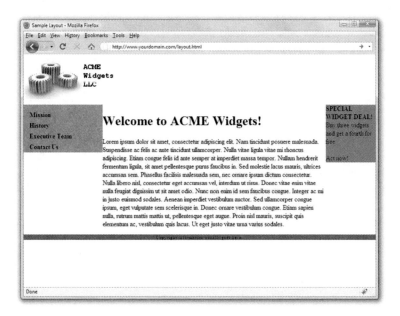

Since you cannot count on a user's browser being a specific height, or that the content will always be the same length, you might think this poses a problem with the fixed/liquid hybrid layout. Not so. If you think a little outside the box, you can apply a few more styles that will bring all the pieces together.

First, add the following declarations in the style sheet entries for the `left_side`, `right_side`, and `content_area` IDs:

```
margin-bottom: -2000px;
padding-bottom: 2000px;
```

These declarations add a ridiculous amount of padding and assign a ridiculously large margin to the bottom of all three elements. You must also add `position:relative` to the footer ID in the style sheet so that it is visible despite this padding.

At this point, the page would look like that which is shown in Figure 19.12—still not what we want, but closer.

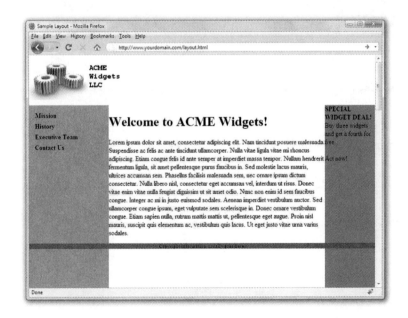

FIGURE 19.12
Color fields are now visible despite the amount of content in the columns.

To clip off all that extra color, add the following to the style sheet for the wrapper ID:

```
overflow: hidden;
```

Figure 19.13 shows the final result: a fixed-width/liquid hybrid layout with the necessary column spacing.

FIGURE 19.13
Congratulations! It's a fixed-width/liquid hybrid layout.

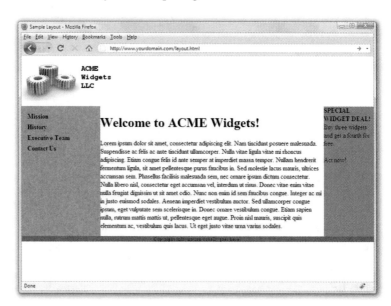

The full HTML code can be seen in Listing 19.2 and the final style sheet is shown in Listing 19.3.

Listing 19.2   Basic Fixed/Liquid Hybrid Layout Structure (with content)

```
<?xml version="1.0" encoding="UTF-8"?>
<!DOCTYPE html PUBLIC "-//W3C//DTD XHTML 1.1//EN"
  "http://www.w3.org/TR/xhtml11/DTD/xhtml11.dtd">

<html xmlns="http://www.w3.org/1999/xhtml" xml:lang="en">
  <head>
    <title>Sample Layout</title>
    <link href="layout.css" rel="stylesheet" type="text/css" />
  </head>

  <body>
    <div id="header"><img src="acmewidgets.jpg" alt="ACME Widgets
      LLC"/></div>
    <div id="wrapper">
      <div id="content_area">
        <h1>Welcome to ACME Widgets!</h1>
```

Listing 19.2   Basic Fixed/Liquid Hybrid Layout Structure (with content)

```
      <p>Lorem ipsum dolor sit amet, consectetur adipiscing elit.
      Nam tincidunt posuere malesuada. Suspendisse ac felis ac ante
      tincidunt ullamcorper. Nulla vitae ligula vitae mi rhoncus
      adipiscing. Etiam congue felis id ante semper at imperdiet
      massa tempor. Nullam hendrerit fermentum ligula, sit amet
      pellentesque purus faucibus in. Sed molestie lacus mauris,
      ultrices accumsan sem. Phasellus facilisis malesuada sem, nec
      ornare ipsum dictum consectetur. Nulla libero nisl,
      consectetur eget accumsan vel, interdum ut risus. Donec
      vitae enim vitae nulla feugiat dignissim ut sit amet odio.
      Nunc non enim id sem faucibus congue. Integer ac mi in justo
      euismod sodales. Aenean imperdiet vestibulum auctor. Sed
      ullamcorper congue ipsum, eget vulputate sem scelerisque in.
      Donec ornare vestibulum congue. Etiam sapien nulla, rutrum
      mattis mattis ut, pellentesque eget augue. Proin nisl mauris,
      suscipit quis elementum ac, vestibulum quis lacus. Ut eget
      justo vitae urna varius sodales. </p>
    </div>
    <div id="left_side">
      <ul>
      <li><a href="#">Mission</a></li>
      <li><a href="#">History</a></li>
      <li><a href="#">Executive Team</a></li>
      <li><a href="#">Contact Us</a></li>
    </ul>
    </div>
    <div id="right_side"><strong>SPECIAL WIDGET DEAL!</strong><br/>
      Buy three widgets and get a fourth for free.<br/><br/>
      Act now!
    </div>
  </div>
  <div id="footer"> Copyright information usually goes here.</div>
  </body>
</html>
```

Listing 19.3   Full Style Sheet for Fixed/Liquid Hybrid Layout

```
body {
  margin:0;
  padding:0;
  min-width: 525px;
}
#header {
  float: left;
  width:100%;
  background-color: #ffffff;
}
#footer {
  float: left;
  width:100%;
```

Listing 19.3   Full Style Sheet for Fixed/Liquid Hybrid Layout

```
  background-color: #7152f4;
  font-size: 8pt;
  font-weight: bold;
  text-align: center;
  position: relative;
}
#wrapper {
  float: left;
  padding-left: 200px;
  padding-right: 125px;
  overflow: hidden;
}
#left_side {
  position: relative;
  float: left;
  width: 200px;
  background-color: #52f471;
  right: 200px;
  margin-left: -100%;
  padding-bottom: 2000px;
  margin-bottom: -2000px;
}
#right_side {
  position: relative;
  float: left;
  width: 125px;
  background-color: #f452d5;
  margin-right: -125px;
  padding-bottom: 2000px;
  margin-bottom: -2000px;
}
#content_area {
  position: relative;
  float: left;
  background-color: #ffffff;
  width: 100%;
  padding-bottom: 2000px;
  margin-bottom: -2000px;
}
#left_side ul {
  list-style: none;
  margin: 12px 0px 0px 12px;
  padding: 0px;
}
#left_side li a:link, #nav li a:visited {
  font-size: 12pt;
  font-weight: bold;
  padding: 3px 0px 3px 3px;
  color: #000000;
  text-decoration: none;
  display: block;
```

Listing 19.3   Full Style Sheet for Fixed/Liquid Hybrid Layout

```
}
#left_side li a:hover, #nav li a:active {
  font-size: 12pt;
  font-weight: bold;
  padding: 3px 0px 3px 3px;
  color: #ffffff;
  text-decoration: none;
  display: block;
}
```

Summary

In this hour, you saw some practical examples of the three main types of layouts: fixed, liquid, and a fixed/liquid hybrid. In the third section of the hour, you saw an extended example that took you through the process bit-by-bit for creating a fixed/liquid hybrid layout in which the HTML and CSS all validate properly. Remember, the most important part of creating a layout is figuring out the sections of content you think you might need to account for in the design.

Q&A

Q I've heard about something called an elastic layout. How is that different than the liquid layout?

A An elastic layout is a layout whose content areas resize when the user resizes the text. Elastic layouts use ems, which are inherently proportional to text and font size. An em is a typographical unit of measurement equal to the point size of the current font. When ems are used in an elastic layout, if a user forces the text size to increase or decrease in size using Ctrl and the mouse scroll wheel, the areas containing the text increase or decrease proportionally. Elastic layouts are very difficult to achieve and are more commonly found in portfolios rather than actual practice due to the number of hours involved in perfecting them.

Q You've spent a lot of time talking about liquid layouts or hybrid layouts—are they better than a purely fixed layout?

A "Better" is a subjective term; in this book the concern is with standards-compliant code. Most designers will tell you that liquid layouts take longer to create (and perfect), but the usability enhancements are worth it. When might the time not be worth it? If your client does not have an opinion and if they are paying you a flat rate rather than an hourly rate. In that case, you are working only to showcase your own skills—that might be worth it to you, however.

Workshop

The workshop contains quiz questions and activities to help you solidify your understanding of the material covered. Try to answer all questions before looking at the "Answers" section that follows.

Quiz

1. Which is the best layout to use, in general: fixed, liquid, or a hybrid?

2. Can you position a fixed layout anywhere on the page?

3. What does `min-width` do?

Answers

1. This was a trick question; there is no "best" layout. It depends on your content and the needs of your audience.

2. Sure. Although most fixed layouts are flush-left or centered, you could assign a fixed position on an XY axis where you could place a `<div>` that contains all the other layout `<div>`s.

3. The `min-width` property sets the minimum width of an element, not including padding, borders, or margins.

Exercises

▶ Figure 19.13 shows the "finished" fixed/liquid hybrid layout, but notice there are a few areas for improvement: there isn't any space around the text in the right-side column, there aren't any margins between the body text and either column, the footer strip is a little sparse, and so on. Take some time to fix up these design elements.

▶ After you've added margin or padding as appropriate in the first exercise, spruce up this page with a horizontal navigation strip and fancier vertical navigation based on what you learned in Hour 17.

Creating Print-Friendly Web Pages

If you've ever used an online mapping tool such as MapQuest or Google Maps, you've no doubt experienced the need to print a web page. Similarly, the proliferation of coupons offered only online, purchase receipts for items from online resellers, and web-based flight check-in and the ability to print boarding passes from your home computer have increased the need for print-friendly pages. It's true, not all web pages are designed entirely for viewing on the screen. You might not realize this, but it's possible to specifically design and offer print-friendly versions of your pages for users who want to print a copy for offline reading—something that Google Maps offers after showing you the on-screen version of content. CSS makes it easy to create web pages that will change appearance based on how they are viewed. In this hour, you learn how to create such pages.

As you work your way through this hour, consider any of your own web pages that might look good in print. Then think about what you would want to change about them to make them look even better on the printed page. Here are some ideas to consider:

▶ Even against warnings in previous lessons, do you have pages that use a patterned background image or an unusual background color with contrasting text? This kind of page can be difficult to print because of the background, so you might consider offering a print version of the page that doesn't use a custom background image or color and simply uses black text. When preparing a page for printing, stick to black text on a white background if possible.

WHAT YOU'LL LEARN IN THIS HOUR:

▶ What makes a page print-friendly

▶ How to apply a media-specific style sheet

▶ How to create a style sheet for print pages

▶ How to view your web page in print preview mode

TRY IT YOURSELF ▼

Review Your Content for Print-Friendliness

▶ Do your pages include lots of links? If so, you might consider changing the appearance of links for printing so that they don't stand out—remove any underlining, for example. Remember, you can't click a piece of paper!

▶ Finally, is every image on your pages absolutely essential? Colorful images cost valuable ink to print on most printers, so you might consider leaving some, if not all, images out of your print-friendly pages.

What Makes a Page Print-Friendly?

I already touched on this topic a bit in the preceding Try It Yourself, but it's worth a more thorough exploration of what constitutes a print-friendly web page. First off, it's important to point out that some web pages are print-friendly already. If your pages use white backgrounds with dark contrasting text and few images, you might not even need to concern yourself with a special print-friendly version. On the other hand, pages with dark backgrounds, dynamic links, and several images might prove to be unwieldy for the average printer.

The main things to keep in mind as you consider what it takes to make your pages more print-friendly are the limitations imposed by the medium. In other words, what is it about a printed page that makes it uniquely different from a computer screen? The obvious difference is size—a printed page is at a fixed size, typically 8 ½ by 11 inches, whereas the size of screens can vary greatly. In addition to size, printed pages also have color limitations (even on color printers). Very few users want to waste the ink required to print a full-color background when they really just want to print the text on the page.

Most users also aren't interested in printing more than the text that serves as the focus on the page. For example, Figure 20.1 shows a travel route mapped out from San Jose, California to Pullman, Washington.

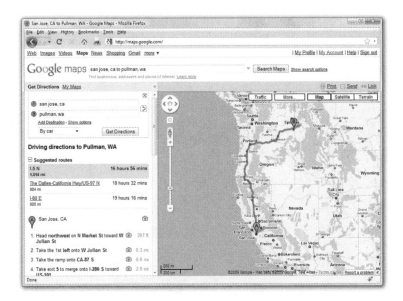

FIGURE 20.1
This page isn't very print-friendly due to the form inputs and large image with its own display controls.

The page shown in Figure 20.1 contains form input fields, a large image that can itself be controlled (moved, zoomed), and other ancillary items that you come to expect in web content. Above the map appears a set of Actions that you can perform, one of which is a link to print the page. At this point, you might wonder why you can't just click the Print button on your web browser. You certainly can do this, but that command prints the page as it is shown on your screen—complete with the form input fields and graphical elements, when all you really want to know are the turns you need to make when driving this route.

If you click the Print link in the body of the page, your web browser will display a page (see Figure 20.2) that Google has formatted specifically to be printed.

FIGURE 20.2
The print-friendly version of the page isolates the text of the driving instructions so that it can be printed by itself.

NOTE

If the font of printer-specific pages is Sans-Serif, some web designers recommend changing the font to Serif, which is considered easier to read in print. If you use a Sans-Serif font on your pages, it's up to you to decide whether you want to maintain the core look of a page when it's printed—which means you don't change the font to Serif.

As shown in the figure, the print-friendly version of this page represents a significant improvement over the original, at least from the perspective of a printer. All the form inputs and images were removed.

In the spirit of giving you a better grasp on what, specifically, to consider as you move toward creating print-friendly pages, following is a list of changes you should at least consider:

▶ Remove the background of the page, which effectively gives the printed page a white background.

▶ Change text colors to black; it's okay to have some color in the text but black is preferred.

▶ Make sure that the font size is large enough that the page can be easily read when printed. You might have to test some different sizes.

▶ Remove link formatting or simply revert to a basic underlined link. Some designers like to retain an underline just so a visitor knows that a link exists in the original page.

▶ Remove any and all nonessential images. This typically includes any images that aren't critical to conveying the content in the page, such as navigation buttons, most ads, and animated images.

In addition to these suggestions, you might find it useful to add a byline with information about the author of the page, along with a URL for the page and copyright information. This is information that could potentially get lost after the user leaves your web site and has only the printed version of the page in hand.

You probably don't need to make these changes to your pages just yet. The idea is to plant the seed of what constitutes a print-friendly page so that you can do a better job of creating a printer-specific style sheet. That's right, it's possible to create a style sheet that is applied to pages only when they are printed. You learn this in the next section.

Applying a Media-Specific Style Sheet

Figure 20.1 showed how a small printer icon with a link allows you to view a special print-friendly version of a page. This type of icon is popular on many news sites, and it's an important feature because you otherwise might not want to hassle with printing a page and wasting paper and ink on the graphics and ads that accompany articles. Although the printer icon and link approach is intuitive and works great, there is an option that does not require these specific links to print-friendly content.

This option involves using a print-specific style sheet that is automatically applied to a page when the user elects to print the page. CSS supports the concept of *media-specific style sheets*, which are style sheets that target a particular medium, such as the screen or printer. CSS doesn't stop with those two forms of media, however. Check out the following list of specific media types that CSS 2 allows you to support with a unique style sheet:

- ▶ all: for all devices
- ▶ aural: for speech synthesizers (called speech in CSS 1 media types)
- ▶ braille: for Braille tactile feedback devices
- ▶ embossed: for paged Braille printers
- ▶ handheld: for handheld devices with limited screen size and bandwidth
- ▶ print: for printed material and documents viewed on screen in Print Preview mode
- ▶ projection: for projected presentations

- ▶ screen: for color computer screens
- ▶ tty: for devices using a fixed-pitch character grid (such as a terminal, teletype, or handheld devices with limited displays).
- ▶ tv: for television-type devices, which are typically low resolution, color, and have limited ability to scroll.

Perhaps the most interesting of these media is the aural type, which allows for web pages that can be read aloud or otherwise listened to. Clearly, the architects of CSS envision a Web with a much broader reach than we currently think of as we design pages primarily for computer screens. While you probably don't need to worry too much about aural web page design just yet, it serves as a good heads-up as to what might be on the horizon.

The good news about style sheets as applied to other media is that they don't require you to learn anything new. Okay, maybe in the case of aural web pages you'll need to learn a few new tricks, but for now you can use the same style properties you've already learned to create print-specific style sheets. The trick is knowing how to apply a style sheet for a particular medium.

If you recall, the `<link />` tag is used to link an external style sheet to a web page. This tag supports an attribute named `media` that you haven't seen yet. This attribute is used to specify the name of the medium to which the style sheet applies. By default, this attribute is set to `all`, which means that an external style sheet will be used for all media if you don't specify otherwise. The other acceptable attribute values correspond to the list of media provided in the previous list.

Establishing a print-specific style sheet for a web page involves using two `<link />` tags, one for the printer and one for each remaining medium. Following is code that handles this task:

```
<link rel="stylesheet" type="text/css" href="standard.css" media="all" />
<link rel="stylesheet" type="text/css" href="for_print.css" media="print" />
```

NOTE

You can also use the @import command to link media-specific style sheets. For example, the following code works just like the previous `<link />` code:

```
@import url(player.css) all;
@import url(player_print.css) print;
```

In this example, two style sheets are linked into a web page. The first sheet targets all media by setting the `media` attribute to `all`. If you did nothing else, the `standard.css` style sheet would apply to all media. However, the presence of the second style sheet results in the `for_print.css` style sheet being used to print the page.

You can specify multiple media types in a single `<link />` tag by separating the types with a comma, like this:

```
<link rel="stylesheet" type="text/css" href="for_pp.css" media="print,
projector" />
```

This code results in the for_pp.css style sheet applying solely to the print and projector media types and nothing else.

Designing a Style Sheet for Print Pages

Using the recommended list of modifications required for a print-friendly web page, it's time to take a stab at creating a print-friendly style sheet. Let's first take a look at a page that is displayed using a normal (screen) style sheet (see Figure 20.3).

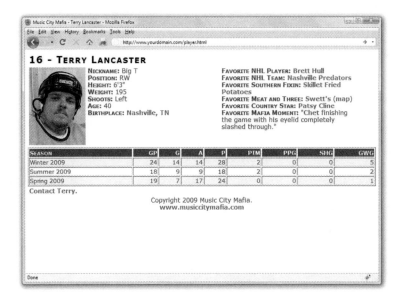

WARNING

You might have been tempted to specify media="screen" in the first linked style sheet in the previous code. Although this would work for viewing the page in a normal web browser, it would cause problems if a user viewed the page using a handheld browser or any of the other types of media. In other words, a style sheet applies only to the specific media types mentioned in the media attribute, and nothing more.

FIGURE 20.3
A CSS-styled page as viewed in a normal web browser.

NOTE

You can specify a media type for your style sheets even if you aren't linking to external versions. The <style> tag also uses the same media attribute as the <link /> tag.

This figure reveals how the page looks in a normal web browser. In reality, this page isn't too far from being print-ready, but it could still benefit from some improvements.

The following changes can help make this web page more print-friendly:

▶ Change the color of all text to black.

▶ Remove link formatting (bold and color).

► Stack the two player information sections vertically because they are unlikely to fit horizontally on the printed page.

► Remove the contact link entirely.

The first two changes to the normal style sheet are fairly straightforward; they primarily involve changing or undoing existing styles. The third change, however, requires a bit of thought. Because you know that printed pages are a fixed size, you should use absolute positioning for all the elements on the printed page. This makes it much easier to place the content sections exactly where you want them. Finally, the last item on the list is very easy to accommodate by simply setting the `display` style property of the `contact` element to `none`.

Listing 20.1 shows the CSS code for the `player_print.css` style sheet, which incorporates these changes into a style sheet that is perfectly suited for printing hockey player pages.

Listing 20.1   CSS Code for the Print-Specific Hockey Player Style Sheet

```css
body {
  font-family:Verdana, Arial;
  font-size:12pt;
  color:black;
}

div {
  padding:3px;
}

div.title {
  font-size:18pt;
  font-weight:bold;
  font-variant:small-caps;
  letter-spacing:2px;
  position:absolute;
  left:0in;
  top:0in;
}

div.image {
  position:absolute;
  left:0in;
  top:0.5in;
}

div.info {
  position:absolute;
  left:1.75in;
```

Listing 20.1   CSS Code for the Print-Specific Hockey Player Style Sheet

```
  top:0.5in;
}

div.favorites {
  position:absolute;
  left:1.75in;
  top:2in;
}

div.footer {
  position:absolute;
  text-align:left;
  left:0in;
  top:9in;
}

table.stats {
  width:100%;
  text-align:right;
  font-size:11pt;
  position:absolute;
  left:0in;
  top:3.75in;
}

div.contact {
  display:none;
}

.label {
  font-weight:bold;
  font-variant:small-caps;
}

tr.heading {
  font-variant:small-caps;
  background-color:black;
  color:white;
}

tr.light {
  background-color:white;
}

tr.dark {
  background-color:#EEEEEE;
}

th.season, td.season {
  text-align:left;
}
```

Listing 20.1   CSS Code for the Print-Specific Hockey Player Style Sheet

```
a, a:link, a:visited {
  color:black;
  font-weight:normal;
  text-decoration:none;
}
```

Probably the neatest thing about this code is how it uses inches (in) as the unit of measure for all the absolute positioning code. This makes sense when you consider that we think of printed pages in terms of inches, not pixels. If you study the code carefully, you'll notice that the text is all black, all special style formatting has been removed from the links, and content sections are now absolutely positioned (so that they appear exactly where you want them).

Viewing a Web Page in Print Preview

Figure 20.4 shows the print-friendly version of a hockey player page as it appears in Internet Explorer's Print Preview window.

FIGURE 20.4
You can use Print Preview to view the print-friendly version of a web page before you print it.

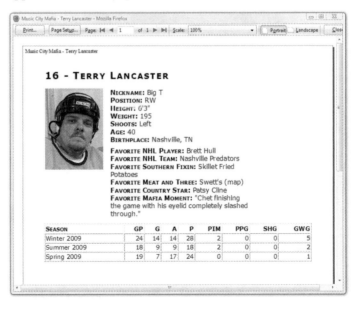

If Figure 20.4 had shown the entire page—all 11 inches of height and then some—you would have noticed that the print-friendly version of the page now includes the footer at the very bottom of the page (see Figure 20.5).

Just to show you how print-friendly pages can be used in a practical situation, check out Figure 20.5. This figure shows the same hockey player page as a PDF document that can be viewed in Adobe Acrobat Reader.

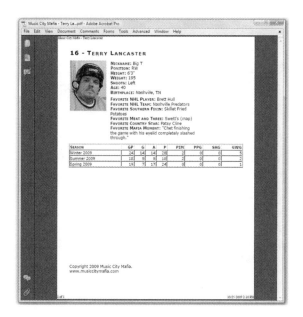

FIGURE 20.5
The hockey player page was converted to a PDF document by printing it as an Adobe PDF.

Adobe's virtual printer can be used to "print" the hockey player web page to a PDF document. You might also find PDF converters such as DoPDF (`http://www.dopdf.com/`) will work for you for at a lower cost than the Adobe Acrobat software. Printing to a PDF effectively creates a version of the print-friendly web page in a format that can be easily shared electronically for printing.

NOTE

To learn more about Acrobat, visit `http://www.adobe.com/ products/acrobat/`.

Summary

This hour focused on a practical application of CSS that solves a common need: printing web pages. You began the hour by learning what exactly constitutes a print-friendly web page. From there, you learned about the mechanism built into CSS that allows a page to distinguish between the media in which it is being rendered, and then you learned how to select a style sheet accordingly. And finally, you created a print-specific style sheet that was used to style a page just for printing. Although most users prefer viewing a page on a large computer screen to reading it on paper, there are times when a printed web page is a necessity. Be sure to give your web page visitors the utmost in flexibility by offering print-friendly pages.

Q&A

Q Can I use the `media` attribute of the `<link />` tag to create a style sheet specifically for viewing a web page on a handheld device?

A Yes. By setting the `media` attribute of the `<link />` tag to `handheld`, you specifically target handheld devices with a style sheet. You will likely see all mobile web sites eventually shift toward this approach to serving mobile pages, as opposed to using specialized markup languages such as WML (Wireless Markup Language).

Q Do I still need to provide printer icons on my pages so that they can be printed?

A No. The linked style sheet technique you learned about in this hour allows you to support print-friendly web pages without any special links on the page. However, if you want to enable the user to view a print-friendly version of a page in a browser, you can link to another version of the page that uses the print-specific style sheet as its main (browser) style sheet. Or you can provide some "fine print" on the page that instructs the user to use the browser's Print Preview feature to view the print-friendly version of the page.

Workshop

The workshop contains quiz questions and activities to help you solidify your understanding of the material covered. Try to answer all questions before looking at the "Answers" section that follows.

Quiz

1. Does having a button to a print-friendly page mean the page is actually print-friendly?

2. What happens to an external style sheet that is linked to a page without any `media` attribute specified?

3. How would you link a style sheet named `freestyle.css` to a page so that it applies only when the page is viewed on a television?

Answers

1. No—you still have to link to a page with a specific stylesheet applied to the content such that it appears "print-friendly."

2. The `media` attribute assumes its default value of `all`, which causes the style sheet to target all media types.

3. `<link rel="stylesheet" type="text/css" href="freestyle.css" media="tv" />`

Exercises

▶ Create a print-friendly style sheet for a page that has a fair number of colors and images. Be sure to add an extra `<link />` tag to the page that links in the print-specific style sheet.

▶ If you're feeling really ambitious, try using the `handheld` value of the `<link />` tag's `media` attribute to create a handheld-specific version of one of your web pages. The concept is the same as creating a print-friendly page, except in this case you're dealing with an extremely constrained screen size instead of a printed page. You can test the page by publishing it and then opening it on a mobile phone or handheld browser.

Understanding Dynamic Web Sites

The term *dynamic* means something active or something that motivates another to become active.

When talking about web sites, a dynamic web site is one that incorporates interactivity into its functionality and design, but also motivates a user to take an action—read more, purchase a product, and so on. In this hour, you'll learn a little bit about the different types of interactivity that can make a site dynamic, including information about both server-side and client-side scripting (as well as some practical examples of the latter).

I've mentioned client-side scripting elsewhere in this book and you used a little of it in Hour 18 when you used event attributes and JavaScript to change the styles of particular elements—that is called manipulating the Document Object Model (DOM). You will do a bit more of that type of manipulation in this chapter. Specifically, after learning about the different technologies, you'll use JavaScript to display a random quote upon page-load and swap images based on user interaction.

WHAT YOU'LL LEARN IN THIS HOUR:

▶ How to conceptualize different types of dynamic content

▶ How to include JavaScript in your HTML

▶ How to display randomized text with JavaScript

▶ How to change images using JavaScript and user events

Understanding the Different Types of Scripting

In web development, there are two different types of scripting: server-side and client-side. Both types of scripting—which is, in fact, computer programming—are beyond the scope of this book. However, they are not *too* far beyond this book. Two very useful and popular books in the Sams Teach Yourself series are natural extensions of this one: *Sams Teach Yourself PHP, MySQL and Apache All-in-One* (for server-side scripting) and *Sams Teach Yourself JavaScript in 24 Hours* (for client-side scripting).

Server-side scripting refers to scripts that run on the web server, which then sends results to your web browser. If you have ever submitted a form at a web site, which includes using a search engine, you have experienced the results of a server-side script. Popular server-side scripting languages include the following; to learn more, visit the web sites listed here:

▶ PHP (PHP: Hypertext Preprocessor)—http://www.php.net/

▶ JSP (Java Server Pages)—http://java.sun.com/products/jsp/

▶ ASP (Active Server Pages)—http://www.asp.net/

▶ Perl—http://www.perl.org/

▶ Python—http://www.python.org/

▶ Ruby—http://www.ruby-lang.org/

NOTE

Despite its name, JavaScript is not a derivation or any other close relative to the object-oriented programming language called Java. Released by Sun Microsystems in 1995, Java is very closely related to the server-side scripting language JSP. JavaScript was created by Netscape Communications, also in 1995, and given the name to indicate a similarity in appearance to Java but not a direct connection with it.

On the other hand, *client-side scripting* refers to scripts that run within your web browser—there is no interaction with a web server in order for the scripts to run. The most popular client-side scripting language, by far, is *JavaScript*. For several years, research has shown that more than 93 percent of all web browsers have JavaScript enabled.

Another client-side scripting language is Microsoft's *VBScript (Visual Basic Scripting Edition)*. This language is only available with Microsoft Internet Explorer web browser, and therefore should not be used unless you are very sure that users will access your site with that web browser (such as in a closed corporate environment). Given a desire to reach the largest possible audience, this hour assumes the use of JavaScript for client-side scripting; the coding examples in this lesson are all JavaScript.

Including JavaScript in HTML

JavaScript code can live in one of two places within your files:

▶ In its own file with a .js extension.

▶ Directly in your HTML files.

External files are often used for script libraries (code you can reuse throughout many pages), while code appearing directly in the HTML files tends to achieve functionality specific to those individual pages. Regardless of where your JavaScript lives, your browser learns of its existence through the use of the `<script></script>` tag pair.

When you store your JavaScript in external files, it is referenced in this manner:

```
<script type="text/javascript" src="/path/to/script.js">
```

These `<script></script>` tags are typically placed between the `<head></head>` tag because it is not, strictly speaking, content that belongs in the `<body>` of the page. Instead, the `<script>` tag makes available a set of JavaScript functions or other information that the rest of the page can then use. However, you can also just encapsulate your JavaScript functions or code snippets with the `<script>` tag and place them anywhere in the page, as needed. Listing 21.1 shows an example of a JavaScript snippet placed in the `<body>` of an HTML document.

Listing 21.1   Using JavaScript to Print Some Text

```
<?xml version="1.0" encoding="UTF-8"?>
<!DOCTYPE html PUBLIC "-//W3C//DTD XHTML 1.1//EN"
  "http://www.w3.org/TR/xhtml11/DTD/xhtml11.dtd">

<html xmlns="http://www.w3.org/1999/xhtml" xml:lang="en">
  <head>
    <title>JavaScript Example</title>
  </head>

  <body>
    <h1>JavaScript Example</h1>
    <p>This text is HTML.</p>
    <script type="text/javascript">
    <!-- Hide the script from old browsers
    document.write('<p>This text comes from JavaScript.</p>');
    // Stop hiding the script -->
    </script>
  </body>
</html>
```

Between the `<script></script>` tags is a single JavaScript command that outputs the following HTML:

```
<p>This text comes from JavaScript.</p>
```

When the browser renders this HTML page, it sees the JavaScript between the `<script></script>` tags, stops for a millisecond to execute the command, then returns to rendering the output that now includes the HTML output from the JavaScript command. Figure 21.1 shows that this page appears as any other HTML page appears. It's an HTML page, but only a small part of the HTML comes from a JavaScript command.

FIGURE 21.1
The output of a JavaScript snippet looks like any other output.

NOTE

You might have noticed these two lines in Listing 21.1:

```
<!-- Hide the script from old
browsers
// Stop hiding the script -->
```

This is an HTML comment. Anything between the `<!--` start and the `-->` end will be visible in the source code but will not be rendered by the browser. In this case, JavaScript code is surrounded by HTML comments on the off chance that your visitor is running a very old web browser or has JavaScript turned off.

Displaying Random Content

You can use JavaScript to display something different each time a page is loaded. Maybe you have a collection of text or images that you find interesting enough to include in your pages?

I'm a sucker for a good quote. If you're like me, you might find it fun to incorporate an ever-changing quote into your web pages. To create a page with a quote that changes each time the page loads, you must first gather all your quotes together, along with their respective sources. You'll then place these quotes into a JavaScript *array*, which is a special type of storage unit in programming languages that is handy for holding lists of items.

After the quotes are loaded into an array, the JavaScript used to pluck out a quote at random is fairly simple. You've already seen the snippet that will print the output into your HTML page.

Listing 21.2 contains the complete HTML and JavaScript code for a web page that displays a random quote each time it loads.

Listing 21.2   A Random-Quote Web Page

```
<?xml version="1.0" encoding="UTF-8"?>
<!DOCTYPE html PUBLIC "-//W3C//DTD XHTML 1.1//EN"
  "http://www.w3.org/TR/xhtml11/DTD/xhtml11.dtd">

<html xmlns="http://www.w3.org/1999/xhtml" xml:lang="en">
  <head>
```

Listing 21.2   A Random-Quote Web Page

```html
<title>Quotable Quotes</title>

<script type="text/javascript">
  <!-- Hide the script from old browsers
  function getQuote() {
    // Create the arrays
    quotes = new Array(4);
    sources = new Array(4);

    // Initialize the arrays with quotes
    quotes[0] = "When I was a boy of 14, my father was so " +
    "ignorant...but when I got to be 21, I was astonished " +
    "at how much he had learned in 7 years.";
    sources[0] = "Mark Twain";
    quotes[1] = "Everybody is ignorant. Only on different " +
    "subjects.";
    sources[1] = "Will Rogers";
    quotes[2] = "They say such nice things about people at " +
    "their funerals that it makes me sad that I'm going to " +
    "miss mine by just a few days.";
    sources[2] = "Garrison Keilor";
    quotes[3] = "What's another word for thesaurus?";
    sources[3] = "Steven Wright";

    // Get a random index into the arrays
    i = Math.floor(Math.random() * quotes.length);

    // Write out the quote as HTML
    document.write("<dl style='background-color: lightpink'>\n");
    document.write("<dt>" + "\"<em>" + quotes[i] + "</em>\"\n");
    document.write("<dd>" + "- " + sources[i] + "\n");
    document.write("<dl>\n");
  }
  // Stop hiding the script -->
</script>
</head>

<body>
  <h1>Quotable Quotes</h1>
  <p>Following is a random quotable quote. To see a new quote just
  reload this page.</p>
  <script type="text/javascript">
    <!-- Hide the script from old browsers
    getQuote();
    // Stop hiding the script -->
  </script>
</body>
</html>
```

Although this code looks kind of long, if you look carefully, you'll see that a lot of it consists of the four quotes available for display on the page. After you get past the length, the code itself isn't too terribly complex.

The large number of lines between the first set of `<script></script>` tags is creating a function called `getQuote()`. Once a function is defined, it can be called in other places in the same page. Note that if the function existed in an external file, the function could be called from all of your pages.

If you look closely at the code you will see some lines like this:

```
// Create the arrays
```

and

```
// Initialize the arrays with quotes
```

These are code comments. The developer uses these comments to leave notes in the code so that anyone reading it has an idea of what the code is doing in that particular place. After the first comment about creating the arrays, you can see that two arrays are created—one called quotes and one called sources—each containing four elements:

```
quotes = new Array(4);
sources = new Array(4);
```

After the second comment (about initializing the arrays with quotes), four items are added to the arrays. We'll look closely at one of them, the first quote by Mark Twain:

```
quotes[0] = "When I was a boy of 14, my father was so " +
"ignorant...but when I got to be 21, I was astonished at " +
"how much he had learned in 7 years.";
sources[0] = "Mark Twain";
```

You already know that the arrays are named quotes and sources. But the variable to which values are assigned (in this instance) are called `quotes[0]` and `sources[0]`. Because quotes and sources are arrays, the items in the array will each have their own position. When using arrays, the first item in the array is not in slot #1, it is in slot #0. In other words, you begin counting at 0 instead of 1. Therefore, the text of the first quote (a value) is assigned to `quotes[0]` (a variable). Similarly, the text of the first source is assigned to `source[0]`.

Text strings are enclosed in quotation marks. However, in JavaScript, a line break indicates an end of a command, such that the following would cause problems in the code:

```
quotes[0] = "When I was a boy of 14, my father was so
ignorant...but when I got to be 21, I was astonished at
how much he had learned in 7 years.";
```

Therefore, you see that the string is built as a series of strings enclosed in quotation marks, with a plus sign (+) connecting the strings.

The next chunk of code definitely looks the most like programming; this line gets a random number:

```
i = Math.floor(Math.random() * quotes.length);
```

But you can't just pick any random number, because the purpose of the random number is to determine which of the quotes and sources should be printed—and there are only four quotes. So, this line of JavaScript:

- ▶ Uses `Math.random()` to get a random number between 0 and 1. For example, 0.5482749 might be a result of `Math.random()`.

- ▶ Multiplies the random number by the length of the quotes array, which is currently 4; the length of the array is the number of elements in the array. If the random number is 0.5482749 (as shown previously), multiplying that by 4 results in 2.1930996.

- ▶ Uses `Math.floor()` to round the result down to the nearest whole number. In other words, 2.1930996 turns into 2.

- ▶ Assigns the variable `i` a value of 2.

The rest of the function should look familiar, with a few exceptions. First, as you learned earlier this hour, `document.write()` is used to write HTML which is then rendered by the browser. Next, the strings are separated in such a way as to make it clear when something needs to be handled differently, such as escaping the quotation marks with a backslash when they should be printed literally (\") or when the value of a variable is substituted. The actual quote and source that is printed is the one that matches `quotes[i]` and `sources[i]`, where `i` is the number determined by the mathematical functions above.

But the act of simply writing the function doesn't mean that any output will be created. Further on in the HTML, you can see `getQuote();` between two `<script></script>` tags—that is how the function is called. Wherever that function call is made, that is where the output of the function will be placed. In this example, the output displays below a paragraph that introduces the quotation.

Figure 21.2 shows the Quotable Quotes page as it appears when loaded in a web browser. When the page reloads, there is a one in four chance a different quote displays—it is random, after all!

FIGURE 21.2
The Quotable Quotes page displays a random quote each time it is loaded.

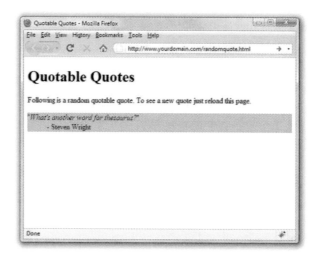

Keep in mind that you can easily modify this page to include your own quotes or other text that you want to display randomly. You can also increase the number of quotes available for display by adding more entries in the quotes and sources arrays in the code.

If you use the Quotable Quotes page as a starting point, you can easily alter the script and create your own interesting variation on the idea. And if you make mistakes along the way, so be it. The trick to getting past mistakes in script code is to be patient and carefully analyze the code you've entered. You can always remove code to simplify a script until you get it working, and then add new code one piece at a time to make sure each piece works.

Understanding the Document Object Model

Client-side interactivity using JavaScript typically takes the form of manipulating the Document Object Model (DOM) in some way. The DOM is the invisible structure of all documents—not the HTML structure or the way in which you apply levels of formatting, but a sort of overall framework or container. If this description seems vague, that's because it is; it's not a tangible object.

The overall container object is called the `document`. Any container within the document that has an ID is referenced by that ID. For example, if you have a `<div>` with an ID called wrapper, then in the DOM that element is referenced by:

```
document.wrapper
```

In Hour 17, you changed the visibility of a specific element by changing something in the `style` object associated with it. If you wanted to access the background-color style of the `<div>` with an ID called wrapper, it would be referred to as:

```
document.wrapper.style.background-color
```

To change the value of that style to something else, perhaps based on an interactive user event, use the following to change the color to white:

```
document.wrapper.style.background-color="#ffffff"
```

The DOM is the framework behind your ability to refer to elements and their associated objects in this way. Obviously, this is a brief overview of something quite complicated, but at least you can now begin to grasp what this document-dot-something business is all about. To learn a lot more about the DOM, visit the World Wide Web Consortium's information about the DOM at http://www.w3.org/DOM/.

Changing Images Based on User Interaction

In Hour 18 you were introduced to the different types of user interaction events, such as `onclick`, `onmouseover`, `onmouseout`, and so on. In that hour, you invoked changes in text based on user interaction; in this section, you'll see an example of a visible type of interaction that is both practical and dynamic.

Figure 21.3 shows a page from an online catalog for a collectibles company. Each page in the catalog shows a large image, information about the item, and a set of smaller images at the bottom of the page. In this type of catalog, close-up images of the details of each item are important to the potential buyer, but several large images on a page becomes unwieldy from both a display and bandwidth point of view.

FIGURE 21.3
The catalog item page when first loaded by the user.

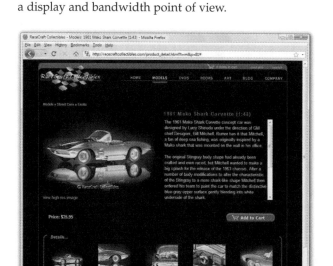

The large image on the page is called using this `<img/>` tag:

```
<img name="product_img" src="/path/to/image.jpg" alt="photo" />
```

As you can see, this image is given a name of `product_img`. Therefore, this image exists in the DOM as `document.product_img`. This is important because a little bit of JavaScript functionality allows us to dynamically change the value of `document.product_img.src`, which is the source (`src`) of the image.

The following code snippet creates the fourth small image in the group of five images shown at the bottom of Figure 21.3. The `onmouseover` event indicates that when the user rolls over this small image, the value of `document.product_img.src`—the large image slot—is filled with the path to a matching large image.

```
<a href="#" onmouseover="javascript:document.product_img.src =
'/path/to/large4.jpg'"><img src="/path/to/small4.jpg"
width="104" height="104" style="padding: 4px; border: 0px"
alt="photo" /></a>
```

Figure 21.4 shows the same page—not reloaded by the user—whereby the slot for the large image is filled by a different image when the user rolls over a smaller image at the bottom of the page. The mouse pointer hovers over the second image from the right. As the user rolls over the small version of the interior photo, the large version of it is shown in the top area on the page.

FIGURE 21.4
The large image is replaced when the user rolls over a smaller one.

Summary

In this hour, you've learned about the differences between server-side scripting and client-side scripting and you've learned how to include JavaScript in your HTML files in order to add a little interactivity to your web sites. You also learned how to use the JavaScript `document.write()` method to display random quotes upon page load. Lastly, you learned what the Document Object Model is all about.

By applying the knowledge you've gained from previous hours, you've learned how to use client-side scripting to make images on a web page respond to mouse movements. None of these tasks requires much in the way of programming skills, but they might inspire you to learn more about JavaScript or a server-side programming language so you can give your pages more complex interactive features.

Q&A

Q If I want to use the random quote script from this lesson, but I want to have a library of a lot of quotes, do I have to put all the quotes in each page?

A Yes. Each item in the array has to be there. This is where you can begin to see a bit of a tipping point between something that can be client-side and something that is better dealt with on the server side. If you have a true library of random quotations and only one is presented at any given time, it's probably best to store those items in a database table and use a little piece of server-side scripting to connect to that database, retrieve the text, and print it on the page. Alternately, you can always continue to carry all the quotes with you in JavaScript, but you should at least put that JavaScript function into a different file that can be maintained separately from the text.

Q I've seen some online catalogs that display a large image in what looks to be a layer on top of the web site content — I can see the regular web site content underneath it, but the focus is on the large image. How is that done?

A The description sounds like an effect created by a JavaScript library called "Lightbox." The Lightbox library allows you to display an image, or a gallery of images, in a layer that is placed over your site content. This is a very popular library used to show the details of large images or just a set of images deemed important enough to showcase "above" the content, as it were. The library is freely available from its creator at http://www.huddletogether.com/projects/lightbox/. To install and use it, follow the instructions included with the software. You will be able to integrate it into your site using the knowledge you've gained in this book so far.

Workshop

Quiz

1. You've made a picture of a button and named it button.gif. You've also made a simple GIF animation of the button whereby it flashes green and white. You've named that GIF flashing.gif. What HTML and JavaScript code would you use to make the button flash whenever a user moves the mouse pointer over it and also link to a page named gohere.html when a user clicks the button?

2. How would you modify the code you wrote for Question 1 so that the button flashes when a user moves his mouse over it and continues flashing even if he moves the mouse away from it?

3. What does the plus sign mean in the following context:

```
document.write('This is a text string ' + 'that I have created.');
```

Answers

1. Your code might look something like this:

```
<a href="gohere.html"
onmouseover="javascript:document.flasher.src='flashing.gif'"
onmouseout="javascript:document.flasher.src='button.gif'">
<img src="button.gif" id="flasher" style="border-style:none" /></a>
```

2. Your code might look something like this:

```
<a href="gohere.html"
onmouseover="javascript:document.flasher.src='flashing.gif'">
<img src="button.gif" id="flasher" style="border-style:none" /></a>
```

3. The plus sign (+) is used to join two strings together.

Exercises

▶ Do you have any pages that would look flashier or be easier to understand if the navigation icons or other images changed when the mouse passed over them? If so, try creating some highlighted versions of the images, and try modifying your own page using the information presented in this hour.

▶ You can display random images—such as graphical banners or advertisements—in the same way you learned to display random content using JavaScript earlier in this chapter. Instead of printing text, just print the `<img/>` tag for the images you want to display.

Working with Web-Based Forms

To this point, pretty much everything in this book has focused on getting information out to others. But you can also use your web pages to gather information from the people who read them.

Web forms allow you to receive feedback, orders, or other information from the users who visit your web pages. If you've ever used a search engine such as Google, Yahoo!, or Bing, you're familiar with HTML forms—those single field entry forms with one button that, when pressed, give you all the information you are looking for and then some. Product order forms are also an extremely popular use of forms; if you've ordered anything from Amazon.com or purchased something from an eBay seller, you've used forms. In this hour, you learn how to create your own forms, but you learn only how to create the front-end of those forms. Working with the back-end of forms requires the knowledge of a programming language and is beyond the scope of this book.

An HTML form is part of a web page that includes areas where users can enter information to be sent back to you, sent to another e-mail address that you specify, sent to a database that you manage, or sent to another system altogether such as a third-party management system for your forms such as Salesforce.com.

How HTML Forms Work

Before you learn the HTML tags that are used to make your own forms, you should at least conceptually understand how the information from those forms makes its way back to you. The actual behind-the-scenes (the *server-side* or *back-end*) process requires knowledge of at least one programming language or at least the ability to follow specific instructions when

NOTE

PHP is the most popular server-side programming language; it's supported by any web-hosting provider worth their salt. You can learn more about PHP at `http://www.php.net/` or you can just dive right in to learning this programming language (plus database interactivity, as discussed in Hour 21) from the ground up in *Sams Teach Yourself PHP, Apache, and MySQL All-in-One*. Although several other books on PHP and related technologies are available, I am partial to this one because I wrote it. It is geared toward the absolute beginners with PHP or any other programming language.

NOTE

Technically, there is a way to send form data without a server-side script, but that method—which uses a mailto link in the `action` attribute of the `<form>`—produces inconsistent results. Individual web browsers, as well as personal security settings, will cause that action to respond differently than you intended and certainly not as the user expects. When users submit a form, they expect it to invoke a script, perform a process that is invisible to them, and then return a message stating that the process has been completed. That is not the case with a form that invokes a mailto.

using someone else's server-side script to handle the form input. At that point in the process, you should either work with someone who has the technical knowledge or you should learn the basics on your own. Simple form-processing is not difficult at all and it is likely that your web-hosting provider has several back-end scripts that you can use with minimal customization.

Forms include a button for the user to submit the form; that button can be an image that you create yourself or a standard HTML form button that is created when a form `<input>` tag is created and given a `type` value of `submit`. When someone clicks a form submission button, all the information typed in the form is sent to a URL that you specify in the `action` attribute of the `<form>` tag . That URL should point to a specific script that will process your form, sending the form contents via email or performing another step in an interactive process (such as requesting results from a search engine or placing items in an online shopping cart).

Once you start thinking about doing more with form content than simply e-mailing results to yourself, additional technical knowledge is required. For example, if you want to create an online store that accepts credit cards and processes transactions, there are some well-established practices for doing so, all geared toward ensuring the security of your customers' data. That is not an operation that you'll want to enter into lightly; you'll need more knowledge than that which is provided in this book.

Before you put a form online, you should look in the user guide for your web-hosting provider and see what they offer in the way of form-processing scripts. A keyword you might search for is **CGI** (Common Gateway Interface). *CGI* is a standard way for programs (such as form-handling scripts) to interact with web servers.

Creating a Form

Every form must begin with a `<form>` tag, which can be located anywhere in the body of the HTML document. The `<form>` tag normally has two attributes, `method` and `action`:

```
<form method="post" action="mailto:me@mysite.com">
```

The most common `method` is `post`, which sends the form entry results as a document. In some situations, you might need to use `method="get"`, which submits the results as part of the URL header instead. For example, `get` is sometimes used when submitting queries to search engines from a web form. Because you're not yet an expert on forms, just use post unless your web-hosting provider's documentation tells you to do otherwise.

The action attribute specifies the address to which to send the form data. You have two options here:

▶ You can type the location of a form-processing program or script on a web server and the form data will then be sent to that program.

▶ You can type mailto: followed by your email address and the form data will be sent directly to you whenever someone fills out the form. However, this approach is completely dependent on the user's computer being properly configured with an email client. People accessing your site from a public computer without an email client will be left out in the cold.

The form created in Listing 22.1 and shown in Figure 22.1 includes just about every type of user input component you can currently use on HTML forms. Refer to this figure and listing as you read the following explanations of each type of input element.

Listing 22.1   A Form with Various User-Input Components

```
<?xml version="1.0" encoding="UTF-8"?>
<!DOCTYPE html PUBLIC "-//W3C//DTD XHTML 1.1//EN"
  "http://www.w3.org/TR/xhtml11/DTD/xhtml11.dtd">

<html xmlns="http://www.w3.org/1999/xhtml" xml:lang="en">
  <head>
    <title>Guest Book</title>

    <style type="text/css">
      .formlabel {
        font-weight:bold;
        width: 250px;
        margin-bottom: 12px;
        float: left;
        text-align: left;
        clear: left;
      }
      .formfield {
        font-weight:normal;
        margin-bottom: 12px;
        float: left;
```

Listing 22.1   A Form with Various User-Input Components

```
            text-align: left;
        }

    input, textarea, select {
        border: 1px solid black;
    }
    </style>
</head>
<body>
    <h1>My Guest Book</h1>
    <p>Please sign my guest book. Thanks!</p>
    <form method="post" action="URL_to_script">

    <div class="formlabel">What is your name?</div>
    <div class="formfield"><input type="text" name="name"
        size="50" /></div>

    <div class="formlabel">What is your e-mail address?</div>
    <div class="formfield"><input type="text" name="email"
        size="50" /></div>

    <div class="formlabel">Please check all that apply:</div>
    <div class="formfield">
        <input type="checkbox" name="website_response[]" value="I
        really like your Web site." />I really like your Web site.<br />
        <input type="checkbox" name="website_response[]" value="One
        of the best sites I've seen." />One of the best sites I've
        seen.<br />
        <input type="checkbox" name="website_response[]" value="I sure
        wish my site looked as good as yours." />I sure wish my site
        looked as good as yours.<br />
        <input type="checkbox" name="website_response[]" value="I have
        no taste and I'm pretty dense, so your site didn't do much for
        me." />I  have no taste and I'm pretty dense, so your site
        didn't do much for me.<br />
    </div>

    <div class="formlabel">Choose the one thing you love best about my
    web site:</div>
    <div class="formfield">
        <input type="radio" name="lovebest" value="me" />That gorgeous
        picture of you.<br />
        <input type="radio" name="lovebest" value="cats" />All the
        beautiful pictures of your cats.<br />
        <input type="radio" name="lovebest" value="childhood" />The
        inspiring recap of your suburban childhood.<br />
        <input type="radio" name="lovebest" value="treasures" />The
        detailed list of all your Elvis memorabilia.<br />
    </div>
```

Listing 22.1   A Form with Various User-Input Components

```
<div class="formlabel">If my web site were a book, how many copies
would it sell?</div>
<div class="formfield">
  <select size="3" name="sales">
    <option value="Millions, for sure." selected="selected">Millions,
      for sure.</option>
    <option value="100,000+ (would be Oprah's favorite)">100,000+
      (would be Oprah's favorite)</option>
    <option value="Thousands (an under-appreciated classic)">Thousands
      (an under-appreciated classic)</option>
    <option value="Very few: not banal enough for today's public">Very
      few: not banal enough for today's public.</option>
    <option value="Sell? None. Everyone will download it for free.">Sell?
      None. Everyone will download it for free.</option>
  </select>
</div>

<div class="formlabel">How can I improve my web site?</div>
<div class="formfield">
  <select name="suggestion">
    <option value="Couldn't be better." selected="selected">Couldn't
      be better.</option>
    <option value="More about the cats.">More about the cats.</option>
    <option value="More about the family.">More about the family.</option>
    <option value="More about Elvis.">More about Elvis.</option>
  </select>
</div>

<div class="formlabel">Feel free to type more praise, gift offers, etc.
    below:</div>
<div class="formfield">
  <textarea name="comments" rows="4" cols="55"></textarea>
</div>

<div style="float:left;">
  <input type="submit" value="Click Here to Submit" />
  <input type="reset" value="Erase and Start Over" />
</div>
</form>
</body>
</html>
```

The code in Listing 22.1 uses a `<form>` tag that contains quite a few `<input />` tags. Each `<input />` tag corresponds to a specific user input component, such as a check box or radio button. The input, select, and text area elements contain borders in the style sheet, so it is easy to see the outline of the elements in the form. Keep in mind that you can apply all sorts of CSS to those elements.

The next few sections dig into the `<input />` and other form-related tags in detail.

Accepting Text Input

To ask the user for a specific piece of information within a form, use the `<input />` tag. This tag must fall between the `<form>` and `</form>` tags, but it can be anywhere on the page in relation to text, images, and other HTML tags. For example, to ask for someone's name, you could type the following:

```
What's your name? <input type="text" size="50" maxlength="100"
name="name" />
```

The `type` attribute indicates what type of form element to display—a simple, one-line text entry box in this case. (Each element type is discussed individually in the following sections.)

The `size` attribute indicates approximately how many characters wide the text input box should be. If you are using a proportionally spaced font, the width of the input will vary depending on what the user enters. If the input is too long to fit in the box, most web browsers will automatically scroll the text to the left.

The `maxlength` attribute determines the number of characters the user is allowed to type into the text box. If a user tries to type beyond the specified length, the extra characters won't appear. You can specify a length that is longer, shorter, or the same as the physical size of the text box. `size` and `maxlength` are used only for `type="text"` because other input types (check boxes, radio buttons, and so on) have fixed sizes.

Naming Each Piece of Form Data

No matter what type an input element is, you must give a name to the data it gathers. You can use any name you like for each input item, as long as each one on the form is different (except in the case of radio buttons and checkboxes, which are discussed later in this hour). When the form is processed by a back-end script, each data item is identified by name. This name becomes a variable, which is filled with a value. The value is either what the user typed in the form or the value associated with the element the user selected.

For example, if a user enters **Jane Doe** in the text box defined previously, a variable is sent to the form processing script; the variable is name and the value of the variable is *Jane Doe*. Form-processing scripts work with these types of variable names and values.

Additional examples of name/value pairs are covered in the following sections.

Including Hidden Data in Forms

Want to send certain data items to the server script that processes a form but don't want the user to see those data items? Use an `<input />` tag with a `type="hidden"` attribute. This attribute has no effect on the display; it just adds any name and value you specify to the form results when they are submitted.

If you are using a form-processing script provided by your web-hosting provider, you might use this attribute to tell a script where to email the form results. For example, the following code will e-mail the results to me@mysite.com:

```
<input type="hidden" name="mail_to" value="me@mysite.com" />
```

Scripts often use at least one or two hidden input elements to carry additional data along for the ride that might be useful when you receive the results of the form submission; some examples include an e-mail address and a subject for the e-mail. If you are using a script provided by your web hosting provider, consult the documentation provided with that script for additional details about potential required hidden fields.

Exploring Form Input Controls

Various input controls are available for retrieving information from the user. You've already seen one text-entry option, and the next few sections introduce you to most of the remaining form-input options you can use to design forms.

Check Boxes

The simplest input type is a *check box*, which appears as a small square. Users can click checkboxes to select or deselect one or more items in a group. For example, the checkboxes listed in Listing 22.1 display after a label that reads "Please check all that apply," implying that the user could indeed check all that apply.

The HTML for the checkboxes in Listing 22.1 shows that the value of the name attribute is the same for all of them: website_response[].

```
<input type="checkbox" name="website_response[]" value="I
    really like your Web site." /> I really like your Web site.<br />
<input type="checkbox" name="website_response[]" value="One
    of the best sites I've seen." /> One of the best sites
    I've seen.<br />
<input type="checkbox" name="website_response[]" value="I sure
    wish my site looked as good as yours." /> I sure wish my site
    looked as good as yours.<br />
<input type="checkbox" name="website_response[]" value="I have
    no taste and I'm pretty dense, so your site didn't do much for
    me." /> I  have no taste and I'm pretty dense, so your site
    didn't do much for me.<br />
```

The use of the brackets (`[]`) indicates to the processing script that a series of values will be placed into this one variable, instead of just one value (well, it might just be one value if the user only selects one checkbox). If a user selects the first checkbox, the text string "I really like your Web site." will be placed in the `website_response[]` bucket. If the user selects the third checkbox, the text string "I sure wish my site looked as good as yours." will also be put into the `website_response[]` bucket. The processing script will then work with that variable as an array of data rather just a single entry.

However, you might see groups of checkboxes that do use individual names for the variables in the group. For example, the following is another way of writing the checkbox group:

```
<input type="checkbox" name="liked_site" value="yes" /> I really like
    your Web site.<br />
<input type="checkbox" name="best_site" value="yes" /> One of the best
    Sites I've seen.<br />
<input type="checkbox" name="my_site_sucks" value="yes" />I sure wish my
    site looked as good as yours.<br />
<input type="checkbox" name="am_dense" value="yes" />I have no taste and
    I'm pretty dense, so your site didn't do much for me.<br />
```

In the previous checkboxes, the variable name of the first checkbox is "liked_site" and the value (if checked) is "yes."

If you want a check box to be checked by default when the form is rendered by the web browser, include the `checked` attribute. For example, the following code creates two check boxes and the first is checked by default:

```
<input type="checkbox" name="website_response[]" value="I
    really like your site." checked="checked"/> I really like your
    site.<br />
<input type="checkbox" name="website_response[]" value="One
    of the best sites I've seen." /> One of the best sites I've
    seen.<br />
```

The check box labeled "I really like your site." is checked in this example. The user would have to click the checkbox to indicate they had another opinion of your site. The checkbox marked "One of the best I've seen." would be unchecked to begin with, so the user would have to click it to turn it on.

Check boxes that are not selected do not appear in the form output at all.

TIP

If you find that the label for an input element is displayed too close to the element, just add a space between the close of the `<input />` tag and the start of the label text, like this:

```
<input type="checkbox"
name="mini" /> Mini Piano
Stool
```

WARNING

XHTML requires all attributes to have an equal sign followed by a value. This explains why `checked="checked"` is used to indicate that a check box is checked (as opposed to just `checked`). This rule applies to all Boolean (`true`/`false`, `on`/`off`, yes/no, and so on) attributes that you might come across in HTML.

NOTE

If you look at other web designers' forms, you might see checkboxes use the same names but with different values, as in the following code:

```
<input type="checkbox"
name="pet" value="dog">
dog<br />
<input type="checkbox"
name="pet" value="cat">
cat<br />
<input type="checkbox"
name="pet" value="iguana">
iguana<br />
```

If the user checks more than one checkbox, it is more than likely only the last value will be processed by the script. This is one reason why you should give some thought to your checkbox groups, the name of the group, and the individual values you want sent to the script before you submit it.

Radio Buttons

Radio buttons, for which only one choice can be selected at a time, are almost as simple to implement as check boxes. The simplest use of a radio button is for yes/no questions or for voting when only one candidate can be selected.

To create a radio button, just use `type="radio"` and give each option its own `<input />` tag. Use the same `name` for all the radio buttons in a group, but don't use the [] that you used with the checkbox:

```
<input type="radio" name="vote" value="yes" checked="checked" /> Yes<br
/>
<input type="radio" name="vote" value="no" /> No <br/>
```

The `value` can be any name or code you choose. If you include the `checked` attribute, that button is selected by default. No more than one radio button with the same `name` can be checked.

When designing your form and choosing between checkboxes and radio buttons, ask yourself: is the question being asked or implied one that could be answered only one way? If so, use a radio button.

Selection Lists

Both *scrolling lists* and *pull-down pick lists* are created with the `<select>` tag. You use this tag together with the `<option>` tag, as the following example shows:

```
<select name="extras" size="3" multiple="multiple">
  <option value="Electric windows" selected="selected">Electric
windows</option>
  <option value="Sunroof">Sunroof</option>
  <option value="AM/FM Radio">AM/FM Radio</option>
  <option value="CD Player">CD Player</option>
  <option value="GPS">GPS</option>
</select>
```

No HTML tags other than `<option>` and `</option>` should appear between the `<select>` and `</select>` tags.

Unlike the `text` input type, the `size` attribute here determines how many items show at once on the selection list. If `size="2"` were used in the preceding code, only the first two options would be visible and a scrollbar would appear next to the list so the user could scroll down to see the third option.

Including the `multiple` attribute allows users to select more than one option at a time; the `selected` attribute makes an option initially selected by default. When the form is submitted, the text specified in the `value` attribute for each option accompanies the selected option.

Text Areas

The `<input type="text">` attribute mentioned earlier this hour allows the user to enter only a single line of text. When you want to allow multiple lines of text in a single input item, use the `<textarea>` and `</textarea>` tags. Any text you include between these two tags is displayed as the default entry. Here's an example:

```
<textarea name="comments" rows="4" cols="20">Please send more
information.
</textarea>
```

As you probably guessed, the `rows` and `cols` attributes control the number of rows and columns of text that fit in the input box. The `cols` attribute is a little less exact than `rows` and approximates the number of characters that fit in a row of text. Text area boxes do have a scrollbar, however, so the user can enter more text than what fits in the display area.

Submitting Form Data

Every form must include a button that submits the form data to a script on the server. You can put any label you like on this button with the `value` attribute:

```
<input type="submit" value="Place My Order Now!" />
```

A gray button will be sized to fit the label you put in the `value` attribute. When the user clicks it, all data items on the form are sent to the email address or program script specified in the form's `action` attribute.

You can also include a Submit Reset button that clears all entries on the form so users can start over if they change their minds or make mistakes. Use the following:

```
<input type="reset" value="Clear This Form and Start Over" />
```

If the standard Submit and Reset buttons look a little bland to you, remember that you can style them using CSS. If that's not good enough, you'll be glad to know that there is an easy way to substitute your own graphics for

TIP

If you leave out the `size` attribute or specify `size="1"`, the list creates a drop-down pick list. Pick lists don't allow for multiple choices; they are logically equivalent to a group of radio buttons. The following example shows another way to choose yes or no for a question:

```
<select name="vote">
  <option
value="yes">Yes</option>
  <option
value="no">No</option>
</select>
```

these buttons. To use an image of your choice for a Submit button, type the following:

```
<input type="image" src="button.gif" alt="Order Now!" />
```

The `button.gif` image will display on the page and the form will be submitted when a user clicks the `button.gif` image. You can also include any attributes normally used with the `<img />` tag, such as `alt` and `style`.

Summary

This hour demonstrated how to create HTML forms, which allow your web page visitors to enter specific information. We stopped short of doing anything with that information because form-handling requires an external script to process that form.

You learned about all the major form elements, as well as how form-processing scripts interpret the names and value attributes of those elements. When you are ready to try a back-end form processing script, you're now well-versed in the front-end details.

Table 22.1 summarizes the HTML tags and attributes covered in this hour.

Table 22.1   HTML Tags and Attributes Covered in Hour 22

Tag/Attribute	Function
`<form>...</form>`	Indicates an input form.
Attributes	
`action="scripturl"`	The address of the script to process this form input.
`method="post/get"`	How the form input will be sent to the server. Normally set to `post`, rather than `get`.
`<input />`	An input element for a form.
Attributes	
`type="controltype"`	The type for this input widget. Possible values are `checkbox`, `hidden`, `radio`, `reset`, `submit`, `text`, and `image`.
`name="name"`	The unique name of this item, as passed to the script.
`value="value"`	The default value for a text or hidden item. For a check box or radio button, it's the value to be submitted with the form. For reset or submit buttons, it's the label for the button itself.

Tag/Attribute	Function
`src="imageurl"`	The source file for an image.
`checked="checked"`	For check boxes and radio buttons. Indicates that this item is checked.
`size="width"`	The width, in characters, of a text input region.
`maxlength="maxlength"`	The maximum number of characters that can be entered into a text region.
`<textarea>...</textarea>`	Indicates a multiline text entry form element. Default text can be included.

Attributes

`name="name"`	The name to be passed to the script.
`rows="numrows"`	The number of rows this text area displays.
`cols="numchars"`	The number of columns (characters) this text area displays.
`<select>...</select>`	Creates a menu or scrolling list of possible items.

Attributes

`name="name"`	The name that is passed to the script.
`size="numelements"`	The number of elements to display. If `size` is indicated, the selection becomes a scrolling list. If no `size` is given, the selection is a drop-down pick list.
`multiple="multiple"`	Allows multiple selections from the list.
`<option>...</option>`	Indicates a possible item within a `<select>` element.

Attributes

`selected="selected"`	With this attribute included, the `<option>` will be selected by default in the list.
`value="value"`	The value to submit if this `<option>` is selected when the form is submitted.

Q&A

Q I've heard that it's dangerous to send credit card numbers over the Internet. Can't thieves intercept form data on its way to me?

A It is possible to intercept form data (and any web pages or email messages) as it travels through the Internet. If you ask for credit card numbers or other sensitive information on your forms, you should implement secure web browsing on a secure server using an SSL (Secure Sockets Layer) certificate. These SSL certificates are available from companies such as VeriSign (`http://www.verisign.com/`), but you should check with your web-hosting provider for the types of SSL certificates they install and resell.

To put the level of risk in perspective, remember that it is much more difficult to intercept information traveling through the Internet than it is to look over someone's shoulder in a restaurant or retail store. Even so, you should always utilize secure pages anytime you're handling sensitive financial information such as credit card numbers, especially when someone else is trusting you to handle their sensitive information.

Q Can I put forms on a CD/DVD-ROM or do they have to be on the Internet?

A You can put a form anywhere you can put a web page. If it's on a disk or CD-ROM instead of a web server, it can be filled out by users whether or not they are connected to the Internet. Of course, they must be connected to the Internet (or your local intranet) when they click the Submit button or the information won't reach the processing script.

Workshop

The workshop contains quiz questions and activities to help you solidify your understanding of the material covered. Try to answer all questions before looking at the "Answers" section that follows.

Quiz

1. What HTML code would you use to create a guestbook form that asks someone for his or her name, sex, age, and email address? Assume that you have a form-processing script set up at `/cgi/generic` and that you need to include the following hidden input element to tell the script where to send the form results:

```
<input type="hidden" name="mailto" value="you@yoursite.com" />
```

2. If you created an image named `sign-in.gif`, how would you use it as the Submit button for the guestbook you created in Question 1?

Answers

1. You would use HTML code similar to the following (with the appropriate DOCTYPE declaration, of course):

```html
<html>
  <head>
    <title>My Guestbook</title>
  </head>

  <body>
    <h1>My Guestbook: Please Sign In</h1>
    <form method="post" action="/cgi/generic">
      <p>
        <input type="hidden" name="mailto" value="you@yoursite.com" />
        Your name: <input type="text" name="name" size="20" /><br />
        Your sex: <input type="radio" name="sex" value="male" /> male
        <input type="radio" name="sex" value="female" /> female<br />
        Your age: <input type="text" name="age" size="4" /><br />
        Your e-mail address: <input type="text" name="email"
size="30" />
        <br />
        <input type="submit" value="sign in" />
        <input type="reset" value="erase" />
      </p>
    </form>
  </body>
</html>
```

2. Replace the following code:

```html
<input type="submit" value="Sign In" />
```

with this code:

```html
<input type="image" src="sign-in.gif" alt="Sign In" />
```

Exercises

▶ Create a form using all the different types of input elements and selection lists to make sure you understand how each of them works.

▶ Investigate the form-handling options at your web-hosting provider and use a script made available to you by the web-hosting provider to process the form you created in the previous exercise.

HOUR 23
Organizing and Managing a Web Site

The bulk of this book has led you through the design and creation of your own web content, from text to graphics and multimedia. Along the way I've noted some of the ways you can think about the lifecycle of that content, but in this hour you'll learn how to look at your work as a whole.

This hour shows you how to think about organizing and presenting multiple web pages so that visitors will be able to navigate among them without confusion. You'll also learn about ways to make your web site memorable enough to visit again and again. Web developers use the term "sticky" to describe pages that people don't want to leave. Hopefully this chapter will help you to make your web sites downright gooey!

Because web sites can be (and usually should be) updated frequently, it's essential to create pages that can be easily maintained. This hour shows you how to add comments and other documentation to your pages so that you—or anyone else on your staff—can understand and modify your pages.

WHAT YOU'LL LEARN IN THIS HOUR:

▶ How to determine when one page is enough to handle all your content

▶ How to organize a simple site

▶ How to organize a larger site

▶ How to write maintainable HTML code

By this point in the book, you should have enough HTML and CSS knowledge to produce most of your web site. You probably have created a number of pages already, and perhaps even published them online.

As you read this hour, think about how your pages are organized now and how you can improve that organization. Have you used comments in your HTML, or a document for future web site maintainers regarding your organization? If not, this would be a good time to start. Along the way, don't be surprised if you decide to do a redesign that involves changing almost all of your pages—the results are likely to be well worth the effort!

TRY IT YOURSELF

Evaluate Your Organization

When One Page Is Enough

Building and organizing an attractive and effective web site doesn't always need to be a complex task. If you are creating a web presence for a single entity (such as a local event) that requires only a brief amount of very specific information, you can effectively present that information on a single page without a lot of flashy graphics. In fact, there are several positive features to a single-page web presence:

▶ All the information on the site downloads quicker than on more extensive sites.

▶ The whole site can be printed on paper with a single print command, even if it is several paper pages long.

▶ Visitors can easily save the site on their hard drives for future reference, especially if it uses a minimum of graphics.

▶ Links between different parts of the same page usually respond more quickly than links to other pages.

Figure 23.1 shows the first part of a web page that serves its intended audience better as a single lengthy page than it would as a multipage site. The page begins, as most introductory pages should, with a succinct explanation of what the page is about and who would want to read it. A detailed table of contents allows visitors to skip directly to the reference material in which they are most interested. It contains about eight paper pages worth of text explaining how to begin the process of buying a house—something a visitor might think about printing out and reading later, perhaps while also taking notes.

FIGURE 23.1
A good table of contents can make a lengthy page easy to navigate.

As Figure 23.2 shows, each short section of the page is followed by a link back up to the table of contents, so navigating around the page feels much the same as navigating around a multipage site. Because the contents of the page are intended as a handy reference, visitors will definitely prefer the convenience of bookmarking or saving a single page instead of eight or 10 separate pages.

Having seen all the fancy graphics and layouts in this book, you might be tempted to forget that a good, old-fashioned outline is often the clearest and most efficient way to organize long web pages within a site.

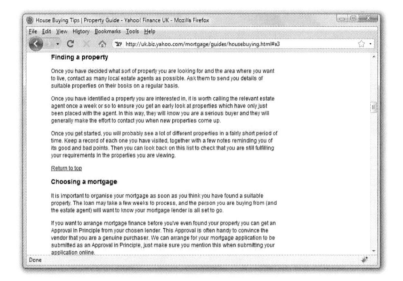

FIGURE 23.2
Always provide a link back to the table of contents after each section of a long web page.

Organizing a Simple Site

Although single-page sites have their place, most companies and individuals serve their readers better by dividing their site into short, quick-read pages surrounded by graphical navigation that allows them to reach almost all the information they could want within a few clicks. Furthermore, using multiple pages instead of a series of very long pages minimizes scrolling around on the page, which can be especially bothersome for visitors who are using mobile devices to view the site or who have relatively low-resolution monitors (less than 800×600).

The goal of the "home" page is simply to make the organization "visible" on the Internet, but also—and more importantly—act as a portal to the information contained within the site itself. The main page of a site should provide the user with enough information to provide a clear picture of the organization, as well as traditional address and telephone contact information and an e-mail address to contact with questions or feedback. It should also provide clear pathways into the highly structured information that should be contained on other pages in the site. The main page shown in Figure 23.3 provides examples of all these good features: basic information, contact information, and paths to information for multiple audiences.

FIGURE 23.3
This university main page uses a basic design, minimal but useful graphics, and clear structure to entice users to explore for more information.

TIP

Regardless of how large your site is, it's a good idea to carefully organize your resources. For example, place the images for your web pages in a separate folder named `images`. Similarly, if you have files that are available for download, place them in a folder called `downloads`. This makes it much easier to keep track of web page resources based on their particular types (HTML pages, GIF images, and so on). Additionally, if you organize your site into sections, such as "Company," "Products," "Press," and so on, put the individual pages into similarly-named directories (`company`, `products`, `press`, and so on) for the same organizational reasons.

One of the most common mistakes beginning web site developers make is creating pages that look different than other pages on the site. Another equally serious mistake is using the same, publicly available clip art that thousands of other web authors are also using. Remember that on the Internet, one click can take you around the world. The only way to make your pages memorable and recognizable as a cohesive site is to make all your pages adhere to a unique, unmistakable visual theme. In other words, strive for uniqueness as compared to other web sites, yet uniformity within the site itself.

As an example of how uniformity can help make a site more cohesive, think about large, popular sites you might have visited, such as ESPN.com. If you visit the MLB section at ESPN.com (see Figure 23.4) and the NFL section (see Figure 23.5), you'll notice a very similar structure.

FIGURE 23.4
The MLB section at ESPN.com.

FIGURE 23.5
The NFL section at ESPN.com.

In both examples, you see navigation elements at the top of the page (including some sub-navigation elements), a large area in the middle of the page for the featured item graphic, a rectangle on the right side containing links to top stories at the moment, and a second rectangle under the top stories links for the display of an advertisement. The only difference between the MLB section and the NFL section is the color scheme: the MLB section is part of a predominantly blue color scheme, while the NFL section is predominantly green. However, in both sections, you know that if you want to read the popular news stories, you look to the right of the page. If you want to navigate to another section in the site or to the site's main page, you look to a navigational element in the top left of the page.

These consistent elements help ensure your users will be able to navigate throughout your content with confidence. From a maintenance perspective, the consistent structural template enables you to reuse pieces of the code. This code reuse typically happens through dynamic programming outside the scope of this book, but in general it means that instead of copying and pasting the same HTML over and over, the HTML only exists in one place and is applied dynamically to the content. Therefore, instead of making changes to thousands of files, you would only need to make a change once.

Organizing a Larger Site

For complex sites, sophisticated layout and graphics can help organize and improve the looks of your site when used consistently throughout all of your pages. To see how you can make aesthetics and organization work hand-in-hand, let's look at examples of navigation (and thus underlying organization) for a few sites that present a large volume of information to several different audiences.

Figure 23.6 shows the main page of Amazon.com, specifically with the side navigation selected. Amazon is in the business of selling products, plain and simple. Therefore, it makes sense for Amazon to show product categories as the main navigational elements, as shown in this figure.

FIGURE 23.6
Amazon.com shows product categories as primary navigation elements.

Although Amazon is in the business of selling products, it still has to provide information regarding who they are, how to contact them, and other ancillary yet important information to enhance the business-to-consumer relationship. Links to this sort of information appear in the footer, or bottom portion, of the Amazon.com web site—outside of the viewing area of this screenshot. When creating your site template, you must determine the most important content areas and how to organize that content; also, remember to provide users with basic information—especially if that information will enhance your image and make the user feel as if you value what they have to say.

The next example is of a secondary page within the Starbucks.com web site. All of the pages in the Starbucks.com web site follow one of the common types of presenting navigation and sub-navigation: a horizontal strip for main navigation, with secondary elements for that section placed in a vertical column on the left. As shown in Figure 23.7, the section the user is currently browsing ("about us") is highlighted. This visual indicator helps users orient themselves within the site. Using a visual indicator is a useful tactic because your users might arrive at a page via a search engine or by a link from another web site. Once your users arrive, you want them to feel at home—or at least feel as if they know where they are in relation to your site—once they get there.

FIGURE 23.7
This Starbucks.com secondary page shows a main navigation element selected with secondary navigation on the left side of the page.

As you can see by the different main navigation elements—"our coffees," "our stores," "starbucks card," "at home," "for business," "about us," and "shop online"—the Starbucks web site has to serve the needs of many different types of people coming to the web site for many different reasons. As you organize your own site content, determine the information that is most important to you, as well as that which is most important to your users, and create a navigation scheme that finds a happy medium between the two.

Figure 23.8 shows another example of a navigation style, this time with a twist on the standard top navigation/left-side navigation scheme. In this example, the left side navigation (secondary navigation in this case) also appears in a drop-down menu under the main navigation (refer to Hour 17 for information on how to do something like this). Hovering the mouse over any of the other main navigation elements shows similar menus. This scheme allows users to have an entire site map at their fingertips, since they would be able to reach any place in the site within one click of any other page.

FIGURE 23.8
The BAWSI.org web site shows
sub-navigation attached to each
main navigation element.

You will also notice that the "Overview" link in the side navigation window is styled a bit differently—with heavier purple text—than the other links in the window, indicating to visitors what page they are on. This visual detail, similar to what you saw on the Starbucks site, is an unobtrusive way to provide users with a sense of where they are within the current navigational scheme.

There are many different types of navigation styles and ways of indicating to users just where they are and where they might want to go next. Keep in mind the following fact: studies have repeatedly shown that people become confused and annoyed when presented with more than seven choices at a time, and people feel most comfortable with five or fewer choices. Therefore, you should avoid presenting more than five links (either in a list or as graphical icons) next to one another if at all possible, and definitely avoid presenting more than seven at once. Amazon.com gets a pass here, because they are an Internet superstore and users expect a lot of "departments" in which to shop when they get there. But when you need to present more than seven links in a navigation list, break them into multiple lists with a separate heading for each of the five to seven items, as you saw in the Amazon.com example in Figure 23.6.

It will also help your readers navigate your site without confusion if you avoid putting any page more than two (or, at most, three) links away from the main page. You should also always send readers back to a main category page (or the home page) after they've read a subsidiary page. In other words, try to design somewhat of a flat link structure in which most pages are no more than one or two links deep. You don't want visitors to have to rely heavily, if at all, on their browsers' Back buttons to navigate through your site.

Writing Maintainable HTML Code

If you've ever done any programming, you already know how important it is to write code that can be maintained—that is, you or someone else should be able look at your code later and not be utterly confused by it. The challenge is to make your code as immediately understandable as possible. There will come a time when you'll look back on a page that you wrote and you won't have a clue what you were thinking or why you wrote the code the way you did. Fortunately, there is a way to combat this problem of apparent memory loss!

Documenting Code with Comments

NOTE

To include comments in a JavaScript script, put // at the beginning of each comment line. (No closing tag is needed for JavaScript comments.) In style sheets, start comments with /* and end them with */.

The HTML <!— and —> tags will not work properly in scripts or style sheets!

You can and should, however, include one <!-- tag just after a <script> or <style> tag, with a --> tag just before the matching </script> or </style>. This hides the script or style commands from older browsers that would otherwise treat them as regular text and display them on the page.

Whenever you develop an HTML page, keep in mind that you or someone else will almost certainly need to make changes to it someday. Simple text web pages are usually fairly easy to read and revise, but complex pages with graphics, tables, and other layout tricks can be quite difficult to decipher.

To see what I'm talking about, visit just about any page in a web browser and view its source code. Using Internet Explorer, click the View menu and then click Source. Using Firefox, click the View menu and then click Page Source. You might see a jumbled bunch of code that is tough to decipher as pure HTML. This might be due to the fact that the markup has been generated dynamically by content management software systems. Or it might be due to the fact that its human maintainer has not paid attention to structure, ease of reading, code commenting, and other methods for making the code readable by humans. For the sake of maintaining your own pages, I encourage you to impose a little more order on your HTML markup.

As you have seen in several different hours, you can enclose comments to yourself or your co-authors between <!-- and --> tags. These comments will not appear on the web page when viewed with a browser but can be read by anyone who examines the HTML code in a text editor or via web browser's View Source (or View Page Source) function. The following example provides a little refresher just to show you how a comment is coded:

```
<!-- This image needs to be updated daily. -->
<img src="headline.jpg" alt="Today's Headline" />
```

As this code reveals, the comment just before the <img /> tag provides a clue as to how the image is used. When someone reads this code, they know immediately that this is an image that must be updated every day. The text in the comment is completely ignored by web browsers.

TIP

One handy usage of comments is to hide parts of a web page that are currently under construction. Rather than making the text and graphics visible and explaining that they're under construction, you can hide them from view entirely with some carefully placed opening and closing comment tags around the HTML you do not want to appear. This is a great way to work on portions of a page gradually and show only the end result to the world when you're finished.

It will be well worth your time now to go through all the web pages, scripts, and style sheets you've created so far and add any comments that you or others might find helpful when revising them in the future. Here's what to do:

TRY IT YOURSELF ▼

Comment Your Code

1. Put a comment explaining any fancy formatting or layout techniques before the tags that make it happen.

2. Use a comment just before an <img /> tag to briefly describe any important graphic whose function isn't obvious from the alt message.

3. Consider using a comment (or several comments) to summarize how the cells of a <table> are supposed to fit together visually.

4. If you use hexadecimal color codes (such as <div style="color: #8040B0">), insert a comment indicating what the color actually is (bluish-purple).

5. Indent your comments to help them stand out and make both the comments and the HTML easier to read. Don't forget to use indentation in the HTML itself to make it more readable, too, as we'll discuss in the next section.

Indenting Code for Clarity

I have a confession. Throughout the book I've been carefully indoctrinating you into an HTML code development style without really letting on. It's time to spill the beans. You've no doubt noticed a consistent pattern with respect to the indentation of all the HTML code in the book. More specifically, each child tag is indented to the right two spaces from its parent tag. Furthermore, content within a tag that spans more than one line is indented within the tag.

The best way to learn the value of indentation is to see some HTML code without it. You know how the song goes—"you don't know what you've got [']til it's gone." Anyway, here's a very simple table coded without any indentation:

```
<table>
<tr><td>Cell One</td><td>Cell Two</td></tr>
<tr><td>Cell Three</td><td>Cell Four</td></tr>
</table>
```

Not only is there no indentation, there also is no delineation between rows and columns within the table. Now compare this code with the following code, which describes the same table:

```
<table>
  <tr>
    <td>Cell One</td>
    <td>Cell Two</td>
  </tr>
  <tr>
    <td>Cell Three</td>
    <td>Cell Four</td>
  </tr>
</table>
```

This heavily indented code makes it plainly obvious how the rows and columns are divided up via `<tr>` and `<td>` tags.

Consistent indentation might even be more important than comments when it comes to making your HTML code understandable and maintainable. And you don't have to buy into this specific indentation strategy. If you'd rather use three or four spaces instead of two, that's fine. And if you want to tighten things up a bit and not indent content within a tag, that also works. The main thing to take from this is that it's important to develop a coding style of your own and then ruthlessly stick to it.

Summary

This hour has given you examples and explanations to help you organize your web pages into a coherent site that is informative, attractive, and easy to navigate. Web users have grown to become quite savvy in terms of expecting well-designed web sites, and they will quickly abandon your site if they experience a poor design that is difficult to navigate.

This hour also discussed the importance of making your HTML code easy to maintain by adding comments and indentation. Comments are important not only as a reminder for you when you revisit code later but also as instruction if someone else should inherit your code. Indentation might seem like an aesthetic issue, but it can truly help you to quickly analyze and understand the structure of a web page at a glance.

Q&A

Q I've seen pages that ask viewers to change the width of their browser window or adjust other settings before proceeding beyond the home page. Why do they do this?

A The snarky response is that the site creators do not care about their users. Never force your users to do something differently than they are doing with their browsers, and especially never, ever resize the browser automatically. Those are some of the biggest usability no-no's. When sites tell you to change your settings, it is because the site creators think they can offer a better presentation if they're given that specific control over the size of users' windows or fonts. Of course, few people bother to change their settings when told to do so (as they shouldn't), so these sites often look weird or unreadable. You'll be much better off using the tips you learn in this book to make your site readable and attractive using any window size and using a wide variety of browser settings. The better organized your site is, the more usable it will be for visitors.

Q Won't lots of comments and spaces make my pages load slower when someone views them?

A The size of a little extra text in your pages is negligible when compared to other, chunkier web page resources (such as images and multimedia). Besides, slower dial-up modem connections typically do a decent job of compressing text when transmitting it, so adding spaces to format your HTML doesn't usually change the transfer time at all. You'd have to type hundreds of comment words to cause even one extra second of delay in loading a page. And keep in mind that with the broadband connections (cable, DSL, and so on) that many people now have, text travels extremely fast. It's the graphics that slow pages down, so squeeze your images as tightly as you can (refer to Hour 10), but use text comments freely.

Workshop

The workshop contains quiz questions and activities to help you solidify your understanding of the material covered. Try to answer all questions before looking at the "Answers" section that follows.

Quiz

1. What are three ways to ensure all your pages form a single cohesive web site?

2. What two types of information should always be included in your home page?

3. You want to say, "Don't change this image of me. It's my only chance at immortality," to future editors of a web page, but you don't want users who view the page to see that message. How would you do it?

Answers

1. Use consistent background, colors, fonts, and styles. Repeat the same link words or graphics on the top of the page that the link leads to. Repeat the same small header, buttons, or other element on every page of the site.

2. Use enough identifying information so that users can immediately see the name of the site and what it is about. Also, whatever the most important message you want to convey to your intended audience is, state it directly and concisely. Whether it's your mission statement or trademarked marketing slogan, make sure that it is in plain view here.

3. Put the following comment immediately before the `<img />` tag:

```
<!-- Don't change this image of me.
     It's my only chance at immortality. -->
```

Exercises

▶ Grab a pencil (the oldfangled kind) and sketch out your web site as a bunch of little rectangles with arrows between them. Sketch a rough overview of what each page will look like by putting squiggles where the text goes and doodles where the images go. Each arrow should start at a doodle icon that corresponds to the navigation button for the page the arrow leads to. Even if you have the latest whiz-bang web site management tools (which are often more work than just creating the site itself), sketching your site by hand can give you a much more intuitive grasp of which pages on your site will be easy to get to and how the layout of adjacent pages will work together—all before you invest time in writing the actual HTML to connect the pages together. Believe it or not, I still sketch out web sites like this when I'm first designing them. Sometimes you can't beat a pencil and paper!

▶ Open the HTML files that make up your current web site, and check them all for comments and code indentation. Are there areas in which the code needs to be explained to anyone who might look at it in the future? If so, add explanatory comments. Is it difficult for you to tell the hierarchy of your code—is it difficult to see headings and sections? If so, indent your HTML so that the structure matches the hierarchy and thus allows you to jump quickly to the section you need to edit.

Helping People Find Your Web Pages

Your web pages are ultimately only as useful as they are accessible—if no one can find your pages, your hard work in creating a useful architecture, providing interesting content, and coding them correctly will be for naught. The additional HTML tags you'll discover in this hour won't make any visible difference in your web pages, but they are extremely important in that they will help your audience more easily find your web pages. For most web site creators, this might be the easiest—but most important— hour in the book. You'll learn how to add elements to your pages and how to construct your site architecture in such a way as to increase the possibility that search engines will return links to your site when someone searches for words related to your topic or company; this is called search engine optimization (SEO). Contrary to what you might hear from companies who try to sell these services to you, there are no magic secrets that guarantee you'll be at the top of every search list. However, there are a series of *free* best practices that you can do on your own to make sure your site is as easy to find as possible.

Publicizing Your Web Site

Presumably, you want your web site to attract someone's attention, or you wouldn't bother to create it in the first place. However, if you are placing your pages only on a local network or corporate intranet, or you are distributing your site exclusively on removable storage media, helping users find your pages might not be much of a problem. But if you are adding the content of your web site to the billions of other pages of content indexed by search engines, bringing your intended audience to your site is a very big challenge indeed.

To tackle this problem, you need a basic understanding of how most people decide which pages they will look at. There are basically three ways people become aware of your web site:

▶ Somebody tells them about it and gives them the address; they enter that address directly into their web browser.

▶ They follow a link to your site from someone else's site.

▶ They find your site indexed in the databases that power the Google, Bing, or Yahoo! search engines (among others).

You can increase your web site traffic with a little time and effort. To increase the number of people who hear about you through word-of-mouth, well, use your mouth—and every other channel of communication available to you. If you have an existing contact database or mailing list, announce your web site to those people. Add the site address to your business cards or company literature. If you have the money, go buy TV and radio ads broadcasting your Internet address. In short, do the marketing thing. Good old-fashioned word-of-mouth marketing is still the best thing going, even on the Internet.

Increasing the number of incoming links to your site from other sites is also pretty straightforward—though that doesn't mean it isn't a lot of work. If there are specialized directories on your topic, either online or in print, be sure you are listed. Participate in social networking, including the implementation of Facebook "fan" pages (if applicable) for your service or business. Create a Twitter account to broadcast news and connect with customers—again, if that is applicable to your online presence. Go into the spaces where your customers might be, such as blogs that comment on your particular topic of interest, and participate in those communities. That is not to say that you should find a forum on your topic or service and spam its users with links to your site. Act as an expert in your given field, offering advice and recommendations along with your own site URL. There's not much I can say in this book to help you with that, except to go out and do it.

The main thing I can help you with is making sure your content has been gathered and indexed correctly by search engines. It's a fair assumption that if your content isn't in Google's databases, you're in trouble.

Search engines are basically huge databases that index as much content on the Internet as possible—including videos and other rich media. They use automated processing to search sites, using programs called robots or spiders to search pages for content and build the databases. After the content is indexed, the search applications themselves use highly sophisticated techniques of ranking pages to determine which content to display first, second, third, and so on when a user enters a search term.

When the search engine processes a user query, it looks for content that contains the key words and phrases that the user is looking for. But it is not a simple match, as in "if this page contains this phrase, return it as a result," because content is ranked according to frequency and context of the keywords and phrases, as well as the number of links from other sites that lend credibility to it. This hour will teach you a few ways to ensure that your content appears appropriately in the search engine, based on the content and context you provide.

Listing Your Pages with the Major Search Sites

If you want users to find your pages, you absolutely must submit a request to each of the major search sites to index your pages. Even though search engines index web content automatically, this is the best way to ensure your site has a presence on their sites. Each of these sites has a form for you to fill out with the URL address, a brief description of the site, and, in some cases, a category or list of keywords with which your listing should be associated. These forms are easy to fill out; you can easily complete all of them in an hour with time left over to list yourself at one or two specialized directories you might have found as well. (How do you find the specialized directories? Through the major search sites, of course!)

Before You List Your Pages

But wait! Before you rush off this minute to submit your listing requests, read the rest of this hour. Otherwise, you'll have a very serious problem, and you will have already lost your best opportunity to solve it.

To see what I mean, imagine this scenario: You publish a page selling automatic cockroach flatteners. I am an Internet user who has a roach problem, and I'm allergic to bug spray. I open my laptop, brush the roaches off the keyboard, log on to my favorite search site, and enter *cockroach* as a search term. The search engine promptly presents me with a list of the first 10 out of 10,254 Internet pages containing the word *cockroach*. You have submitted your listing request, so you know that your page is somewhere on that list.

Did I mention that I'm rich? And did I mention that two roaches are mating on my foot? You even offer same-day delivery in my area. Do you want your page to be number 3 on the list, or number 8,542? Okay, now you understand the problem. Just getting listed in a search engine isn't enough—you need to work your way up the rankings.

TIP

There are sites that provide one form that automatically submits itself to all the major search engines, plus several minor search engines. These sites—such as http://www.scrubtheweb.com/, http://www.submitexpress.com/, and http://www.hypersubmit.com/—are popular examples of sites that attempt to sell you a premium service that lists you in many other directories and indexes as well. Depending on your target audience, these services might or might not be of value, but I strongly recommend that you go directly to the major search sites listed previously in this hour and use their own forms to submit your requests to be listed. That way you can be sure to answer the questions (which are slightly different at every site) accurately, and you will know exactly how your site listing will appear at each search engine.

Even though listing with the major search engines is easy and quick, it can be a bit confusing: Each search engine uses different terminology to identify where you should click to register your pages. The following list might save you some frustration; it includes the addresses of some popular search engines which will include your site for free, along with the exact wording of the link you should click to register:

▶ Google—Visit http://www.google.com/addurl/, enter the address of your site and a brief description, and then enter the squiggly verification text, called a CAPTCHA, (or Completely Automated Public Turing test to tell Computers and Humans Apart) shown on the page. Then click the Add URL button to add your site to Google.

▶ Yahoo! Search—Visit http://siteexplorer.search.yahoo.com/submit, enter the address of your site, and then click the Submit URL button.

▶ Bing—Visit http://www.bing.com/docs/submit.aspx, enter the verification text, enter the address of your site, and then click the Submit URL button.

▶ AllTheWeb—AllTheWeb search results are provided by Yahoo! Search, so just be sure to submit your site to Yahoo! Search, as explained previously.

▶ AltaVista—AltaVista search results are also provided by Yahoo! Search, so just be sure to submit your site to Yahoo!.

Providing Hints for Search Engines

Fact: There is absolutely nothing you can do to guarantee that your site will appear in the top 10 search results for a particular word or phrase in any major search engine (short of buying ad space from the search site, that is). After all, if there were such guarantees, why couldn't everyone else who wants to be number 1 on the list do it, too? What you can do is avoid being last on the list and give yourself as good a chance as anyone else of being first; this is called search engine optimization (SEO), or optimizing the content and structure of your pages so that search engines will favor your pages over others.

Each search engine uses a different method for determining which pages are likely to be most relevant and should therefore be sorted to the top of a search result list. You don't need to get too hung up on the differences, though, because they all use some combination of the same basic criteria.

The following list includes almost everything any search engine considers when trying to evaluate which pages best match one or more keywords.

- Do keywords appear in the `<title>` tag of the page?
- Do keywords appear in the first few lines of the page?
- Do keywords appear in a `<meta />` tag in the page?
- Do keywords appear in `<h1>` headings in the page?
- Do keywords appear in the names of image files and `alt` text for images in the page?
- How many other pages within the web site link to the page?
- How many other pages in other web sites link to the page? How many other pages link to those pages?
- How many times have users chosen this page from a previous search list result?

Clearly, the most important thing you can do to improve your position is to consider the keywords your intended audience are most likely to enter. I'd recommend that you not concern yourself with common, single-word searches like "food"; the lists they generate are usually so long that trying to make it to the top is like playing the lottery. Focus instead on uncommon words and two- or three-word combinations that are most likely to indicate relevance to your topic (for instance, "Southern home-style cooking" instead of simply "food"). Make sure that those terms and phrases occur several times on your page, and be certain to put the most important ones in the `<title>` tag and the first heading or introductory paragraph.

Of all the search-engine evaluation criteria just listed, the use of `<meta />` tags is probably the least understood. Some people rave about `<meta />` tags as if using them could instantly move you to the top of every search list. Other people dismiss `<meta />` tags as ineffective and useless. Neither of these extremes is true.

A `<meta />` *tag* is a general-purpose tag you can put in the `<head>` portion of any document to specify some information about the page that doesn't belong in the `<body>` text. Most major search engines look at `<meta />` tags to provide them with a short description of your page and some keywords to identify what your page is about. For example, your automatic cockroach flattener order form might include the following two tags:

```
<meta name="description"
content="Order form for the SuperSquish cockroach flattener." />
<meta name="keywords"
content="cockroach,roaches,kill,squish,supersquish" />
```

NOTE

Some over-eager web page authors put dozens or even hundreds of repetitions of the same word on their pages, sometimes in small print or a hard-to-see color, just to get the search engines to position that page at the top of the list whenever users search for that word. This practice is called *search engine spamming.*

Don't be tempted to try this sort of thing—all the major search engines are aware of this practice and immediately delete any page from their database that sets off a "spam detector" by repeating the same word or group of words in a suspicious pattern. It's still fine (and quite beneficial) to have several occurrences of important search words on a page, in the natural course of your content. Make sure, however, that you use those words in normal sentences or phrases—then the spam police will leave you alone.

WARNING

Always place `<meta />` tags *after* the `<head>`, `<title>`, and `</title>` tags but *before* the closing `</head>` tag.

According to XHTML standards, `<title>` must be the very first tag in the `<head>` section of every document.

The first tag in this example ensures that the search engine has an accurate description of the page to present on its search results list. The second `<meta />` tag slightly increases your page's ranking on the list whenever any of your specified keywords are included in a search query.

You should always include `<meta />` tags with `name="description"` and `name="keywords"` attributes in any page that you want to be indexed by a search engine. Doing so might not have a dramatic effect on your position in search lists, and not all search engines look for `<meta />` tags, but it can only help.

To give you a concrete example of how to improve search engine results, consider the page shown in Listing 24.1.

This page *should* be fairly easy to find because it deals with a specific topic and includes several occurrences of some uncommon technical terms for which users interested in this subject would be likely to search. However, there are several things you could do to improve the chances of this page appearing high on a search engine results list.

Listing 24.1   A Page That Will Have Little Visibility During an Internet Site Search

```
<?xml version="1.0" encoding="UTF-8"?>
<!DOCTYPE html PUBLIC "-//W3C//DTD XHTML 1.1//EN"
  "http://www.w3.org/TR/xhtml11/DTD/xhtml11.dtd">

<html xmlns="http://www.w3.org/1999/xhtml" xml:lang="en">
  <head>
    <title>Fractal Central</title>
  </head>

  <body>
    <div style="text-align:center">
      <img src="fractalaccent.gif" alt="" />
    </div>
    <div style="width:133px; float:left; padding:6px; text-align:center;
    border-width:4px; border-style:ridge">
      Discover the latest software, books and more at our online store.<br />
      <a href="orderform.html"><img src="orderform.gif" alt="Order Form"
      style="border-style:none" /></a>
    </div>
    <div style="float:left; padding:6px">
      <h2>A Comprehensive Guide to the<br />
      Art and Science of Chaos and Complexity</h2>
      <p>What's that? You say you're hearing about "fractals" and "chaos" all
      over the place, but still aren't too sure what they are? How about a
      quick summary of some key concepts:</p>
      <ol>
        <li><p>Even the simplest systems become deeply complex and richly
        beautiful when a process is "iterated" over and over, using the
        results of each step as the starting point of the next. This is how
        Nature creates a magnificently detailed 300-foot redwood tree from a
```

```
        seed the size of your fingernail.</p></li>
        <li><p>Most "iterated systems" are easily simulated on computers,
        but only a few are predictable and controllable. Why? Because a tiny
        influence, like a "butterfly flapping its wings," can be strangely
        amplified to have major consequences such as completely changing
        tomorrow's weather in a distant part of the world.</p></li>
        <li><p>Fractals can be magnified forever without loss of detail, so
        mathematics that relies on straight lines is useless with them.
        However, they give us a new concept called "fractal dimension" which
        can measure the texture and complexity of anything from coastlines to
        storm clouds.</p></li>
        <li><p>While fractals win prizes at graphics shows, their chaotic
        patterns pop up in every branch of science. Physicists find beautiful
        artwork coming out of their plotters. "Strange attractors" with
        fractal turbulence appear in celestial mechanics. Biologists diagnose
        "dynamical diseases" when fractal rhythms fall out of sync. Even pure
        mathematicians go on tour with dazzling videos of their
        research.</p></li>
      </ol>
      <p>Think all these folks may be on to something?</p>
    </div>
    <div style="text-align:center">
      <a href="http://netletter.com/nonsense/"><img src="findout.gif"
      alt="Find Out More" style="border-style:none" /></a>
    </div>
  </body>
</html>
```

Now compare the page in Listing 24.1 with the changes made to the page in Listing 24.2. The two pages look almost the same, but to search robots and search engines, these two pages appear quite different. The following list summarizes what was changed in the page and how those changes affected indexing:

► Important search terms were added to the `<title>` tag and the first heading on the page. The original page didn't even include the word *fractal* in either of these two key positions.

► `<meta />` tags were added to assist search engines with a description and keywords.

► A very descriptive `alt` attribute was added to the first `<img />` tag. Not all search engines read and index `alt` text, but some do.

► The quotation marks around technical terms (such as `"fractal"` and `"iterated"`) were removed because some search engines consider *"fractal"* to be a different word than *fractal*. The quotation marks were replaced with the character entity ", which search robots simply disregard. This is also a good idea because XHTML urges web developers to use the " entity instead of quotation marks anyway.

▶ The keyword *fractal* was added twice to the text in the order-form box.

It is impossible to quantify how much more frequently users searching for information on fractals and chaos were able to find the page shown in Listing 24.2 versus the page shown in Listing 24.1, but it's a sure bet that the changes could only improve the page's visibility to search engines. As is often the case, the improvements made for the benefit of the search spiders probably made the page's subject easier for humans to recognize and understand as well. This makes optimizing a page for search engines a win-win effort!

Listing 24.2   An Improvement on the Page in Listing 24.1

```
<?xml version="1.0" encoding="UTF-8"?>
<!DOCTYPE html PUBLIC "-//W3C//DTD XHTML 1.1//EN"
  "http://www.w3.org/TR/xhtml11/DTD/xhtml11.dtd">

<html xmlns="http://www.w3.org/1999/xhtml" xml:lang="en">
  <head>
    <title>Fractal Central: A Guide to Fractals, Chaos, and Complexity</title>
    <meta name="description" content="A comprehensive guide to fractal
    geometry, chaos science and complexity theory." />
    <meta name="keywords"  content="fractal,fractals,chaos science,chaos
    theory,fractal geometry,complexity,complexity theory" />
  </head>

  <body>
    <div style="text-align:center">
      <img src="fractalaccent.gif" alt="Fractal Central: A Guide to Fractals,
      Chaos, and Complexity" />
    </div>
    <div style="width:133px; float:left; padding:6px; text-align:center;
    border-width:4px; border-style:ridge">
      Discover the latest fractal software, books and more at the
      <span style="font-weight:bold">Fractal Central</span> online store.<br />
      <a href="orderform.html"><img src="orderform.gif" alt="Order Form"
      style="border-style:none" /></a>
    </div>
    <div style="float:left; padding:6px">
      <h2>A Comprehensive Guide to Fractal Geometry,<br />
      Chaos Science, and Complexity Theory</h2>
      <p>What's that? You say you're hearing about &quot;fractals&quot; and
      &quot;chaos&quot; all over the place, but still aren't too sure what
      they are? How about a quick summary of some key concepts:</p>
      <ol>
        <li><p>Even the simplest systems become deeply complex and richly
        beautiful when a process is &quot;iterated&quot; over and over, using
        the results of each step as the starting point of the next. This is
        how Nature creates a magnificently detailed 300-foot redwood tree from
        a seed the size of your fingernail.</p></li>
```

```
    <li><p>Most &quot;iterated systems&quot; are easily simulated on
    computers, but only a few are predictable and controllable. Why?
    Because a tiny influence, like a &quot;butterfly flapping its
    wings,&quot; can be strangely amplified to have major consequences
    such as completely changing tomorrow's weather in a distant part of
    the world.</p></li>
    <li><p>Fractals can be magnified forever without loss of detail, so
    mathematics that relies on straight lines is useless with them.
    However, they give us a new concept called &quot;fractal
    dimension&quot; which can measure the texture and complexity of
    anything from coastlines to storm clouds.</p></li>
    <li><p>While fractals win prizes at graphics shows, their chaotic
    patterns pop up in every branch of science. Physicists find beautiful
    artwork coming out of their plotters. &quot;Strange attractors&quot;
    with fractal turbulence appear in celestial mechanics. Biologists
    diagnose &quot;dynamical diseases&quot; when fractal rhythms fall out
    of sync. Even pure mathematicians go on tour with dazzling videos of
    their research.</p></li>
  </ol>
  <p>Think all these folks may be on to something?</p>
</div>
<div style="text-align:center">
  <a href="http://netletter.com/nonsense/"><img src="findout.gif"
  alt="Find Out More" style="border-style:none" /></a>
</div>
</body>
</html>
```

These changes will go a long way toward making the content of this site more likely to be appropriately indexed. In addition to good, indexed content, remember that the quality of content—as well as the number of other sites linking to yours—is important as well.

Additional Tips for Search Engine Optimization

The most important tip I can give you regarding search engine optimization is to not pay an SEO company to perform your SEO tasks if that company promises specific results for you. If a company promises that your site will be the number one result in a Google search, run for the hills and take your checkbook with you—no one can promise that, as the search algorithms have so many variables that the number one result might change several times over the course of a given week. That is not to say that all SEO companies are scam artists. Some legitimate site content and architect consultants who perform SEO tasks get lumped in with the spammers who send unsolicited e-mail, such as this:

```
"Dear google.com,
I visited your website and noticed that you are not listed in most of the
major search engines and directories..."
```

This sample e-mail is used as an example in Google's own guidelines for webmasters, along with the note to "reserve the same skepticism for unsolicited email about search engines as you do for burn fat at night diet pills or requests to help transfer funds from deposed dictators." Yes, someone actually sent Google a spam e-mail about how to increase their search ranking...in Google. For more good advice from Google, visit http://www.google.com/webmasters/.

Here are some additional actions you can take, for free, to optimize your content for search engines:

▶ Use accurate page titles. Your titles should be brief, but descriptive and unique. Do not try to stuff your titles with keywords.

▶ Create human-friendly URLs, such as those with words in them that users can easily remember. It is a lot easier to remember—and it's easier for search engines to index in a relevant way—a URL such as http://www.mycompany.com/products/super_widget.html compared to something like http://www.mycompany.com?c=p&id=4&id=49f8sd7345fea.

▶ Create URLs that reflect your directory structure. This assumes you have a directory structure in the first place, which you should.

▶ When possible, use text—not graphical elements—for navigation.

▶ If you have content several levels deep, use a breadcrumb trail so users can find their way back home. A breadcrumb trail also provides search engines with more words to index. For example, if you are looking at a recipe for biscuits in the Southern Cooking category of a food-related web site, the breadcrumb trail for this particular page might look like this:

Home > Southern Cooking > Recipes > Biscuits

▶ Within the content of your page, use headings (<h1>, <h2>, <h3>) appropriately.

In addition to providing rich and useful content for your users, you should follow these tips to increase your site's prominence in page rankings.

Summary

This hour covered some extremely important territory by exploring how to provide hints to search engines (such as Google, Bing, and Yahoo!) so users can find your pages more easily. You also saw an example of the HTML behind a perfectly reasonable web page *redone* to make it more search engine friendly. Finally, you learned a few more tips to optimize the indexing of your site overall.

Table 24.1 lists the tags and attributes covered in this hour.

Table 24.1 HTML Tags and Attributes Covered in Hour 24

Tag/Attribute	Function
`<meta />`	Indicates meta-information about this document (information about the document itself). Most commonly used to add a page description and to designate keywords. Used in the document `<head>`.
Attributes	
`name="name"`	Can be used to specify which type of information about the document is in the `content` attribute. For example, `name="keywords"` means that keywords for the page are in `content`.
`content="value"`	The actual message or value for the information specified in `http-equiv` or `name`. For example, if the `http-equiv` attribute is set to `refresh`, the `content` attribute should be set to the number of seconds to wait, followed by a semicolon and the address of the page to load.

Q&A

Q I have lots of pages in my site. Do I need to fill out a separate form for each page at each search site?

A No. If you submit just your home page (which is presumably linked to all the other pages), the search spiders will crawl through all the links on the page (and all the links on the linked pages, and so on) until they have indexed all the pages on your site.

Q I submitted a request to be listed with a search engine, but when I search for my page, my page never comes up—not even when I enter my company's unique name. What can I do?

A Most of the big search engines offer a form you can fill out to instantly check whether a specific address is included in their database. If you find that it isn't included, you can submit another request form. Sometimes it takes days or even weeks for the spiders to get around to indexing your pages after you submit a request.

Q When I put keywords in a `<meta />` tag, do I need to include every possible variation of spelling and capitalization?

A Don't worry about capitalization; almost all searches are entered in all lowercase letters. Do include any obvious variations or common spelling errors as separate keywords. Although simple in concept, there are more advanced strategies available when it comes to manipulating the `<meta />` tag than I've been able to cover in this hour. Visit http://en.wikipedia.org/wiki/Meta_element for good information on the various attributes of this tag and how to use it.

Q I've heard that I can I use the `<meta />` tag to make a page automatically reload itself every few seconds or minutes. Is this true?

A Yes, but there's no point in doing that unless you have some sort of program or script set up on your web server to provide new information on the page. And if that is the case, the chances are good that you can go about that refresh in a different way using AJAX (see Hour 21 for basic information on AJAX). For usability reasons, the use of `<meta />` to refresh content is frowned upon by the W3C and users in general.

Workshop

The workshop contains quiz questions and activities to help you solidify your understanding of the material covered. Try to answer all questions before looking at the "Answers" section that follows.

Quiz

1. If you publish a page about puppy adoption, how could you help make sure that the page can be found by users who enter puppy, dog, and/or adoption at all the major Internet search sites?

2. Suppose you decide to paste your keywords hundreds of times in your HTML code, using a white font on a white background, so that your readers cannot see them. How would search engine spiders deal with this?

3. Is it better to throw all your content in one directory, or to organize it into several directories?

Answers

1. Make sure that *puppy*, *dog*, and *adoption* all occur frequently on your main page (as they probably already do) and title your page something along the lines of Puppy Dog Adoption. While you're at it, put the following `<meta />` tags in the `<head>` portion of the page:

```
<meta name="description"
content="dog adoption information and services" />
<meta name="keywords" content="puppy, dog, adoption" />
```

Publish your page online and then visit the site submittal page for each major search engine (listed earlier in the hour) to fill out the site submission forms.

2. Search engine spiders would ignore the duplications and possibly blacklist you from their index and label you as a spammer.

3. Definitely organize your content into directories. This will provide easier maintenance of your content, but will also give you the opportunity to create human-readable URLs with directory structures that make sense, and also to create a navigational breadcrumb trail.

Exercises

▶ You've reached the end of the hours. If you have a site that is ready for the world to see, review the content and structure for the best possible optimizations and then submit the address to all the major search engines.

APPENDIX A
HTML and CSS Resources on the Internet

The links in this appendix represent only a few of the numerous resources you'll find with a simple keyword search. But if you're overwhelmed by the options, these are good starting places.

General HTML, XHTML, and CSS Information

The World Wide Web Consortium (W3C):

http://www.w3.org/

The W3C Markup Validation Service:

http://validator.w3.org/

W3Schools.com Web Building Tutorials:

http://www.w3schools.com/

The Web Standards Project:

http://www.webstandards.org/

The HTML Writer's Guild:

http://www.hwg.org/

The Web Developer's Virtual Library:

http://www.wdvl.com/

Web Browsers

Apple Safari:

http://www.apple.com/safari/

Google Chrome:

http://www.google.com/chrome/

Microsoft Internet Explorer:

http://www.microsoft.com/windows/ie/

Mozilla Firefox:

http://www.getfirefox.com/

Opera:

http://www.opera.com/

Web Page Design

Web Monkey:

http://webmonkey.wired.com/webmonkey/

A List Apart ("for people who make web sites"):

http://www.alistapart.com/

Web Pages That Suck:

http://www.webpagesthatsuck.com/

HTML Help (Web Design Group):

http://www.htmlhelp.com/

Software

Adobe Creative Suite

http://www.adobe.com/products/creativesuite/

Corel PaintPro:

http://www.corel.com/

GIMP (GNU Image Manipulation Program):

http://gimp.org/

Picasa:

http://picasa.google.com/

Mapedit:

http://www.boutell.com/mapedit/

Shareware.com:

http://shareware.cnet.com/

Classic FTP:

http://www.nchsoftware.com/classic/

Cyberduck (FTP client):

http://cyberduck.ch/

FileZilla (FTP client):

http://filezilla-project.org/

Colors and Graphics

Microsoft Clip Art Gallery:

http://dgl.microsoft.com/

Barry's Art Server:

http://www.barrysclipart.com/

HTML Color Picker:

http://www.pagetutor.com/pagetutor/makapage/picker/

HTML Color Codes:

http://htmlcolorcodes.org/

Color Scheme Designer:

http://colorschemedesigner.com/

Kuler by Adobe:

http://kuler.adobe.com/

Color Blender:

http://www.meyerweb.com/eric/tools/color-blend/

Multimedia

Apple QuickTime:

http://www.apple.com/quicktime/

Windows Movie Maker:

http://www.microsoft.com/windowsxp/using/moviemaker/default.mspx

RealAudio:

http://www.real.com/

Adobe Flash:

http://www.adobe.com/products/flash/

Sound Central:

http://www.soundcentral.com/

MIDIworld:

http://www.midiworld.com/

Advanced Developer Resources

WebReference:

http://www.webreference.com/

JavaScript.com:

http://www.javascript.com/

IRT.org developer resource:

http://www.irt.org/

Web Site Hosting

Web Hosting Geeks (reviews of hosting providers):

http://webhostinggeeks.com/

A Small Orange (hosting provider):

http://asmallorange.com/hosting/shared/

Bluehost (hosting provider):

http://www.bluehost.com/tell_me_more.html

Daily Razor (hosting provider):

http://www.dailyrazor.com/php/promo.php

DreamHost (hosting provider):

http://www.dreamhost.com/hosting.html

Just Host (hosting provider):

http://www.justhost.com/web-hosting

Lunar Pages (hosting provider):

http://www.lunarpages.com/starter-hosting/

Web Site Services

Google's Webmaster Tools:

http://www.google.com/webmasters/

Open Directory Project:

http://dmoz.org/about.html

Freedback.com (free form processing service):

http://www.freedback.com/

XHTML 1.1 and CSS 2 Quick Reference

XHTML 1.1 represents a modern reformulation of HTML as an XML application, allowing extensions to the language to be more easily defined and implemented. This appendix provides a quick reference to the elements and attributes of XHTML 1.1 that you are most likely to see and use, as well as the style properties that CSS 2 comprises. For the complete specifications, visit http://www.w3.org/.

To make the information readily accessible, this appendix organizes HTML elements by their function in the following order:

- ▶ Structure
- ▶ Text phrases and paragraphs
- ▶ Text formatting elements
- ▶ Lists
- ▶ Links
- ▶ Tables
- ▶ Embedded content
- ▶ Style
- ▶ Forms
- ▶ Scripts

The elements are listed alphabetically within each section, and the following information is presented:

- ▶ Usage–Gives a general description of the element.
- ▶ Start/End Tag–Indicates whether these tags are required, optional, or illegal.

▶ Attributes–Lists the attributes of the element with a short description of their effect. Any attributes that are used for mouse control or to invoke client-side scripting are not indicated here; please see the full specification at the W3C web site for those action-oriented attributes.

▶ Empty–Indicates whether the element can be empty.

▶ Notes–Relates any special considerations for using the element.

NOTE

XHTML 1.1 includes several fundamental attributes that apply to a significant number of elements. These are referred to within each element listing as `core`, `i18n`, and `events`. These attribute groups are covered in detail after all the XHTML elements are presented. There you'll find the specific attributes associated with each of these attribute groups.

The CSS style properties follow a similar arrangement except that they are listed with acceptable values, as opposed to attributes.

XHTML Structure

XHTML relies on several elements to provide structure to a document (as opposed to structuring the text within) as well as to provide information that is used by the browser or search engines.

Comments `<!-- ... -->`

Usage	Used to insert notes or scripts that are not displayed by the browser.
Start/End Tag	Required/Required.
Attributes	None.
Empty	Yes.
Notes	Comments are not restricted to one line and can be any length. The end tag is not required to be on the same line as the start tag.

`<!doctype...>`

Usage	Version information appears on the first line of an HTML document and is an SGML declaration rather than an element.

`<body>...</body>`

Usage	Contains the document's content.
Start/End Tag	Optional/Optional.
Attributes	`core, i18n, events`.
Empty	No.
Notes	There can be only one `<body>` and it must follow the `<head>`. If you are using frames (please try not to), the `<body>` element can be replaced by a `<frameset>` element.

`<div>...</div>`

Usage	The division element is used to add structure to a block of text.
Start/End Tag	Required/Required.
Attributes	`core, i18n, events`.
Empty	No.
Notes	Cannot be used within a p element.

NOTE

You might run across HTML web pages that use the `<div>` element with an attribute named `align`. This attribute was removed in XHTML and HTML 5, with the new approach to alignment involving the `text-align` CSS style property. This style property is covered later in this appendix.

`<h1>...</h1>` Through `<h6>...</h6>`

Usage	The six headings (h1 is uppermost, or most important) are used in the body to structure information in a hierarchical fashion.
Start/End Tag	Required/Required.
Attributes	`core, i18n, events`.
Empty	No.
Notes	Visual browsers will display the size of the headings in relation to their importance; `<h1>` is the largest and `<h6>` is the smallest.

<head>...</head>

TIP

The `profile` attribute is not allowed in HTML 5.

Usage	This is the document header and it contains other elements that provide information to users and search engines.
Start/End Tag	Optional/Optional.
Attributes	i18n.
	`profile="url"`–URL specifying the location of `meta` data.
Empty	No.
Notes	There can be only one <head> per document. It must follow the opening <html> tag and precede the <body>.

<hr />

Usage	Horizontal rules are used to separate sections of a web page.
Start/End Tag	Required/Illegal.
Attributes	`core`, `events`, `i18n`.
Empty	Yes.

<html>...</html>

Usage	The `html` element contains the entire document.
Start/End Tag	Optional/Optional.
Attributes	`i18n`.
Empty	No.
Notes	The version information is duplicated in the <!doctype...> declaration and is therefore not essential.

`<meta />`

Usage	Provides information about the document.
Start/End Tag	Required/Illegal.
Attributes	i18n.
	`http-equiv="servercmd"`–HTTP response header name.
	`name="name"`–Name of the meta information.
	`content="value"`–Content of the meta information.
	`scheme="scheme"`–Assigns a scheme to interpret the meta data.
Empty	Yes.

TIP

The scheme attribute is not allowed in HTML 5.

`<span>...</span>`

Usage	Organizes the document by defining a span of text.
Start/End Tag	Required/Required.
Attributes	core, i18n, events.
Empty	No.

`<title>...</title>`

Usage	The name you give your web page. The `<title>` tag is placed in the `<head>` tag and is displayed in the browser window title bar.
Start/End Tag	Required/Required.
Attributes	i18n.
Empty	No.
Notes	Only one title allowed per document.

XHTML Text Phrases and Paragraphs

Text phrases (or blocks) can be structured to suit a specific purpose, such as creating a paragraph. This should not be confused with modifying the formatting of the text.

`<blockquote>...</blockquote>`

Usage	Used to display long quotations.
Start/End Tag	Required/Required.
Attributes	core, i18n, events.
	cite="*url*"—The URL of the quoted text.
Empty	No.

`<br />`

Usage	Forces a line break.
Start/End Tag	Required/Illegal.
Attributes	core, i18n, events.
Empty	Yes.

`<cite>...</cite>`

Usage	Cites a reference.
Start/End Tag	Required/Required.
Attributes	core, i18n, events.
Empty	No.

`<code>...</code>`

Usage	Identifies a code fragment for display.
Start/End Tag	Required/Required.
Attributes	core, i18n, events.
Empty	No.

`<h1>...</h1>` Through `<h6>...</h6>`

Usage	Text heading.
Start/End Tag	Required/Required.
Attributes	core, i18n, events.
Empty	No.

`<p>...</p>`

Usage	Defines a paragraph.
Start/End Tag	Required/Optional.
Attributes	`core`, `i18n`, `events`.
Empty	No.

`<pre>...</pre>`

Usage	Displays preformatted text.
Start/End Tag	Required/Required.
Attributes	`core`, `i18n`, `events`.
Empty	No.

`<strong>...</strong>`

Usage	Stronger emphasis.
Start/End Tag	Required/Required.
Attributes	`core`, `i18n`, `events`.
Empty	No.

`<sub>...</sub>`

Usage	Creates subscript.
Start/End Tag	Required/Required.
Attributes	`core`, `i18n`, `events`.
Empty	No.

`<sup>...</sup>`

Usage	Creates superscript.
Start/End Tag	Required/Required.
Attributes	`core`, `i18n`, `events`.
Empty	No.

XHTML Text Formatting Elements

General text characteristics (such as the size, weight, and style) can be modified using these elements, but the preferred approach is to use CSS style properties. Later in the appendix, you'll find a complete reference for these properties, which provide an incredible amount of control over text formatting.

`<b>...</b>`

Usage	Bold text.
Start/End Tag	Required/Required.
Attributes	core, i18n, events.
Empty	No.

`<big>...</big>`

Usage	Large text.
Start/End Tag	Required/Required.
Attributes	core, i18n, events.
Empty	No.

TIP

This element has been removed in HTML 5 because its effect is purely presentational and thus better handled by CSS.

`<i>...</i>`

Usage	Italicized text.
Start/End Tag	Required/Required.
Attributes	core, i18n, events.
Empty	No.

`<small>...</small>`

Usage	Small text.
Start/End Tag	Required/Required.
Attributes	core, i18n, events.
Empty	No.

`<tt>...</tt>`

Usage	Teletype (or monospaced) text.
Start/End Tag	Required/Required.
Attributes	`core`, `i18n`, `events`.
Empty	No.

XHTML Lists

You can organize text into a more structured outline by creating lists. Lists can be nested.

`<dd>...</dd>`

Usage	The definition description used in a `<dl>` (definition list) element.
Start/End Tag	Required/Optional.
Attributes	`core`, `i18n`, `events`.
Empty	No.
Notes	Can contain block-level content, such as the `<p>` element.

`<dl>...</dl>`

Usage	Creates a definition list.
Start/End Tag	Required/Required.
Attributes	`core`, `i18n`, `events`.
Empty	No.
Notes	Must contain at least one `<dt>` or `<dd>` element in any order.

`<dt>...</dt>`

Usage	The definition term (or label) used within a `<dl>` (definition list) element.
Start/End Tag	Required/Optional.
Attributes	`core`, `i18n`, `events`.
Empty	No.
Notes	Must contain text (which can be modified by text markup elements).

`<li>...</li>`

Usage	Defines a list item within a list.
Start/End Tag	Required/Optional.
Attributes	core, i18n, events.
Empty	No.

`<ol>...</ol>`

Usage	Creates an ordered list.
Start/End Tag	Required/Required.
Attributes	core, i18n, events.
Empty	No.
Notes	Must contain at least one list item.

`<ul>...</ul>`

Usage	Creates an unordered list.
Start/End Tag	Required/Required.
Attributes	core, i18n, events.
Empty	No.
Notes	Must contain at least one list item.

XHTML Links

Hyperlinking is fundamental to XHTML. These elements enable you to link to other documents, other locations within a document, or external files.

`<a>...</a>`

Usage	Used to define links and anchors.
Start/End Tag	Required/Required.
Attributes	core, i18n, events.
	`charset="encoding"`–Character encoding of the resource.
	`name="name"`–Defines an anchor.
	`href="linkurl"`–The URL of the linked resource.

rel="*linktype*"–Forward link types.

rev="*linktype*"–Reverse link types.

shape="*value*"–Enables you to define client-side imagemaps using defined shapes (default, rect, circle, poly).

coords="*values*"–Sets the size of the shape using pixel or percentage lengths.

Empty	No.

TIP

The charset, name, rev, shape, and coords attributes are not allowed in HTML 5.

<base />

Usage	All other URLs in the document are resolved against this location.
Start/End Tag	Required/Illegal.
Attributes	href="*linkurl*"–The URL of the linked resource.
Empty	Yes.
Notes	Located in the document <head>.

<link />

Usage	Defines the relationship between a link and a resource.
Start/End Tag	Required/Illegal.
Attributes	core, i18n, events.
	charset="*encoding*"–The character encoding of the resource.
	href="*linkurl*"–The URL of the resource.
	rel="*linktype*"–The forward link types.
	rev="*linktype*"–The reverse link types.
	type="*contenttype*"–The Internet content type.
	media="*media*"–Defines the destination medium (such as screen, print, projection, braille, speech, all).
	target="*placement*"–Determines where the resource is displayed (user-defined name, blank, parent, self, top).
Empty	Yes.
Notes	Located in the document <head>.

TIP

The charset, rev, and target attributes are not allowed in HTML 5.

XHTML Tables

Tables are meant to display data in a tabular format. Prior to XHTML, tables were widely used for page layout purposes, but with the advent of style sheets, this is officially discouraged by the W3C as well as the authors of this book.

<caption>...</caption>

Usage	Displays a table caption.
Start/End Tag	Required/Required.
Attributes	core, i18n, events.
Empty	No.
Notes	Optional.

TIP

The width, align, char, charoff, and valign attributes have been removed in HTML 5 because their effects are purely presentational and thus better handled by CSS.

<col />

Usage	Groups individual columns within column groups in order to share attribute values.
Start/End Tag	Required/Illegal.
Attributes	core, i18n, events.
	span="*numcols*"–The number of columns the group contains.
	width="*width*"–The column width as a percentage, pixel value, or minimum value.
	align="*alignment*"–Horizontally aligns the contents of cells (left, center, right, justify, char).
	char="*charalignment*"–Sets a character on which the column aligns.
	charoff="*charoffset*"–Offset to the first alignment character on a line.
	valign="*verticalalignment*"–Vertically aligns the contents of a cell (top, middle, bottom, baseline).
Empty	Yes.

`<colgroup>...</colgroup>`

Usage	Defines a column group.
Start/End Tag	Required/Optional.
Attributes	core, i18n, events.
	span=`"numcols"`–The number of columns in a group.
	width=`"width"`–The width of the columns.
	align=`"alignment"`–Horizontally aligns the contents of cells (left, center, right, justify, char).
	char=`"charalignment"`–Sets a character on which the column aligns.
	charoff=`"charoffset"`–Offset to the first alignment character on a line.
	valign=`"verticalalignment"`–Vertically aligns the contents of a cell (top, middle, bottom, baseline).
Empty	No.

TIP

The width, align, char, charoff, and valign attributes have been removed in HTML 5 because their effects are purely presentational and thus better handled by CSS.

`<table>...</table>`

Usage	Creates a table.
Start/End Tag	Required/Required.
Attributes	core, i18n, events.
	width=`"width"`–Table width.
	cols=`"numcols"`–The number of columns.
	border=`"borderwidth"`–The width in pixels of a border around the table.
	frame=`"frame"`–Sets the visible sides of a table (void, above, below, hsides, lhs, rhs, vsides, box, border).
	rules=`"rules"`–Sets the visible rules within a table (none, groups, rows, cols, all).
	cellspacing=`"cellspacing"`–Spacing between cells.
	cellpadding=`"cellpadding"`–Spacing in cells.
	summary=`"description"`–Provides a text description of the table for accessibility purposes.
Empty	No.

TIP

The width, align, border, frame, rules, cellspacing, cellpadding, and summary attributes have been removed in HTML 5 because their effects are purely presentational and thus better handled by CSS.

`<tbody>...</tbody>`

Usage	Defines the table body.
Start/End Tag	Optional/Optional.
Attributes	core, i18n, events.
	align="*alignment*"—Horizontally aligns the contents of cells (left, center, right, justify, char).
	char="*charalignment*"—Sets a character on which the column aligns.
	charoff="*charoffset*"—Offset to the first alignment character on a line.
	valign="*verticalalignment*"—Vertically aligns the contents of cells (top, middle, bottom, baseline).
Empty	No.

`<td>...</td>`

Usage	Defines a cell's contents.
Start/End Tag	Required/Optional.
Attributes	core, i18n, events.
	abbr="*name*"—Abbreviated name.
	axis="*axisnames*"—axis names listing row and column headers pertaining to the cell.
	rowspan="*numrows*"—The number of rows spanned by a cell.
	colspan="*numcols*"—The number of columns spanned by a cell.
	align="*alignment*"—Horizontally aligns the contents of cells (left, center, right, justify, char).
	char="*charalignment*"—Sets a character on which the column aligns.
	charoff="*charoffset*"—Offset to the first alignment character on a line.
	valign="*verticalalignment*"—Vertically aligns the contents of cells (top, middle, bottom, baseline).

headers=`"`*`headers`*`"`–Header information for a cell.

scope=`"`*`scope`*`"`-Indicates whether a cell provides header information for other cells.

Empty	No.

`<tfoot>...</tfoot>`

Usage	Defines the table footer.
Start/End Tag	Required/Optional.
Attributes	core, i18n, events.
	align=`"`*`alignment`*`"`–Horizontally aligns the contents of cells (`left`, `center`, `right`, `justify`, `char`).
	char=`"`*`charalignment`*`"`–Sets a character on which the column aligns.
	charoff=`"`*`charoffset`*`"`–Offset to the first alignment character on a line.
	valign=`"`*`verticalalignment`*`"`–Vertically aligns the contents of cells (`top`, `middle`, `bottom`, `baseline`).
Empty	No.

TIP

The `align`, `char`, `charoff`, and `valign` attributes have been removed in HTML 5 because their effects are purely presentational and thus better handled by CSS.

`<th>...</th>`

Usage	Defines the cell contents of the table header.
Start/End Tag	Required/Optional.
Attributes	core, i18n, events.
	axis=`"`*`name`*`"`–Abbreviated name.
	axes=`"`*`axisnames`*`"`–axis names listing row and column headers pertaining to the cell.
	rowspan=`"`*`numrows`*`"`–The number of rows spanned by a cell.
	colspan=`"`*`numcols`*`"`–The number of columns spanned by a cell.
	align=`"`*`alignment`*`"`–Horizontally aligns the contents of cells (`left`, `center`, `right`, `justify`, `char`).
	char=`"`*`charalignment`*`"`–Sets a character on

TIP

The `axis`, `axes`, `align`, `char`, `charoff`, and `valign` attributes have been removed in HTML 5 because their effects are purely presentational and thus better handled by CSS.

which the column aligns.

charoff=*"charoffset"*–Offset to the first alignment character on a line.

valign=*"verticalalignment"*–Vertically aligns
the contents of cells (top, middle, bottom, baseline).

headers=*"headers"*–Header information for a
cell.

scope=*"scope"*–Indicates whether a cell provides
header information for other cells.

Empty	No.

`<thead>...</thead>`

TIP

The align, char, charoff, and
valign attributes have been
removed in HTML 5 because
their effects are purely presentational and thus better handled by CSS.

Usage	Defines the table header.
Start/End Tag	Required/Optional.
Attributes	core, i18n, events.
	align=*"alignment"*–Horizontally aligns the con-tents of cells (left, center, right, justify, char).
	char=*"charalignment"*–Sets a character on which the column aligns.
	charoff=*"charoffset"*–Offset to the first align-ment character on a line.
	valign=*"verticalalignment"*–Vertically aligns the contents of cells (top, middle, bottom, base-line).
Empty	No.

`<tr>...</tr>`

TIP

The align, char, charoff, and
valign attributes have been
removed in HTML 5 because
their effects are purely presentational and thus better handled by CSS.

Usage	Defines a row of table cells.
Start/End Tag	Required/Optional.
Attributes	core, i18n, events.
	align=*"alignment"*–Horizontally aligns the con-tents of cells (left, center, right, justify, char).
	char=*"charalignment"*–Sets a character on which the column aligns.

	`charoff="`*`charoffset`*`"`–Offset to the first alignment character on a line.
	`valign="`*`verticalalignment`*`"`–Vertically aligns the contents of cells (`top`, `middle`, `bottom`, `base-line`).
Empty	No.

XHTML Embedded Content

Also called *inclusions*, embedded content applies to images, imagemaps, Java applets, Flash animations, and other multimedia or programmed content that is placed in a Web page to provide additional functionality.

`<area />`

Usage	The `<area>` element is used to define links and anchors.
Start/End Tag	Required/Illegal.
Attributes	`core`, `i18n`, `events`.
	`shape="`*`value`*`"`–Enables you to define client-side imagemaps using defined shapes (`default`, `rect`, `circle`, `poly`).
	`coords="`*`values`*`"`–Sets the size of the shape using pixel or percentage lengths.
	`href="`*`linkurl`*`"`–The URL of the linked resource.
	`nohref="`*`nohref`*`"`–Indicates that the region has no action.
	`alt="`*`alttext`*`"`–Displays alternative text.
Empty	Yes.

`<img />`

Usage	Includes an image in the document.
Start/End Tag	Required/Illegal.
Attributes	`core`, `i18n`, `events`.
	`src="`*`sourceurl`*`"`–The URL of the image.
	`alt="`*`alttext`*`"`–Alternative text to display.
	`height="`*`height`*`"`–The height of the image.

TIP

The `hspace` and `vspace` attributes have been removed in HTML 5 because their effects are purely presentational and thus better handled by CSS.

width="*width*"–The width of the image.

border="*border*"–Border width.

hspace="*horizontalspace*"–The horizontal space separating the image from other content.

vspace="*verticalspace*"–The vertical space separating the image from other content.

usemap="*mapurl*"–The URL to a client-side imagemap.

ismap="ismap"–Identifies a server-side imagemap.

Empty	Yes.

<map>...</map>

Usage	When used with the <area> element, creates a client-side imagemap.
Start/End Tag	Required/Required.
Attributes	core, i18n, events.
	name="*name*"–The name of the imagemap to be created.
Empty	No.

TIP

The hspace and vspace attributes have been removed in HTML 5 because their effects are purely presentational and thus better handled by CSS.

<object>...</object>

Usage	Includes an object.
Start/End Tag	Required/Required.
Attributes	core, i18n, events.
	declare="declare"–A flag that declares but doesn't create an object.
	classid="*objecturl*"–The URL of the object's location.
	codebase="*codebaseurl*"–The URL for resolving URLs specified by other attributes.
	data="*dataurl*"–The URL to the object's data.
	type="*datatype*"–The Internet content type for data.

codetype="*codetype*"–The Internet content type for the code.

standby="*waitmsg*"–Show message while loading.

height="*height*"–The height of the object.

width="*width*"–The width of the object.

border="*border*"–Displays the border around an object.

hspace="*horizontalspace*"–The space between the sides of the object and other page content.

vspace="*verticalspace*"–The space between the top and bottom of the object and other page content.

usemap="*mapurl*"–The URL to an imagemap.

shapes="shapes"–Enables you to define areas to search for hyperlinks if the object is an image.

name="*nameurl*"–The URL to submit as part of a form.

Empty	No.

<param />

Usage	Initializes an object.
Start/End Tag	Required/Illegal.
Attributes	name="*name*"–Defines the parameter name.
	value="*value*"–The value of the object parameter.
	valuetype="*valuetype*"–Defines the value type (data, ref, object).
	type="*contenttype*"–The Internet medium type.
Empty	Yes.

XHTML Style

Style sheets (both inline and external) are incorporated into an HTML document through the use of the `<style>` element

`<style>...</style>`	
Usage	Creates an internal style sheet.
Start/End Tag	Required/Required.
Attributes	i18n.
	type="*contenttype*"–The Internet content type.
	media="*media*"–Defines the destination medium (screen, print, projection, braille, speech, all).
	title="*title*"–The title of the style.
Empty	No.
Notes	Located in the `<head>` element.

XHTML Forms

Forms create an interface for the user to select options, enter information, and return data to the Web server for processing.

`<button>...</button>`	
Usage	Creates a button.
Start/End Tag	Required/Required.
Attributes	core, i18n, events.
	name="*name*"–The button name.
	value="*value*"–The value of the button.
	type="*type*"–The button type (button, submit, reset).
	disabled="disabled"–Sets the button state to disabled.
Empty	No.

`<fieldset>...</fieldset>`

Usage	Groups related controls.
Start/End Tag	Required/Required.
Attributes	core, i18n, events.
Empty	No.

`<form>...</form>`

Usage	Creates a form that holds controls for user input.
Start/End Tag	Required/Required.
Attributes	core, i18n, events.
	action="*actionurl*"–The URL for the server action.
	method="*post/get*"–The HTTP method (get, post). get is deprecated.
	enctype="*mediatype*"–Specifies the MIME (Internet media) type.
	accept="*contenttypes*"–The list of content types acceptable by the server.
	accept-charset="*encodings*"–The list of character encodings.
Empty	No.

`<input />`

Usage	Defines controls used in forms.
Start/End Tag	Required/Illegal.
Attributes	core, i18n, events.
	type="*controltype*"–The type of input control (text, password, checkbox, radio, submit, reset, file, hidden, image, button).
	name="*name*"–The name of the control (required except for submit and reset).
	value="*value*"–The initial value of the control (required for radio and check boxes).
	checked="checked"–Sets the radio buttons to a checked state.

disabled="disabled"–Disables the control.

readonly="readonly"–For text password types.

size="*size*"–The width of the control in pixels except for text and password controls, which are specified in number of characters.

maxlength="*maxlength*"–The maximum number of characters that can be entered.

src="*imageurl*"–The URL to an image control type.

alt="*alttext*"–An alternative text description.

usemap="*mapurl*"–The URL to a client-side imagemap.

accept="*filetypes*"–File types allowed for upload.

Empty	Yes.

`<label>...</label>`

Usage	Labels a control.
Start/End Tag	Required/Required.
Attributes	core, i18n, events.
	for="*control*"–Associates a label with an identified control.
Empty	No.

` <option>...</option>`

Usage	Specifies choices in a `<select>` element.
Start/End Tag	Required/Optional.
Attributes	core, i18n, events.
	selected="selected"–Specifies whether the option is selected.
	disabled="disabled"–Disables control.
	label="*label*"–Defines a label for the group of options.
	value="*value*"–The value submitted if a control is submitted.
Empty	No.

`<select>...</select>`

Usage	Creates choices for the user to select.
Start/End Tag	Required/Required.
Attributes	`core`, `i18n`, `events`.
	`name="name"`—The name of the element.
	`size="size"`—The width in number of rows.
	`multiple="multiple"`—Allows multiple selections.
	`disabled="disabled"`—Disables the control.
Empty	No.

`<textarea>...</textarea>`

Usage	Creates an area for user input with multiple lines.
Start/End Tag	Required/Required.
Attributes	`core`, `i18n`, `events`.
	`name="name"`—The name of the control.
	`rows="numrows"`—The width in number of rows.
	`cols="numcols"`—The height in number of columns.
	`disabled="disabled"`—Disables the control.
	`readonly="readonly"`—Sets the displayed text to read-only status.
Empty	No.
Notes	Text to be displayed is placed within the start and end tags.

XHTML Scripts

Scripts make it possible to process data and perform other dynamic events. Scripts are included in web pages thanks to the `<script>` element, which also identifies the specific scripting language being used (JavaScript, VBScript, and so on.).

\<noscript\>...\</noscript\>

Usage	Provides alternative content for browsers unable to execute a script.
Start/End Tag	Required/Required.
Attributes	`core`, `i18n`, `events`.
Empty	No.

\<script\>...\</script\>

Usage	The `<script>` element contains client-side scripts that are executed by the browser.
Start/End Tag	Required/Required.
Attributes	`type="scripttype"`–Script language Internet content type.
	`src="scripturl"`–The URL for the external script.
	`defer="defer"`–Indicates that the script doesn't alter document content.
Empty	No.
Notes	You can set the default scripting language in the `<meta />` element.

XHTML Common Attributes

The following six attributes are abbreviated as `core` in the preceding sections:

- ▶ `id="id"`–A global identifier.

- ▶ `class="styleclasses"`–A list of classes separated by spaces.

- ▶ `style="styles"`–Style information.

- ▶ `title="title"`–Provides more information for a specific element (as opposed to the `<title>` element, which titles the entire Web page).

- ▶ `accesskey="shortcut"`–Sets the keyboard shortcut used to access an element.

- ▶ `tabindex="taborder"`–Sets the tab order of an element.

The following two attributes for internationalization are abbreviated as i18n in the preceding sections:

▶ lang="*lang*"–The language identifier.

▶ dir="*textdir*"–The text direction (ltr, rtl).

The following intrinsic events are abbreviated events. For more information on their application in specific elements, see the W3C specification:

▶ onclick="*eventcode*"–A pointing device (such as a mouse) was single-clicked.

▶ ondblclick="*eventcode*"–A pointing device (such as a mouse) was double-clicked.

▶ onmousedown="*eventcode*"–A mouse button was clicked and held down.

▶ onmouseup="*eventcode*"–A mouse button that was clicked and held down was released.

▶ onmouseover="*eventcode*"–A mouse moved the cursor over an object.

▶ onmousemove="*eventcode*"–The mouse was moved.

▶ onmouseout="*eventcode*"–A mouse moved the cursor off an object.

▶ onkeypress="*eventcode*"–A key was pressed and released.

▶ onkeydown="*eventcode*"–A key was pressed and held down.

▶ onkeyup="*eventcode*"–A key that was pressed has been released.

CSS Dimension Style Properties

Quite a few CSS style rules rely on dimensional properties in one form or another. It would be difficult to size elements with them.

height	
Usage	Sets the height of an element.
Values	auto, *length*, %.

line-height

Usage	Sets the distance between lines of elements.
Values	normal, *length*, %.

max-height

Usage	Sets the maximum height of an element.
Values	none, *length*, %.

max-width

Usage	Sets the maximum width of an element.
Values	none, *length*, %.

min-height

Usage	Sets the minimum height of an element.
Values	*length*, %.

min-width

Usage	Sets the minimum width of an element.
Values	*length*, %.

width

Usage	Sets the width of an element.
Values	auto, *length*, %.

CSS Text and Font Style Properties

The heart of CSS styling lies in the text and style properties, which give you an incredible amount of control over the appearance of Web page text.

color

Usage	Sets the color of text.
Values	*color*.

direction

Usage	Sets the direction of text, as in left-to-right or right-to-left.
Values	`ltr, rtl.`

font

Usage	A shorthand property that allows you to set all the font properties in one declaration.
Values	`font-style, font-variant, font-weight, font-size/line-height, font-family.`

font-family

Usage	A prioritized list of font family names and/or generic family names for an element.
Values	`family-name, generic-family.`

font-size

Usage	Sets the size of a font.
Values	`xx-small, x-small, small, medium, large, x-large, xx-large, smaller, larger,` *length*, `%.`

font-style

Usage	Sets the style of the font.
Values	`normal, italic, oblique.`

font-variant

Usage	Displays text in a small-caps font or a normal font.
Values	`normal, small-caps.`

font-weight

Usage	Sets the weight (boldness) of a font.
Values	`normal, bold, bolder, lighter, 100, 200, 300, 400, 500, 600, 700, 800, 900.`

letter-spacing

Usage	Increases or decreases the space between characters of text.
Values	normal, *length*.

text-align

Usage	Aligns the text within an element.
Values	left, right, center, justify.

text-decoration

Usage	Applies a decoration to text.
Values	none, underline, overline, line-through, blink.

text-indent

Usage	Indents the first line of text in an element.
Values	*length*, %.

text-transform

Usage	Controls the capitalization of letters of text.
Values	none, capitalize, uppercase, lowercase.

white-space

Usage	Establishes the handling of white space within an element.
Values	normal, pre, nowrap.

word-spacing

Usage	Increases or decreases the space between words.
Values	normal, *length*.

CSS Background Style Properties

There are several CSS style properties that can be used to alter the backgrounds of pages and individual elements on pages.

background

Usage	A shorthand property that allows you to set all the background properties in one declaration.
Values	`background-color, background-image, background-repeat, background-attachment, background-position.`

background-attachment

Usage	Determines whether a background image is fixed or scrolls with the rest of the page.
Values	`scroll, fixed.`

background-color

Usage	Sets the background color of an element.
Values	`color-rgb, color-hex, color-name, transparent.`

background-image

Usage	Sets an image as the background.
Values	`url`, `none.`

background-position

Usage	Sets the starting position of a background image.
Values	`top left, top center, top right, center left, center center, center right, bottom left, bottom center, bottom right, x-% y-%, x-pos y-pos.`

background-repeat

Usage	Sets whether and how a background image is repeated.
Values	`repeat, repeat-x, repeat-y, no-repeat`.

CSS Border Style Properties

Every block element has a border that can be styled. Although you can certainly leave borders invisible, there are several styles that can be applied to element borders.

border

Usage	A shorthand property that allows you to set all the properties for the four borders in one declaration.
Values	`border-width, border-style, border-color`.

border-bottom

Usage	A shorthand property that allows you to set all the bottom border properties in one declaration.
Values	`border-bottom-width, border-style, border-color`.

border-bottom-color

Usage	Sets the color of the bottom border.
Values	`border-color`.

border-bottom-style

Usage	Sets the style of the bottom border.
Values	`border-style`.

border-bottom-width

Usage	Sets the width of the bottom border.
Values	`thin, medium, thick, length`.

border-color

Usage	Sets the color of the four borders.
Values	*color*.
Notes	Can be specified using from one to four colors.

border-left

Usage	A shorthand property that allows you to set all the left border properties in one declaration.
Values	`border-left-width, border-style, border-color`.

border-left-color

Usage	Sets the color of the left border.
Values	`border-color`.

border-left-style

Usage	Sets the style of the left border.
Values	`border-style`.

border-left-width

Usage	Sets the width of the left border.
Values	`thin, medium, thick,` *length*.

border-right

Usage	A shorthand property that allows you to set all the right border properties in one declaration.
Values	`border-right-width, border-style, border-color`.

border-right-color

Usage	Sets the color of the right border.
Values	`border-color`.

border-right-style

Usage	Sets the style of the right border.
Values	`border-style`.

border-right-width

Usage	Sets the width of the right border.
Values	`thin, medium, thick,` *`length`*.

border-style

Usage	Sets the style of the four borders.
Values	`none, hidden, dotted, dashed, solid, double, groove, ridge, inset, outset`.
Notes	Can be specified using from one to four styles.

border-top

Usage	A shorthand property that allows you to set all the top border properties in one declaration.
Values	`border-top-width, border-style, border-color`.

border-top-color

Usage	Sets the color of the top border.
Values	`border-color`.

border-top-style

Usage	Sets the style of the top border.
Values	`border-style`.

border-top-width

Usage	Sets the width of the top border.
Values	`thin, medium, thick,` *`length`*.

border-width

Usage	A shorthand property for setting the width of the four borders in one declaration.
Values	`thin`, `medium`, `thick`, *length*.
Notes	Can be specified using one to four widths.

CSS Margin Style Properties

Margins allow you to add a bit of spacing around the outer edge of an element, outside of the element's border.

margin

Usage	A shorthand property that allows you to set all the margin properties in one declaration.
Values	`margin-top`, `margin-right`, `margin-bottom`, `margin-left`.

margin-bottom

Usage	Sets the bottom margin of an element.
Values	`auto`, *length*, %.

margin-left

Usage	Sets the left margin of an element.
Values	`auto`, *length*, %.

margin-right

Usage	Sets the right margin of an element.
Values	`auto`, *length*, %.

margin-top

Usage	Sets the top margin of an element.
Values	`auto`, *length*, %.

CSS Padding Style Properties

Padding allows you to add space around an element, inside of the element's border.

padding

Usage	A shorthand property that allows you to set all the padding properties in one declaration.
Values	`padding-top`, `padding-right`, `padding-bottom`, `padding-left`.

padding-bottom

Usage	Sets the bottom padding of an element.
Values	*length*, %.

padding-left

Usage	Sets the left padding of an element.
Values	*length*, %.

padding-right

Usage	Sets the right padding of an element.
Values	*length*, %.

padding-top

Usage	Sets the top padding of an element.
Values	*length*, %.

CSS Layout and Display Style Properties

The layout and display properties in CSS play an extremely important role in determining how elements are laid out and arranged on the page.

bottom

Usage	Sets the offset between the bottom edge of the element and the bottom edge of its parent element.
Values	auto, *length*, %.

clear

Usage	Determines the sides of an element where other floating elements are not allowed.
Values	left, right, both, none.

clip

Usage	Sets the shape of an element.
Values	auto, *shape*.
Notes	The element is clipped to this shape when displayed.

cursor

Usage	Specifies the type of mouse cursor to be displayed.
Values	*url*, auto, crosshair, default, pointer, move, e-resize, ne-resize, nw-resize, n-resize, se-resize, sw-resize, s-resize, w-resize, text, wait, help.

display

Usage	Sets whether and how an element is displayed.
Values	none, inline, block, list-item, run-in, compact, marker, table, inline-table, table-row-group, table-header-group, table-footer-group, table-row, table-column-group, table-column, table-cell, table-caption.

float

Usage	Sets where an image or text will appear relative to another element.
Values	left, right, none.

left

Usage	Sets the offset between the left edge of the element and the left edge of its parent element.
Values	auto, *length*, %.

overflow

Usage	Determines what happens if the content of an element overflows its area.
Values	auto, visible, hidden, scroll.

position

Usage	Specifies the layout of an element as using static, relative, absolute, or fixed positioning.
Values	static, relative, absolute, fixed.

right

Usage	Sets the offset between the right edge of the element and the right edge of its parent element.
Values	auto, *length*, %.

top

Usage	Sets the offset between the top edge of the element and the top edge of its parent element.
Values	auto, *length*, %.

vertical-align	
Usage	Sets the vertical alignment of an element.
Values	`baseline`, `sub`, `super`, `top`, `text-top`, `middle`, `bottom`, `text-bottom`, *length*, %.

visibility	
Usage	Determines whether an element should be shown (visible) or hidden (invisible).
Values	`visible`, `hidden`, `collapse`.

z-index	
Usage	Sets the z-order (stacking order) of an element.
Values	`auto`, *number*.

CSS List and Marker Style Properties

You might not have realized how much flexibility there is when it comes to the styling of lists via CSS. Several CSS styles apply to lists and the list-item markers (or bullets) within the lists.

list-style	
Usage	A shorthand property that allows you to set all the list properties in one declaration.
Values	`list-style-type`, `list-style-position`, `list-style-image`.

list-style-image	
Usage	Sets an image as the list-item marker (bullet) for the list.
Values	`none`, *url*.

list-style-position

Usage	Sets where the list-item marker (bullet) is placed in the list.
Values	`inside, outside`.

list-style-type

Usage	Sets the type of the list-item marker (bullet).
Values	`none, disc, circle, square, decimal, decimal-leading-zero, lower-roman, upper-roman, lower-alpha, upper-alpha, lower-greek, lower-latin, upper-latin, hebrew, armenian, georgian, cjk-ideographic, hiragana, katakana, hiragana-iroha, katakana-iroha`.

CSS Table Style Properties

There are a few advanced table properties that enable you to fine-tune the manner in which tables are rendered and displayed.

border-collapse

Usage	Sets the border model of a table.
Values	`collapse, separate`.

border-spacing

Usage	Sets the distance between the borders of adjacent cells.
Values	`length length`.

caption-side

Usage	Sets the position of the caption relative to the table.
Values	`top, bottom, left, right`.

empty-cells

Usage	Determines whether cells with no visible content should have borders.
Values	show, hide.

table-layout

Usage	Determines how the table is laid out.
Values	auto, fixed.
Notes	Speeds up browser rendering for fixed-size tables if you set it to fixed.

INDEX

U - V

FREE Online Edition

Your purchase of **Sams Teach Yourself HTML and CSS in 24 Hours** includes access to a free online edition for 45 days through the Safari Books Online subscription service. Nearly every Sams book is available online through Safari Books Online, along with more than 5,000 other technical books and videos from publishers such as Addison-Wesley Professional, Cisco Press, Exam Cram, IBM Press, O'Reilly, Prentice Hall, and Que.

SAFARI BOOKS ONLINE allows you to search for a specific answer, cut and paste code, download chapters, and stay current with emerging technologies.

Activate your FREE Online Edition at www.informit.com/safarifree

STEP 1: Enter the coupon code: CQVGNCB.

STEP 2: New Safari users, complete the brief registration form.
Safari subscribers, just log in.

If you have difficulty registering on Safari or accessing the online edition, please e-mail customer-service@safaribooksonline.com